Praise for *Advanced ASP.NET AJAX*

"If you're an ASP.NET developer looking for the shortest road to delivering AJAX-enabled, Web 2.0 applications, *Advanced ASP.NET AJAX Server Controls* has what you need. Deliver interactive AJAX functionality that today's web applications demand, using tools and methods you already know."

> —*Shawn Burke*
> *AJAX Control Toolkit Director, Microsoft*

"You know what is frustrating? When I read or hear about a technology, start playing with it, and then dead end because the documentation only covers simple concepts or a reference book just gives you an introduction that is nothing more than a glorified regurgitation of the documentation. Adam Calderon and Joel Rumerman take you to the next level as you begin or refine building ASP.NET AJAX Server Controls. They not only show you how, but dive deep to give you insight and guidance. This book is intended for those who want to go beyond UpdatePanel and build their own controls. If you are looking for a primer, then look for another book on the shelf—this is hardcore."

> —*Thomas Lewis*
> *Web User Experience Evangelism Manager, Microsoft*

"*Advanced ASP.NET AJAX Server Controls* is the most complete and thorough resource available for this powerful AJAX framework. The authors have provided tremendous depth into the flexibility and extensibility of the technology for beginning and advanced developers alike, going far beyond the simple cases covered in other sources."

> —*Jason Schmitt*
> *Vice President of Products, Steelbox Networks*

"Kudos to Adam Calderon and Joel Rumerman for tackling the subject of building AJAX Server Controls. This book is *The Red Pill* for ASP.NET AJAX Developers (see the *Matrix* movie). Custom Controls and components are the .NET Developer's best opportunity for code reuse, and this book takes controls building into the AJAX era."

> —*Joe Stagner*
> *Senior Program Manager, Developer Tools & Platforms, Microsoft*

Advanced ASP.NET AJAX
Server Controls

Microsoft .NET Development Series

John Montgomery, *Series Advisor*
Don Box, *Series Advisor*
Brad Abrams, *Series Advisor*

The award-winning Microsoft .NET Development Series was established in 2002 to provide professional developers with the most comprehensive and practical coverage of the latest .NET technologies. It is supported and developed by the leaders and experts of Microsoft development technologies, including Microsoft architects, MVPs, and leading industry luminaries. Books in this series provide a core resource of information and understanding every developer needs to write effective applications.

Titles in the Series

For more information go to www.informit.com/msdotnetseries/

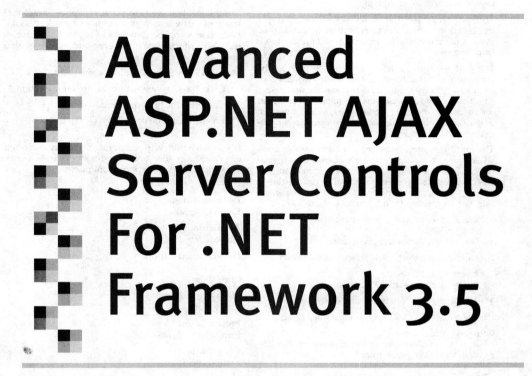

Advanced ASP.NET AJAX Server Controls For .NET Framework 3.5

- Adam Calderon
- Joel Rumerman

✦ Addison-Wesley

Upper Saddle River, NJ • Boston • Indianapolis • San Francisco
New York • Toronto • Montreal • London • Munich • Paris
Madrid • Cape Town • Sydney • Tokyo • Singapore • Mexico City

Many of the designations used by manufacturers and sellers to distinguish their products are claimed as trademarks. Where those designations appear in this book, and the publisher was aware of a trademark claim, the designations have been printed with initial capital letters or in all capitals.

The .NET logo is either a registered trademark or trademark of Microsoft Corporation in the United States and/or other countries and is used under license from Microsoft.

The authors and publisher have taken care in the preparation of this book, but make no expressed or implied warranty of any kind and assume no responsibility for errors or omissions. No liability is assumed for incidental or consequential damages in connection with or arising out of the use of the information or programs contained herein.

The publisher offers excellent discounts on this book when ordered in quantity for bulk purchases or special sales, which may include electronic versions and/or custom covers and content particular to your business, training goals, marketing focus, and branding interests. For more information, please contact:

U.S. Corporate and Government Sales
(800) 382-3419
corpsales@pearsontechgroup.com

For sales outside the United States please contact:

International Sales
international@pearson.com

Visit us on the web: www.informit.com/aw

Library of Congress Cataloging-in-Publication Data:

Calderon, Adam, 1964-
  Advanced ASP.Net Ajax server controls for .Net 3.5 / Adam Calderon, Joel Rumerman.
    p. cm.
  ISBN 0-321-51444-0 (pbk. : alk. paper) 1. Internet programming. 2. Active server pages. 3. Microsoft .NET. 4. Ajax (Web site development technology) 5. Web servers. I. Rumerman, Joel, 1980- II. Title.

  QA76.625.C34 2008
  006.7'882—dc22
                                        2008013462

ISBN-13: 978-0-321-51444-8
ISBN-10: 0-321-51444-0
Text printed in the United States on recycled paper at RR Donnelly in Crawfordsville, Indiana.
First printing: July 2008

This Book Is Safari Enabled

The Safari® Enabled icon on the cover of your favorite technology book means the book is available through Safari Bookshelf. When you buy this book, you get free access to the online edition for 45 days.

Safari Bookshelf is an electronic reference library that lets you easily search thousands of technical books, find code samples, download chapters, and access technical information whenever and wherever you need it.

To gain 45-day Safari Enabled access to this book:

- Go to http://www.informit.com/onlineedition.
- Complete the brief registration form.
- Enter the coupon code DWNQ-VHHL-H21A-XGL8-34YC.

If you have difficulty registering on Safari Bookshelf or accessing the online edition, please e-mail customer-service@safaribooksonline.com.

Editor-in-Chief
Karen Gettman

Acquisitions Editor
Joan Murray

Development Editors
Sheri Cain
Chris Zahn

Managing Editor
Kristy Hart

Project Editor
Jovana San Nicolas-Shirley

Copy Editor
Keith Cline

Indexer
WordWise Publishing Services

Proofreader
Geneil Breeze

Publishing Coordinator
Olivia Basegio

Cover Designer
Chuti Prasertsith

Compositor
Bronkella Publishing

To my wife, Gayle, and my son, Derek: You were already accustomed to my hard work ethic, but I think writing this book took things to the next level. Your patience and understanding during this long journey provided the foundation I needed to get through the rough times. I am truly blessed to have the both of you in my life.

—Adam

To my wife, Stacey: You make even the hard days easy. And to my parents: I truly am 50 percent of each of you.

—Joel

Contents

II Controls

Figures

Tables

Foreword

THE ASP.NET PLATFORM POWERS millions of websites around the world today, and is perhaps one of the most productive platforms for web development. During the nearly ten years of its development and use, ASP.NET has formed around itself a strong community and vibrant ecosystem of developers.

The page framework and the associated server controls framework are quintessential to the success of ASP.NET and its developer experience, programming model, and extensibility. Writing this Foreword brings back memories of early ASP.NET days, and reminds me of the continued evolution of the framework as a platform alongside the Web.

In the late 1990s, the Web was very much a nascent application platform. Browsers brought potential for new levels of reach, but offered few and varying degrees of capabilities (remember HTML 3.2?), and concepts such as "stateless programming model" presented an odd paradigm shift. Server controls provided a set of familiar abstractions and created a component-based rapid application development (RAD) programming experience for the Web (à la Visual Basic) and allowed developers to feel at home as they started to look to the Web to build the next generation of data-driven applications.

Flash forward a few years, and in 2006, the AJAX buzz created a renewed interest in the Web as *the* application platform. Today, AJAX is mainstream and, quite literally, everywhere. It enables building interactive experiences that users have come to expect. Still, it brings new but similar challenges: varying browser APIs and an unfamiliar script-based programming model. Once again, ASP.NET (and in particular, server controls) provided a mechanism for creating a productive development model for incorporating AJAX-based techniques, and for encapsulating server and client behaviors into a familiar and consistent component model.

ASP.NET provides an end-to-end AJAX story. Traditional server controls create a simple server-centric AJAX programming model, but they are just a part of the story. This new generation of server controls leverages an AJAX script framework that independently enables a client-centric AJAX programming model. The core framework is complemented by the AJAX Control Toolkit, which offers both a compelling set of out-of-the-box components and an open source project for further developing the ASP.NET AJAX stack. I am excited to see this end-to-end story uncovered and unfold itself over the course of this book.

In this book, Adam and Joel focus on providing a beyond-the-basics drill down of the inner workings and extensibility of the ASP.NET AJAX framework by covering the programming patterns established by the script framework, the architecture, and the techniques to create AJAX-enabled server controls. They also cover advanced but still relevant topics such as localization and error handling. By providing a conceptual guide to understanding and extending the framework, this book is sure to serve any application or component developer who is looking to unlock the true potential of ASP.NET AJAX.

—*Nikhil Kothari*
Software Architect
.NET Developer Platform, Microsoft

Preface

Introduction

SERVER CONTROLS ARE AN INTEGRAL aspect of every ASP.NET application we build. They encapsulate browser appearance and server functionality in a reusable object. They can be used across multiple pages within a single ASP.NET application and across multiple ASP.NET applications. ASP.NET comes with a lot of prebuilt server controls. We have simple controls such as the label, and we have complex controls such as the GridView. We can also create our own server controls to meet a need not met by one of the existing controls by inheriting from the appropriate base class and overriding its methods as needed.

This model of using server controls to encapsulate browser appearance and server functionality has served our needs well since the inception of ASP.NET 1.0, but our server control needs are changing.

A new server control need that has recently surfaced is the ability to incorporate AJAX functionality directly into the server control.

This need arose because our web applications need to be more responsive and visually interactive than the traditional ASP.NET repaint-the-entire-screen model and therefore the traditional server control supplies. This requirement has emerged because users are using websites such as Gmail, Live.com, Yahoo! Mail, and others that don't repaint the screen every time they click a button or need to receive fresh data. Rather, they rely on AJAX to fetch fresh data and then update or add to a portion of the screen based on that data. Because these websites are heavily used and users really enjoy their experience while using these websites, they expect other websites to perform with the same elegance as their favored sites do. When a website doesn't perform with the same elegance, the user often moves on to another website that does. Those popular applications have raised the bar for what is an acceptably user-friendly website.

Because our users are demanding a website experience that essentially uses AJAX and we build our ASP.NET websites using server controls, we need a way of easily creating server controls that not only encapsulate browser appearance and server functionality, but also include AJAX functionality so that the server control itself is AJAX-enabled.

Taking a step back for a moment, unlike other technologies you might have read books about, ASP.NET AJAX server controls don't provide you with anything that you couldn't already do. We've always been able to embed AJAX functionality into server controls… it was just a real pain.

There were a few different methods we could use to include the JavaScript with our server control such as embedding it as a resource, but we eventually ended up having to do the same three tasks. To make our server control have some serious client capabilities, we always had to concatenate strings together to form JavaScript statements and functions, write browser sniffing statements to make sure that the JavaScript was cross-browser compatible, and add attributes or render out HTML that attached the JavaScript functionality to the client versions of our server controls. It wasn't impossible, but it was error-prone, and there was always this mingling of server code and JavaScript that was hard to maintain and even harder to read.

Furthermore, if you had multiple server controls that had client capabilities, it was difficult (but not impossible) to ensure that the client functions that each server control required didn't overwrite each other when rendered on the browser. Tracking down that problem was always a fun hour or so.

The difficulty grew exponentially if we wanted to include a mechanism for asynchronously communicating with the server when the user pressed a button embedded in the server control. Even with a helper communication library, there were always tricks to getting your control to communicate properly with the server.

These hindrances were problematic enough to lead to some bad programming habits and bad code and to scare programmers away from even attempting to include AJAX functionality in their server controls.

These problems are what Microsoft ASP.NET AJAX solves.

In this book, we teach you how to use ASP.NET AJAX to create server controls that encapsulate AJAX functionality. ASP.NET AJAX provides both server and client programming constructs that make adding AJAX capabilities to our server controls easy. Not to sound cliché, but with ASP.NET AJAX reducing the complexity of adding AJAX capabilities to our server controls, we can create server controls whose AJAX capabilities are limited only by our creativity. If we want a listbox that self-updates with fresh data, if we want a type-ahead textbox that dynamically populates from the server, or if we want a button that submits an address for verification, we can easily accomplish these things through ASP.NET AJAX.

The ASP.NET AJAX Components

As we go through the book we'll be talking about the three parts of ASP.NET AJAX: the Microsoft AJAX Library, the ASP.NET 2.0 AJAX Extensions, and the ASP.NET AJAX Control Toolkit. Here's a quick rundown of the different components.

Microsoft AJAX Library

The Microsoft AJAX Library is the JavaScript programming framework of ASP.NET AJAX. It provides all the client programming constructs you'll use to create new client objects and components. It's contained within the MicrosoftAjax.js JavaScript file that's embedded in the System.Web. Extensions DLL.

ASP.NET 2.0 AJAX Extensions

The ASP.NET 2.0 AJAX Extensions are server objects such as the `Script Manager`, `ScriptControl`, and `ScriptDescriptor`, which provide a connection between the Microsoft AJAX Library and our server ASP.NET development. These server objects provide an important distinction between ASP.NET AJAX and other AJAX frameworks because they provide a server programming model for manipulating client code (and allow us to make AJAX-enabled server controls!). Like the Microsoft AJAX Library, they are included in the System.Web.Extensions DLL.

ASP.NET AJAX Control Toolkit

The ASP.NET AJAX Control Toolkit is a shared source project that is built on top of ASP.NET AJAX. It's an effort shared between Microsoft and the ASP.NET AJAX community with the goal of developing powerful and reusable ASP.NET AJAX extenders and controls.

It's not actually part of ASP.NET AJAX, but because it provides so many great server and extender controls, it's invaluable to the ASP.NET AJAX community. Creating new extender controls through it is a topic we cover fully.

Book Breakdown

The book is divided into four major parts. In the first part, we focus on the basics of the Microsoft AJAX Library and JavaScript, the programming language that powers it. We call this part "Client Code." In the second part, we focus on a creating distributable AJAX-enabled controls, and we call this part "Controls." In the third part, called "Communication," we focus on the different ways your client control can communicate with the server. Finally, in the fourth part, we focus on the AJAX Control Toolkit, a slightly higher-level model of creating AJAX-enabled server controls. This final part is aptly named "AJAX Control Toolkit."

Client Code

Chapter 1, "Programming with JavaScript," focuses on JavaScript, the programming language that powers the Microsoft AJAX Library. We spend a full chapter on JavaScript because so many developers (ourselves included) have glossed over key details when working with the language; and because you're going to be writing so much JavaScript to AJAX-enable your server controls, a solid background is important.

In Chapter 2, "Microsoft AJAX Library Programming," we continue where we left off in Chapter 1 by taking a look at how the Microsoft AJAX Library builds on JavaScript to provide a programming platform a .NET developer will find familiar.

Controls

Starting in Chapter 3, "Components," we begin our path to creating fully encapsulated AJAX-enabled controls by learning how to use and derive from three key client types: components, controls, and behaviors. We talk theory and provide a couple of practical examples.

In Chapter 4, "Sys.Application," we cover maybe the most important portion of the Microsoft AJAX Library as we discuss Sys.Application and how it acts like a client runtime with which we can interact.

In Chapter 5, "Adding Client Capabilities to Server Controls," we bring the server into the mix when we cover how to create server components that automatically create corresponding components.

In Chapter 6, "ASP.NET AJAX Localization," we continue adding control capabilities with an in-depth examination of localization in ASP.NET AJAX.

Finally, in Chapter 7, "Control Development in a Partial Postback Environment," we wrap up the "Controls" part with a look at the concerns surrounding how the UpdatePanel affects control development.

Communication

With Chapter 8, "ASP.NET AJAX Communication Architecture," we start looking at communication in ASP.NET AJAX using Windows Communication Foundation (WCF) services, page methods, and the client web service proxies.

In Chapter 9, "Application Services," we cover the application services and include a demonstration of how to build your own application service.

AJAX Control Toolkit

Beginning with Chapter 10, "ASP.NET AJAX Control Toolkit Architecture," we start our look at the AJAX Control Toolkit. We cover the base classes that are used by toolkit controls and the support and designer classes that provide additional features.

Finally, we conclude the book with Chapter 11, "Adding Client Capabilities to Server Controls Using the ASP.NET AJAX Control Toolkit," as we attach client capabilities to server controls using the AJAX Control Toolkit. This chapter includes how to build a new extender control and provide design-time features for it.

What Is Not Covered?

You might find it strange to see a note that talks about what we're not covering. We're including it for two reasons.

First, this book covers a pretty narrow topic when compared to ASP.NET AJAX at large. Because of this, we don't have the normal introductory chapter where we walk you through the basics or history of ASP.NET AJAX. Instead, we're making the assumption, good or bad, that you've got some ASP.NET AJAX knowledge under your belt. If you don't, don't worry; getting your ASP.NET AJAX knowledge to the point where you feel comfortable doesn't take long, and this book will pick up right where that basic knowledge leaves off. For this type of information, the Microsoft ASP.NET AJAX website located at http://asp.net/ajax is an excellent source.

Second, we're leaving out a familiar ASP.NET AJAX subject, and we wanted a chance to tell you and defend our decision before we got too far. This is something that we've repeatedly debated between the two of us and asked many colleagues for their opinion and was a decision that we didn't come to easily.

There are no chapters in which we cover how to use the `UpdatePanel` server control.

Okay, you haven't closed the book? Good. Let us explain how and why we came to this decision.

Simply put, the `UpdatePanel` is a server control. It comes with ASP.NET AJAX and provides a quick and dirty way to refresh a portion of a page such that the page goes through its normal lifecycle, but doesn't refresh the entire page when the page processing is done. Using it, we don't have to alter the way we've been programming web pages since ASP.NET 1.0 came out. This is a good thing and was a "quick win" for Microsoft. It allowed ASP.NET AJAX to be adopted quickly by ASP.NET developers and provided a unique advantage against other AJAX frameworks.

However, the `UpdatePanel` is just a server control and it's developed in such a way that it doesn't have a whole lot of comparative properties with the type of ASP.NET AJAX server control development we're covering.

We're not saying it's not an important server control and that it has no place in the AJAX world. Rather, it is an extremely valuable tool whose complexity and correct usage is worthy of a small book; just not this one.

Finally, although we do not cover how to use the `UpdatePanel`, we do cover how to create server controls so that they work correctly in an `UpdatePanel`, or more specifically a partial-postback, environment. We expect that you want your new server controls to work in any ASP.NET environment, and a partial-postback environment is no exception. The partial-postback environment, however, requires us to use some different methods, the new `ScriptManager.RegisterXXX` methods being the most common, and take some care in how we create our server controls. So, we've dedicated Chapter 7 to this topic.

Why Just Server Controls?

Writing a book on just server controls allows us to delve deeply into a narrow topic that is extremely important to web application developers. The ASP.NET AJAX books currently available all generally focus on the technology as a whole. Because they cover a broad range of topics, giving a taste of everything, they have trouble really getting into how certain parts of ASP.NET AJAX work and tend to give shallow coverage of topics that we think are key to creating server controls. It's been our experience that developers tend to move past the content of the more general books fairly quickly because nonbasic situations arise almost immediately when working on a real-life web application.

Target Audience

This book is primarily targeted at the experienced ASP.NET developer who has developed custom web server controls. We expect that you're reading this book to enhance your already proficient ASP.NET development skill set with new ASP.NET AJAX skills. The applications you develop demand elegance and professionalism and easy maintenance and scalability, so you tend to use server controls to your advantage wherever possible.

Besides your experience with ASP.NET, we expect that you're familiar with JavaScript and the basics of ASP.NET AJAX. Therefore, we don't cover how to set up a new ASP.NET AJAX-enabled web application, and although we do cover JavaScript, we start our coverage at a level where we assume some existing knowledge.

Our goal is to provide you with the tools you need to build reusable ASP.NET AJAX server controls or AJAX Control Toolkit extender controls. Our feeling is that reasonably knowledgeable ASP.NET developers will be able to learn the skills necessary to create new ASP.NET AJAX server controls through this book and then add that skill to their ASP.NET development tool bag.

Prerequisites

This book requires ASP.NET 3.5 AJAX and Visual Studio 2008. We heavily cover features included in ASP.NET 3.5 AJAX not included in ASP.NET 2.0 AJAX and C#'s and Visual Studio 2008's new capabilities such as automatic properties and JavaScript IntelliSense.

Source Code

The source code for the book's examples can be found on the book's website: www.informit.com/title/9780321514448.

Acknowledgments

WE ARE TOTALLY AMAZED AT HOW much effort it took so many people to make this book. From the editor to the technical reviewers, copy editors, and marketing folks, there are a lot of people responsible for creating a quality book other than the authors.

We first want to thank all our technical reviewers: Joe Stagner, Jason Schmitt, Milan Negovan, and Russel Gauthier. This book wouldn't be anywhere near as good as it is without the massive time and effort you put into each chapter. The early drafts were rough, real rough, and your reviews let us know it. If you hadn't been so truthful, we would have thought that what we had written was ready to publish, which would have been a huge mistake. Your ability to take all our jumbled thoughts and see what we were trying to say and put us on the path to a comprehensible, useful book is simply amazing. There is no way we could have done this without every piece of input you provided.

We also want to thank our project editor, Jovana San Nicolas-Shirley, for letting us make last-minute changes and answering all our seemingly endless questions (and those we have still yet to ask!).

Also, we want to thank our copy editor, Keith Cline, for asking for clarifications when our writing was unclear, correcting our errant grammar, and making us sound like seasoned writers (when we're really not!).

A special thanks goes out to our marketing team of Curt Johnson, Nancy Valentine, and Andrea Bledsoe for getting our book out to the public.

We also want to thank Joan Murray, our wonderful editor who not only guided two brand new authors through their first book-writing experience, but also managed to have a baby during it all. Congratulations again, and thanks for providing all the support and leeway we needed to craft a quality book.

Thanks also to everyone else at Addison-Wesley who has worked on the book, including Emily Frey, our temporary editor; Kristy Hart and Sheri Cain, who performed early development edits; Karen Opal, who got us into the Library of Congress; and everyone else who we've either forgotten or didn't know about!

From Adam

First, I want to thank my coauthor, Joel, for his never-ending pursuit of excellence, both professionally and personally. Our endless discussions about technology and life in general made writing this book a truly awesome experience. I also want to thank the great team at InterKnowlgy for providing an environment that motivates someone to keep pursuing his technical passions. The cutting-edge work that InterKnowlgy continues to attract makes it a most challenging and exciting place to work.

From Joel

Although this book is dedicated to my wife, Stacey, I want to acknowledge her here, too. We share an office at home and spent countless hours together while she studied for licensing exams and I wrote. There is no way that I would have stayed sane if you had not been there to break the monotony and distract me when I got frustrated. Bouncing ideas and analogies off of you was one of the most fun aspects of writing this book. You truly are an amazing woman, a wonderful wife, an accomplished professional, and a fantastic officemate.

Although my wife was my officemate for most evenings and weekends of the past year, this book wouldn't have happened and I wouldn't be as advanced in my career as I am without my coauthor, Adam. Adam approached me to coauthor this book when we worked together at Inter-Knowlgy because I had shown a greater interest in the technology than required to just get the job done. Because I was really into the technology, but more because I respect him so much both as a professional and a person, I was immediately onboard. Although I left InterKnowlogy shortly after we started the book, our personal and professional relationship has only gotten stronger; and without his leadership, dedication, technical knowledge, and industry connections, this book would have never gotten very far nor be nearly as good as it is. Thanks, Adam, for putting up with my endless phone calls, circular ideas, and overall pain-in-the-ass self.

My parents: Mom and Dad. Who would've thought that I would actually end up 50 percent Mom and 50 percent Dad? Dad, your "don't guess, think" advice when I was programming Pascal in high school taught me to step back from a problem. Mom, the endless hours you dedicated working with me on my reports, essays, and papers has made me a halfway decent writer and not scared of the copy editor's red pen. Also, previous opportunities I had to write for you instilled confidence in me that I could do this.

Keri, Seth, Riley, and Cameron. Thanks for always asking about the book and encouraging me. Remember, it'll make a good bedtime story for the kids, and I'm sure it'll put you to sleep, too.

All the developers at the CoStar Group, especially my teammates Jason, Louise, and John. You guys have helped me grow as a developer and a team member, and together we delivered a mapping solution second to none. I'm sure the coming years will be as rewarding as the past one as we branch into new uncharted territories.

Finally, to all my friends who have shared a beer with me in the past 14 months and heard me either cheer in happiness for completing a milestone or curse an upcoming deadline, thanks. Believe it or not, your support throughout this whole process has meant a lot to me.

About the Authors

Adam Calderon is a C# MVP and the Application Development Practice Lead at InterKnowlogy. He is an accomplished software developer, author, teacher, and speaker with more than 14 years of experience designing and developing solutions on the Microsoft platform. His involvement with ASP.NET AJAX began in late 2005 with his participation in the ASP.NET ATLAS First Access program and later as a member of the UI Server Frameworks Advisory Council. Adam was one of the fortunate few who were able to work on a production application that utilized ASP.NET AJAX in its alpha form and experienced firsthand the trials and tribulations of working in "beta land" on this exciting technology. Visit Adam's blog at http://blogs.interknowlogy.com/adamcalderon.

Joel Rumerman is a Senior .NET Developer at the CoStar Group, where he develops ASP.NET applications to support the company's commercial real estate information business. He is an adept software developer with more than eight years of experience developing .NET applications and is active in the San Diego .NET community as an author and speaker. Joel has been working with ASP.NET AJAX since late 2005 when he started work on a large-scale application for a worldwide independent software vendor. This initial entry into the ASP.NET AJAX world provided him invaluable experience as he worked closely with Microsoft as a member of the ATLAS First Access program and participated in a Strategic Design Review of the technology. Joel has gone on to implement many more solutions using ASP.NET AJAX, including a Virtual Earth mash-up that maps commercial real estate properties. Visit Joel's blog at http://seejoelprogram.wordpress.com.

PART I
Client Code

1

Programming with JavaScript

A S WE COVERED IN THE PREFACE, ASP.NET AJAX is composed of three distinct sections: the Microsoft AJAX Library, ASP.NET 2.0 AJAX, and the ASP.NET AJAX Control Toolkit. In this chapter, we focus on the programming language that powers the Microsoft AJAX Library, JavaScript.

We're spending some time on JavaScript rather than jumping directly into programming with the Microsoft AJAX Library because successfully programming using the Microsoft AJAX Library requires a solid foundation of JavaScript, the language it was written in and extends. As much as the Library provides to ease client-side development and turn JavaScript programming into an object-oriented development experience ASP.NET developers can relate to, we still need rock-solid JavaScript skills when we program within it. Otherwise, we won't be able to take full advantage of its abilities and won't understand how to use it properly.

Because JavaScript is a full programming language, covering it completely requires a full book. If you want to master it completely, we recommend *JavaScript: The Definitive Guide* by David Flanagan and *Pro JavaScript Techniques* by John Resig. Because this book is about ASP.NET AJAX and not JavaScript, however, we cannot cover every nook and cranny of the language. Instead, we try to tackle concepts that you might have glossed over in your day-to-day development. Topics we cover are functions as first-class objects, primitive data types, objects, equality, variable scope, and function arguments.

From there, we transition into developing a few objects that act like a classic object-oriented system. We cover this because the Microsoft AJAX Library acts like a classic object-oriented system, and it's important to understand the basics of how Microsoft created this system so that we can be prepared for and understand its programming model.

Generally JavaScript

JavaScript Introduction

JavaScript can be separated into two categories: client-side JavaScript (CSJS) and server-side JavaScript (SSJS). SSJS is used infrequently when compared to its client-side sibling. Because we're looking at client technologies, when we refer to JavaScript in this book we refer to CSJS.

JavaScript is actually the Mozilla Foundation implementation of the ECMAScript standard, but the term is more commonly used to refer to all implementations of the ECMAScript standard rather than to the Mozilla Foundation-specific implementation. When we refer to JavaScript in this book, we are referring to the ECMAScript standard, not the Mozilla-specific implementation. Keep in mind, however, that different browsers have implemented the standard in moderately different ways.

Despite its name, JavaScript is completely unrelated to the Sun Microsystem Java programming language. Netscape changed the language name from LiveScript to JavaScript as a co-marketing deal between Netscape and Sun when Java was bundled with the Netscape browser, back when Netscape was the dominate browser. In retrospect, it is a horrible name that has been the source of confusion for many developers.

Language Attributes

Dynamically Typed

In dynamically typed languages, the data types are not declared and are not known until execution time. This is in contrast to statically typed languages, such as C# or Java, where data types are declared and known at compile type. Dynamically typed languages can lead to more flexible applications when compared to statically typed languages, but developers often prefer the clarity and error checking that declared and compiled data types provide in a statically typed language. The example in Listing 1.1 shows legal statements in JavaScript, a dynamically typed language, which would be illegal in a statically typed language.

LISTING 1.1   Dynamic Typing

```
var x = 5; // set x to 5
x = "hello!"; // set x to 'hello!'
```

In JavaScript, this is perfectly legal because the type is associated to the value of the variable rather than the variable itself. In contrast, this is illegal in a statically typed language because the type is associated to the variable and the compiler wouldn't allow x to change its associated type from an integer to a string.

Interpreted

Like most scripting languages, JavaScript is interpreted rather than compiled. Its code is stored as text and interpreted into machine instructions and stored in memory as the program runs. This is in contrast to compiled languages, such as C# and Java, where the code is compiled into machine instructions or an intermediate form such as IL or bytecode in a discrete step before program execution begins.

Functions as First-Class Objects

In JavaScript, Function is a type of built-in object. It has a property that contains executable code and can be invoked using its name followed by parentheses, (). The Function object is important because it enables us to group code into a callable block. We actually use the Function type unknowingly whenever we declare a new function. Whenever the keyword function is used, it actually creates a new object of type Function passing in the function's body to Function's constructor. Listing 1.2 demonstrates this concept. The two methods, newMethod and newMethod2, are exactly the same thing (other than their names) once interpreted and executed by the JavaScript runtime.

LISTING 1.2 Creating Functions

```
var newMethod = new Function("alert ('new method');");
newMethod(); // alerts "new method"

function newMethod2() {
  alert ("new method");
}
newMethod2(); // alerts "new method"
```

Because we can create an object of type Function, we can declare functions wherever we want without enclosing them inside another concept such as a class, as we normally do in class-based object-oriented programming languages. The ability to do this makes the function a first-class citizen (or object) of the language.

This idea has important ramifications. It means that functions act as the bounding construct of the language and displace what we might consider a normal object-oriented principle, classes. No keyword represents the common class idea found in most modern object-oriented programming languages such as Java or C#. (The class keyword in JavaScript refers to a CSS class.) Rather, as we discuss in the "Object-Oriented JavaScript Programming" section later in this chapter, functions act as the boundary for new types.

An important aspect of JavaScript functions is that they are unique only by name, not by name plus arguments as in other languages. If we declare one function and then declare another function with the same name, the second function overwrites the first one.

Primitive Data Types

JavaScript has three primitive data types: boolean, number, and string. It also has two special values: undefined and null. (We cover null and undefined later in this section and explain the differences between undefined the value and undefined the type.) Everything else is a variation of the Object type, which we cover in detail in this chapter's "Objects" section.

booleans

A boolean has two possible values: true or false. booleans can be created by assigning true, false, 1 (indicating true), or 0 (indicating false) to a variable, as shown in Listing 1.3.

LISTING 1.3 Declaring boolean Variables

```
var x = false;
var y = true;
var z = 1;
alert (y === z); // alerts 'true'
```

Numbers

Numbers are always stored as 64-bit values, similar to doubles in .NET. Because of this single number type, division between any two numbers can produce fractional results. The number type also contains a series of special values shown in Table 1.1. A number can be manipulated through normal mathematical and bitwise expressions, and normal order-of-operations precedence is applied (parentheses, exponents, multiplication, division, addition, and subtraction). If the current value has a decimal value and a bitwise expression is used, the number is first converted to a 32-bit integer using rounding, the bitwise expression is applied, and then the number is converted back to a 64-bit double.

TABLE 1.1 Special Number Values

Constant	Definition
Number.NaN or Nan	Not a number. Useful for determining whether a variable can be coerced into a Number type.
Number.Infinity or Infinity	Represents the greatest possible value, but has no numeric value.
Number.MAX_VALUE	Largest possible number represented within the 64 bits.
Number.MIN_VALUE	Smallest possible number represented within the 64 bits.
Number.POSITIVE_INFINITY	Represents positive infinity.
Number.Negative_INFINITY	Represents negative infinity.

Strings

A string is a sequence of zero or more Unicode values used to represent text. They are immutable (modification produces a new string), and there is no separate character type that represents a string of length one.

Strings are created using quotation marks. They can be either single (') or double (") quotation marks, but they have to be paired properly. The forward slash (\) is used for escaping quotes and special characters within a string. Listing 1.4 demonstrates some patterns used to create strings.

LISTING 1.4　Declaring String Variables

```
var x = "Hello!";
var y = 'Hello Again!';
var z = 'Hello, I\'m Bob';
```

Table 1.2 shows the other special characters that use the forward slash to escape them.

TABLE 1.2　Special Characters

Escape Sequence	Output
\'	Single quote (')
\"	Double quote (")
\\	Backslash (\)
\b	Backspace
\t	Horizontal tab
\n	New line character
\r	Carriage return character
\f	Form feed character
\ddd	Octal sequence (3 digits)
\xdd	Hexadecimal sequence (2 hex digits)
\udddd	Unicode sequence (4 hex digits)

> **■ NOTE**   **String Concatenation Is Expensive!**
>
> Any time you assign a string to a variable, memory is allocated from the heap to store that string. This occurs because strings are immutable. They cannot change after they have been assigned to a variable. Therefore, take care, where possible, to avoid concatenating strings. Certain techniques are available, which the Microsoft AJAX Library makes readily accessible through the `Sys.StringBuilder` type, to avoid string concatenations through the use of arrays to store string parts. We strongly suggest that if you want to write string concatenation code that performs well, use the `Sys.StringBuilder` class just as you would on the server.

Objects

Besides variables that are primitive data types, every other variable in JavaScript is an object. Functions, dates, and Document Object Model (DOM) elements, among many others, are all objects. Objects are how we extend the language with our own types, write modular code, and generally make our code easier to understand. We use objects extensively throughout the rest of this book, and we discuss how to use them in a classic object-oriented system later in this chapter. For now, however, let's go over some object basics.

Basics

First, we can create new objects in two different ways. We can use the built-in `Object` type with the `new` keyword, or we can use an object literal. An object literal is a string that defines the object and is begun with a left curly brace ({) and ended with a right curly brace (}). Listing 1.5 demonstrates using these two methods to create two new object instances.

LISTING 1.5   Creating New Object Instances

```
var myCar = new Object();
var myCar2 = { };
```

These objects already have a function available just because they're objects. The toString function is attached to the object's prototype (we explain what a prototype is in a bit), and therefore it is subsequently available on all instances that inherit from Object, which is everything.

Besides having the toString function, which would require an override to make it output anything interesting, these objects are a bit plain because they have no properties assigned. We can assign properties to an object using either the Object Literal notation or through a dot notation. Listing 1.6 shows both ways as we add the make and model properties to the two object instances we created in Listing 1.5.

LISTING 1.6   Object Properties

```
var myCar = new Object();
myCar.make = 'Ford';
myCar.model = 'Explorer';

var myCar2 = { make: "Ford", model: "Explorer" };
```

JavaScript stores an object's properties using an associative array, which is an array that is accessed by key rather than index. The dot notation that we used in Listing 1.6 is just another way of accessing the values in the associative array. We could have just as easily added the properties using array syntax. Listing 1.7 demonstrates this concept.

LISTING 1.7   Object Properties as Associative Arrays

```
var myCar = new Object();
myCar.make = 'Ford';
myCar["model"] = 'Explorer';

alert (myCar.make === myCar["make"]); // alerts true.
```

> ■ **NOTE**   Associative Arrays
>
> Associative arrays are a great way of accessing a property on an object by name. Whenever you're tempted to use an eval statement to access the property on an object, you can most likely access it by array position instead.

Because objects store their properties in an associative array, we can iterate over the properties using a for...in loop. Listing 1.8 demonstrates this concept as we iterate over the properties of our myCar object.

LISTING 1.8   Using a for...in Loop

```
var myCar = new Object();
myCar.make = 'Ford';
myCar["model"] = 'Explorer';
myCar.year = 2003;
myCar.mileage = 60000;

var propValues;
for (var propName in myCar) {
  propValues = propValues + " " + myCar[propName];
}

alert (propValues); / alerts "Ford Explorer 2003 60000 ";
```

Just as we defined properties, we can define functions. Listing 1.9 adds the print function to our myCar object.

LISTING 1.9   Object Functions

```
myCar.print = function() {
  alert (this.make + " " + this.model);
};
myCar.print(); // alerts 'Ford Explorer'
```

We could have done all of this using the Object Literal notation, too. Listing 1.10 shows how to create the same object using Object Literal notation.

LISTING 1.10   Object Literal Notation

```
var myOtherCar = {
  make: "Ford",
  model: "Explorer",
  year: 2003,
  mileage: 60000
  print: function() {
    alert (this.make + " " + this.model);
  }
}

myOtherCar.print // alerts 'Ford Explorer'
```

Adding properties and functions to an existing object is useful in many cases, but has serious drawbacks because those properties and functions are added only to that particular instance. If we wanted to create another object that has the same properties and functions, we would have to re-add them to the new object instance. Fortunately, JavaScript provides other ways of attaching properties and functions to an object so that they have to be defined only one time. We cover this mechanism in the "Object-Oriented JavaScript Programming" section of this chapter.

> ### ■ NOTE   Expando Properties
>
> Adding properties and functions to an object in the manner we just discussed is called adding an Expando property. Expando properties tend to be slow performing when compared to custom objects; so although they have some useful purposes, their use should be limited to those situations where you have no choice but to use them. Instead, you should use the custom object technique we cover in the "Object-Oriented JavaScript Programming" section of this chapter.

After we add a property or a function to an object, we can set its value back to `null` by assigning `null` to it, as shown here:

```
myCar.print = null;
```

This is useful, but if we iterate over this object using the `for...in` loop, `print` will still be included in the loop. If you don't want the property at all anymore and want to completely remove it, you can delete it from the object using the `delete` command as follows:

```
delete myCar.print;
```

Deleting a property removes it from the object so that it will no longer be returned from the `for...in` loop, and if accessed, it returns `undefined`.

JavaScript Object Notation (JSON)

JSON is a data interchange format similar to XML in purpose, but lighter than XML when compared on the number of characters needed to define an object with the same content. Listing 1.11 shows the JSON and XML needed to create an object with the same content.

LISTING 1.11   JSON versus XML

```
[
  {
    "Make":"Ford",
    "Model":"Explorer",
    "Year": 2003,
    "Type": "SUV",
    "PreviousOwners" : ["Tony","Mark","Susan"]
  },
  {
    "Make":"Honda",
    "Model":"Accord",
    "Year": 1999,
    "Type": "Sedan",
    "PreviousOwners" : ["Stacey","Bailey","Robin"]
  }
]
<Cars>
 <Car>
  <Make>Ford</Make>
  <Model>Explorer</Model>
  <Year>2003</Year>
  <Type>SUV</Type>
  <PreviousOwners>
   <Owner>Tony</Owner>
   <Owner>Mark</Owner>
   <Owner>Susan</Owner>
  </PreviousOwners>
 </Car>
 <Car>
  <Make>Honda</Make>
  <Model>Accord</Model>
  <Year>1999</Year>
  <Type>Sedan</Type>
  <PreviousOwners>
   <Owner>Stacey</Owner>
   <Owner>Bailey</Owner>
   <Owner>Robin</Owner>
  </PreviousOwners>
 </Car>
</Cars>
```

JSON's syntax is based on the Object Literal notation briefly covered earlier, but the rules for creating valid JSON are stricter in comparison.

The first rule difference is that property names must be enclosed in full quotation marks. In Object Literal notation, they can be enclosed in full quotation marks, single quotation marks, or nothing at all as long as they don't conflict with a reserved word. In JSON, every property name must be enclosed in quotes.

The other rule difference is the type of objects that can be assigned to properties. In Object Literal notation any primitive type or object can be assigned to a property. Not so in JSON. In JSON, only primitive data types, arrays, null, and object literals can be assigned to properties. Because it's used as a data interchange format, it makes sense that functions and other objects aren't allowed to be assigned to properties.

> ■ **NOTE**   JSON in ASP.NET AJAX
>
> JSON is the default response format for web services that are made callable to client code.

Primitive Data Type Wrapper Objects

Each of the primitive data types, boolean, number, and string, has a wrapper object that's accessed through the capitalized version of the primitive data type: `Boolean`, `Number`, and `String`. The wrapper objects derive from the `Object` data type and contain the methods (`substring`, `length`, `toString`, and so on) that we seemingly use directly off variables that point to primitive data types. Because the primitive data types just store data and don't have any methods or properties available to them, JavaScript silently converts the primitive data types to and from the wrapper objects so that we can use methods without having to cast to another object first.

As an example of this implicit conversion, consider the `length` property that we use on the `string` data type shown in Listing 1.12.

LISTING 1.12 Implicit Conversion to Primitive Wrapper Object

```
var x = "Hello!";
var len = x.length;
```

Now when we use the `length` property of the x variable, JavaScript actually converts the primitive string data type to its wrapper `String` object and then executes the `length` property on it.

instanceof

instanceof determines whether an object derives from a particular type. This operation can prove useful when programming systems that work with inherited and derived types, but it works only with objects and does not work with the primitive types. Listing 1.13 demonstrates instanceof in action.

LISTING 1.13   instanceof

```
var x = new Date();
alert (x instanceof Date); // alerts true
alert (x instanceof Object); // also returns true.
```

As you might expect, x is an instance of a Date and an Object because the Date type derives from Object.

The constructor Property

The constructor property references the function that created an object. It can be used to determine an object's type. It is similar to the instanceof operator, but instead of testing to see whether the object is derived or is of a particular type, the constructor property returns the name of the function that created the object, which is really the object's exact type. Listing 1.14 shows how to use the constructor property.

LISTING 1.14   The constructor Property

```
var x = new Number();
if (x.constructor === Number) {
  alert ("x is a number!");
}
```

This code snippet will alert "x is a number!" because we used the Number constructor method to create our object.

The constructor property is key to mimicking a classic object-oriented system, and we cover how to use it for this purpose in the "Object-Oriented JavaScript Programming" section.

> **▪ TIP**   constructor Property of Primitive Data Types
>
> Because the primitive data types don't inherit from Object, you might be wondering what's returned when we examine their constructor properties. Well, at least in Internet Explorer 7 and Firefox, the wrapper object's constructor that's associated to each primitive data type is returned. It seems that even when attempting to access the constructor property, JavaScript casts the primitive types to their wrapper objects.

Variables and Function Arguments

Equality

JavaScript provides two different types of equality models: strict and not strict. The strict equality operators compare both the value and type of the operands and are accessed through the operators === and !==, which are often referred to as strict equal and strict not equal. The not strict equality operators, accessed through the operators == and !=, compare the operands based solely on value. If the operands are not the same type, such as a number and a string, JavaScript attempts to perform a type conversion to an appropriate type before performing the comparison. Both equality models are useful depending on what you're trying to accomplish, but the strict equality operators perform a bit better because they don't require any type conversions before they're executed. Most of the JavaScript code that we'll write and that Microsoft wrote in the Microsoft AJAX Library uses the strict equality operators when a comparison is required.

Scope

Variables in JavaScript are scoped differently than in other block-scoped languages such as C# or Java. In JavaScript, only the global object (the window object in browsers) and functions are variable scope boundaries. Other blocks, such as if-then-else statements and while loops, don't provide a variable scope boundary. This is in contrast to other languages such as C#, where scope can be created anywhere by enclosing code within a pair of curly braces ({}).

Not having the ability to scope variables within a block other than a function means that variables declared inside a block other than the function block will be accessible outside that block. Listing 1.15 shows how we can access a variable declared within an if-then statement from outside the block and how a function acts as a scoping boundary as we unsuccessfully attempt to access a variable declared inside the function from the outside.

LISTING 1.15 Function-Level Variable Scope

```
function myMethod() {
  var insideVariable = 3;
  if (true) {
    var unscopedVariable = new Date();
  }

  // successfully alerts the year
  alert (unscopedVariable.getFullYear());
}

myMethod();
alert (insideVariable); // alerts undefined
```

As mentioned, the scoping element other than a function is the global window. The global window is the root of the DOM and is accessed through the window keyword. Everything that we program in JavaScript is in some way or another attached to the global window object, and if you've been procedurally programming with JavaScript, you've been unknowingly (or maybe knowingly) using the global window object a lot. Every time you create a variable in procedural code, you are adding that variable to the window object. In fact, all global variables and functions can be accessed through the window keyword, but we normally leave it off for brevity and just use the variable or function name. To demonstrate this, Listing 1.16 first declares a global variable and then accesses it with and without the window prefix.

LISTING 1.16 Globally Scoped Variables

```
var myGlobalVariable = "I'm global!!";

alert (window.myGlobalVariable); // alerts "I'm global!!"
alert (myGlobalVariable); // also alerts "I'm global!!"
```

As you can see, there's no difference in accessing global variables with or without the window prefix. We half-heartedly suggest, however, that you use the window prefix when accessing global JavaScript variables. It provides clarity on variable scope.

As for global variable usage in JavaScript, they act like global variables in other languages and are accessible from within all scopes. They serve a purpose, but as discussed in the "Object-Oriented JavaScript" section later in this chapter, we can encapsulate our variables in objects, which provide us with benefits such as preventing variable-name collisions.

Finally, variables that aren't declared before they are used, as shown in Listing 1.17, are dynamically declared as a global variable by the JavaScript runtime. Having the runtime create a global variable automatically for us is expensive because the runtime searches for the variable's declaration in all valid scopes before creating a new variable. To eke out the most performance of our code and to avoid frustrating, hard-to-track-down bugs, we should always declare variables before they are used.

LISTING 1.17 Undeclared Variables

```
myVariable = "Hello!"; // missing var keyword
alert (myVariable) // alerts "Hello!"
function myMethod() {
  myOtherVariable = "hi!"; // missing var keyword
}

myMethod();
alert (myOtherVariable); // alerts "hi!";
```

null and undefined

null and undefined are two reserved words that deserve special attention.

null is a reserved word that means no value and is used to point a variable to no data so that memory can be reused. Unlike the .NET languages, however, null (or Nothing in VB) is not the default value of a newly declared variable. Rather, undefined is the default value of a newly declared variable.

undefined is a primitive value *and* a type. Both styles of undefined are supported by all modern browsers, but they serve different purposes. As a primitive value, undefined refers to a newly declared variable's default value. As a type, undefined refers to a variable that has never been declared and is accessed using the typeof keyword. Listing 1.18 demonstrates the different usages of null and undefined.

LISTING 1.18 Comparing null and the undefined Value

```
var x = null;
var y;

alert (x); // alerts 'null'
alert (y); // alerts 'undefined'-this is a value.
alert (typeof(z)); // alerts-'undefined' this is a type.
alert (y == typeof(z)); // alerts 'false'
```

Comparing a null valued variable and an undefined valued variable will evaluate to true when using the nonstrict comparison and evaluate to false when using the strict comparison, as shown in Listing 1.19.

LISTING 1.19 Comparing null to Itself

```
var x;
alert (x == null); // alerts 'true'
alert (x === null); // alerts 'false'
```

This typeof comparison is using undefined as a primitive value. If we were to use undefined as a type, using the keyword typeof to return us a type, comparing to null will evaluate to false, using either strict or nonstrict. Listing 1.20 demonstrates this.

LISTING 1.20 Comparing Using the undefined Type

```
var x;
alert (typeof(x) == null); // alerts 'false'
alert (typeof(x) === null); // alerts 'false'
```

As shown in the "Function Arguments" section later in the chapter, undefined is useful for determining whether an argument was passed into a function.

typeof

typeof returns a string based on the data type of its operand. The operand can be a variable, string, object, or keyword. typeof is most commonly used to determine whether a variable has been declared and/or assigned to by testing it against the undefined type we described earlier. Listing 1.21 demonstrates this type of usage.

LISTING 1.21   Using typeof to Test Variable Declaration and Assignment

```
var x;
alert (typeof(x)); // alerts "undefined"

function abc (param1) {
  if (typeof(param1) === "undefined") {
    alert ("param1 was not supplied.");
  }
}

// execute abc, but leave out the parameter
abc();
```

Using typeof on variables can produce some interesting results. Table 1.3 displays the results of executing typeof on variables of the stated types.

TABLE 1.3 typeof Evaluations

Statement	Output
alert (typeof(new Array()));	"object"
alert (typeof(new Object ()));	"object"
alert (typeof(new Date()));	"object"
alert (typeof(new String("hi!")));	"object"
alert (typeof (33));	"number"
alert (typeof (true));	"boolean"
alert (typeof ("hi!"));	"string"
alert (typeof (null));	"object"
alert (typeof (undefined));	"undefined"

Notice how the `null`, `Array`, and `Date` types return `"object"` as their data types. This might seem a bit odd at first because we expect the method call to return something more representative of the actual object, such as `"Array"` or `"Date"`. This is a quirk of the `typeof` function. It returns only the base type of the operand. Because all variables at their base types are fundamentally either a primitive data type, an object, or undefined, those are the only types of values that `typeof` returns.

Function Arguments

You can explicitly define a function's arguments using the following common pattern:

```
function fn(var1, var2)
```

However, explicit definition isn't required because method arguments are always supplied to the function in a special local `arguments` variable. This local variable is accessible once inside the function through the `arguments` keyword. Each function has its own local `arguments` variable, including functions that are contained within other functions. The `arguments` local variable acts like a quasi-array but without any of the array methods such as `join` or `split`. It has two properties: `length` and `callee`. `length` refers to the number of entries in the array, and `callee` refers to currently executing function.

arguments Variable

Let's take a look at some code that uses the local `arguments` variable. Listing 1.22 shows a function where the arguments aren't explicitly specified, but they are still available.

LISTING 1.22 Implicit Arguments

```
function myMethod() {
  var firstArgument = arguments[0];
  alert (firstArgument); // alerts "Ford"
}

myMethod ("Ford");
```

The execution of this block of code will alert "Ford" because it was the first argument supplied to the argument list of the method. If we had supplied other arguments in the method call, they would be available in the subsequent array positions.

We can also code functions that explicitly name parameters as they are passed into the method. Parameters are named based on the position in which they are listed and the order in which they are passed. The code in Listing 1.23 explicitly names parameters as they are passed into the method and also compares the argument at the first position in the arguments variable with the named make parameter to demonstrate that they are the same thing.

LISTING 1.23 Explicit Arguments

```
function myMethod2(make, model) {
  alert (make); // alerts "Ford"
  alert (model); // alerts "Explorer"
  alert (make === arguments[0]); alerts "true"
}

myMethod2("Ford", "Explorer");
```

Finally, if we name a parameter, but one isn't passed in, our parameter's type will be undefined, as shown in Listing 1.24.

LISTING 1.24 Undefined Arguments

```
function myMethod2(make, model) {
  alert (make); // alerts "Ford"
  alert (typeof(model) === "undefined"); // alerts true.
}

myMethod2("Ford");
```

Having the ability to pass in an arbitrary range of arguments enables us to handle arguments in a dynamic manner. For instance, we can define a worker method that executes another method with an arbitrary number of parameters. Listing 1.25 demonstrates this idea.

LISTING 1.25 Dynamic Arguments

```
function executeOtherFunction () {
  if (arguments.length > 0) {
    var method = arguments[0] + "("
    for (var i=1; i<arguments.length; i++) {
      method = method + arguments [i];
      if (i < arguments.length-1) {
        method = method + ",";
      }
    }
    method = method + ");";
    eval (method);
  }
}

function otherFunction () {
  if (arguments.length > 0) {
    for (var i=0; i<arguments.length; i++) {
      alert (arguments[i]);
    }
  }
}

executeOtherFunction ("otherFunction", "Ford", "Explorer", 1999);
```

Although this code demonstration is a bit contrived, this ability is useful in real-world examples, such as in a dynamic code execution engine.

callee

The `callee` property available on a function's local `arguments` variable accesses the function being executed. Listing 1.26 shows an example of using `arguments.callee` to access the `sayHello` method.

LISTING 1.26 arguments.callee

```
function sayHello(name) {
  alert ("Hi " + name);
  alert ("My method name is: " + arguments.callee);
}
sayHello("Bob")
```

This might seem like an unnecessary feature, but when we use anonymous methods, the `callee` property can prove especially useful because we have no name to refer to our anonymous method if it needs to be called again. Listing 1.27 demonstrates this idea; we implement a factorial function through recursion, which relies on an anonymous function to perform the factorial work.

LISTING 1.27   Recursive Anonymous Methods with arguments.callee

```
function doFactorial() {
  return function(x) {
    if (x<=1) {
      return 1;
    }
    else {
      return x*arguments.callee(x-1);
    }
  }
}

alert ("Factorial of 5: " + doFactorial()(5)); // alerts 120(5*4*3*2*1)
```

> **■ NOTE   arguments.caller**
>
> `caller` is another property that might be available on the local `arguments` variable. It refers to the method that called the currently executing method. However, because not all modern browsers support `arguments.caller`, use it carefully.

this

`this` in JavaScript points to the current owner of the executing method. It functions much like `this` in C# and can point to the global window object if the executing method is procedural, a DOM element if the executing method is handling a DOM event, or an object if the executing method is contained within the object's definition. Listing 1.28 displays the described scenarios.

LISTING 1.28 The Different Uses of this

```
function proceduralFunction() {
  // in a procedural function, this points to the window
}
proceduralFunction();

function clickFunction() {
  // in a function that handles an event, this points to the
  // DOM element (myButton)
}
myButton.onclick = clickFunction;

MyObject = function MyObject() {
  this.method = function() {
    // in a function contained within an object,
    // this points to MyObject
  }
}

var my = new MyObject();
my.method();
```

Error Handling

JavaScript provides two different mechanisms for trapping and handling errors. It provides a try-catch-finally mechanism for catching and handling errors and a global error event for handling uncaught errors.

Try-Catch-Finally Mechanism

The try-catch-finally mechanism works similarly to the one available in C# and other languages. Code wrapped in a `try` block that causes an error to be thrown transfers control to the `catch` block, which receives as a parameter an instance of the built-in `Error` type describing the error that occurred. Listing 1.29 displays a basic `try-catch` block.

LISTING 1.29 Basic try-catch Statement

```
try {
  var a = null;
  a.prop = "bad value.";
}
catch (e) { }
```

In our example, because a is null and we try to assign a value to the prop property, an error is thrown. When the error is thrown, the catch block takes control. The catch block accepts a single parameter, e, which is an instance of the Error type. The Error type has two standard properties, as listed in Table 1.4.

TABLE 1.4 Standard Error Properties

Property Name	Description
name	The type of the error that occurred. The possible types vary from browser to browser, but the most common ones are Error, EvalError, RangeError, SyntaxError, TypeError, and URIError.
message	Information about the error that actually occurred.

Browsers also implement useful nonstandard error properties. Just be careful to check for a property's existence before accessing it. Table 1.5 details the properties.

TABLE 1.5 Nonstandard Error Properties

Property Name	Browser	Description
number	Internet Explorer	A proprietary number that indicates the type of error that occurred
description	Internet Explorer	A string property that can hold different information than the message property
fileName	Firefox	The path of the file that contains the code that caused the error
lineNumber	Firefox	The line on which the error occurred
stack	Firefox	A stack trace of all method calls up until the error occurred
line	Safari	The line on which the error occurred
sourceURL	Safari	The URL of the file that contains the code that caused the error

Once the `catch` block has control, it can use the error parameter for whatever purpose you define, such as displaying a message to the user or publishing the error back to the server using AJAX.

TIP   Error Publishing

With the increasingly large amount of JavaScript code we're writing for our web applications, more errors are occurring at the browser level. Although we've had general error logging mechanisms at the server level for a while now, we're normally blind to the errors that crop up on client machines resulting from bad JavaScript. If you're writing an AJAX application, a good idea is to plan a client error publishing mechanism to send client errors back to the server so that you're notified of them. Just make sure it doesn't cause any errors itself!

We cover a client error handling component in Chapter 3, "Components," and you can find its source in Appendix D, "Client Error Handling Code."

Besides catching runtime exceptions, you can create and throw your own errors. You do this by creating a new `Error` object and then throwing it using the `throw` command. Listing 1.30 shows how to do so.

LISTING 1.30   Throwing an Error

```
function fn (param1) {
  if (typeof(param1) === "undefined") {
    var err = new Error();
    err.message = "Param1 was not supplied";
    err.name = "Missing Parameter";
    throw err;
  }
}

try {
  fn();
}
catch (e) {
  alert ("Name: " + e.name + "\nMessage: " + e.message);
}
```

Figure 1.1 displays the output of Listing 1.30.

FIGURE 1.1 Output of caught error alert

The last part of the try-catch-finally mechanism is the finally block. As with C#, the finally block always executes after either the try block or the catch block execution is complete. It's useful for cleaning up any variables or objects that might have been affected by either the try or catch blocks. Listing 1.31 shows how to use the finally block; we update a global variable to the current date when the finally block executes.

LISTING 1.31 Using the finally Block

```
window.lastExecutionCompletedDate = null;

function fn (param1) {
    ...
}

try {
    fn();
}
catch (e) {
    alert ("Name: " + e.name + "\nMessage: " + e.message);
}
finally {
    window.lastExecutionCompletedDate = new Date();
}
```

Unhandled Exceptions

The other error handling mechanism is the global error event attached to the window, which can be used as a catchall for unhandled errors. We can trap unhandled errors by creating a function that handles the error event. Listing 1.32 shows how to wire up to the error event.

LISTING 1.32   **The Error Event Handler**

```
function errorHandler (message, errorURL, lineNumber) {}
window.onerror = errorHandler;
```

The signature for the error handler function takes three parameters: the error message, the URL of the page where the error occurred, and the line number of where the error occurred.

> ■ **NOTE**   **Line Number**
>
> The line number is notoriously wrong in Internet Explorer.

Now, when an unhandled error occurs, our `errorHandler` method takes over. Listing 1.33 shows a more complete version of the error handler and code that causes an unhandled error.

LISTING 1.33   **Globally Handling an Error**

```
function errorHandler (message, errorURL, lineNumber) {
  var outputMessage =
    "Message: " + message +
    "\nURL: " + errorURL +
    "\nLine Number: " + lineNumber;
  alert (outputMessage);
}
window.onerror = errorHandler;

var a = null;
a.value = "bad value.";
```

Figure 1.2 shows the output of executing Listing 1.32.

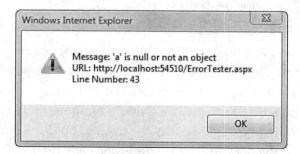

FIGURE 1.2   Output of unhandled error alert

Delayed Code Execution Using Timeouts and Intervals

JavaScript provides two ways to register code for delayed execution through timeouts and intervals. Some common uses of timeouts and intervals are animation, helping to check a session's activeness at various points in time, delayed response to a DOM event such as a mouseover, and a whole host of other applications.

Timeouts and intervals are identical except for one difference. Timeouts execute only after the delay expires, whereas intervals execute when the time delay expires *and* then reset themselves so that they will continually execute after the delay expires. In this sense, the time delay is really an interval.

Timeouts

Creating a timeout is done through the `window.setTimeout` method. When you call the `setTimeout` method, you pass in the code you want to execute after the delay expires and the amount of the delay in milliseconds:

```
window.setTimeout("alert('x');", 1000);
```

The preceding code registers the statement `alert('x');` to execute after 1,000 milliseconds has expired.

The `setTimeout` method returns a unique number called the timeout ID. The timeout ID can be used to prevent the code from executing when the delay expires by executing the `window.clearTimeout` method with the timeout ID as its argument. Listing 1.34 demonstrates how to cancel the timeout.

LISTING 1.34   Canceling a Timeout

```
var timeoutId = window.setTimeout("alert('x');", 1000);
window.clearTimeout(timeoutId);
```

If the `window.clearTimeout` method executes before the 1,000 millisecond delay expires, the timeout is canceled, and its code won't execute.

Understanding how the code registered with the timeout (as well as interval) executes when the delay expires is tantamount to using timeouts successfully. In Listing 1.34, we used a string to hold the code we wanted to execute when the delay expired. This is one code registration option that `setTimeout` supports. In the background, JavaScript automatically wraps our string in an anonymous function when it creates the timeout and then executes the function when the delay expires. Listing 1.35 displays the code that JavaScript actually executes.

LISTING 1.35 Automatically Generated Function

```
function anonymous()
{
  alert('x');
}
```

The other code registration option that `setTimeout` supports is using a function. The function can be either a predefined function or an anonymous function we define inline. Listing 1.36 displays the `setTimeout` call using an anonymous function as its code registration method, and Listing 1.37 shows the same functionality using a predefined function.

LISTING 1.36 Explicit Anonymous Function

```
window.setTimeout(
  function () {
    alert ("x");
  },
1000);
```

LISTING 1.37 Predefined Function

```
function preDefined() {
  alert ("x");
}
window.setTimeout(preDefined, 1000);
```

> **■ NOTE   Zero Parameter Methods**
>
> The automatic calls to the functions registered in the `setTimeout` or `setInterval` methods will not pass in any parameters. The methods we specify can be defined with parameters for use in other cases, but if we try to access the parameters in our function after the `setTimeout` or `setInterval` automatically calls it, the values will be undefined.

One advantage of using a function, either anonymous inline or a pre-defined, instead of a string expression is avoiding the complexity of concatenating a string. In Listing 1.38, we create two timeouts that produce the same result. The first uses the string concatenation method, and the second uses an anonymous function.

LISTING 1.38 Explicit Anonymous Function

```
var a = new Date();
var b = "Hello!";

window.setTimeout ("alert ('" + b + " today is " + a + "');", 1000);

window.setTimeout(
  function () {
    alert (b + " today is " + a);
  },
  1000);
```

As Listing 1.38 shows, because we're trying to use a string in the code we want to register, the string concatenation needed to create the valid string expression gets complicated very quickly even when working with our simple example. On the other hand, using a function allows us to program normally and keep the code readable. When we execute the code in Listing 1.38, we receive two identical alerts that look something like what's shown in Figure 1.3.

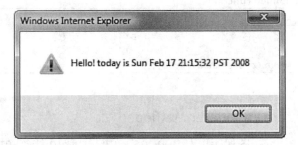

FIGURE 1.3 Output of alert registered with timeout

There are some difficulties, however, with using a function rather than a string. The difficulties lie in what the parameter values are when the method executes after the delay.

The fact that the two alerts created by Listing 1.38 are identical is actually just luck. The only reason they're identical is because the variables do not change once we create the second timeout. We can see how fragile the identical methods are by altering our code slightly. Listing 1.39 adds a statement that updates variable b to "boo!" once we create the second timeout.

LISTING 1.39 Problems with Functions and Variables

```
var a = new Date();
var b = "Hello!";

window.setTimeout ("alert ('" + b + " today is " + a + "');", 1000);

window.setTimeout(
  function () {
    alert (b + " today is " + a);
  },
1000);

b = "Boo!";
```

Now when our timeouts execute they do not produce the same alerts. The first timeout still produces the same alert shown in Figure 1.3, but the second timeout produces an alert similar to Figure 1.4.

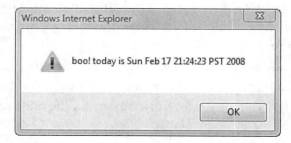

FIGURE 1.4 Output of alert after we modified variable b

The reason this happens is because of a subtlety in how the string expression treats variables. As mentioned earlier, when JavaScript encounters the string, it wraps the string in an anonymous method, and that's what is executed when the delay expires. When JavaScript creates this anonymous method and there are variables included in the string used to create the method as there are in our example, it evaluates those parameters at the time that the function is created. So, rather than create a function that looks similar to the one used in the second `setTimeout` method, it looks like the one shown in Listing 1.40.

LISTING 1.40   Automatically Generated Anonymous Function

```
function anonymous()
{
  alert ('Hello! today is Sun Feb 17 21:28:36 PST 2008');
}
```

Now when our timeout expires it alerts the predetermined string, and even though we've modified the b's value before the timeout expires, the modification has no effect.

In comparison, when a function is used, the function attached to the timeout and the variable references inside the function are evaluated when the delay expires and the function executes. This different execution pattern means that the variables used inside the function could have been modified since the timeout was created.

As you might have guessed, this could be an undesirable characteristic of our timeout because we might want our timeout to use the variable's value as it was when the timeout was created. Yet, we also don't want to resort to using a string for our timeout, because it's hard to work with.

Don't worry; there is a way around this problem. First, let's fix the anonymous function version of our code, and then we can cover how to fix the predefined function version.

If we wrap our `setTimeout` in a function and then immediately execute it, we can create scope and thus remember the original values of our variables. Listing 1.41 demonstrates how we can fix the anonymous function method.

LISTING 1.41   Inducing Scope for Our Anonymous Function

```
var fn = function(c,d) {
  window.setTimeout(
    function () {
      alert (d + " today is " + c);
    },
    1000);
}(a,b);
```

Here we define the function fn that expects the two parameters c and d. As soon as we declare fn, we immediately execute it, passing in the variables a and b, which at this point haven't been modified. Those values are then assigned to fn's parameters c and d, respectively. Then our setTimeout method executes, creating our timeout. We've replaced the variables a and b in the timeout's anonymous function with c and d. We are able to do this because of a JavaScript feature called closures. Because fn's execution will be complete by the time the anonymous method inside the timeout executes, you might think that the timeout's anonymous method wouldn't have access to c and d. But because of JavaScript's closure feature, c and d are still available to the timeout's anonymous method. The general closure principle that we use here is that a function declared inside another function will have access to the outer functions arguments even after the outer function's execution has completed. We talk some more about closures later on in this chapter when we cover object-oriented JavaScript programming.

Now, when our second timeout executes, the alert will use b's initial "Hello!" value instead of the latter "Boo!" value.

> **■ NOTE   Scope Problems**
>
> Another problem with setTimeout and setInterval is that when the code that is registered with the timeout executes, this will always be the global window object, even if we create our timeout from within an object. This is the case because both methods are attached to the window object and therefore our registered code executes with the window object as its owner. With window as the method's owner, the window becomes this.
>
> Maintaining scope is a larger problem than just dealing with timeouts and intervals. The section "Maintaining Scope" in Chapter 2, "Microsoft AJAX Library Programming," explains how to overcome this problem using features in the Microsoft AJAX Library.

Fixing the predefined version is similar to the anonymous version, but is a bit more complicated. Listing 1.42 displays the fixed version.

LISTING 1.42 Inducing Scope for Our Predefined Function

```javascript
var a = new Date();
var b = "Hello!";

function preDefined(c, d) {
  alert (d + " today is " + c);
}

function curry(func, a,b) {
  return function() {
    func(a,b);
  }
}
window.setTimeout(curry(preDefined,a,b), 1000);

b = "Boo!";
```

When the `window.setTimeout` method executes, the first parameter to the `setTimeout` call is actually a method call into `curry`, which is defined above it. The parameters passed into the `curry` method are the `predefined` function, a, and b. `curry` then proceeds to create and return an anonymous function that will execute the predefined function with values a and b. This anonymous function gets registered with the timeout. By passing a and b into the `curry` function, we've again created a closure; so when the anonymous method executes, values a and b are what they were when the `curry` method executed.

■ **TIP** Curry Methods

Curry methods are a common tool in functional programming. In our case, we're using a curry method to reduce the number of parameters. We need to get a and b into our anonymous method, but `setTimeout` accepts only methods with no parameters. To get around this, we curry our parameters into our anonymous method early. Doing this also enables us to retain the original values of a and b.

When Will a Timeout Execute?

Unlike .NET, the current versions of JavaScript are single threaded. It doesn't have the capabilities to execute more than one statement at a time. Given that, a timeout executes when the following conditions are true:

1. The timeout's delay has expired.
2. No older expired timeouts are waiting to be executed.
3. The current call stack is completed.

The first condition is straightforward. The timeout's delay must have expired for it to be added to the list of things to execute.

The second condition, when there are no other older expired timeouts waiting to execute, pretty much means that our expired timeout needs to get in line. If there are other expired timeouts waiting to execute and they've been in line longer than our expired timeout has, they go first.

The third condition, when the current call stack is completed, means that while the current call stack still has instructions to execute, JavaScript will not switch to another call stack. Example call stacks are all the code executed by a single event handler, the callback of an AJAX method, and a timeout's anonymous method. When JavaScript starts executing a call stack, it won't stop until it has finished. When it has finished, it will be available to execute another call stack that's been added to the queue of call stacks to be processed, which could be our expired timeout.

The following code illustrates how a timeout's execution is delayed because the current call stack hasn't completed:

```
window.setTimeout ("alert ('" + b + " today is " + a + "');", 1000);

var x="";
for (var i=0; i<75000;i++) {
    x+= i.toString();
}
```

Because the loop doesn't complete for quite a while, the timeout can't execute, even though it has expired.

Intervals

Intervals are identical to timeouts except that the function or string expression is continuously evaluated at the specified interval until the interval is canceled, instead of executing only one time when the delay expires. We create an interval in Listing 1.43 using a `window.setInterval` method that continually appends `"hello!"` to the `div` tag `"abc"`.

LISTING 1.43   Using an Interval

```
<body>
  <form id="form1" runat="server">
    <div id="abc" />
  </form>

  <script type="text/javascript">
    var div = document.getElementById("abc");
    var intervalId = window.setInterval(
      "div.innerHTML += 'hello!';", 1000);
  </script>
</body>
```

Figure 1.5 displays the effects of the interval executing seven times.

```
hello!hello!hello!hello!hello!hello!hello!
```

FIGURE 1.5   Output of the abc div tag after 7 seconds

Just as with timeouts, intervals can be canceled using the ID that is returned and the `clearInterval` method.

LISTING 1.44   Clearing an Interval

```
var intervalId = window.setInterval("alert('x');", 1000);
window.clearInterval(timeoutId);
```

Other than that, there really aren't any other differences between an interval and a timeout. The same rules apply to when an interval will execute and the intricacies of using expressions and functions.

Object-Oriented JavaScript Programming

Because most ASP.NET programmers have backgrounds in classic, class-based object-oriented systems, the Microsoft AJAX Library was designed to mimic a classic object-oriented system in JavaScript to provide a development experience most of its audience would find welcoming. The Microsoft AJAX Library implements new programming constructs to achieve this classic object-oriented system, but those constructs all rely on JavaScript language features, some of which were described in the preceding section, for their implementations. These constructs are available for use without understanding how they were implemented, but it's our opinion that one can't successfully develop within the Microsoft AJAX Library, even with the new, more familiar constructs, without understanding the basics of how a classic object-oriented system can be created using out-of-the-box JavaScript.

So, in this section, we walk through how we can achieve two common object-oriented principles, abstract data types and inheritance in JavaScript, without using the Microsoft AJAX Library. This should set you up for success when you start using the constructs provided by the Microsoft AJAX Library to create new systems.

> **■ NOTE   A Word about JavaScript and Classic Object-Oriented Systems**
>
> JavaScript is a prototypal object language. It can be coerced into mimicking a classic system, but we're not advocating that mimicking a classic object-oriented system is in fact the best way to program with JavaScript. In fact, some JavaScript purists believe that coercing JavaScript in this way is sacrilegious. However, because this book is looking at JavaScript through the ASP.NET AJAX lens and the Microsoft AJAX Library mimics a classic object-oriented system, it seems appropriate that we consider JavaScript in a classic system manner only rather than introduce other ways of working with it.
>
> Furthermore, there are a few different approaches to coerce JavaScript so that it mimics a classic object-oriented system. The way we describe in this section is just one way, and a not full-baked way at that. A cursory Internet search on "object-oriented JavaScript" will show that opinions differ greatly about how best to achieve a classic system in JavaScript and that the idea is continually evolving.

Abstract Data Types

As stated earlier in the section "Generally JavaScript," JavaScript doesn't support the `class` keyword as conventional object-oriented languages such as Java, C#, and C++ do. Instead, JavaScript relies on functions having double duty as both procedural entry points and abstract data type definitions. In fact, every JavaScript programmer who has created a function has already created a new abstract data type. Let's take a look at the simple example in Listing 1.45. The first thing we do is declare a new empty function: `Book`. Then we execute the function and assign it to the variable `execResult`. Then we do something a bit different and use the `Book` function as an object constructor.

LISTING 1.45   Defining Types

```
function Book() {}

var execResult = Book();
var myBook = new Book();
```

We can do this because the `function` keyword doubles as both a constructor function and a procedural method declaration. This allows us to both create a new object using the function and execute it as a procedural method. The `new` keyword determines which path the `function` keyword takes: Execute the method as a constructor or a procedural method that returns a result.

After we have an object, `myBook`, we can dynamically add properties to the instance as shown in Listing 1.46.

LISTING 1.46   Adding Properties to an Instance

```
myBook.publisher = 'Addison & Wesley';
myBook.subject = 'ASP.NET';

alert (myBook.subject === 'ASP.NET'); // alerts true
```

As we described earlier, the problem with adding properties this way is that if we create another instance of type `Book`, we no longer have access to the properties we just defined because they were only added to the instance of that object, not to the abstract data type's definition. Listing 1.47

demonstrates that if we determine the typeof the subject property on another instance of the Book type, we're returned the undefined type.

LISTING 1.47 Undefined Properties

```
var myOtherBook = new Book();
alert (typeof(myOtherBook.subject)); // alerts 'undefined';
```

If we want properties to be available to all instances of the object, we have to define them in the constructor, which in turn adds to the abstract data type's definition. Listing 1.48 demonstrates this as we add the publisher, subject, and publishYear properties to the Book type.

LISTING 1.48 Defining Type Members

```
function Book() {
  this.publisher = null;
  this.subject= null;

  var publishYear = 1998;
}
```

The this keyword that we use to define the publisher and subject members is used to add members to the object so that they are publicly visible. The publishYear member defined using the var keyword is actually private to the Book's constructor. If we try to access it from outside Book, we'll receive undefined as the result.

Now, when we create another Book, the publisher and subject members will be defined and initialized to null. Listing 1.49 demonstrates the null publisher property and the undefined publishYear member.

LISTING 1.49 Default Values and Private Members

```
var myGoodBook = new Book();
alert (myGoodBook.publisher == null);
alert(typeof(myGoodBook.publishYear) === 'undefined');
```

If we want to supply parameters to our constructor, we can just specify them as we normally would for a method, as shown in Listing 1.50.

LISTING 1.50 Constructor Parameters

```
function Book(publisher, subject, publishYear) {
  this.publisher = publisher;
  this.subject = subject;

  var publishYear = publishYear;
}
```

Now, when we create a new Book, we can specify the publisher, subject, and publish year, as shown in Listing 1.51.

LISTING 1.51 Creating an Instance with Parameters

```
var myAJAXBook = new Book("A&W", "ASP.NET AJAX", 2007);
alert (myAJAXBook.subject === "ASP.NET AJAX");
```

Finally, we can assign new methods to our class to support behavior, as shown in Listing 1.52. The two methods prefixed with this, IsSubjectDotNet, and IsBookNewAndCool will be publicly available on instances of the object. The methods really aren't any different from the publisher and subject properties. They just point to functions rather than strings (remember, functions are objects, too). The other method, WasPublishedThisYear, is private to the Book constructor and can be accessed by public methods, but is not visible externally. It can, however, access the private variable publishYear and be accessed by public members as shown in the IsBookNewAndCool method.

LISTING 1.52 Defining Publicly Visible Methods

```
Book = function (publisher, subject, publishYear) {
  this.publisher = publisher;
  this.subject = subject;

  var publishYear = publishYear;

  this.IsSubjectDotNet = function() {
    return (this.subject.indexOf('NET') !== -1);
  }

  this.IsBookNewAndCool = function() {
    return (WasPublishedThisYear() && this.IsSubjectDotNet ());
  }

  WasPublishedThisYear = function () {
```

```
      var currdate = new Date();
      return (currdate.getFullYear() === publishYear);
  }
}

var myFinalBook = new Book('A&W', '.NET', 2007);

// alerts true
alert (typeof(myFinalBook.WasPublishedThisYear) === "undefined");
// alerts true
alert (myFinalBook.IsSubjectDotNet());
// alerts false
alert (myFinalBook.IsBookNewAndCool());
```

This is a complete definition of an abstract data type in JavaScript. We could use this abstract data type on any page in a repetitive, consistent manner, but it has a major problem. Every time the Book constructor is executed, it assigns the publisher and subject properties their respective values, but it also creates and assigns the IsSubjectDotNet and IsBookNewAndCool functions to the current object, this. Creating and assigning the functions this way is actually quite expensive in terms of execution time and resources. However, there is a better way to create and assign functions to an abstract data type. From the "Generally JavaScript" section, you know that the objects in JavaScript are prototype based. If we edit the Book's prototype and add the IsSubjectDotNet and IsBookNewAndCool methods to it, when we create a new Book instance we will use its prototype as the template. This will reduce the execution time for creating a Book instance and also reduce the memory footprint each instance holds. Listing 1.53 demonstrates adding the methods to the Book's prototype instead of creating them and assigning them to each Book instance.

LISTING 1.53 Defining Prototype-Based Methods

```
Book = function (publisher, subject, publishYear) {
  this.publisher = publisher;
  this.subject = subject;

  var publishYear = publishYear;
  WasPublishedThisYear = function() {
    var currdate = new Date();
    return (currdate.getFullYear() === publishYear);
  }
}
```

LISTING 1.53 continued

```
Book.prototype.IsSubjectDotNet = function() {
  return (this.subject.indexOf('NET') !== -1);
}

Book.prototype.IsBookNewAndCool = function() {
  return (WasPublishedThisYear() && this.IsSubjectDotNet ());
}

var myFinalBook = new Book('A&W', '.NET', 2007);

// alerts "true"
alert (myFinalBook.IsSubjectDotNet());
// alerts "false"
alert (myFinalBook.IsBookNewAndCool());
```

Now, whenever a new Book instance is created, its methods are cloned from its prototype. Using the prototype method is the best performing way to create methods and assign them to an abstract data type's definition because only one copy of the methods is created and stored versus creating them for each object instance.

Prototyping in a Prototype Language

The concept of prototyping is the major tenet of prototype-based languages, of which JavaScript is one. In prototype-based languages, objects are not instantiated by creating an instance of a particular class from a class definition, but rather are cloned from existing objects and thus copy the behavior (the prototype) of the existing object, preserving the same qualities as the original. To create a new object type, we modify the prototype of an object and then clone it as needed. In JavaScript, we modify an object's prototype by manipulating a special property called prototype. This is what we did in the example in Listing 1.53. An interesting property of prototypes is that when we manipulate an object's prototype, all instances of that object recognize the change immediately. For instance, if we add a new function to our Book's prototype, when we have an instance of the object the instance of the object will be able to access the new function. Listing 1.54 demonstrates this idea as we add a new method, toArray, and access it from our previously created myFinalBook variable.

LISTING 1.54 Modifying an Existing Object's Prototype

```
...
// create the object.
var myFinalBook = new Book('A&W', '.NET', 2007);

// modify the prototype
Book.prototype.toArray = function() {
  return [this.publisher, this.subject];
}

// new method is available on object
alert (myFinalBook.toArray().length);
```

> **■ NOTE   A Word about Closures**
>
> The "Abstract Data Types" section we just went over relies heavily on the idea of closures. We didn't mention them by name because explaining them and how they work can be a bit difficult, and we really wanted to relate this section to an object-oriented principle with which you might be more familiar.
>
> For those who care, however, a closure is defined as a method that contains local variables and inner functions that still exist after the outer method has completed its execution. Put into more practical terms, a closure is implemented by having one function contain another with a pointer to the inner function being available after the outer function has exited. The `IsBookNewAndCool` function in Listing 1.52 is an example of an inner function declared inside an outer one that's available after the `Book` constructor exited, and thus a new closure was formed when we created an instance of the `Book` type. Important to note is that a new closure is formed every time we create a `Book` instance, and hence the memory footprint of a creating a `Book` closure that contains a lot of inner functions is large as we explained in the discussion of Listing 1.52.
>
> Closures can be used for many different programming tasks other than what we've used them for in this section and also have some serious caveats when it comes to garbage collection, performance, and usage. For more information, we suggest reading the excellent blog entry at http://blog.morrisjohns.com/javascript_closures_for_dummies. For the more theoretical ideas, check out www.jibbering.com/faq/faq_notes/closures. html.

Inheritance

Another important principle of object-oriented development is inheritance. Inheritance is defined as a derived object taking over (inheriting) the data and behavior of another object. This is a common feature in most object-oriented languages and something we assume you're familiar with. JavaScript presents some unique challenges when it comes to inheritance because it doesn't provide an apparent inheritance mechanism directly in the language, and it's left up to the developer to implement an inheritance pattern. Let's take a look at one way we can implement the inheritance pattern in JavaScript by continuing with our Book example.

Using our Book type we defined in Listing 1.53, we want to define a new type called TextBook that inherits from Book. We also want to add a new gradeLevel property to TextBook. To achieve the inheritance, we have to follow three steps. First, we have to define our new TextBook type and chain its constructor to Book's constructor so that when a TextBook is created and its constructor executed, Book's constructor also executes. Second, we need to have our class functions accessible to our derived type, and finally we need to ensure that when queried our derived type returns the correct information regarding its type.

To start, we need to chain our derived type's constructor to our base type's constructor. To do this, we write a helper function called initializeBaseType that will execute our base type's constructor. We're going to attach initializeBaseType to Object's prototype so that we can use it from any object. Listing 1.55 shows the code for initializeBaseType.

LISTING 1.55 Defining initializeBaseType

```
Object.prototype.initializeBaseType = function (baseType, args) {
  if (arguments.length > 1) {
    baseType.apply(this, args);
  }
  else {
    baseType.call(this);
  }
}
```

initializeBaseType uses either apply or call to execute the baseType's constructor in the scope of this, which will be the derived type, thus creating all the base class's elements on the derived type.

We can then use this helper method when we define our new `TextBook` type, as shown in Listing 1.56.

LISTING 1.56 Calling a Base Constructor Using initializeBaseType

```
TextBook = function(publisher, subject, publishYear, gradeLevel) {
  this.gradeLevel = gradeLevel;
  this.initializeBaseType (Book, [ publisher, subject, publishYear ]);
}
```

Now, when we create a new `TextBook`, the `initializeBaseType` method is executed, and all of `Book`'s properties are assigned to `this`, the current object. Listing 1.57 shows the base property publisher available to the `myTextBook` variable that was created using the `TextBook` constructor.

LISTING 1.57 Accessing Inherited Properties

```
var myTextBook = new TextBook("A&W", "ASP.NET AJAX", 2007, 11);
alert (myTextBook.publisher);
alert (myTextBook.gradeLevel);
```

This works for inheriting properties and functions attached to an object as properties (i.e., using `this`), but we also need to attach methods that are attached to the base type's prototype to the derived type so that we can inherit behavior and data. There are a couple of ways to accomplish this, but a simple way is to assign a new instance of the base type to the prototype of the derived type. The following code shows an example of this pattern with `TextBook`'s prototype being assigned an instance of a `Book`:

```
TextBook.prototype = new Book();
```

In assigning an instance of `Book` to `TextBook`'s prototype, we are in essence assigning `Book`'s public prototype to `TextBook`'s private prototype. Whenever we attempt to access one of `Book`'s methods on a `TextBook` instance, JavaScript will search for that method in the public prototype of `TextBook`. When it determines that the method doesn't exist on its own prototype, it walks to the next prototype in the chain, in this case `Book`'s, and attempts to locate the method there. If it finds it there, the method is executed; but if it doesn't find it there, it continues walking the prototype chain until the chain is exhausted or the method is found and executed. The chain is exhausted when `Object`'s prototype is reached and searched. Initially,

`Object`'s prototype is `null`, but like any other object, `Object`'s prototype can be extended.

> **■. WARNING   Inheritance Implementation**
>
> Defining inheritance this way is a bit limited because we need to ensure that executing a parameterless constructor on `Book` has no undesirable side effects. There are other ways to associate `Book`'s methods to `TextBook` that are more robust and have less potential for problems; for the purposes of this example, however, associating the methods through instance assignment is sufficient.

This prototype chain walk we just described also gives us a way to override base methods in a derived type. If our derived type redefines a method that is defined on the base type, our prototype walk stops at the derived instance's method instead of continuing to the base type's prototype. Listing 1.58 demonstrates an example of redefining the `IsBookNewAndCool` method.

LISTING 1.58 Redefining a Base Class Method

```
TextBook.prototype.IsBookNewAndCool = function() {
   return (this.gradeLevel > 7 && WasPublishedThisYear());
}
```

The final feature of inheritance is the ability to execute a base class method from the inherited class. For instance, what if we want to execute `Book`'s `IsBookNewAndCool` method from within `TextBook`'s `IsBookNewAndCool` method? Unfortunately, this isn't a trivial problem, and it can be a bit cumbersome to solve in a super clean way within JavaScript. For the purposes of our simplistic inheritance example, we can use the code shown in Listing 1.59.

LISTING 1.59 Executing a Base Class Method

```
TextBook.prototype.IsBookNewAndCool = function() {
   return (this.gradeLevel > 7
      && Book.prototype.IsBookNewAndCool.call(this));
}
```

The problem with this code is that it limits us to hard coding our base class's name in the derived class method. It would be much cleaner to use a keyword such as base or super as other object-oriented languages do, but because JavaScript lacks the ability for a class *to know* about its base class, we would have to implement our own base or super keyword and its associated functionality. This isn't impossible—after all, ASP.NET AJAX and other frameworks do it—but it's beyond the scope of this book.

Finally, now that we've pointed TextBook's prototype at an instance of Book, the public constructor property that points back to the method that created the object is broken. If we test Textbook.prototype.constructor, we'll receive the result Book because we've cloned its prototype and assigned it to TextBook's. To fix this, we need to repoint our TextBook's constructor property back to itself:

```
TextBook.prototype.constructor = TextBook;
```

To recap our new code, Listing 1.60 displays the full code listing for creating a new TextBook type that inherits from Book.

LISTING 1.60 Complete Code Sample

```
// Define our new helper method
Object.prototype.inherits = function (parentType) {
  if (arguments.length > 1) {
    baseType.apply(this, arguments);
  }
  else
  {
    baseType.call(this);
  }
}

// define our new TextBook type
TextBook = function (publisher, subject, publishYear, gradeLevel) {
  this.Inherits (Book, publisher, subject, publishYear);
  this.gradeLevel = gradeLevel;
}

TextBook.prototype.IsBookNewAndCool = function() {
  return (this.gradeLevel > 7
    && Book.prototype.IsBookNewAndCool.call(this));

TextBook.prototype = new Book();
TextBook.prototype.constructor = TextBook;
```

SUMMARY

In this chapter, we walked through JavaScript, the programming language of the Microsoft AJAX Library. We began with some JavaScript features and continued by mimicking a classic object-oriented system. Understanding how JavaScript works and how to use it is tantamount to successfully programming using the Microsoft AJAX Library and understanding the code and features we discuss in the rest of the book. The language's nuances and prototypal object pattern can seem a bit odd at first, but it also provides a unique programming experience once accustomed to. As we move through the rest of the book, we use what we've worked through and add it to other JavaScript tidbits of information.

2

Microsoft AJAX Library Programming

NOW THAT WE'VE COMPLETED our dive into JavaScript and object-oriented concepts as implemented in JavaScript, let's start to examine the Microsoft AJAX Library.

The Microsoft AJAX Library is a JavaScript framework that exists to make JavaScript programming easier and quicker. It provides objects and programming constructs that we can use to build applications at a more abstract level than if we had to manipulate plain JavaScript. It's designed to be approachable to ASP.NET developers, so you'll see many concepts and types that look similar to ones an ASP.NET developer will have come across when building pages and controls.

There's nothing magical about the Microsoft AJAX Library, and there's nothing in it that we couldn't have written using plain JavaScript ourselves. The beauty of it is that a bunch of JavaScript experts got together and crafted something that the rest of us could understand and reuse to produce code that is cross-browser compliant, less error-prone, better performing, and easier to read and maintain.

In this chapter, we examine the types and objects that provide the benefits we just mentioned. We start out by exploring new features attached to the built-in types that address some of their shortcomings. We move on to covering a development pattern called the Prototype Model that enables you to build custom object-oriented types to extend the Library. While covering the Prototype Model, we cover how we're using a new type system that's defined in the Library that enables inheritance and interface implementation. Finally, we wrap up this chapter with a look at five new important types—Sys.EventHandlerList, Sys.StringBuilder, Sys.Debug, Sys.UI.DomElement, and Sys.UI.DomEvent—which are available within the Library.

Extending the Built-In JavaScript Types

As discussed in Chapter 1, "Programming with JavaScript," JavaScript contains a series of built-in types: objects, arrays, dates, strings, errors, booleans, numbers, and functions, among others. These built-in types, however, have some faults. Sometimes they lack key capabilities such as trimming a string, and sometimes they make performing a simple task, such as inserting an item into the middle of an array, more difficult than it needs to be.

The Microsoft AJAX Library attempts to overcome some of the built-in types' problems by extending them with new features.

Booleans

The Microsoft AJAX Library extends the built-in Boolean type with a single method: parse. parse converts a string representation of a logical value into a Boolean object. It's used with the following syntax:

```
var myBool = Boolean.parse(stringValue);
```

The result of the parse operation depends on the stringValue. Table 2.1 lists the possible values for the stringValue argument and what their parse result is.

TABLE 2.1 Results of the parse Method

stringValue	Parse Output
`"true"`	true
`"false"`	false
`"True"`	true
`"False"`	false
`true`	Error, value must be `string`
`false`	Error, value must be `string`
`0`	Error, value must be `string`
`1`	Error, value must be `string`
`23432`	Error, value must be `string`
`"test"`	Error, value must be `true` or `false`

As you can tell from the results, only `"True"` and `"False"`—both upper-case and lowercase—are parsed successfully. This feature might seem shallow, but it really comes in handy when we need to accept user input and don't want to be too picky about the format in which they provide it.

> ■ **NOTE**   Wrapper Objects
>
> The new methods that we're discussing here are all attached to objects. Remember, the primitive data types: number, boolean, and string, only hold data. It's their respective wrapper objects: Number, Boolean, and String that have attached functions.

Dates and Numbers

The new methods for working with dates and numbers all have to do with formatting and localization. We cover these topics in detail in Chapter 6, "ASP.NET AJAX Localization," so we defer to that chapter for information about the extensions provided to the date and number types.

Strings

The Microsoft AJAX Library extends the built-in `String` type to include some new methods that .NET developers will find familiar. Table 2.2 lists the methods and syntax.

TABLE 2.2 New String Type Methods

Method Name	Description	Syntax
`startsWith`	Determines whether a `String` object begins with the specified string	var beginsWith = *stringObject*.startsWith (*prefix*);
`endsWith`	Determines whether a `String` object ends with the specified string	var endsWith = *stringObject*.endsWith (*suffix*);
`trim`	Removes leading and trailing whitespace from a `String` object	var trimmedString = *stringObject*.trim();
`trimEnd`	Removes trailing whitespace from a `String` object	var trimmedString = *stringObject*.trimEnd();
`trimStart`	Removes leading whitespace from a `String` object	var trimmedString = *stringObject*.trimStart();

`format`	Replaces each format item in the `String` object with a corresponding value	var formattedString = String.format(*format, args*);
		
		var formatted = String.format("{0:d} items", 6);
		
		// formatted = "6 items"

`localeFormat`	Replaces each format item in the `String` object with a corresponding value, calculating that value based on the current culture	var formattedString = String.localeFormat (*format,args*);
		var formatted = String.localeFormat ("{0:d} items", 6);
		// formatted = "6 items"

> **▪ NOTE**   format and localeFormat
>
> The format and localeFormat methods deserve a little more attention than Table 2.2 provides. Rather than cover it here, we cover it in Chapter 6 when we cover the localization and globalization of all objects, including dates, numbers, and strings.

The methods are pretty self-explanatory, so we leave the examples to you.

Arrays

As with the String object, the Microsoft AJAX Library extends the built-in Array object with useful methods that will be familiar to .NET developers. Table 2.3 details the new methods. Notice that all the methods are static.

TABLE 2.3 New Array Type Methods

Method Name	Description	Syntax
add	Adds an item to the end of the Array object.	`Array.add(arrayObject, item);`
addRange	Adds a series of items to the end of the Array object.	`Array.add(arrayObject, [a,b,c]);`
insert	Inserts an item into an Array object at the specified position.	`Array.insert(arrayObject, item, 3);`
enqueue	Adds an item to the end of the Array object.	`Array.enqueue(arrayObject, item);`
remove	Removes an item from an Array object and returns a Boolean value indicating whether the item was removed successfully.	`var success = Array.remove (arrayObject, item);`
removeAt	Removes an item from an Array object at the specified position.	`Array.removeAt(arrayObject, 3);`

TABLE 2.3 continued

Method Name	Description	Syntax
dequeue	Removes and returns the first of the Array object.	var dequeuedItem = Array.dequeue(*arrayObject*);
contains	Determines whether an item is in the Array object.	var isContained = Array.contains(*arrayObject*, *item*);
indexOf	Returns the index of an item in the Array object. If it isn't found, -1 is returned.	var indexOfItem = Array.indexOf(*arrayObject*, *item*);
foreach	Executes a function against each item in the Array object.	Array.forEach(*arrayObject*, *fn*, *context*);
clone	Creates and returns a shallow copy of the Array object.	var clonedArray = Array.clone(*arrayObject*);
clear	Clears the Array object.	Array.clear(*arrayObject*);
parse	Converts a string into an Array object.	var newArray = Array.parse("[1,2,3,4]");

Most of the new methods attached to the Array type aren't really new. Instead, they wrap single-statement calls on an array instance. For instance, the removeAt method just calls a single line of code:

```
arrayVar.splice(index, 1);
```

Good or bad, the Microsoft AJAX Library wraps the native array methods with ones that are more familiar to the .NET developer.

One of the new array methods that provide functionality other than wrapping a single statement is the forEach method.

forEach

As stated in Table 2.3, the forEach method executes a function against each element of an array, and its syntax is as follows:

```
Array.forEach(arrayObject, fn, context);
```

The array containing the elements is the first parameter, and the function we want to apply to each array element is the second parameter. The third parameter can be anything we want it to be, and it will be available as the current context (i.e., `this`) whenever the function we've defined gets executed.

The function that we define to apply to each array element has a specific syntax we follow. The syntax is this:

```
function fn(element, index, arrayObject) { }
```

With this function, the first parameter is the current element, the second parameter is the index of the current element in the array, and the third parameter is the array containing all the elements.

Within the function, `this` is the context parameter that we originally passed into our `forEach` method call. Listing 2.1 demonstrates a full example of the `forEach` method.

LISTING 2.1   Using Array.forEach

```
var myArray = Array.parse(
  "[
    'Joel@example.com',
    'Adam@example.com',
    'Bob@example.com'
  ]");
var emailTo = '';
function buildEmailTo (emailAddress, index, arrayObject) {
  emailTo += emailAddress + this;
}

Array.forEach(myArray, buildEmailTo, ';');

// alerts 'Joel@example.com;Adam@example.com;Bob@example.com;'
alert (emailTo);
```

The purpose of the `forEach` method is to help you write less code by providing a logical loop structure that allows you to execute an arbitrary method on each element. If used properly, you can avoid writing the same loop more than once.

Errors

We covered JavaScript's built-in error handling framework in the "Error Handling" section of Chapter 1. The Microsoft AJAX Library extends the error handling framework with .NET-like concepts and includes a set of predefined errors. Table 2.4 details the new error types provided by the Microsoft AJAX Library.

TABLE 2.4 Existing Error Types

Name	Similar .NET Exception	Description
argumentNull	System.ArgumentNullException	Argument is null.
argumentOutOfRange	System.ArgumentOutOfRangeException	Argument was outside the range of valid values.
argumentType	None	Argument cannot be converted to an expected type.
argumentUndefined	System.NullReferenceException	Argument is unexpectedly undefined.
invalidOperation	System.InvalidOperationException	Cannot execute operation at the current state of an object.
notImplemented	System.NotImplementedException	Method isn't implemented.
parameterCount	None	Parameter count mismatch.

Creating New Error Types

You might want to create a new reusable error type, and you can follow the Microsoft AJAX Library's pattern of error creation to accomplish this. To start, let's define our new error. Our new error is going to be called the nonPositive error, and it is intended to be thrown when it is determined that a number is less than zero. Listing 2.2 details our code.

LISTING 2.2 Defining an Error Type

```
Error.nonPositive = function(value) {
  var displayMessage = "NonPositive Exception: " + value;
  var e = Error.create(displayMessage,
    {"name": "NonPositive" }
  );
  e.popStackFrame();
  return e;
}
```

Our nonPositive error is just a new object type. It is considered a new Error type because it returns an Error object as its return value. In the method body, the Error.create statement creates the Error object. It creates it with an error message string, and then adds an object that contains additional information about the error. Then, the e.popStackFrame call attempts to attach the current call stack to the error.

> **▪ NOTE** popStackFrame
>
> The popStackFrame error has an effect only when the browser supports a stack property on the Error object. Current browsers are Mozilla Firefox and Opera.

Finally, the error is returned as the function's return value.

> **▪ NOTE** Error Object
>
> We attached the nonPositive error to the global Error object, but doing this was just a design decision for this particular error. We could have left it as a standalone object, or we could have attached it to some other namespace.

Now that we've defined our error, let's use it. Listing 2.3 creates and throws the error if it determines that the value passed in is less than zero.

LISTING 2.3 Throwing an Error

```
function runTest(value) {
  try {
    if (value < 0) {
      throw Error.nonPositive(value);
    }
  }
  catch (e) {
    if (e.name === "NonPositive") {
      alert (e.message);
    }
  }
}

runTest(-2);
runTest(2);
```

Extending the Microsoft AJAX Library

The Microsoft AJAX Library was designed to be extensible so that it can be adapted to your application's needs. We extend it by creating custom objects through a development pattern called the Prototype Model and the Library's type system. We can extend it with new types of classes, interfaces, and enumerations.

The Prototype Model consists of four steps:

1. Namespace declaration
2. Type declaration
3. Public interface declaration
4. Type registration

Each individual step is straightforward, with the bulk of the programming work residing in the type and public interface declaration. Let's look at each step in detail as we build a simple class.

Classes

Classes are used to define objects that contain attributes and behaviors. These attributes and behaviors are normally linked to form a logical grouping of information and behavior.

Namespace Declaration

A namespace declaration is completely optional, just as it is in .NET programming, but using it provides the same benefits as it does in .NET. It helps group our types into logical blocks that are easier for us to comprehend and manage. We might have a utilities namespace or a controls namespace. Using a namespace also helps prevent naming collisions.

Creating a namespace is done through a single line of code. The syntax for creating a namespace is as follows:

```
Type.registerNamespace("namespace");
```

> **■ NOTE   The Type System**
>
> The type system (or Type object depending on how you look at it) is a new global object supplied by the Microsoft AJAX Library. It's responsible for registering classes and namespaces, implementing inheritance and interfaces, and a whole host of other tasks. It is similar in functionality to the type system in the .NET Framework. We use the type system extensively as we walk through creating new types.

Listing 2.4 demonstrates a few different namespace declarations.

LISTING 2.4 Declaring Namespaces

```
Type.registerNamespace ("Books.Publishers");
Type.registerNamespace ("Books.Authors");
Type.registerNamespace ("Some.Other.Namespace");
```

There are two important points to understand when declaring namespaces. First, declaring a namespace as we did with `Type.register Namespace("Books.Publishers")` actually declares two namespaces: `Books` and `Books.Publishers`. The outer namespace, `Books`, is implicitly created when we declare the more specific namespace `Books.Publishers`. This means that we don't have to explicitly declare the `Books` namespace to use it. Figure 2.1 shows how Visual Studio's IntelliSense picks up the inner namespace's availability, although we didn't explicitly declare it, and Figure 2.2 shows the availability of the full namespace, `Books.Publishers`, that we explicitly declared.

FIGURE 2.1 IntelliSense in Visual Studio 2008 of an implicit namespace

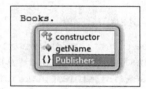

FIGURE 2.2 IntelliSense in Visual Studio 2008 of a declared namespace

The second point is that registering the same namespace more than once is okay. When you are working with a system of JavaScript files, more than one file might require a specific namespace such as Web.Behaviors. Because the file creator won't know whether both files will always be used together, each file needs to declare the namespace within itself to guarantee its availability. Because of this requirement, the Microsoft AJAX Library keeps track of which namespaces are already created and ignores namespaces that are declared more than once.

> ■ **NOTE**   IntelliSense in Visual Studio 2008
>
> IntelliSense in Visual Studio 2008 has improved dramatically. We cover it in detail in Appendix A, "JavaScript in Visual Studio 2008."

Type Declaration

In pure technical terms, a type declaration is a variable name assigned to a Function object whose purpose is to act as a constructor method and create an object of that type (a concept we covered in Chapter 1). The type declaration also contains members that should be created and assigned to each instance of that type and are meant to be accessed through the public interface. Listing 2.5 defines a new type, Publisher, using the Books. Publishers namespace we declared in Listing 2.4. The code also attaches two new members to the type: _name and _city.

LISTING 2.5 Defining a Type

```
Books.Publishers.Publisher = function() {
  this._name = null;
  this._city = null;
}
```

▪ TIP   Classes Are Functions!

The importance of understanding that a class is a variable assigned to a Function object is something that we can't stress enough. It is perhaps the most crucial piece of information you need to understand to comprehend the Prototype Model.

▪ NOTE   Capitalizing Constructor

When defining methods that are intended to be used as constructor methods, we use PascalCase, resulting in each word in the function's name being capitalized.

We can also pass in parameters to the constructor method as shown in Listing 2.6.

LISTING 2.6 Defining a Constructor with Parameters

```
Books.Publishers.Publisher = function(name, city) {
  this._name = name;
  this._city = city;
}
```

▪ NOTE   Privacy

When defining types in this manner, there is no real concept of privacy. Our want-to-be private members can be accessed from an instance of that type just by requesting the member name. We can't declare the name and city members we just defined as private, as we can in .NET, and have the JavaScript runtime enforce the privacy. The best we can do using this style of programming is have privacy by convention. Privacy by convention is naming things in a certain way such that when a tool such as IntelliSense or a person reads the code, it is understood that the variable was intended to be private. In the case of ASP.NET AJAX, members and functions that are prefixed with an underscore (_) are considered private members, and their use by other objects should be avoided. If you do decide to access a private member or method, understand that its implementation may change in future releases or be completely removed. We should use private members and methods with the same consideration and care that we access private members and methods in .NET through reflection.

Finally, in the case that our type inherits from another type, we need to call the base class's constructor when our constructor is executed. This is done using the `initializeBase` method, as shown in Listing 2.7.

LISTING 2.7 Initializing Inheritance

```
Books.Publishers.Publisher = function(name, city) {
  Books.Publishers.Publisher.initializeBase(this, [name]);
  this._name = name;
  this._city = city;
}
```

The `initializeBase` method takes as a parameter the pointer to the current object, `this`, and an argument array. In cases where there are no arguments to pass to the base type's constructor, the argument array can be set to null or not passed in at all. In other cases, we can selectively pass the arguments our base class requires, as we do in the Listing 2.7, by creating a new array.

■ **TIP** Executing initializeBase

Even if our type doesn't inherit from another type, executing `initializeBase` is recommended. It won't hurt anything, and because we define what our type inherits from in another section of code, it's possible that we'll change its inheritance at a later point and forget to include the `initializeBase` method. If we just include it from the beginning, we won't have this problem.

> **TIP** Extension of the Function Object
>
> The `initializeBase` method is available to our `Books.Publishers.Publisher` class because in the Microsoft AJAX Library, the `Function` object type's prototype has been extended to include the `initializeBase` method. Because our `Books.Publishers.Publisher` object is a pointer to a `Function` object, the `initializeBase` method is available to it. (The Microsoft AJAX Library does this in a roundabout way using the previously mentioned type system to extend the `Function`'s prototype, but it has the same effect as directly extending the `Function`'s prototype.)

> **NOTE** Code Repeat!
>
> If the code examples we just covered look familiar, don't worry, you're not going crazy. A type declaration is similar to the object-oriented JavaScript programming model we detailed in Chapter 1. You'll see more patterns repeated as we walk through the "Public Interface Declaration" section.

Public Interface Declaration

Now that we've defined our new type and declared its private members, we need to define the type's public interface. We do this by extending the type's prototype just as we did in Chapter 1. We could use the same syntax for extending the type's prototype as we did previously, but we can use a more concise syntax. Listing 2.8 adds the `get` and `set` properties to our `Publisher`'s public interface using the concise syntax.

LISTING 2.8 Defining the Public Interface

```
Books.Publishers.Publisher.prototype = {
  get_name: function() {
    return this._name;
  },
  set_name: function(value) {
    this._name = value;
  },
  get_city: function() {
    return this._city;
  },
  set_city: function(value) {
```

LISTING 2.8 continued

```
    this._city = value;
  },

  toString: function() {
    return this.getLocation();
  },

  getLocation: function() {
    return this._name + " in " + this._city;
  }
}
```

> ■ **NOTE** Property Prefixes
>
> The get_ and set_ prefixes that we use on our getter and setter properties, respectively, are considered a naming convention. Normally, naming conventions are useful from a readability and comprehension aspect, but don't serve a functional purpose within the language. In the Microsoft AJAX Library, however, some naming conventions also serve a functional purpose.
>
> The get_ and set_ prefixes fall into this category of having a functional purpose. When we cover creating components in Chapter 3, "Components," we discuss the functional purpose of the get_ and set_ prefixes.

The public interface accesses the private members that we declared in our type definition. As we walk through more features of the Microsoft AJAX Library, we continually enhance our public interface to provide features to our type.

Type Registration

The final step, type registration, is how we attach our type to the Microsoft AJAX Library runtime. It's also the point where we can specify a base class to inherit from and interfaces that our type implements. Registering a type is as straightforward as registering a namespace and is completed through a single line of code. The following code demonstrates how to register the

`Book.Publishers.Publisher` type we've coded in the previous code examples:

```
Books.Publishers.Publisher.registerClass("Books.Publishers.
Publisher");
```

With this code, we register our class with the Microsoft AJAX Library, but don't specify a base class that it inherits from or any interfaces it implements. Later in this chapter, in the "Inheritance and Interface Implementation" section, we go over inheritance and interface implementation.

NOTE   Registration Requirements

When we are passing the name of a class into the `registerClass` method, the name passed in must be the same as the function we are using as the type declaration. The Microsoft AJAX Library evaluates this name to ensure that it is available as a type before it registers the class with the runtime.

We also need to make sure that we don't register a class more than one time. Doing so will cause an `invalidOperation` error to be thrown by the runtime.

The requirements just mentioned also hold true for `register Interface` and `registerEnum`.

Now that we've covered the four basic steps of the Prototype Model to build a class, let's look at how we can use the Prototype Model to build the other different types of objects we can register with the Microsoft AJAX Library, an interface and an enumeration.

Interfaces

Interfaces are a formal contract that a class can implement to expose behavior it promises to provide. They are a common concept in object-oriented languages, but are foreign to JavaScript. However, the Microsoft AJAX Library brings the interface concept to the client programming environment, albeit in a dynamic language kind of way.

An interface in the Microsoft AJAX Library works similarly to a .NET interface and is easily declared following the same basic steps as a class declaration. Let's take a quick look at a simple interface, `IComparable`, which defines a single method `compareTo`. Our `IComparable` interface is displayed in Listing 2.9.

LISTING 2.9 Defining an Interface

```
IComparable = function() { };
IComparable.prototype = {
  compareTo: function(obj) {throw Error.notImplemented(); }
};
IComparable.registerInterface("IComparable");
```

First, `IComparable`'s type declaration takes no parameters. Because interfaces do not maintain state themselves, private members aren't allowed, and therefore there is no need for function parameters.

Second, the constructor method does not call `initializeBase` as we did in the class's constructor. Interfaces *cannot inherit* from another interface, so there is no possibility of a base class or base interface.

Moving to the public interface declaration, the single `compareTo` function throws the predefined `notImplemented` error. In the .NET Framework, there is no method body when we declare an interface method, just the method's signature. However, there is no equivalent code construct in JavaScript, where we can just declare a method's signature, so we're forced to include a method body. Because we're forced to include a method body, we need to ensure that if the method is called directly on the interface versus an implementation of the interface that we throw an error.

Finally, when we register our interface, we use the `registerInterface` method that is available on the `Function` type. The `registerInterface` method takes a single parameter, which is the name of the interface.

To test our new `IComparable` interface, we apply it to a couple of test classes: `Book` and `Newspaper`. Then, we create a `bubbleSort` function that is designed to sort any array whose items implement `IComparable`. To test our `bubbleSort` method, we create a list of `Book`s and a list of `Newspaper`s and sort them using the method.

To start, Listing 2.10 defines our `Book` and `Newspaper` types.

LISTING 2.10   Defining Book and Newspaper

```
// Book Declaration
Book = function(text) {
    this._text = text;
};
Book.prototype = {
  get_text: function() { return this._text; },

  // compare a book to another book
  // returns -1 if this book text's length is less than obj
  // returns 0 if the book text's length is the same as obj
  // returns 1 if the book text's length is the greater than obj
  compareTo: function(obj) {
    var objLen = obj.get_text().length;
    var thisLen = this.get_text().length;
    if (thisLen === objLen) {
      return 0;
    }
    else if (thisLen > objLen) {
      return 1;
    }
    return -1;
  },
  toString: function() { return this._text; }
};
Book.registerClass("Book", null, IComparable);

// Newspaper Declaration
Newspaper= function(numberOfPages) {
  this._numberOfPages = numberOfPages;
};
Newspaper.prototype = {
  get_numberOfPages: function() { return this._numberOfPages; },

  // compare a newspaper to another newspaper
  // return -1 if this newspaper's number of pages is less than obj
  // return 0 if they're the same
  // return 1 if this newspaper's number of pages is greater than obj.
  compareTo: function (obj) {
    var objPages = obj.get_numberOfPages();
    if (this._numberOfPages === objPages) {
      return 0;
    }
    else if (this._numberOfPages > objPages) {
      return 1;
    }
    return -1;
  },
  toString: function () { return this._numberOfPages; }
}
Newspaper.registerClass("Newspaper", null, IComparable);
```

Both types implement the IComparable interface and its compareTo function. The compareTo function rudimentarily compares one instance to another and returns the numeric value -1, 0, or 1.

With our types defined, we can craft our generic bubbleSort function, which is shown in Listing 2.11.

LISTING 2.11   Defining the bubbleSort method

```
// sorts anything that implements IComparable
function bubbleSort(toSort) {
  var sortedArray = [];
  for (var i=0; i< toSort.length; i++) {
    var itemToSort = toSort[i];

    // test to make sure that IComparable is supported.
    if (!IComparable.isImplementedBy(itemToSort)) {
      throw Error.invalidOperation(
        "Item does not implement IComparable");
    }

    for (var j=0; j<sortedArray.length; j++) {
      var itemToCompare = sortedArray[j];

      if (itemToSort.compareTo(itemToCompare) < 0) {
        break;
      }
    }
    Array.insert(sortedArray, j, itemToSort);
  }
  return sortedArray;
}
```

Our bubbleSort function works like a normal bubble sort and iterates through the toSort array, creating a sorted array as it processes each item.

When it pulls an item to sort out of the array, it checks to make sure that it implements the IComparable interface by using the isImplementBy method. If the item fails to be implemented by IComparable, an invalidationOperation error is created and thrown.

When the sort enters the inner loop, it executes the compareTo method on the itemToSort until it either finds an element that it is less than itself or runs out of items to compare, which means the itemToSort goes at the end of the list.

When the position of the new item is determined, it is inserted into the sortedArray.

We can test our new bubbleSort by creating a list of Books and a list of Newspapers and running them through the bubbleSort. Listing 2.12 shows our test code.

LISTING 2.12   Testing our bubbleSort Method

```
var bookList = [
  new Book("This is the book text"),
  new Book("This is the other book's text"),
  new Book("This is my book's text"),
  new Book("This is my book's text"),
  new Book("This is my other book's text")];

var newspaperList = [
  new Newspaper(15),
  new Newspaper(154),
  new Newspaper(22),
  new Newspaper(65),
  new Newspaper(1),
  new Newspaper(16),
  new Newspaper(87),
  new Newspaper(69),
  new Newspaper(44)];

var sortedBooks = bubbleSort(bookList);
var sortedNewspapers = bubbleSort(newspaperList);

alert (sortedBooks.join(" ó "));
alert (sortedNewspapers.join(" ó "));
```

Figure 2.3 and Figure 2.4 show the output of the sortedBooks alert call and the sortedNewspapers alert call.

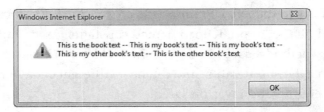

FIGURE 2.3 Output of sorted books list

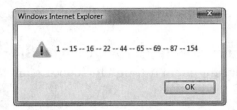

FIGURE 2.4 Output of sorted newspaper list

Although interfaces in the Microsoft AJAX Library are beneficial, as evidenced in the preceding code example, when compared with interfaces in .NET, they have a few significant drawbacks worth mentioning.

First, an interface cannot inherit from another interface, as is possible in the .NET Framework. This is a bit limiting because we can't combine behaviors from multiple interfaces into a single concept.

Second, when a class implements an interface, no check is done to ensure that the class implements all the interface's methods. This is the main reason why it's important for the interface's methods to throw `notImplemented` errors. In case a class doesn't implement an interface method and the method is executed, an error is thrown versus silently failing. Finally, as a corollary to the previous point, there's no guarantee that an interface definition won't include a method declaration whose body is not empty or does not throw the `notImplemented` error. Having a method that performs a task other than throw an error breaks the rules of an interface.

Enumerations

Believe it or not, enumerations in ASP.NET AJAX are interesting. An enumeration in ASP.NET AJAX mimics the `Enumeration` type in the .NET Framework. As in the .NET Framework, an ASP.NET AJAX enumeration is composed of a set of predefined named constants. An enumeration also exposes two methods, `parse` and `toString`, which can be used to evaluate values against the enumeration and can have different behavior depending on how the enumeration was declared.

> **█ NOTE** **Modifiable Enumerations**
>
> Unlike the .NET Framework where an enumeration is constrained to its predefined values, an enumeration in ASP.NET AJAX can be modified at runtime, so you need to protect yourself from unexpected results when working with an enumeration.

To define an enumeration, we follow the same four basic steps outlined earlier: declare a namespace, declare the enumeration type, modify the public interface definition, and register the enumeration with the Microsoft AJAX Library. Listing 2.13 is a full example of an enumeration declaration.

LISTING 2.13 Defining an Enumeration

```
Type.registerNamespace("Books");
Books.BookType = function() {};
Books.BookType.prototype =
{
  TextBook: 1,
  Biography: 2,
  CookBook: 4,
  HowTo: 8,
  SelfHelp: 16
};
Books.BookType.prototype.Fantasy = 32;
Books.BookType.registerEnum("Books.BookType", true);
```

After our enumeration has been registered, we access the enumeration's items as shown in Listing 2.14.

LISTING 2.14 Accessing an Enumeration's Items

```
var bookType1 = Books.BookType.TextBook;
var bookType2 = Books.BookType.Biography;
// alerts "true"
alert (bookType1 !== bookType2);
```

Using the enumeration is similar to using one that was declared in .NET. The main difference is that once assigned to a variable, an enumeration item is evaluated to its integer value. So, if we were to examine `bookType1`'s value, we would receive the value 1, not the strongly typed `Books.BookType.TextBook` as we would in .NET.

Looking at our enumeration's declaration, there are a few differences between it and the class declaration we previously covered. Let's examine the differences between the two and the steps we took to create our enumeration.

First, our constructor method is empty. Enumerations don't have any instance members and don't inherit from another type. There really isn't anything that makes sense to execute when our enumeration is instantiated, and the constructor should always be empty.

Second, we declare the public interface in a slightly different way. Instead of declaring and adding Function objects to the prototype, we assign other types of objects to the prototype. In the Books.BookType enumeration declared in Listing 2.13, we can see that there are five public members added—TextBook, Biography, CookBook, HowTo, and SelfHelp—using the concise prototype syntax. However, rather than have these public members point to functions as we would when we declared a class, we point them to integer values. This means that when we access the value Books.BookType.TextBook, we don't access a function, we access an integer. The sixth public member, Fantasy, is added using the more verbose prototype method to help clarify this point.

Finally, we register our enumeration using the registerEnum function that is available on the Books.BookType object. Similar to the register Class method we used to register a class, the registerEnum is available from the Books.BookType object because the JavaScript Function object has been extended to include a registerEnum method and Books.BookType is just a variable that points to a Function object.

Registering the enumeration using the registerEnum method has the effect of assigning the members that are attached to the prototype of the enumeration back to the type as expando properties. To better clarify this idea, Listing 2.15 displays the code from within the registerEnum method that performs this action.

LISTING 2.15 Adding Expando Properties

```
for (var i in this.prototype) {
  this[i] = this.prototype[i];
}
```

The code iterates over the members that are attached to the prototype and assigns them as expando properties to the enumeration.

When we register our enumeration, we include two parameters. The first is a string that is the name of the enumeration, and the second is a boolean that indicates whether the enumeration should run in flags mode or nonflags mode. As you might expect, if the second parameter's value is true, the enumeration runs in flags mode; if it is false, the enumeration runs in nonflags mode. An enumeration that is set up to run in flags mode allows bit operations to be applied to the enumeration's items. In most cases, the usage of the flags mode affects only the parse and toString methods associated to the enumeration. Let's cover the parse and toString methods and see how they perform when our enumeration is both in the nonflags mode and in the flags mode.

Parse

The parse method syntax is as follows:

```
EnumType.parse(value, ignoreCase);
```

Depending on whether the enumeration is in flags mode or nonflags mode, parse behaves differently.

Parse Nonflags Mode

When you use parse on an enumeration that is in nonflags mode, parse attempts to convert the string into one of the enumeration's items and then return its value. To do this, parse just takes the string that was passed into the method through the first parameter and attempts to find it the enumeration's prototype. If it can't find the string in the enumeration, parse throws an invalid value error. Listing 2.16 demonstrates the common usage of the parse method.

LISTING 2.16 Parsing a Value to an Enumeration

```
var value = Books.BookType.parse("HowTo");
alert (value); // alerts 8
try {
  Books.BookType.parse("Gardening");
} // throws an error
catch (e) {}
```

parse also optionally takes a second parameter, `ignoreCase`, which determines whether the parsing should be case sensitive. By default, the `ignoreCase` value is `false`, and the parsing is case sensitive. Listing 2.17 demonstrates the use of this parameter.

LISTING 2.17   Parsing a Value Ignoring Case

```
try {
  Books.BookType.parse("howto", false);
}
catch (e) { }
// throws an error because the lower-case string "howto" wasn't found.

var value = Books.BookType.parse("howto", true);
alert (value); // alerts 8
```

This is the functionality of `parse` when the enumeration is marked to run in nonflags mode.

Parse Flags Mode

When you use `parse` on an enumeration that is marked to run in flags mode, multiple string values can be passed in through the first parameter using a comma-separated list, and the method returns a bitwise OR'd value of those strings' parsed values. If we attempt to pass in a comma-separated list to an enumeration that isn't set to run in flags mode, `parse` attempts to parse the string as a whole entity. Listing 2.18 demonstrates `parse`'s capability to parse multiple values when using an enumeration that is set to run in flags mode.

LISTING 2.18   Parsing Multiple Values Using a Flag-Enabled Enumeration

```
var value = Books.BookType.parse("HowTo,SelfHelp");
alert (value); // alerts 24.
```

In this code example, the two values passed in, `"HowTo"` and `"SelfHelp"`, are parsed and are evaluated to their respective enumeration items, `Books.BookType.HowTo` and `Books.BookType.SelfHelp`. Then, their values are bitwise OR'd together to form the resulting value 24. In this particular example, the resulting value 24 is returned because the `Books.BookType.HowTo` has the value of 8, or in binary format 00001000, and the `Books.BookType.`

SelfHelp has the value 16, or in binary format 00010000. When they are bit-wise OR'd together, they form the value 00011000, which is equivalent to the integer value 24.

> **NOTE   Not Found Values**
>
> If one of the strings included in the comma-separated string wasn't found on the enumeration, parse throws an error. Also, if we had only passed in one value, as we did in Listing 2.16, the result would have been the same.

toString

The toString method syntax is as follows:

EnumType.toString(value);

Depending on whether the enumeration is in flags mode or in nonflags mode, toString behaves differently.

toString Nonflags Mode

In nonflags mode, toString attempts to convert a number to one of the enumeration items by looping through the values of the enumeration and attempting to find the matching value. Listing 2.19 demonstrates the common usage for toString.

LISTING 2.19   Converting a Value to an Enumeration Item Using toString

```
var howTo = Books.BookType.toString(8);
alert (howTo); // alerts "HowTo"
```

Just like with the parse method, if you attempt to execute the toString method passing in a value that doesn't exist on the enumeration, an ArgumentOutOfRangeException is thrown.

toString Flags Mode

In flags mode, toString attempts to convert a number into one or more enumeration items by treating the value passed in as a parameter as a bit-wise value. An example best exemplifies this idea. Listing 2.20 shows the process in action.

LISTING 2.20 Converting a Value to Multiple Enumeration Items Using toString

```
var enumValues = Books.BookType.toString(26);
alert (enumValues); // outputs "Biography, HowTo, SelfHelp";
```

To see how the enumeration items "SelfHelp", "HowTo", and "Biography" were encoded in the 26 value; we first need to write out 26 in binary format, which is 00011010. Looking at the binary representation of 26, we can see that there is a 1 in the 16, 8, and 2 positions in the 8-bit byte. This means that those positions are "on" and that the enumeration items corresponding to these values are also "on." That is how 26, even though it doesn't correspond to a particular enumeration item in the enumeration, actually includes three values.

Inheritance and Interface Implementation

Although we can now create a new class, interface, or enumeration, the Microsoft AJAX Library really starts to become an object-oriented programming language that is familiar to .NET developers when we're able to inherit from a base class and implement interfaces.

Class inheritance and interface implementation are two important, commonly found features of object-oriented languages that allow ideas to be generalized into human-comprehensible packages. Throughout the object-oriented universe, there are different ways to generalize ideas. In the .NET Framework, however, generalization is provided through the ability for classes to inherit from a single base class and implement multiple interfaces.

The Microsoft AJAX Library follows the same rules of inheritance and interface implementation in that classes can inherit from one base class and implement multiple interfaces. Which base class a class inherits from and which interfaces a class implements are specified in the registerClass statement that we execute when we register our type with the Microsoft AJAX Library.

Inheritance

Inheritance is used to define new classes that are based on a class that has already been defined. The new classes inherit the attributes and behavior of the base class, but can override the behavior of the base class if it decides to.

Setting Up Inheritance

Setting up a class that inherits from another is straightforward. Let's define a new class, `Books.Publishers.NewspaperPublisher`, that inherits from our previously defined class `Books.Publishers.Publisher`. Listing 2.21 shows the new class inheriting from the previous one.

LISTING 2.21 Setting Up Inheritance

```
Books.Publishers.Publisher = function(name, city) {
  ...
}
...
Books.Publishers.Publisher.registerClass('Books.Publishers.Publisher');

Books.Publishers.NewspaperPublisher = function(name, city, state) {
  Books.Publishers.NewspaperPublisher.initializeBase
    (this, [name, city]);
  this._state = state;
}
Books.Publishers.NewspaperPublisher.prototype = {
  ...
}
Books.Publishers.NewspaperPublisher.registerClass(
  'Books.Publishers.NewspaperPublisher', Books.Publishers.Publisher);
```

> ▪▪ **NOTE** Class Registration Order
>
> When defining a class that inherits from another, you need to ensure that the base class is defined and registered before you register the derived class. JavaScript is a translated language and is therefore read and processed from top to bottom and left to right. If you attempt to reference a base class that is defined and registered below your derived class, you'll receive runtime errors. Depending on the mistake you make, you'll either receive a JavaScript undefined error or a "type not registered" error.

Setting up the inheritance was a two-step process, and the code required is highlighted in the code example. First, we chained the derived class's constructor to the base class's constructor by executing the `initializeBase` method in the derived class's constructor. Then, when we executed the `registerClass` method, we specified the base class as the second parameter. Notice that when we specified the base class, we used the variable that points to the base class rather than the string version of the name, as we do with the first parameter.

Accessing Base Class Methods

Now that we've set up our new class's inheritance, we can access the base class's attributes and methods. We have two sets of properties available on our base class, "city" and "name", and after we declare an instance of our derived class, we can access these methods just by executing them on our instance. Listing 2.22 demonstrates how we're able to execute the get_city method on our instance.

LISTING 2.22 Accessing Base Class Methods

```
var instance = new Books.Publishers.NewspaperPublisher
  ("A&W", "Boston", "MA");
alert (instance.getLocation()); // alerts 'A&W in Boston'
```

We're able to access any of the methods that our base class exposes in this way. In fact, if we look at the IntelliSense available on our instance variable, we're able to see the get_*, set_*, and getLocation methods are available to us. Figure 2.5 shows how these methods are available to us inside Visual Studio.

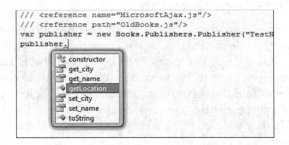

FIGURE 2.5 Availability of base class methods

What IntelliSense won't show you is that the members _city and _name are also available to our instance variable. Because they're prefixed with the underscore, they're intended to be private members of the base class and inaccessible to the inherited class. However, as mentioned earlier, there are no true private members in JavaScript using the development pattern we're using, and therefore we can execute the code shown in Listing 2.23 without any problems.

LISTING 2.23 Accessing Private Members

```
var instance =
  new Books.Publishers.NewspaperPublisher("A&W", "Boston", "MA");
alert (instance._city);
```

Overriding Base Class Methods

In C#, if we want to override a base class's method in a derived class, we first mark the base class method with the keyword virtual, and then mark the derived class method with the keyword override. In the Microsoft AJAX Library, all methods are overridable and don't need to be marked with a special keyword either in the base class or in the derived class. Listing 2.24 demonstrates how to override the getLocation method of our base class.

LISTING 2.24 Overriding a Base Class Method

```
Books.Publishers.NewspaperPublisher.prototype = {
  getLocation: function() {
    return
      this.get_name() + " in " +
      this.get_city() + ", " +
      this._state;
  }
}
```

Now, when we execute the getLocation method on our instance object, the derived class's getLocation method is executed rather than the base class version. Figure 2.6 shows the output of executing the code in Listing 2.24.

FIGURE 2.6 Output of the overridden base class method

Calling Base Class Methods

In object-oriented languages, derived classes often override methods of the base class, and this is possible in the JavaScript, as we demonstrated in the previous section. It is also common for derived classes to override base class methods and also execute the base class method in the overridden method's body. We constantly use this idea whenever we work within ASP.NET and override any of the page's lifecycle methods. An example is shown in Listing 2.25, where we execute the base class's OnPreRender from within the overridden OnPreRender method.

LISTING 2.25 Calling a Base Method in C#

```
...
public void override OnPreRender(EventArgs e)
{
   base.OnPreRender(e);
   // add some extra functionality here
}
```

As is shown in the example, C# uses the base keyword to execute a method as it is attached to the base class when working inside a derived class. Unfortunately, JavaScript lacks this keyword or a suitable replacement, and executing a base class method isn't as easy as it is in C#. However, the Microsoft AJAX Library helps us out and provides a way to execute a base class method using the callBaseMethod method, as shown in Listing 2.26.

LISTING 2.26 Calling a Base Method

```
Books.Publishers.NewspaperPublisher.prototype = {
   getLocation: function() {
     var baseLocation =
       Books.Publishers.NewspaperPublisher.callBaseMethod(this,
       'getLocation');
     return baseLocation + this._state;
   }
}
```

The syntax for executing the base method is as follows:

derivedType.callBaseMethod(instance, 'methodname', [parameter Array]);

In our example, the derived type is Books.Publishers.Newspaper Publisher, the instance is this, the method name is getLocation, and there are no parameters required by the method, so we leave off the parameter array parameter.

The Microsoft AJAX Library executes the base method using a simple algorithm. First, it determines the base type from the derived type's registration information. If the base type is found, it searches for the method within the base type's prototype that matches the method name. If it finds the method name, it executes the associated method using the built-in apply JavaScript method.

Working with Inheritance

The Microsoft AJAX Library provides some methods to query an instance or a type for inheritance hierarchy information. For the subsequent code snippets, we rely on a new type called TestType that is defined in Listing 2.27.

LISTING 2.27 TestType Definition

```
TestType = function(element) {
  TestType.initializeBase(this, [element]);
}

// inherit from Sys.UI.Control, a Microsoft AJAX Library built-in type
// Sys.UI.Control inherits from Sys.Component
TestType.registerClass("TestType", Sys.UI.Control);
```

inheritsFrom

inheritsFrom (see Listing 2.28) determines whether a type inherits from another type somewhere on its inheritance hierarchy:

var inherits = *Type*.inheritsFrom(*baseType*);

LISTING 2.28 Using inheritsFrom

```
var a = TestType.inheritsFrom(Sys.UI.Control);
var b = TestType.inheritsFrom(Sys.Component);
var c = Sys.Component.inheritsFrom(TestType);
var d = TestType.inheritsFrom(Object);

alert (a); // true
```

LISTING 2.28   continued

```
alert (b); // true
alert (c); // false
alert (d); // false.
// Inheritance in the framework does not propagate to the
// built-in Object type, but is only for types
// registered with the framework.
```

getBaseType

getBaseType (see Listing 2.29) returns the base type of a type if there is one; otherwise, it returns null. The object returned isn't the name of the base type, but is actually the constructor function for the type:

```
var baseType = Type.getBaseType();
```

LISTING 2.29   Using getBaseType

```
var a = TestType.getBaseType();
var b = Books.Publishers.NewspaperPublisher.getBaseType();
var c = Sys.Component.getBaseType();

alert (a == null ? "null" : a.getName()); // Sys.UI.Control
alert (b == null ? "null" : b.getName()); // Books.Publishers.Publisher
alert (c == null ? "null" : c.getName()); // null
```

isInstanceOfType

isInstanceOfType (see Listing 2.30) determines whether an instance inherits from a type somewhere in the instance type's inheritance tree:

```
var inherits = Type.isInstanceOfType(instanceVar);
```

LISTING 2.30   Using isInstanceOfType

```
// TestType inherits from Sys.UI.Control, which requires
// a DOM element in its constructor.
// For now, assume we have an element on the page with id 'abc'
var instanceVar = new TestType(document.getElementById("abc"));

var a = TestType.isInstanceOfType(instanceVar);
var b = Sys.Component.isInstanceOfType(instanceVar);
var c = Books.Publishers.Publisher.isInstanceOfType(instanceVar);

alert (a); // true
alert (b); // true
alert (c); // false
```

The methods that we just described are important because they provide type information that can be used to control execution flow and other tasks. Listing 2.31 demonstrates how you can use `isInstanceOfType` to control execution flow.

LISTING 2.31   Controlling Flow by Type

```
function processObject(obj) {
  if (Sys.UI.Behavior.isInstanceOfType(obj) ||
    (Sys.UI.Control.isInstanceOfType(obj)) {
    processElement(obj.get_element());
  }
  else if (Sys.Component.isInstanceOfType(obj)) {
    processNonElement(obj);
  }
  else {
    alert ("obj does not inherit from a supported type.");
  }
}

var instanceVar = new TestType(document.getElementById("abc"));
processObject(instanceVar);
```

Implementing Multiple Interfaces

We already showed how to implement a single interface, in Listing 2.10, but a common practice in .NET is to implement more than one interface. We can do the same using the Microsoft AJAX Library. All we have to do is append the interface name to the end of our `registerClass` method. Listing 2.32 defines a new interface, `ICloneable`, and applies it to our previously defined Book class.

LISTING 2.32   Implementing Multiple Interfaces

```
ICloneable: function() {};
ICloneable.prototype = {
  clone:function() { throw Error.notImplemented(); }
};
ICloneable.registerInterface("ICloneable");

… // IComparable Declaration

Book = function(text) {
    this._text = text;
};
```

LISTING 2.32   continued

```
Book.prototype = {
  get_text: function() { return this._text; },

  compareTo: function(obj) {
...
  },
  clone: function() {
    return new Book(this._text);
  },
  toString: function() { return this._text; }
};
Book.registerClass("Book", null, IComparable, ICloneable);
```

The differences between the previous declaration of Book and the one in Listing 2.32 are the clone method and the registerClass statement. The clone method is the implementation of the ICloneable interface, and in the registerClass statement, we include the ICloneable interface.

The full syntax for registering a class that implements an interface is as follows:

```
className.registerClass("className", baseClass, interface1,
interface2, … ,interfaceN);
```

Notice that the final value of the registerClass method can have zero to many interface names. This is how we can tell the Microsoft AJAX Library that this class implements the following interfaces.

Using an Interface

Our previous bubble sort example walked us through how to implement an interface, and there isn't much more to an interface than that. The Microsoft AJAX Library does, however, provide us some methods for working with interfaces that are useful for type reflection.

implementsInterface

implementsInterface (see Listing 2.33) determines whether a class implements a particular interface:

```
var implementsInterface = className.implementsInterface(inter
faceName);
```

LISTING 2.33   Using implementsInterface

```
var a = Books.implementsInterface(ICloneable);

var b = ICloneable.implementsInterface(ICloneable);

//using some built-in types
var c = Sys.Component.
implementsInterface(Sys.INotifyPropertyChange);

alert (a); // outputs true
alert (b); // outputs false; interfaces are not self-implementing
alert (c); // outputs true
```

isImplementedBy

isImplementedBy (see Listing 2.34) determines whether an instance variable implements a particular interface:

```
var implementsInterface = interfaceName.isImplementedBy
(instanceVar);
```

LISTING 2.34   Using isImplementedBy

```
var book = new Book("abc");
var numberVar = new Number(4);

var a = ICloneable.isImplementedBy(book);
var b = IComparable.isImplementedBy(numberVar);

//using some built-in types
var comp = new Sys.Component();
var c = Sys.INotifyPropertyChange.isImplementedBy(comp);

alert (a); // outputs true
alert (b); // outputs false
alert (c); // outputs true
```

getInterfaces

getInterfaces (see Listing 2.35) returns an array of interfaces that a type implements:

```
var interfaces = className.getInterfaces();
```

LISTING 2.35   Using getInterfaces

```
// for this example we'll use Sys.Component because it implements
// multiple interfaces

var interfaces = Sys.Component.getInterfaces();
for (var i=0; i<interfaces.length; i++) {
  alert (interfaces[i].getName());
}

// alerts
// Sys.IDisposable
// Sys.INotifyPropertyChange
// Sys.INotifyDisposing
```

Important New Types

Besides extending the built-in JavaScript types, the Microsoft AJAX Library provides new types that help us develop better code and implement more complex features. This section tackles a few of these new types. These new types include Sys.EventHandlerList, which provides .NET-style events, Sys.StringBuilder, which provides performant string concatenation capabilities, Sys.Debug, which provides new debugging capabilities; Sys.UI. DomElement, which provides DOM element manipulation methods; and Sys.UI.DomEvent, which provides DOM event methods.

Sys.EventHandlerList

The Sys.EventHandlerList type provides a way for us to create, maintain, and raise custom events.

So far, when we've written JavaScript code that responds to events, the events being raised are either DOM events or attached to built-in objects. A DOM element was *clicked*, the window was *resized*, and an XmlHttpRequest object's *ready state changed* are all examples of events provided to us through the DOM or by existing objects.

But what if we wanted to raise our own custom events so objects could respond to a change in state of another object? An item was *removed* from the list, a component was *destroyed* from the application, and a property on an object was *changed* are all examples of scenarios in which we might want to raise an event. There is no preexisting JavaScript object that allows us to do this. The ability to create, maintain, and raise custom events is what `Sys.EventHandlerList` provides.

> **■ NOTE**   System.ComponentModel.EventHandlerList
>
> `Sys.EventHandlerList` was designed to mimic the .NET-type `System.ComponentModel.EventHandlerList`.

To add custom events to an object, you add an instance of `Sys.Event HandlerList` into another object and expose public methods off that object that manipulate the instance. (Table 2.5 details the methods we use to manipulate the `Sys.EventHandlerList` type.)

To illustrate how to add the custom events capability, we enhance our `Books.Publishers.Publisher` object with an instance of `Sys.Event HandlerList`. Listing 2.36 shows our enhanced type definition.

TABLE 2.5 Sys.EventHandlerList Methods

Method Name	Description	Syntax
addHandler	Adds a handler (a function) to the list of handlers for the event name (string)	`obj.addHandler(eventName, handler);`
removeHandler	Removes a handler from the list of handlers of the event name	`obj.removeHandler(eventName, handler);`
getHandler	Builds and returns a function object that encapsulates all of the handlers assigned to the event name	`var handler = obj.getHandler(eventName);`

LISTING 2.36 Adding the Custom Events Capability

```
Type.registerNamespace ("Books.Publishers");
Books.Publishers.Publisher = function(name, city) {
  Books.Publishers.Publisher.initializeBase(this, [name]);
  this._name = name;
  this._city = city;
  this._editors = [];

  this._events = new Sys.EventHandlerList();
}

Books.Publishers.Publisher.prototype = {
  // … code omitted for brevity … //

  get_editors: function() {
    return this._editors;
  },

  add_editorAdded: function(handler) {
    this._events.addHandler("editorAdded", handler);
  },
  remove_editorAdded: function(handler) {
    this._events.removeHandler("editorAdded", handler);
  },

  addEditor: function(editor) {
    Array.add(this._editors, editor);
    var handler = this._events.getHandler("editorAdded");
    if (handler != null) {
        handler (this, Sys.EventArgs.Empty);
    }
  }
}
Books.Publishers.Publisher.registerClass("Books.Publishers.Publisher");
```

In Listing 2.36, we added two new members and four new methods.

The new members are _events, which is an instance of Sys.Event HandlerList, and _editors, which is an Array.

The first method added, get_editors, is a public property that returns access to the private _editors member.

The second method added, add_editorAdded, provides a way to add an event handler to the editorAdded event. The method takes in a single parameter, handler, which is a function that will be executed when the editorAdded event is raised. The association between the event editorAdded and the event handler function handler is stored using the _events object. The event name and the handler are passed into _events addHandler method to store the association.

The third method added, remove_editorAdded, provides a way to remove an event handler from the editorAdded event. It works exactly the same way as the add_editorAdded method except that rather than call addHandler on the _events object it calls removeHandler.

> **▪ NOTE** **Adding and Removing Multiple Handlers**
>
> If you add the same handler more than once to an event, that handler executes more than once when the event is raised. Similarly, if you add the same handler more than once to an event and then want to remove it, you must remove it more than once, too. Finally, if you remove a handler from an event and that handler is not associated to the event, nothing happens. No error is thrown.

The fourth and final method, addEditor, is responsible for adding the editor to the _editor array and raising the editorAdded event. It accomplishes the first task using Array.add. It then raises the editorAdded event similarly to how it's done in .NET. In .NET, we write code the looks like what is shown in Listing 2.37 to raise the editorAdded event.

LISTING 2.37 Raising the Event

```
if (editorAdded != null)
  editorAdded(this, System.EventArgs.Empty);
```

The JavaScript code is nearly identical except that we have to first retrieve the event handler method from the _events object. We do this by calling the getHandler method on the _events object with the argument editorAdded, the name of the event we want to retrieve. After we retrieve the handler, we execute it passing in a pointer to the current object and the Sys.EventArgs.Empty object. (We cover this call in more detail in a few moments.)

We can test our new event capabilities by creating a function that handles the editorAdded event. Listing 2.38 demonstrates our new event capabilities.

LISTING 2.38 Handling the editorAdded Event

```
function editorAddedHandler(sender, args) {
  alert ("Current Number of Editors: " + sender.get_editors().length);
}

var pub = new Books.Publishers.Publisher("A&W","Boston");
pub.add_editorAdded(editorAddedHandler);
pub.addEditor("Tim");
pub.addEditor("Mark");
```

When the code runs, each time we add an editor to our **pub** object the
editorAddedHandler method executes. Referring back to Listing 2.37 we
can see that when we execute the handler we provide two parameter values: this and Sys.EventArgs.Empty. These are the values available in our
editorAddedHandler method in the sender and args parameters, respectively. Figure 2.7 and Figure 2.8 show the output of **editorAddedHandler**
after each editor has been added.

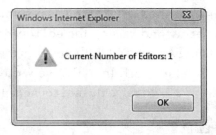

FIGURE 2.7 Output of the editorAddedHandler method after adding Tim

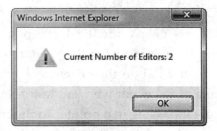

FIGURE 2.8 Output of the editorAddedHandler method after adding Mark

Getting back to the execution of the handler inside the **addEditor**
method, we passed in two arguments to the handler call—**this** and
Sys.EventArgs.Empty—and these arguments translated to the **sender** and
args parameters in our editorAddedHandler method. Passing in the current object so that it is available as the sender parameter in our handler is

customary, just as it is in .NET, but we can actually pass in anything we want to. The second argument is where we're supposed to pass in any relevant data we want our handler to have access to. We do this by inheriting from `Sys.EventArgs` to create our own event arguments type similarly to how we inherit from `System.EventArgs` in .NET. Listing 2.39 shows an example of how to inherit from `Sys.EventArgs` to create an event arguments type that holds the number of editors.

> **■ NOTE   Sys.EventArgs.Empty**
>
> `Sys.EventArgs.Empty` is just a default instantiation of the `Sys.EventArgs` class. Like its .NET counterpart, `System.EventArgs.Empty`, it is used to pass blank empty information to a handler.

LISTING 2.39   Creating a Custom EventArgs Type

```
Books.Publishers.NumberOfEditorsEventArgs = function(numberOfEditors) {
  this._numberOfEditors = numberOfEditors;
}
Books.Publishers.NumberOfEditorsEventArgs.prototype = {
  get_numberOfEditors: function() {
    return this._numberOfEditors;
  }
}
Books.Publishers.NumberOfEditorsEventArgs.registerClass
  ("Books.Publishers.NumberOfEditorsEventArgs", Sys.EventArgs);
```

There's not much to creating our own event arguments type. The declaration and body are similar to any other Microsoft AJAX Library object, and in this particular instance our event argument contains the number of editors. The main difference is that we inherit from `Sys.EventArgs` rather than some other type or none at all.

After we have our event arguments type defined, we can use it instead of `Sys.EventArgs.Empty`. Listing 2.40 shows the modified `addEditor` method that uses the new event arguments type when we raise the `editorAdded` event.

LISTING 2.40 Raising the editorAdded Event Using the NumberOfEditorsEventArgs Type

```
addEditor: function(editor) {
  Array.add(this._editors, editor);
  var handler = this._events.getHandler("editorAdded");
  if (handler != null) {
    var args = new Books.Publishers.NumberOfEditorsEventArgs
               (this._editors.length);
    handler (this, args);
  }
}
```

As the highlighted code shows, we create a new instance of the Books.Publishers.NumberOfEditorsEventArgs type and use it as the second argument in our handler call.

Now, when our handler executes, the second parameter will be of type Books.Publishers.NumberOfEditorsEventArgs rather than Sys.EventArgs. Empty. We can then use this parameter to retrieve the number of editors. Listing 2.41 shows our updated editorAddedHandled method.

LISTING 2.41 Using the NumberOfEditorsEventArgs in the editorAddedHandler Method

```
function editorAddedHandler(sender, args) {
  alert ("Current Number of Editors: " + args.get_numberOfEditors());
}
```

Sys.StringBuilder

A new class to work with strings that the Microsoft AJAX Library includes is the Sys.StringBuilder class. It is a member of the Microsoft AJAX Library's Sys namespace and is created using the following syntax:

```
var sb = new Sys.StringBuilder(optionalInitialText);
```

Its purpose is to provide an efficient way to concatenate multiple strings together. Its availability is important because like in .NET, JavaScript strings are immutable objects. After they've been assigned a value, memory is allocated. Any changes to that value, such as appending more characters, causes a completely new memory space to be allocated to hold the modified string. This isn't very efficient, especially when concatenating a large number of strings together, because memory to hold the entire string will constantly be allocated. To get around the inefficient use of memory, we append string pieces to a StringBuilder, and when we've completed our appending, we use the toString method of the StringBuilder class to create a single string as output. Sys.StringBuilder methods and syntax are explained in Table 2.6.

TABLE 2.6 Sys.StringBuilder Methods

Method Name	Description	Syntax
append	Appends a string to the end of the StringBuilder instance	sb.append("Hello!"); sb.append("My name is :");
appendLine	Appends a string and a blank line to the end of a StringBuilder instance	sb.appendLine("Hello!"); sb.appendLine("My name is :");
clear	Clears the contents of the StringBuilder	sb.clear();
isEmpty	Determines whether the StringBuilder instance contains any content	var isSBEmpty=sb.isEmpty();

toString	Concatenates the string parts together, returning a single string	var fullStr = sb.toString();
		var fullStrSep =
		sb.toString("@");
		// creates a string with an @
		symbol between each string part.

▪ NOTE   Sys.StringBuilder: Under the Hood

Sys.StringBuilder achieves better performance than string concatenation, but how? Whenever you call append or appendLine on your Sys.StringBuilder instance, the text you're appending is actually added to the end of an array rather than directly to a string, increasing the length of the array by one with each appending. When you ask for the concatenated string using the toString method, the array elements are "joined" together using the Array.join method. The join method works by calculating the string version of each array element and then creating a single string containing all the elements. It does this without assigning to memory more than once, and therefore the inefficiencies of constantly reallocating and assigning to memory are eliminated.

Sys.Debug

One of the hardest tasks in JavaScript is debugging. Although the tools have matured in recent years, they are still lacking in many aspects. ASP.NET AJAX attempts to alleviate some of these problems by providing a set of debugging commands that are available through the `Sys.Debug` object.

> **NOTE   Sys._Debug**
>
> `Sys.Debug` is an instance of the private type `Sys._Debug`, which is why we call `Sys.Debug` an object rather than a type.

There isn't an extensive list of commands, but they provide decent coverage of the common debugging scenarios. Table 2.7 details the five public methods available from `Sys.Debug`.

TABLE 2.7 Sys.Debug Methods

Method Name	Description	Syntax
trace	Appends a message to the console and to an HTML `TextArea` named `TraceConsole` if one is present on the page.	`Sys.Debug.trace(message);`
traceDump	Recursively enumerates the properties of an object, appending the properties and their values to the console.	`Sys.Debug.traceDump(object)`
clearTrace	Clears the HTML `TextArea` named `TraceConsole` if one is present on the page.	`Sys.Debug.clearTrace();`
fail	Appends a message to console, and then breaks into the debugger using the JavaScript debugger if that command is supported by the browser.	`Sys.Debug.fail(message);`

Method Name	Description	Syntax
assert	Evaluates a conditional expression. If the expression is false, a JavaScript confirmation is displayed to the user with the message provided in the assert call. If the user confirms the dialog, the message is appended to the console, and if the browser supports the debugger command, the browser breaks into the JavaScript debugger.	Sys.Debug.assert(*condition, message, displayCaller*);

Listing 2.42 provides a test page for the trace methods that we defined in Table 2.7: trace, traceDump, and clearTrace. The code relies on our previously defined Books.Publishers.Publisher object, which is placed in the Publisher.js file but not shown in the listing.

LISTING 2.42   Testing Sys.Debug's Tracing Methods

```
<%@ Page Language="C#" AutoEventWireup="true"
  CodeBehind="DebugTester.aspx.cs" Inherits="Debugging.DebugTester" %>

<html>
<head runat="server">
  <title>Trace in Action!</title>

  <script type="text/javascript">
  function trace() {
    Sys.Debug.trace($get("txtTraceMessage").value);
  }

  function traceDump() {
    var name = $get("txtPublisherName").value;
    var city = $get("txtPublisherCity").value;
    var myPublisher = new Books.Publishers.Publisher(name, city);
    Sys.Debug.traceDump(myPublisher);
  }

  function clearTrace() {
    Sys.Debug.clearTrace();
  }
  </script>
</head>
<body>
```

LISTING 2.42   continued

```
<form id="form1" runat="server">
<asp:ScriptManager ID="SM1" runat="server">
  <Scripts>
    <asp:ScriptReference Path="~/Publisher.js" />
  </Scripts>
</asp:ScriptManager>
<textarea id="TraceConsole"
  style="width: 400px;
  height: 200px;"
  cols="1"
  rows="1">
</textarea>
<br />
<span>Trace Message: </span>
<input type="text" id="txtTraceMessage" />
<input type="button"
       onclick="trace();"
       value="Append Trace" />
<br />
<span>Publisher Name: </span>
<input type="text" id="txtPublisherName" />
<span>Publisher City: </span>
<input type="text" id="txtPublisherCity" />
<input type="button"
       onclick="traceDump();"
       value="Dump Publisher Object" />
<br />
<input type="button"
       onclick="clearTrace();"
       value="Clear Trace" />
</form>
</body>
</html>
```

Figure 2.9 shows the example page in action. Because we defined a textarea with ID TraceConsole in the DebugTester page, the trace commands append their information to the textarea.

Even if we didn't include a textarea on the page, the trace commands still append to the console. What the console is depends on the executing situation. Table 2.8 details the different consoles.

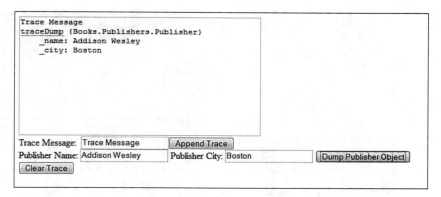

```
Trace Message
traceDump {Books.Publishers.Publisher}
    _name: Addison Wesley
    _city: Boston




Trace Message:  Trace Message          Append Trace
Publisher Name: Addison Wesley    Publisher City: Boston        Dump Publisher Object
  Clear Trace
```

FIGURE 2.9 Debug test page in action

TABLE 2.8 Available Debug Consoles

Browser or Application	Console Information
Visual Studio	When a debugger is attached to Internet Explorer either by directly attaching to the IExplore.exe instance or by running the application through Visual Studio, `trace` messages will appear in the Output window when the window is set to Show Output from Debug.
Web Development Helper	Once it is installed and running on the page, `trace` messages are appended to the script console.
Firefox	With Firebug installed, `trace` messages are appended to its console.
Safari	Once the debug menu has been added to the browser, `trace` messages are appended to the JavaScript console.
Opera	The `trace` messages are appended to the error console.

Figures 2.10 through 2.14 show the various consoles with `trace` messages appended to them.

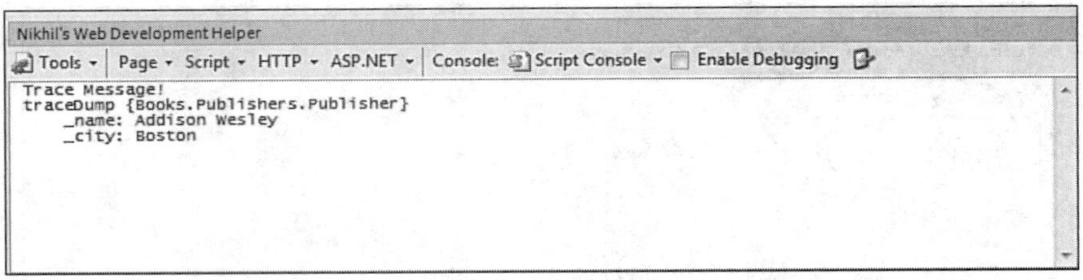

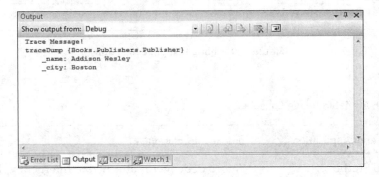

FIGURE 2.10 Web Development Helper displaying the trace messages

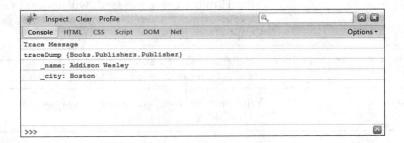

FIGURE 2.11 Visual Studio's output window displaying the trace messages

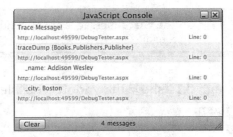

FIGURE 2.12 Firebug's console window displaying the trace messages

FIGURE 2.13 Safari's JavaScript console displaying the trace messages

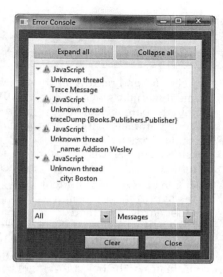

FIGURE 2.14 Opera's error console displaying the trace messages

The other two methods, `fail` and `assert`, work similarly to their .NET counterparts `System.Diagnositcs.Debug.Fail` and `System.Diagnostics.Debug.Assert`. Important to note is that both methods break into the JavaScript debugger only if the browser supports the `debugger` command.

Sys.UI.DomElement

The `Sys.UI.DomElement` class includes commonly used methods for working with DOM elements. Instead of us creating `Sys.UI.DomElement` instances, static methods are attached to the class, and we use those instead. Table 2.9 details the methods and syntax provided by the class.

TABLE 2.9 Sys.UI.DomElement Methods

Method Name	Description	Syntax

getElementById or $get	Searches for and returns an element with the given ID within the parent element (second parameter). If no second parameter is specified, document is assumed.
	
	$get can be used as a shortcut to the Sys.UI.DomElement.getElementById method.
		`var elm = Sys.UI.DomElement.getElementById(elmId, parent);`
		or
		`var elm = $get(elmId, searchRadius);`

getLocation	Gets a JSON-formatted object that contains the x,y coordinates of the object in relation to the owner frame or window.	`var location = Sys.UI.DomElement.getLocation(elm);`
		`var x = location.x;`
		`var y = location.y;`

getBounds	The same as getLocation, and also returns the width and height of the element in pixels.	`var bounds = Sys.UI.DomElement.getBounds(elm);`
		`var x = location.x;`
		`var y = location.y;`
		`var width = location.width;`
		`var height = location.height;`

setLocation	Sets the absolute position of an element relative to the upper-left corner of its containing block. The containing block for an absolutely positioned element is the nearest ancestor with a position value other than static.	`Sys.UI.DomElement.setLocation(elm, x, y);`
addCssClass	Adds a CSS class to the element if the class is not already part of it.	`Sys.UI.DomElement.addCssClass(elm, cssClassName);`

Method Name	Description	Syntax
containsCssClass	Determines whether a CSS class belongs to an element.	`var classApplied = Sys.UI.DomElement. containsCssClass(`*`elm,`* *`cssClassName`*`);`
removeCssClass	Removes a CSS class from an element.	`Sys.UI.DomElement. removeCssClass(`*`elm,`* *`cssClassName`*`);`
toggleCssClass	Adds a CSS class to an element if it is not already added. Removes a CSS class if it is already added.	`Sys.UI.DomElement. toggleCssClass(`*`elm,`* *`cssClassName`*`);`
getVisible	Gets an element's visibility. An element is visible if its visibility is not `'hidden'` and its display is not `'none'`.	`var visible = Sys.UI.DomElement. getVisible(`*`elm`*`);`
setVisible	Sets an element's visibility style-property and updates the display style-property appropriately based on the current visibility mode.	`Sys.UI.DomElement. setVisible(`*`elm, false`*`);`
getVisibilityMode	Gets an element's visibility mode. The possible values are `Sys.UI.VisibilityMode. hide` and `Sys.UI. VisibilityMode.collapse`.	`var mode = Sys.UI.DomElement. getVisibilityMode(elm);`
setVisibilityMode	Sets an element's visibility mode. If the element is already hidden, setting the visibility mode to collapse will set the element's display `style-property` to none. Setting it to hide will set the element's display `style-property` to whatever it was originally: `inline`, `block`, or `inline-block`.	`Sys.UI.DomElement. setVisibilityMode (elmSys.UI. VisibilityMode. collapse);`

> **■ NOTE   getLocation and getBounds Problems**
>
> With elements that are styled with "position:fixed", getLocation and getBounds will not work correctly in all browsers. "fixed" disrupts the layout flow and prevents accurate location and bounds from being calculated.

> **■ NOTE   Shortcut Methods**
>
> The Microsoft AJAX Library exposes a few global methods as shortcuts to commonly used methods. These methods are prefixed with the $ character. Examples of these shortcuts are the $get method, which references the Sys.UI.DomElement.getElementById method, and the $addHandler and $removeHandler methods, which reference the Sys.UI.DomEvent.addHandler and Sys.UI.DomEvent.removeHandler methods, respectively.

As you work through actual code, you'll find that the methods provided by the Sys.UI.DomElement class are useful. Listing 2.43 shows a test page that uses each of the methods listed in Table 2.9.

LISTING 2.43   Sys.UI.DomElement Methods

```
<%@ Page Language="C#" AutoEventWireup="true"
CodeBehind="Default.aspx.cs" Inherits="Chapter_3._Default" %>

<html>
<head>
  <style type="text/css">
    .highLightElement {
      background-color: Yellow;
      color: Green;
      font-weight: bold;
    }
    </style>
</head>
<body>
  <form runat="server">
  <asp:ScriptManager ID="SM1" runat="server" />
  <div id="myDiv" style="position: absolute;
```

```
                        top: 10px;
                        left: 10px;
                        width: 250px;
                        height: 175px;
                        border:solid 1px black">
    <span id="mySpan" />
    <input type="button"
           id="removeHighlight"
           value="Remove Highlight"
           onclick="removeHighlightFn();" />
</div>
</form>

<script type="text/javascript">

    // remove the highLightElement CSS Class from the
    // SPAN element if its present
    function removeHighlightFn() {
        var spanElm = $get("mySpan");
        if (spanElm !== null &&
            Sys.UI.DomElement.containsCssClass
            (spanElm, 'highLightElement')) {

                Sys.UI.DomElement.removeCssClass
                  (spanElm, 'highLightElement');
        }
    }

    // getElementById
    var divElm = Sys.UI.DomElement.getElementById("myDiv");

    // get an element contained within another element.
    var spanElm = $get("mySpan", divElm);

    // use getLocation to write out the bounds of
    // the SPAN element
    var spanLocation = Sys.UI.DomElement.getLocation(spanElm);
    spanElm.innerHTML =
        "Initial Inner span X: "
        + spanLocation.x
        + "<br/>Initial Inner span Y: "
        + spanLocation.y
        + "<br />";

    // use setLocation to move the DIV element
    var divLocation = Sys.UI.DomElement.getLocation(divElm);
    Sys.UI.DomElement.setLocation
        (divElm, divLocation.x + 100, divLocation.y + 100);
```

LISTING 2.43 continued

```
    var spanLocation = Sys.UI.DomElement.getLocation(spanElm);
    spanElm.innerHTML +=
      "<br/> Final Inner Span X: "
      + spanLocation.x
      + "<br/>Final Inner Span Y: "
      + spanLocation.y
      + "<br />";

    // use containsCssClass and addCssClass to add
    // the highLightElement CSS class to the SPAN element
    if (!Sys.UI.DomElement.containsCssClass
      (spanElm, 'highLightElement')) {
        Sys.UI.DomElement.addCssClass(spanElm, 'highLightElement');
    }

    // use getBounds to get the bounds of the DIV element
    var divBounds = Sys.UI.DomElement.getBounds(divElm);
    spanElm.innerHTML +=
      "<br/> The width of the DIV: "
      + divBounds.width
      + "<br/>The height of the DIV: "
      + divBounds.height;
    </script>
</body>
</html>
```

When the code in Listing 2.43 first executes and the SPAN and DIV have been placed and updated, we're presented with the output shown in Figure 2.15.

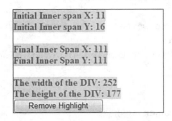

FIGURE 2.15 The div and span with initial x,y coordinates; after moving x,y coordinates; and the div's final width and height

When we click the Remove Highlight button, the removeHighlightFn method executes, and the highlight is removed from the text. Figure 2.16 shows the resulting display.

```
Initial Inner span X: 11
Initial Inner span Y: 16

Final Inner Span X: 111
Final Inner Span Y: 111

The width of the DIV: 252
The height of the DIV: 177
     Remove Highlight
```

FIGURE 2.16 The span with the highlight removed

Sys.UI.DomEvent

The Sys.UI.DomEvent class provides cross-browser access to DOM element event properties and methods to work with DOM element events. This class is useful because it provides a common denominator for the different browser's eventing systems.

Let's start with how event handlers are attached to DOM element events without using the Sys.UI.DomEvent class. Among the four major browsers, there are three common ways of attaching event handlers. Table 2.10 explains them.

TABLE 2.10 Attaching Event Handlers to DOM Element Events

Event Registration Method	Syntax	Supported Browsers
attachEvent	elm.attachEvent(eventName, handler);	Internet Explorer
addEventListenter	elm.addEventListener(eventName, handler, useCapturing);	Firefox, Safari, Opera
oneventname=	elm.oneventname=handler;	All

Right away, we can see that the first two event registration methods, attachEvent and addEventListener, are problematic because they aren't supported by all the major browsers. The final method, assigning a handler to the event using the oneventname= syntax, works across all browsers, but it can prove problematic when you want to assign more than one event handler to a single DOM element event. Although you can overcome this problem fairly easily with some helper code, another annoying problem is that you have to write the event handler code to handle the different ways the browsers builds and passes in the event. Listing 2.44 demonstrates the basic code we have to write to handle an event successfully across different browsers.

LISTING 2.44 Normalizing an Event

```
function handleClickEvent(e) {
  // check to see if there was an event argument passed in.
  if (!e) {
    e = window.event;
  }

  // determine the event's firing element.
  var elmFiringEvent = null;
  if (typeof(e.target) !== 'undefined') {
    elmFiringEvent = e.target;
  }
  else {
    elmFiringEvent = e.srcElement;
  }
}

var button = $get('removeHighlight');
button.onclick = handleClickEvent;
```

As you can see, we have to jump through a few hoops to get a pointer to the event object, and when we have that pointer, we have to jump through more hoops to determine the element that originated the event.

These are the problems that Sys.UI.DomEvent solves. It provides methods that standardize how we attach and detach handlers from DOM element events and internally normalizes all events by having all events pass through it first. Table 2.11 details the methods and syntax that the Sys.UI.DomEvent class provides.

TABLE 2.11 Sys.UI.DomEvent Methods

Method Name	Description	Syntax
.addHandler $addHandler	Attaches a handler to the DOM element event.	Sys.UI.DomEvent.addHandler(*elm, eventName, handler*) or $addHandler(*elm, eventName, handler*);
.addHandlers $addHandlers	Attaches multiple events/handlers to a DOM element.	Sys.UI.DomEvent.addHandlers (*elm, {eventName: handler, eventName2: handler2}*); or $attachHandlers(elm, {eventName: handler, eventName2: handler2);
.clearHandlers $clearHandlers	Removes all the handlers for all events from a DOM element.	Sys.UI.DomEvent. clearHandlers(*elm*); or $clearHandlers(*elm*);
.preventDefault	Prevents the default action from occurring. For instance, if you prevent the default of a keydown event in a textbox, the character won't be appended to the textbox's input.	*event*.preventDefault();
.stopPropagation	Prevents the event from being bubbled up the DOM hierarchy to parent elements.	*event*.stopPropagation();
.removeHandler $removeHandler	Removes a specific handler for a specific event on a specific element.	Sys.UI.DomEvent. removeHandler(*elm, eventName, handler*); or $removeHandler(*elm, eventName, handler*);

Those are the methods available on Sys.UI.DomEvent, but they don't tell the whole story of what Sys.UI.DomEvent does for us. Sys.UI.DomEvent also normalizes the event information across browsers. Normalizing the event information eliminates the problem of searching for the `target` property or `srcElement` property on our event object among other problems caused by the browser's different eventing systems. Listing 2.45 demonstrates an event handler method that uses a normalized event and attaching and detaching an event handler from the DOM element's event.

LISTING 2.45 Attaching and Removing a DOM Element Event Handler

```
function handleClickEvent(e) {
  var elmFiringEvent = e.target;

  // remove the handler from the firing event.
  $removeHandler(elmFiringEvent, "click", handleClickEvent);
}

var button = $get('removeHighlight');

// attach the event handler to the button's click event.
$addHandler(button, "click", handleClickEvent);
```

As the `handleClickEvent` method shows, there is always an argument passed into the event handler, which is of type `Sys.UI.DomEvent`. This is the normalized event object, and it will be the same whether you are running in Firefox, Internet Explorer, or in a different supported browser. Table 2.12 lists the properties that are available on this normalized event object.

TABLE 2.12 Sys.UI.DomEvent Properties

Property Name	Description
altKey	A Boolean value indicating whether the Alt key was pressed when the event fired
button	Gets a `Sys.UI.MouseButton` enumeration property that indicates the state of the mouse when the event fired
charCode	Gets the character code of the key that fired the event
clientX	Gets the x-coordinate of the mouse's position relative to the client window excluding scroll bars
clientY	Gets the y-coordinate of the mouse's position relative to the client window excluding scroll bars

Property Name	Description
ctrlKey	A Boolean value indicating whether the Ctrl key was pressed when the event fired
offsetX	Gets the x-coordinate of the mouse's position relative to the element that raised the event
offsetY	Gets the y-coordinate of the mouse's position relative to the element that raised the event
screenX	Gets the x-coordinate of the mouse's position relative to the user's screen
screenY	Gets the y-coordinate of the mouse's position relative to the user's screen
shiftKey	A Boolean value indicating whether the Shift key was pressed when the event fired
target	The element that raised the event
type	The name of the event

■ NOTE Normalizing the Event Object

In normalizing the event, the Microsoft AJAX Library developers had to decide what to name properties when they expressed the same value across multiple browsers but had different names. Hence, srcElement was renamed target, and other name changes occurred.

They also made a decision to normalize different types of events into a single event object. This means that each event object has *exactly* the same properties no matter what the originating event was. This is useful from a standardization viewpoint, but can lead to some missing information that you might have expected to be available on your event object.

> **■ TIP   Accessing the Raw Event**
>
> If needed, the event as raised by the browser can be accessed through the `Sys.UI.DomEvent` object. It is accessed through the `rawEvent` property. This property can be useful when the normalized event object doesn't contain a particular property that the `rawEvent` will. But be careful, when you access the `rawEvent` object you are writing non-standard code and must write code for each of the browsers you intend to support.

Maintaining Scope

When working with events such as the example we coded in Listing 2.45, maintaining the scope of `this` can become a problem. In Listing 2.45, when the `handleClickEvent` method executed, we had a single parameter, `e`, available to us, which was a normalized `DomEvent` object. We also had `this` available to us, and because the method was executing as an event handler for a DOM element, `this` pointed to the firing element, which was the `removeHighlight` button.

Having `this` point to the DOM element is the default behavior of an event handler method, but it is unwanted behavior when our event handler is contained within an object. In the case where our method is contained within an object, we normally want `this` to point to the current object, not the firing DOM element.

Listing 2.46 demonstrates this problem. In the code example, we define a new test type called `MyObject` that contains a single private member, `_name`, and a single method, `clickEventHandler`, whose purpose is to alert `_name`'s value when it is clicked. We create an instance of the object and then attach the `click` event of a button to the object's `clickEventHandler`.

LISTING 2.46   Demonstrating Problems with this

```
<html>
<body>
  <form id="form1" runat="server">
    <input type="button" value="Test!" id="test" />
    <asp:ScriptManager ID="SM1" runat="server" />
  </form>

  <script type="text/javascript">
```

```
MyObject = function() {
  this._name = "Default Name";
};

MyObject.prototype = {
  clickEventHandler: function(e) {
    alert (this._name);
  }
};

var myObject = new MyObject();
$addHandler($get("test"), "click", myObject.clickEventHandler);
</script>

</body>
</html>
```

The code looks like it would alert "Default Name" when we click the test button, but instead we get the undefined value, as shown in Figure 2.17.

FIGURE 2.17 The undefined error message

We receive this error message rather than the desired "Default Name" because when clickEventHandler executes, this points to the test button and not the current object. To correct this, we can use a construct provided to us by the Microsoft AJAX Library called a delegate.

Delegates

Delegates are another idea brought over from .NET. In .NET, they are objects that encapsulate a reference to another method. The delegate object can be passed to other code, which can execute the referenced method without any knowledge of the method it's executing.

In the Microsoft AJAX Library, delegates work relatively the same way. You create a delegate supplying the reference to the method you want executed and then pass the delegate to other code, which then executes the referenced method.

The main benefit of a Microsoft AJAX Library delegate is that you can supply an instance in which you want the referenced method executed. Simply put, you can point this to any object you want. We can use this feature of delegates to maintain scope during event operations.

To create the delegate, we use the Function.createDelegate method, as follows:

```
var del = Function.createDelegate(instance, method);
```

Altering the relevant portions of Listing 2.46, we can use a delegate to get the clickEventHandler method to alert the desired value. Listing 2.47 displays the alerted code.

LISTING 2.47   Using a Delegate

```
...
   var myObject = new MyObject();
   var del =
     Function.createDelegate(myObject, myObject.clickEventHandler);
   $addHandler($get("test"), "click", del);
...
```

What we did is create a delegate that is executed when the click event fires instead of the directly executing clickEventHandler. When the delegate executes, clickEventHandler will execute, and this will be myObject.

Now when we click our test button, we're presented with the desired output, as shown in Figure 2.18.

FIGURE 2.18 The object's _name member

> **■ NOTE   A Delegate's Internals**
>
> The internals of a delegate are simple.
>
> ```
> return function() {
>   return method.apply(instance, arguments);
> }
> ```
>
> It returns an anonymous function that uses JavaScript's `apply` method to switch the context of this as it executes the method.

Callbacks

Although callbacks aren't directly related to maintaining scope, they are useful for passing extra information to event handlers. In Listing 2.47 we defined the `clickEventHandler` method with a single parameter, which will always be the `DomEvent`. What callbacks enable us to do is send in some other data as a second parameter.

To use a callback, we follow the same pattern as a delegate. We create a callback and add it as the handler method for an event. To create a callback, use the following syntax:

```
var callback = Function.createCallback(method, context);
```

The `method` is the method to execute, and the `context` is the extra data we want to pass into that method. Listing 2.48 updates the previous example in two ways. First, we add an extra parameter to the `clickEvent` `Handler` method. Second, we create a callback and use it in adding the `click` event handler to the test button. When we create the callback, we use the previously defined delegate as the method and supply a simple `"123"` string as the context. One thing that is great about delegates and callbacks is that we can combine them as needed. If we weren't able to, our this problem would return and we wouldn't be able to access _name.

LISTING 2.48   Using a Callback

```
...
  clickEventHandler: function(e, context) {
    alert (this._name + context);
  }
...
...
var a = new MyObject();
var del = Function.createDelegate(a, a.clickEventHandler);
var cb = Function.createCallback(del, "123");
$addHandler($get("test"), "click", cb);
...
```

Now when our clickEventHandler executes, everything is the same except that its context parameter will be "123" and our output will look like Figure 2.19.

FIGURE 2.19 Output of _name and context

One of the drawbacks of a callback is that we can specify only one extra parameter. Because of this, if we want to supply multiple parameters, we need to use a simple object that acts like a dictionary. Listing 2.49 shows how we can supply a dictionary rather than a simple parameter.

LISTING 2.49   Passing in a Dictionary

```
var context = {"Date": new Date().getDate(), "x": 319, "y":483};
var cb = Function.createCallback(del, context);
```

> ### ■ NOTE   Not the Only Use
>
> Using callbacks with event handlers isn't their only use. Another handy use is to use them to pass in the same object over and over again without specifying it for each call.

SUMMARY

In this chapter we walked through the basics of working with the Microsoft AJAX Library. First we covered how to extend the .NET Framework with your own objects. Then, we detailed the Microsoft AJAX Library's base type extensions. From there, we covered how the Microsoft AJAX Library works with DOM elements and events using the `Sys.UI.DomElement` and `Sys.UI.DomEvent` classes, respectively. Finally, we wrapped it up with a walk-through of how to maintain scope using delegates and callbacks.

PART II
Controls

■ 3 ■
Components

IN CHAPTER 2, "MICROSOFT AJAX Library Programming," we began our discussion of the Microsoft AJAX Library and how it extends the built-in JavaScript types with new features, how to use the Prototype Model to extend the Library with our own custom types, and we even covered a few of the important prebuilt types.

In this chapter, we continue our discussion of the Microsoft AJAX Library by covering components and its two derived types, controls and behaviors. This chapter is the start of creating client objects that will be related to server controls.

Components Defined

A component is any object whose client type inherits from `Sys.Component`. They are extremely important because you'll use the `Sys.Component` base type to extend the framework to create new components. You'll want to create new components because `Sys.Component` contains a few distinct characteristics not found in any other Microsoft AJAX Library type.

First, components are designed to bridge the gap between client and server programming. Through server objects called `ScriptDescriptors`, we can instruct ASP.NET AJAX to automatically emit JavaScript that creates instances of our component types. Using this feature, we can attach client capabilities to web server controls without actually writing any JavaScript in our web server control's class.

> **■ NOTE   Creating Components through Server Code**
>
> We cover creating components through server code in detail in Chapter 5, "Adding Client Capabilities to Server Controls."

Second, `Sys.Application`, which is a global object that acts like a client runtime, is set up to manage any type that inherits from `Sys.Component`. This means that your component will go through a predefined lifecycle. You'll know when the component will be created and when it will be disposed, and you can inject your own custom code at these points as needed. This provides you with a great deal of control and safety.

> **■ NOTE   Components and Web Server Controls**
>
> `Sys.Application` managing components is similar to a page managing web server controls. It was designed that way on purpose to give ASP.NET developers a familiar feel when programming within the Microsoft AJAX Library. We cover `Sys.Application` in detail in Chapter 4, "Sys.Application."

Finally, components have a lot of the common functionality that you'll need already built-in. They have a `Sys.EventHandlerList` instance, so you can create, maintain, and raise custom events. They implement the `Sys.INotifyPropertyChanged` interface, which provides property-changed notification methods. And they implement the `Sys.INotifyDisposing` interface so that other objects can be notified easily when they are disposed.

Components, Controls, and Behaviors

As if components weren't already great, there are two special-purpose component types contained within the Microsoft AJAX Library: behaviors, represented by the `Sys.UI.Behavior` class; and controls, represented by the `Sys.UI.Control` class. Figure 3.1 shows the hierarchy between the three types.

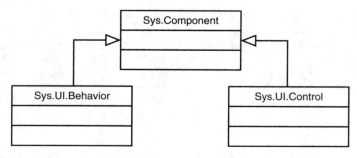

FIGURE 3.1 Class hierarchy between Sys.Component, Sys.UI.Behavior, and Sys.UI.Control

> **■ TIP   Managed Components**
>
> As Figure 3.1 shows, `Sys.Component` is the base type for both `Sys.UI.Control` and `Sys.UI.Behavior`. As stated earlier, `Sys.Application` manages components. It is through inheritance that controls and behaviors are managed, too. When we talk about `Sys.Application`, we refer to it as having managed components, which could be a component, behavior, or control.

Behaviors, controls, and components are mostly the same. This is the case because when compared to the amount of functionality the base component type provides, behaviors and controls don't provide much, and the functionality they do provide doesn't take them in a radically different direction.

The one striking difference that does exist between a base component and a behavior or control is behaviors and controls have a built-in association to a DOM element because they are intended to be visual. In comparison, components do not have a built-in association to a DOM element because they are intended to be nonvisual.

Between behaviors and controls, the major difference is that a DOM element can have only one control associated to it, whereas it can have multiple associated behaviors.

Table 3.1 summarizes the differences between the three types.

TABLE 3.1 Differences between Components, Controls, and Behaviors

Object Type	Can Be Associated to a DOM Element	A DOM Element Can Have More Than One Associated to It	Access to Object from DOM Element
Component	Not allowed	N/A (not directly associated to a DOM element).	N/A (not directly associated to a DOM element).
Control	Must be associated to a DOM element	No, a DOM element can have only one associated control.	Yes, a control can be accessed through a `control` expando property attached to the DOM element.
Behavior	Must be associated to a DOM element	Yes, a DOM element can have one or more associated behaviors.	Yes, a behavior can be accessed through an expando property of the behavior's name from the DOM element if the behavior was named at the time it was initialized. All behaviors attached to an element can be accessed by a private `_behaviors` array attached to the DOM element.

These rules are enforced during the creation of a component, behavior, and control and dictate what base type your new type will inherit from. Figure 3.2 covers the basic decision process when determining what type of new object to create based on the feature's requirements.

Now that we covered the basics of components, controls, and behaviors, let's tackle each type individually.

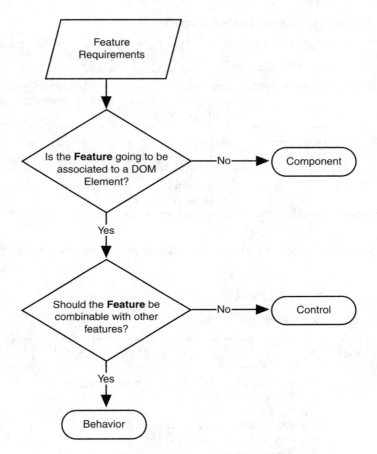

FIGURE 3.2 Decision process between component, control, and behavior

Sys.Component

Sys.Component is the root type of all components and provides the majority of the functionality. It does not inherit from another type, but does implement three interfaces: Sys.IDisposable, Sys.INotifyProperty Changed, and Sys.INotifyDisposing. Table 3.2 details these three interfaces.

TABLE 3.2 Interfaces Implemented by Sys.Component

Interface	Purpose	Methods
`Sys.INotifyPropertyChanged`	Implements property-changed notification event	`add_propertyChanged` `remove_propertyChanged`
`Sys.INotifyDisposing`	Implements disposing event	`add_disposing` `remove_disposing`
`Sys.IDisposable`	Represents a disposable object.	`dispose`

`Sys.Component` also contains five internal members, as detailed in Table 3.3.

TABLE 3.3 Sys.Component Members

Member Name	Purpose	Type
`_id`	The unique identifier of the component. Used to find the component after it's registered with `Sys.Application`. Each component managed by `Sys.Application` must have a unique ID.	`string`
`_idSet`	Indicates whether the `_id` property has been set.	`boolean`
`_initializing`	Indicates whether the component has been through its initialization routine.	`boolean`
`_updating`	Indicates whether the component is updating.	`boolean`
`_events`	Maintains a list of events and event handlers.	`Sys.EventHandlerList`

Besides implementing the methods required by the three interfaces, `Sys.Component` exposes methods that allow interaction with its internal members. Table 3.4 details these methods and the methods required by the three interfaces.

TABLE 3.4 Sys.Component Methods

Method Name	Description	Syntax
beginUpdate	Marks the component as updating. Called during the creation of a component.	`comp.beginUpdate();`
endUpdate	Marks the component as not updating. Called during the creation of a component. Executes the `initialize` method if the component is not initialized. Executes the updated method.	`comp.endUpdate();`
updated	Empty implementation.	`comp.updated();`
get_isUpdating	Getter for the updating member.	`comp.get_isUpdating();`
initialize	Marks the component as initialized.	`comp.initialize();`
get_initialized	Getter for the initialized member.	`comp.get_initialized();`
dispose	Executes the disposing event handlers. Removes the _events property from the component. Unregisters the component from `Sys.Application`.	`comp.dispose();`

TABLE 3.4 continued

Method Name	Description	Syntax
get_events	Getter for the events member.	comp.get_events()
get_id	Getter for the ID member.	comp.get_id();
set_id	Setter for the ID member. ID cannot be changed after it has been set (through this setter) or after the component has been registered with Sys.Application.	comp.set_id(id);
add_disposing	Adds an event handler to the disposing event.	comp.add_disposing(*handler*);
remove_disposing	Removes an event handler from the disposing event.	comp.remove_disposing(*handler*);
add_propertyChanged	Adds an event handler to the propertyChanged event.	comp.add_propertyChanged(*handler*);
remove_propertyChanged	Removes an event handler from the propertyChanged event.	comp.remove_propertyChanged(*handler*)
raisePropertyChanged	Executes registered propertyChanged event handlers passing in the name of the property that changed in the event arguments.	comp.raisePropertyChanged(*propertyName*);

> ■ **NOTE**   **beginUpdate, endUpdate, and initialize**
>
> beginUpdate, endUpdate, and initialize are automatically executed during the component creation process. They are normally not executed by user-defined code, but can be overridden to provide custom functionality.

Defining New Components

Sys.Component is extremely useful, but directly creating instances of it is not its purpose. Instead, it is intended to be used as a base class for user-defined components.

We can define a new component type using the Prototype Model we covered in Chapter 2 and registering our component to inherit from Sys.Component.

ErrorHandler Component

To demonstrate how to define a new component, we create a new error handling component. The ErrorHandler component will be responsible for publishing handled and unhandled errors to an error data service.

Skeleton

To start, we create the skeleton of our new component, as Listing 3.1 shows.

LISTING 3.1 Defining Our ErrorHandler Component

```
/// <reference name="MicrosoftAjax.js"/>
ErrorHandler = function() {
  ErrorHandler.initializeBase(this);
};

ErrorHandler.prototype = {
  initialize: function() {
    ErrorHandler.callBaseMethod(this, 'initialize');
  },
  dispose: function() {
    ErrorHandler.callBaseMethod(this, 'dispose');
  }
}
ErrorHandler.registerClass('ErrorHandler', Sys.Component);
```

Besides calling `initializeBase` in the constructor and registering our class to inherit from `Sys.Component`, we overrode `Sys.Component`'s `initialize` and `dispose` methods. We included these overrides in the skeleton because overriding the `initialize` and `dispose` methods is normally the first step taken in creating a new component, and we suggest doing it right away.

Build Up and Tear Down

We can build on our skeleton definition by providing an implementation of our `initialize` and `dispose` methods.

In the `initialize` method, you build up your component. This includes adding event handlers to DOM elements, appending a new DOM element to the tree, or anything else your component requires.

In the `dispose` method, you tear down your component. This might include detaching an event from a DOM element, destroying a created DOM element, or releasing any other resources that your component created.

■ TIP   dispose May Be Called More Than Once

It's a good habit to write your `dispose` method so that it can be called more than once without causing any runtime errors. With a decently complex application, it's likely you'll get into a situation where when some manager object is disposed it will call `dispose` on its child components. But, each of the child components will have also been registered as a disposable object with `Sys.Application`. When `Sys.Application` disposes and executes `dispose` on each of the registered disposable objects, it will be the second (or more time) that `dispose` will have been called on them. If you're not careful, this can cause a runtime error. Simple if-then checks can prevent most common problems.

For our new `ErrorHandler` component, we need to add a handler to the window's `error` event when the component initializes and then remove the handler when our component disposes. Listing 3.2 shows how we do this.

LISTING 3.2 Adding a Handler to Window's error Event

```
/// <reference name="MicrosoftAjax.js"/>
ErrorHandler = function () {
  ErrorHandler.initializeBase(this);
};

ErrorHandler.prototype = {
  initialize: function () {
    ErrorHandler.callBaseMethod(this, 'initialize');
    window.onerror =
      Function.createDelegate(this, this._unhandledError);
  },

  dispose: function ErrorHandler$dispose() {
    window.onerror = null;
    ErrorHandler.callBaseMethod(this, 'dispose');
  },

  _unhandledError: function(msg, url, lineNumber) {
    try {
      var stackTrace = StackTrace.createStackTrace(arguments.callee);
      ErrorDataService.PublishError
        (stackTrace, msg, url, lineNumber);
    }
    catch (e) { }
  }
}
ErrorHandler.registerClass('ErrorHandler', Sys.Component);
```

As you can see in Listing 3.2, we did some interesting things. First, in the `initialize` method, we created a delegate that pointed to the _unhandled Error method and assigned it to the window's error event using the onerror assignment.

■ **TIP**   **window.onerror**

We used the onerror assignment rather than the $addHandler method because for some reason the window's error event doesn't support adding events through addEventListener or attachEvent, the two browser-specific methods that $addHandler eventually calls.

In the `dispose` method, we went ahead and cleared the window's `error` event handler. This is the buildup and teardown of our component.

In the `unhandledError` method that will execute when an unhandled error occurs, we do two things. First, we generate a stack trace using a global `StackTrace` object passing in the `callee` property of the function's `arguments` variable. After we have our stack trace, we execute the `PublishError` method on our `ErrorDataService` web service proxy, passing to the server the stack trace, the error message, the URL of the page where the error occurred, and the line number of the error message. We also wrapped all the code in a try-catch statement because we don't want the error handling code to throw any runtime errors itself.

> ■ **NOTE**   StackTrace and ErrorDataService
>
> The global `StackTrace` object we used to generate our stack trace of the executing call stack is really useful for debugging, and its full source code is available in Appendix D, "Client Error Handling Code." Similarly, the `ErrorDataService` web service that we used to send the error information back to the server for processing can be found in Appendix D.

Using Base Class Methods and Objects

By inheriting from `Sys.Component`, our type inherits all the attributes and behaviors of `Sys.Component`. Using the base class's `Sys.EventHandlerList` object and its related functionality, we can define new events without having to write much code ourselves. Listing 3.3 expands our basic `Error Handler` component and adds an event that we can register with that will be raised whenever an error occurs.

LISTING 3.3 Using Base Class Methods

```
… // code remains the same as before.

_unhandledError: function (msg, url, lineNumber) {
  try {
    var stackTrace =
    StackTrace.createStackTrace(arguments.callee);
    ErrorDataService.PublishError
      (stackTrace, msg, url, lineNumber);

    var args = new ErrorEventArgs(stackTrace, msg, url, lineNumber);
    this._raiseUnhandledErrorOccured(args);
```

```
      }
      catch (e) { }
    },

    add_unhandledErrorOccurred: function(handler) {
      this.get_events().addHandler("unhandledErrorOccurred", handler);
    },

    remove_unhandledErrorOccurred: function(handler) {
      this.get_events().removeHandler("unhandledErrorOccurred", handler);
    },

    _raiseUnhandledErrorOccured: function(args) {
      var evt = this.get_events().getHandler("unhandledErrorOccurred");
      if (evt !== null) {
        evt(this, args);
      }
    },
  }
  ErrorHandler.registerClass('ErrorHandler', Sys.Component) ;

  ErrorEventArgs = function(stackTrace, message, url, lineNumber) {
    ErrorEventArgs.initializeBase(this);
    this._message = message;
    this._stackTrace = stackTrace;
    this._url = url;
    this._lineNumber = lineNumber;
  }
  ErrorEventArgs.registerClass("ErrorEventArgs", Sys.EventArgs);
```

Starting from the bottom of Listing 3.3, we define the new `ErrorEvent Args` type. This type inherits from `Sys.EventArgs` and turns our error information into an object.

In the `ErrorHandler` type, we added the three methods necessary to add, remove, and raise the `unhandledErrorOccurred` event. We rely on `Sys.Component`'s event handler list, which we access through `this.get_events()` to maintain the list of events.

Finally, in the `_unhandledError`, we added code to create the error event arguments and then pass them on to the method that raises the event.

One final change that we make to our `ErrorHandler` component is to add a property that allows us to enable or disable the error publishing feature. Listing 3.4 shows the code changes.

LISTING 3.4 Adding the Disable Error Publishing Property

```
/// <reference name="MicrosoftAjax.js"/>
ErrorHandler = function () {
```

Listing 3.4 continued

```
    ErrorHandler.initializeBase(this);
    this._disableErrorPublication = false;
};

ErrorHandler.prototype = {
...
  get_disableErrorPublication: function() {
    return this._disableErrorPublication;
  },

  set_disableErrorPublication: function(value) {
    if (!this.get_updating()) {
      this.raisePropertyChanged("disableErrorPublication");
    }
    this._disableErrorPublication = value;
  },

  _unhandledError: function(msg, url, lineNumber) {
    try {
      var stackTrace = StackTrace.createStackTrace(arguments.callee);
      if (!this._disableErrorPublication) {
        ErrorDataService.PublishError
          (stackTrace, msg, url, lineNumber);
      }
      var args =
        new ErrorEventArgs(stackTrace, msg, url, lineNumber);
      this._raiseUnhandledErrorOccured(args);
    }
    catch (e) { }
  },
  ...
}
ErrorHandler.registerClass('ErrorHandler', Sys.Component);
...
```

With that final change, we've created a useful component that we can use to send client error information to the server so that we can be aware of issues our clients are experiencing.

Creating Components

Based on what we've covered so far, you might think that to create a new component you would "new up" a component and assign it to a variable, as shown in Listing 3.5.

LISTING 3.5 Creating an Instance of a Component Using new

```
var errorHandler = new ErrorHandler();
errorHandler.set_disableErrorPublication (false);
```

Although nothing is wrong with this code, after all a component is just a JavaScript object, components should be created through the Sys. Component.create method. Listing 3.6 shows the syntax for using the create method.

LISTING 3.6 Creating an Instance of a Component Using Sys.Component.create

```
var newComponent =
  Sys.Component.create(
    type,
    properties,
    events,
    references,
    element);
```

The Sys.Component.create method, which can also be accessed through the global variable $create, does more than just create a new instance of a particular type. Instead, it creates an instance of a particular type, registers the instance with Sys.Application as a managed component, and automatically calls the component's beginUpdate, endUpdate, updating, and initialize methods. In addition to doing all this automatically, depending on what parameters are provided to the call, $create can assign initial property values, add event handlers to events, assign other components as references, and associate a DOM element to the component. Finally, the $create method returns a pointer to the created instance. So as you can see, the $create method does a lot more than create a new instance of a type.

> ■ **NOTE** Initialize Execution
>
> Initialize always executes after all properties, events, and references have been set.

Importantly, the $create method not only creates instances of types that directly inherit from Sys.Component, but can also create types that have multiple levels of inheritance before reaching the Sys.Component type. This includes controls that inherit from Sys.UI.Control and behaviors that inherit from `Sys.UI.Behavior`. The `$create` method works a little bit differently when creating a behavior or control, and we cover this slight difference when we cover those types later in this chapter.

■ **NOTE**   Parameter Information

The only parameter required by the `$create` method is `type`. The other parameters—`properties`, `events`, `references`, and `element`—are all optional parameters. If you don't want to use them, supply `null`.

Supplying a value other than `null` for the element parameter is valid only when the type you're creating an instance of inherits from `Sys.UI.Control` or `Sys.UI.Behavior`. If you pass in an element when creating a component that does not inherit from either of these types, an error is thrown.

Likewise, if you do not pass in an element when creating an instance of a type that inherits from `Sys.UI.Control` or `Sys.UI.Behavior`, an error will be thrown.

To demonstrate how to use the `$create` method, we walk through a series of `$create` calls changing the parameters around to suit our demonstration purposes.

■ **NOTE**   Sys.Application Is Initialized

The following explanation of the `$create` method assumes that `Sys.Application` has been initialized. Although components will not always be created under this condition, we chose this assumption for the initial walkthrough of the `$create` method so that we could have a clear path through the method without too many branches.

However, there are a couple of significant differences between creating components after `Sys.Application` is initialized and creating components before `Sys.Application` is fully initialized, and we point out how the `$create` method changes when `Sys.Application` isn't fully initialized when we discuss `Sys.Application`'s initialization process in Chapter 4.

Using the type Parameter

First, let's look at the basic call where we only pass in the type we want to create and `null` values for the rest of the parameters. Listing 3.7 shows this call.

LISTING 3.7 The type Parameter

```
var errorHandler =
  Sys.Component.create(
    ErrorHandler,
    null,
    null,
    null,
    null);
```

type

Description: The type of component to create

Expected type: type

Required: Yes

Other requirements: The value assigned to type must inherit from Sys.Component.

Notes: The parameter is not enclosed in quotation marks because it's a Type object, not a string. A Type object is a Function object that has been registered with the Microsoft AJAX Library using the registerClass, registerInterface, or registerEnum method such as we did with the ErrorHandler component.

In this example, the first thing the Sys.Component.create method does is ensure that the parameter value ErrorHandler is a Type and inherits from Sys.Component. After it passes those tests, it creates a new instance of ErrorHandler and assigns it to a local variable.

> **NOTE   Registering as a Disposable Object**
>
> When the new instance is created, it registers as a disposable object with Sys.Application. Doing so ensures that the instance's dispose method is executed when Sys.Application is disposed. We cover this topic further in Chapter 4.

Then, on our new instance, beginUpdate is executed. By default, begin Update does nothing more than set the internal updating flag to true, but it can be overridden by the new component's implementation to do more work if necessary.

Then, on our new instance, endUpdate is executed, which sets the internal _updating flag back to false and then executes the initialize method, which we overrode to attach an event handler to the window's error event. Once the initialize method has executed, the updated method executes. If a method override is not supplied, the updated method doesn't do anything. From there, the component is returned, and you can access it through a variable assigned to the method call.

> ■ **TIP**   _initialized Check
>
> In endUpdate, there is a check to make sure the internal member _initialized is false before initialize is called. In the case of the $create method, initialized will always be false when endUpdate is called. However, if you use endUpdate for a different purpose later in the component's lifecycle, _initialized will be set to true, and the initialize method won't execute again. This allows you to call beginUpdate and endUpdate without having to worry about your component being re-initialized.

This simple example tells us one important thing through the power of omission. Nowhere did we say that the component got added to Sys. Application's managed objects, which is something we claimed the Sys. Component.create method did. This didn't happen because the ID of the component was never set, and only components that have their IDs set are automatically added to Sys.Application's managed components. We can correct this by manually setting the component's ID and then adding it to Sys.Application's list of managed components, as shown in Listing 3.8.

LISTING 3.8 Manually Setting the ID and Calling addComponent

```
var errorHandler =
  Sys.Component.create(
    ErrorHandler,
    null,
    null,
    null,
    null);

errorHandler.set_id("ApplicationErrorHandler");
Sys.Application.addComponent(errorHandler);
```

> ■ **NOTE**   Calling addComponent
>
> If we were to manually add the component to Sys.Application without setting the component's ID, an error would be thrown.

Another way to correct this problem is to initially set the component's ID. If the ID is set using the **properties** parameter, the component will automatically be added to Sys.Application's managed components right after the events parameter is processed. Listing 3.9 shows the change required.

LISTING 3.9 Setting the Component's id Inline

```
var errorHandler =
  Sys.Component.create(
    ErrorHandler,
    {id: "ApplicationErrorHandler"},
    null,
    null,
    null);
```

Because having a value for the component's ID is necessary for it to become a managed component, it should almost always be set in the $create call. There might be special cases where you don't want to set it or want to set it a later time, but these will be rare.

Also, the IDs of components that are managed by Sys.Application must be unique. If you attempt to add two components with the same ID to Sys.Application's managed components either through the $create statement or manually calling addComponent, an error will be thrown.

> ■ **NOTE**   Using the returned Variable
>
> The $create method enables us to access the created component through a pointer returned by the method, but it's useful only in certain situations. Because the component is registered with Sys.Application, we'll be able to get access to the component later by finding it within Sys.Application's managed components using its unique ID.

Using the properties Parameter

In this example let's pass in some simple initial property values. Listing 3.10 shows how we do this.

LISTING 3.10 Passing In Initial Property Values

```
var errorHandler =
  Sys.Component.create(
    ErrorHandler,
    {
      id: "ApplicationErrorHandler",
      disableErrorPublication: true
    },
    null,
    null,
    null);
```

properties

Expected type: Object

Required: No

Description: An object containing key-value pairs, where the key is the name of a property on the component to set, and the value is the value to assign to that property

In this example, the initial steps of the $create method are the same as they were in the previous example. The type is validated, the component is created, and beginUpdate is executed.

The next step is to assign the property values to the component's properties. The properties and their values are passed in using the string-object syntax that is highlighted in Listing 3.10. Instead of using the string-object syntax, we could have used object creation code as shown in Listing 3.11, but the string-object syntax is a shorter and more comprehensible syntax in this situation.

LISTING 3.11 Creating Properties Object Using Variables

```
var initialProperties = new Object;
initialProperties.id = "ApplicationErrorHandler";
initialProperties.disableErrorPublication = true;

var errorHandler =
  $create(
    ErrorHandler,
    initialProperties,
    null,
```

```
    null,
    null);
```

Using either method, our code indicates that we want to set two properties: id and `disableErrorPublication`.

To do this, the `$create` method delegates control to another method, `Sys$Component_setProperties`. This is a global method available within the Microsoft AJAX Library, whose purpose is to set properties on a component. It accepts two parameters: the `target` object and the `properties` object.

Within this method, each of the expando properties attached to the `properties` parameter is accessed and successively processed according to a series of rules.

The first rule determines whether there is a getter method for the property. It does this by prefixing the current property name, id, with the string `get_`. In our example, the `get_id` method exists on the base `Sys.Component` class, so this rule is met.

After the getter method has been established as existing, the setter method is looked for. It does this by prefixing the current property name with the string `set_`. Again, in our example, the `set_id` method exists on the base `Sys.Component` class.

After the setter method has been determined to exist, the setter method is executed on the target, passing in the value of the current property. In our example, the value passed in is `ApplicationErrorHandler`.

The process repeats until all properties have been successfully applied to the component or an error occurs, such as the getter not existing, a setter not taking in the correct number of parameters, or a whole host of other possibilities. In our example, the `disableErrorPublication` property is initialized with the value `true`.

▪▪ **NOTE**   **Iterating over the Properties**

The expando properties attached to the `properties` parameter are accessed by using a for...in loop. As we discussed in Chapter 1, "Programming with JavaScript," the for...in loop iterates over the properties of an object, placing the current property name into a variable.

After the property name is placed in a variable, the value associated to the property name is accessed using the associative array principle discussed in Chapter 1.

Calling the Setter Method

As mentioned, the setter method for a property is executed during the creation of a component. Just as in .NET, the setter method can contain any code it wants. If you write the method to execute a long-running process, the component creation waits until that process has completed.

With that in mind, you need to be careful to make the setter method as efficient as possible for the component creation to complete quickly.

If there is extra code that should not execute during the component creation process, one way to avoid executing it is to check the value of _updating, as shown here:

```
...
set_disableErrorPublication: function(value) {
  if (!this.get_updating()) {
    this.raisePropertyChanged
      ("disableErrorPublication");
  }
  this._disableErrorPublication = value;
},
...
```

In this code example, we make sure that the component is not updating before we raise the propertyChanged event. Checking the _updating flag is less expensive than going through the process of raising the event.

Caution: This is just test code. Make sure that you really don't want the propertyChanged event to be raised when the component is updating before using this code.

Complex Property Setting

Setting the id and the disableErrorPublication of our ErrorHandler instance are simple examples of property settings through the $create method, but there are four advanced scenarios of property setting that we can use to our advantage to create complex components in a single statement.

1. Setting a value that has no setter or getter, such as an attribute on a DOM element or a property attached to a prototype
2. Appending items to an array
3. Setting properties on a subcomponent; a component contained within another component
4. Adding properties to an existing object

Each of these concepts is illustrated with a new dummy component MyComplexComponent:

```
MyComplexComponent = function() {
  MyComplexComponent.initializeBase(this);
  this.city = null;
  this._areaCodes = [];
  this._myObject = { firstName: "Harry" };
  this.subComponent =
    $create(ErrorHandler,
      null,
      null,
      null,
      null);
};

MyComplexComponent.prototype = {
  someExpandoProperty: null,
  get_address: function() {
    return this._address;
  },
  set_address: function(value) {
    this._address = value;
  },
  get_areaCodes: function() {
    return this._areaCodes;
  },
  get_myObject: function() {
    return this._myObject;
  }
};

MyComplexComponent.registerClass(
  "MyComplexComponent",
  Sys.Component);

var newComponent =
  $create(
```

```
MyComplexComponent,
{
  id: "MyNewComplexComponent",
  city: "San Diego",
  areaCodes: [619, 858, 760],
  someExpandoProperty: "My Expando's Value",
  subComponent:
  {
    id: "ApplicationErrorHandler",
    disableErrorPublication: "true"
  },
  myObject: { lastName: "Houdini" }
},
null,
null,
null);
```

1. Setting a value that has no getter or setter

    This scenario is exemplified through the setting of the city and someExpandoProperty properties. These properties can be set because they are existing fields on the object. If they didn't already exist, the setProperties routine wouldn't add them for us.

2. Appending items to an array

    The second advanced scenario is exemplified through the areaCodes property. Here, we define a new array of three elements (619, 858, and 760) and assign it to the areaCodes property. For the elements to be appended to the existing array, there must be a getter for the property, but no setter. If there is a setter, it will be used instead, and it will be up to the setter's code to append the items to the array. Also, the array must already be instantiated. If the variable points to null or undefined, an error is thrown.

3. Setting properties on a subcomponent

    The third advanced scenario is exemplified through the sub Component property. Here, we define a subobject that contains an id and disableErrorPublication property, both properties on our previously defined ErrorHandler component. When the set Properties method encounters this property, it accesses the subcomponent, and then recursively calls the setProperties method using the subcomponent as the target parameter and the subobject containing the id and address properties as the properties parameter. This type of recursive call could continue an infinite number of levels deep if we had set up our properties parameter that way.

We could have supplied a getter here and had the same effect, but if we had supplied a setter, too, setting the properties of the subcomponent would not have worked as expected.

When we call the setProperties method recursively using a component as the target parameter, it calls beginUpdate on that component before it enters the for...in loop and endUpdate when it exits. This is something to be aware of if you're using the get_updating method in your code.

4. Setting properties on a simple JavaScript object

The fourth and final advanced scenario is exemplified through the myObject property. The myObject property defines a simple object containing the property lastName that has the value Houdini. When the setProperties method encounters this property, it makes a recursive call into the setProperties method to apply the new properties to the myObject member. Here, rather than pass in a component as the target, myObject is passed in as the target parameter and the new properties object is passed in as the properties parameter.

As you can see, the properties parameter of the $create method can handle some advanced scenarios. You'll find use for them in your code, if you remember that they're there.

Using the events Parameter

In this example, let's assign an event handler to the available initialized event using the events parameter. The code in Listing 3.12 demonstrates how to do this.

LISTING 3.12 Passing in Event Handlers

```
$create(
  ErrorHandler,
  {
    id:"ApplicationErrorHandler",
    disableErrorPublication: true
  },
  {
    unhandledErrorOccurred:
      function(sender, args) {
        alert(args._stackTrace);
      }
  },
  null,
  null);
```

events

Expected type: `Object`

Required: No

Description: An object containing key-value pairs, where the key is the name of an event on the component to assign to, and the value is an event handler to add to the event

In this example, the initial steps of the `$create` method are the same as they were in the previous `properties` example. The type is validated, the component is created, `beginUpdate` is executed, and then the properties are set.

After the properties are set, the `events` parameter is processed. Similar to the `properties` property, the `events` parameter is an object that contains a series of key-value pairs. The `events` object is iterated over, and each key-value pair is used to add an event handler to an event until they are all added or an error occurs. Again, similar to the `properties` parameter, the event handlers are added to events by executing the appropriate method. In this case, the key, `unhandledErrorOccurred`, is automatically prefixed with `add_` to create `add_unhandledErrorOccurred`. This string is then looked for as a function contained within the component's definition. If the method `add_unhandledErrorOccurred` is successfully found and the value of the key-value pair contained in the object is a `Function` object, the value is passed into the `add_unhandledErrorOccurred` method as its parameter and executed, adding the event handler to the event.

In our example `$create` statement, we defined the event handler in line with the `$create` statement, and our event handler is successfully added to the unhandledErrorOccurred event. Another way to do this is to predefine an event handler function, as we show in Listing 3.13.

LISTING 3.13 Predefining an Event Handler

```
function unhandledErrorHandler(sender, args) {
  alert(args._stackTrace);
}

$create(
  MyComponent,
  {address: "123 N. Fake Street" },
  {
    unhandledErrorOccurred:
      unhandledErrorHandler
    }
  },
  null,
  null);
```

Predefining the event handler allows it to be reused for other components or to be called procedurally.

In addition, if we want to handle an event with a method that is contained within our component, rather than use a global function as we did in Listing 3.13, we have to go through an extra step of creating a delegate to wrap our event handler method so that context gets pointed back to the intended component, as shown in Listing 3.14.

LISTING 3.14 Wrapping an Event Handler in a Delegate

```
MyOtherComponent = function() {
  MyOtherComponent.initializeBase(this);
  this._subComponent = null;
};

MyOtherComponent.prototype = {
  _unhandledErrorOccurred: function(sender, args) {
    var stackTrace = args._stackTrace;
    if (typeof(stackTrace) != "undefined") {
      alert ("The Stack Trace of the error was: " + stackTrace);
    }
  },
```

LISTING 3.14 continued

```
initialize: function() {
  MyOtherComponent.callBaseMethod(this, "initialize");

  this._errorHandler =
    $create(
      ErrorHandler,
      {
        id:"ApplicationErrorHandler",
        disableErrorPublishing: true
      },
      {
        unhandledErrorOccurred:
          Function.createDelegate (
            this,
            this._unhandledErrorOccurred
          )
      },
      null,
      null);

  // cause an error to be thrown
  var nullObj = null;
  nullObj.causeError;
  }
};

MyOtherComponent.registerClass("MyOtherComponent", Sys.Component);
```

As shown in the highlighted text, we create an instance of the Error Handler component in MyOtherComponent's initialize method. When we assign the event handler to the unhandledErrorOccurred event, we wrap it in a delegate so that when the code goes to execute the _unhandled ErrorOccurred method it executes is using the correct context.

■ NOTE   Functional Prefixes

Now that we've covered setting properties and adding event handlers through the $create method, we can see how the property prefixes get_ and set_ and the event handler prefix add_ are not only aesthetic prefixes but also functional.

Using the references Parameter

With the references parameter, we can assign one component to a property on another, thus linking them together. You might wonder why we would need a separate parameter for this when we could already accomplish this using the properties parameter. We need this parameter because when we start using server code to create instances of client components, we won't know what order the components will be created in. If we use a separate parameter, the initialization process that Sys.Application goes through to create our components treats component references differently and delays assigning them until all components have been created. Doing this eliminates the problem of a component attempting to access an uncreated component.

To illustrate how to use the references parameter, we pass in one component as a reference to another component in the $create statement using the references parameter. To do that, we must first create a component that can act as a reference to our second component. Listing 3.15 shows the two $create statements. In this example, we use two fictitious components to keep the example clear.

LISTING 3.15 Assigning References

```
// create the first component
$create(
  MyComponent,
  {
    id: "MyFirstComponent"
  },
  null
  null,
  null
);

// create the second component and assign the first component
// to a property called subComponent
$create(
  MyComponent,
  {
    id: "MySecondComponent"
  },
  null,
  {
    subComponent:"MyFirstComponent"
  },
  null
);
```

references

Expected type: `Object`

Required: No

Description: An object that contains key-value pairs, where the key represents a component property, and the value represents a component to assign to this property. The value is the `id` of the component.

After the `$create` statement has passed the event's assignment code, it processes the `references` parameter. Similar to the `properties` and `events` parameters, the `references` parameter is an object that contains key-value pairs. The key is the property we want to assign, and the value is an `id` of a component we want to assign to the property.

In Listing 3.15, the `references` object is highlighted. The object states that we want to assign the component that has the id `MyFirstComponent` to the `subComponent` property of the component being created. Just like the `setProperties` method we discussed earlier, the `setReferences` method looks for a setter method that's defined by prefixing `set_` to the property name. In our example, this method's name is `set_subComponent`. When this method is found, the component `id`, `MyFirstComponent`, is looked for within `Sys.Application`'s managed components. If the component is found, the setter method is executed with the found component as its parameter.

■ **NOTE**   Finding Managed Components

Through `Sys.Application.find`, we can find registered components by ID. When we cover `Sys.Application` in Chapter 4, we cover the `find` method in detail.

■ **TIP**   Creation Order

As mentioned earlier, for this code sample to work correctly, `MyFirst Component` must be available before the second `$create` statement executes. References to uncreated components can be used if `Sys. Application` is in its initialization phase. This is something we cover in Chapter 4.

Using the element Parameter

The last parameter of the $create method is element, which is used as a pointer to a DOM element. Because the element parameter is valid only when we're creating a new behavior or a new control, we cover the element parameter when we cover defining and creating those types.

Wrapping Up Components

A component is not just defined as an object that inherits from Sys.Component, but also as being managed by Sys.Application. Creating an instance of a type that inherits from Sys.Component using the new keyword will not automatically register the instance with Sys.Application. We have to use the $create method for this to happen. Using $create also facilitates setting properties, wiring up event handlers, assigning references to other components, and associating it with a DOM element, as we see with controls and behaviors. It also automatically calls the initialize method on the component, enabling you to create user-defined code that executes after all the properties have been set, event handlers added, and component references assigned.

Controls

A control is a special type of component directly associated to a DOM element. A DOM element can have *only* one associated control, and a control *must* be associated to a DOM element.

In practical terms, because we can have only one control associated to a given DOM element, their use is intended for situations where you want to have full power over the DOM element. In those cases where you're not sure whether that's your intention, start off with a behavior, and then move to a control if needed. In reality, switching back and forth between a control and a behavior is not too difficult and doesn't require too much code to be altered.

Because a control is directly tied to a DOM element, it has methods that are useful for accessing and manipulating the associated DOM element. Table 3.5 details the methods available to a control that access and manipulate the associated DOM element.

TABLE 3.5 Sys.UI.Control Methods

Method Name	Description	Syntax
set_id	Overrides component's set_id method. Throws an error because a control's id is always the associated DOM element's id.	no valid usage
get_id	Overrides component's get_id method. Returns the id of the associated DOM element.	return ctrl.get_id();
get_visible	Returns the value returned by calling Sys.UI. DOMElement.getVisible on the associated DOM element.	return ctrl.get_visible();
set_visible	Calls Sys.UI.DomElement. setVisible using the control's associated DOM element and the Boolean value passed into the set_visible call.	ctrl.set_visible(*visibility*);
get_visibilityMode	Calls Sys.UI.DomElement. getVisibilityMode using the control's associated DOM element.	return ctrl.get_visibilityMode();
set_visibilityMode	Calls Sys.UI.DomElement. setVisibilityMode using the control's associated DOM element and Sys. UI.VisibilityMode parameter passed in to the set_visibilityMode call.	ctrl.set_visibilityMode(*Sys.UI.VisibilityMode*);
get_element	Returns the associated DOM element.	return ctrl.get_element();

Method Name	Description	Syntax
addCssClass	Calls `Sys.UI.DomElement.addCssClass` using the control's associated DOM element and the name of the CSS class to add.	`ctrl.addCssClass (cssClassName)`
removeCssClass	Calls `Sys.UI.DomElement.removeCssClass` using the control's associated DOM element and the name of the CSS class to remove.	`ctrl.removeCssClass (cssClassName);`
toggleCssClass	Calls `Sys.UI.DomElement.toggleCssClass` using the control's associated DOM element and the name of the CSS class to toggle.	`ctrl.toggleCssClass (cssClassName);`
dispose	Overrides `Sys.Component`'s dispose. Calls base class `dispose`, sets `element`'s control expando property to `undefined`, and deletes reference to the DOM element from the component.	`ctrl.dispose();`

New Concepts

Besides the methods that access and manipulate the associated DOM element, other methods introduce two new concepts: a control's parent and ASP.NET-like event bubbling.

Control's Parent

A control's parent property provides a pointer to another control. The parent can be calculated in one of two ways. If a parent has been explicitly set using the `set_parent` method, that is the control's parent. If a parent has not been explicitly set, the control's associated DOM element's `parentNode` pointer is walked until an element with a control attached to it is reached, and that is considered the control's parent.

Table 3.6 details the methods involved with the parent pointer concept.

TABLE 3.6 Sys.UI.Control Methods Related to Control's Parent

Method Name	Description	Syntax
get_parent	Returns the explicitly set parent or the first control encountered by walking up the DOM element's parentNode pointer	`var parent = ctrl.get_parent();`
set_parent	Explicitly sets the parent	`ctrl.set_parent(otherCtrl);`

Event Bubbling

Event bubbling is a method of passing events up through the parent pointer and giving parent controls the opportunity to handle those events.

Event bubbling in the Microsoft AJAX Library is similar to event bubbling using controls in ASP.NET. A control starts the process by calling `raiseBubbleEvent`, passing in a source and event arguments. In the `raiseBubbleEvent` method, the control's parent is retrieved using the `get_parent` method attached to the control, and `onBubbleEvent` is called on it. The default implementation of `Sys.UI.Control`'s `onBubbleEvent` method returns `false`, which indicates that the control did not handle the event and the bubbling should continue up the hierarchy.

If the control wants to handle the bubbled event, it may do so by overriding the default implementation of `onBubbleEvent`. In the overridden method, it can decide whether the bubbling should continue or stop. If it wants to stop the event's propagation up the parent hierarchy, it returns `true`. If it wants to allow other controls higher up in the control's parent tree the opportunity to handle the event, too, it returns `false`.

Table 3.7 details the methods involved with the event bubbling concept.

TABLE 3.7 Sys.UI.Control Methods Related to Event Bubbling

Method Name	Description	Syntax
onBubbleEvent	Part of the event bubbling framework. Needs to be overridden to provide functionality. Returns false by default.	Is automatically called by raiseBubbleEvent
raiseBubbleEvent	Part of the event bubbling framework. Walks the control's parent list, firing the onBubbleEvent on each parent object.	ctrl.raiseBubbleEvent (source, args);

> **■ NOTE   Additional Methods**
>
> Because Sys.UI.Control inherits from Sys.Component, all the methods available to Sys.Component are available to Sys.UI.Control.

Defining a New Control

Like defining a new component, defining a new control follows the Prototype Model we covered in Chapter 2. To illustrate how to define a new control, we create a new control that attaches to a textbox and allows only numbers to be entered. Listing 3.16 shows the code necessary to define the new NumberOnlyTextBox control.

LISTING 3.16 Defining a New Control Type

```
/// <reference name="MicrosoftAjax.js"/>
NumberOnlyTextBox = function(element) {
  NumberOnlyTextBox.initializeBase(this, [element]);
  this._keyDownDelegate = null;
};

NumberOnlyTextBox.prototype = {
  initialize: function() {
    NumberOnlyTextBox.callBaseMethod(this,'initialize');
    this._keyDownDelegate =
      Function.createDelegate(this, this._keyDownHandler);
    $addHandler(this.get_element(), "keydown", this._keyDownDelegate);
  },
```

LISTING 3.16 continued

```
  dispose: function() {
    $removeHandler
      (this.get_element(), "keydown", this._keyDownDelegate);
    this._keyDownDelegate = null;
    NumberOnlyTextBox.callBaseMethod(this, 'dispose');
  },

  _keyDownHandler: function(e) {
      return ((e.keyCode >= 48 && e.keyCode <= 57) || (e.keyCode == 8));
  }
};

NumberOnlyTextBox.registerClass("NumberOnlyTextBox", Sys.UI.Control);
```

As shown in Listing 3.16, we can see that there are two major differences between our NumberOnlyTextBox control and our ErrorHandler component we declared previously.

First, the base class of our NumberOnlyTextBox control is Sys.UI.Control and not Sys.Component.

Second, the constructor takes an element parameter and passes it to the base class's constructor through the initializeBase method. This parameter is the DOM element that is going to be associated to the control.

When the element is passed to Sys.UI.Control's constructor, three things happen. First, the DOM element is checked to make sure that there is no other control already associated to it. If this test fails, the constructor throws an error, and the control's creation fails. If it passes, the second step the constructor takes is to assign the DOM element to the internal member _element. Finally, the control is assigned to the DOM element using the expando property control. If we created a reference to the associated element, we could access the assigned control using the following code:

```
$get("TextBox1").control;
```

Using our newly minted control type, Listing 3.17 demonstrates the association requirements we just discussed.

LISTING 3.17 Creating an Instance of MyControl Using new

```
<html xmlns="http://www.w3.org/1999/xhtml">
<head runat="server">
  <title>Control Testing!</title>
</head>
```

```
<body>
  <form id="form1" runat="server">
  <asp:ScriptManager ID="SM1" runat="server" />

  // omitted NumberOnlyTextBox definition for brevity.

  <asp:TextBox ID="txtBox1" runat="server" Width="150px" />

  <script type="text/javascript">

    var numberOnlyTextBox =
      new NumberOnlyTextBox($get("txtBox1"));

    // alerts "txtBox1"
    alert ("numberOnlyTextBox's associated element's id: " +
           numberOnlyTextBox.get_element().id);

    // alerts "txtBox1"
    alert ("numberOnlyTextBox's associated control's id: " +
           $get("txtBox1").control.get_id());

    // throws a JavaScript error because a
    // control is already associated to txtBox1.
    var numberOnlyTextBox2 =
      new NumberOnlyTextBox ($get("txtBox1"));
  </script>

  </form>
</body>
</html>
```

Creating a Control

In Listing 3.17, we used the new keyword to create a new instance of our NumberOnlyTextBox type. From our component discussion, we know that the $create method performs a whole host of tasks besides creating a new instance of the type, and because our new type inherits from Sys.UI. Control, which inherits from Sys.Component, we can use the $create statement in the same manner as we did for our ErrorHandler component.

Instead of walking through the entire $create method again, we need to discuss only the use of the element parameter because that's the only difference. Using the example we created in Listing 3.17 as a basis, we can modify the code to use the $create method. Listing 3.18 shows the altered code.

LISTING 3.18 Creating an Instance of MyControl Using $create

```html
<html>
<head runat="server">
  <title>Control Testing!</title>
</head>
<body>
  <form id="form1" runat="server">
  <asp:ScriptManager ID="SM1" runat="server" />

  // omitted NumberOnlyTextBox definition for brevity.

  <asp:TextBox ID="txtBox1" runat="server" Width="150px" />

  <script type="text/javascript">
    $create(
      NumberOnlyTextBox,
      null,
      null,
      null,
      $get("txtBox1")
    );
  </script>

  </form>
</body>
</html>
```

The highlighted code shows the $create method call. Notice how $get("txtBox1") is passed in as the element parameter of the $create method. When the $create method instantiates the new instance of the NumberOnlyTextBox, it determines whether the NumberOnlyTextBox inherits from Sys.UI.Control or Sys.UI.Behavior. If it does, and in our example it does, it uses the element parameter as the parameter for the constructor call; similar to what we did in Listing 3.17 before we used the $create method to create our new control.

> ■ **NOTE** Setting the Control's id
>
> Unlike a component or behavior, setting the id of a control is not allowed. The id of the control is always the id of the associated DOM element.

Wrapping Up Controls

Controls are not too different from their base component type. The main difference is that a control must be associated to a DOM element, whereas a component must not be.

Behaviors

A behavior is another special type of component that is related to DOM elements. Like controls, a behavior must be associated to a DOM element. However, unlike a control, there can be more than one behavior attached to a DOM element.

In a practical sense, behaviors define how we want a DOM element to behave. We want the DOM element to *collapse* to a single line, we want the DOM element to *float* on the page, and we want the DOM element to *fill* all the available screen space. These are all examples of behaviors that we might attach to a DOM element.

To help us define new behaviors and use instantiated behaviors, the base `Sys.Behavior` type includes a few more methods than its base `Sys.Component` type. Table 3.8 details these methods.

TABLE 3.8 Sys.UI.Behavior Methods

Method Name	Description	Syntax
get_element	Returns the DOM element associated to the behavior.	`return behavior.get_element();`
get_name	Returns the name of the behavior. If the name has been explicitly set, that's the name returned. If it has not been explicitly set, the name returned is the short type name of the behavior.	`return behavior.get_name();`

TABLE **3.8** continued

Method Name	Description	Syntax
set_name	Sets the name of the behavior. Explicitly set behavior names must be unique. The name of a behavior cannot be set after the behavior has been initialized. The behavior name must not start with a blank space, end with a blank space, or be an empty string.	behavior.set_ name("HiddenElm");
initialize	Calls the base class's initialize method. Attaches the behavior to its associated DOM element by adding an expando property to the DOM element that's the name of the behavior.	behavior.initialize();
dispose	Overrides Sys. Component's dispose. Calls base class dispose, removes the DOM element's expando property that is in the name of the behavior, and deletes the reference to DOM element from the behavior.	behavior.dispose();
get_id	Returns the underlying component's id if it's set. If it's not set, the value returned is the associated DOM element's id appended with the behavior's name.	return behavior.get_id();

Method Name	Description	Syntax
Sys.UI.Behavior. getBehaviorsByType	Returns all behaviors attached to a DOM element that are of a particular type.	return Sys.UI.Behavior. getBehaviorsByType (*element, typeName*)
Sys.UI.Behavior. getBehaviorByName	Returns a behavior attached to a DOM element if it was found.	return Sys.UI.Behavior. getBehaviorByName (*element, behaviorName*)
Sys.UI.Behavior. getBehaviors	Returns a copy of the behaviors attached to a DOM element. If there are no behaviors for a particular DOM element, returns an empty array.	return Sys.UI.Behavior. getBehaviors (*element*);

Defining a Behavior

Like defining a new component and control, defining a new behavior follows the Prototype Model we covered in Chapter 2. Rather than create a brand new example, we modify the NumberOnlyTextBox control example we used in the previous section to work as a behavior instead. Listing 3.19 shows the code necessary to define the NumberOnlyTextBox behavior.

LISTING 3.19 Defining a Behavior Type

```
/// <reference name="MicrosoftAjax.js"/>
NumberOnlyTextBox = function(element) {
  NumberOnlyTextBox.initializeBase(this, [element]);
  this._keyDownDelegate = null;
};

NumberOnlyTextBox.prototype = {
  initialize: function() {
    NumberOnlyTextBox.callBaseMethod(this,'initialize');
    this._keyDownDelegate =
      Function.createDelegate(this, this._keyDownHandler);
    $addHandler(this.get_element(), "keydown", this._keyDownDelegate);
  },

  dispose: function() {
    $removeHandler
      (this.get_element(), "keydown", this._keyDownDelegate);
```

Listing 3.19 continued

```
    this._keyDownDelegate = null;
    NumberOnlyTextBox.callBaseMethod(this, 'dispose');
  },

  _keyDownHandler: function(e) {
    return ((e.keyCode >= 48 && e.keyCode <= 57) || (e.keyCode == 8));
  }
};
```

```
NumberOnlyTextBox.registerClass("NumberOnlyTextBox", Sys.UI.Behavior);
```

As you can see, the code to define our NumberOnlyTextBox behavior is almost identical to the code necessary to define the NumberOnlyTextBox as a new control. The only difference is that a behavior inherits from Sys.UI.Behavior rather than Sys.UI.Control.

Sys.UI.Behavior's constructor, like Sys.UI.Control's, takes in an element as a parameter. In its constructor, the internal member _element is assigned to the element parameter, associating the DOM element to the behavior. Then, the behavior is added to the element's _behaviors expando property. The _behaviors expando property is like the control's control property except that it is defined as an array so that more than one behavior can be associated to the DOM element.

Creating a Behavior

From our component and control discussion, we know that using the $create method is the correct way of instantiating a new instance of a type that inherits from Sys.Component, and a behavior is no different.

In fact, creating a behavior is exactly the same as creating a control, and the code shown in Listing 3.18 will suffice for an example of how to do this.

Unlike controls, however, a couple of problems could appear when creating behaviors, and they both have to do with the uniqueness of the behavior.

Behavior Uniqueness Problems

The first problem is that if a behavior's id is not set, the id is automatically generated based on the id of the associated DOM element and the name of the behavior. Because this is a generated value, it's likely that it could be the same for more than one behavior. If the same `id` is generated for more than one behavior, when the second behavior attempts to register itself with `Sys.Application`, the registration fails because components managed by `Sys.Application` must have unique `id`s. Listing 3.20 demonstrates this problem.

LISTING 3.20 Creating Behaviors That Have the Same id

```
<html xmlns="http://www.w3.org/1999/xhtml">
<head runat="server">
  <title>Behavior Testing!</title>
</head>
<body>
  <form id="form1" runat="server">
  <asp:ScriptManager ID="SM1" runat="server" />

  // … NumberOnlyTextBox omitted for brevity.

  <asp:TextBox ID="txtBox1" runat="server" Width="150px" />

  <script type="text/javascript">
    $create(
      NumberOnlyTextBox,
      null,
      null,
      null,
      $get("txtBox1")
    );

    // this will cause an error because the id of the component will
    // be the same as the previous behavior.
    $create(
      NumberOnlyTextBox,
      null,
      null,
      null,
      $get("txtBox1")
    );
  </script>

  </form>
</body>
</html>
```

In this example, because we're not explicitly setting the `name` or the `id` of either behavior, the `id` of each behavior is `txtBox1$NumberOnlyTextBox`. The behaviors' `id`s are computed based on the DOM element's `id` (txtBox1), appended with $, followed by the name of the behavior, which when it's not explicitly set is the type name minus any namespaces.

> **■ NOTE   NumberOnlyTextBox**
>
> In our example, the name of our behavior is just the full name of the type: NumberOnlyTextBox.
>
> If we were using a namespace for our behavior, for example MyProject. Behaviors.NumberOnlyTextBox, the calculated name of the behavior would still be NumberOnlyTextBox.

When the second behavior tries to register itself with Sys.Application, an error occurs because a component is already registered with that id.

To rectify this problem, either the name or id of the behavior has to be explicitly set. In either case, the id or the name needs to be unique. In the case of the id, it needs to be unique among all components. In the case of the name, it needs to be unique among behaviors attached to the associated DOM element. Listing 3.21 shows code that would successfully create the two behaviors and attach them to the same textbox.

LISTING 3.21 Setting a Behavior's id

```
<script type="text/javascript">
  $create(
    NumberOnlyTextBox,
    {id: "Behavior1" },
    null,
    null,
    $get("txtBox1")
  );

  $create(
    NumberOnlyTextBox,
    {id: "Behavior2" },
    null,
    null,
    $get("txtBox1")
  );
</script>
```

The second problem with creating behaviors can occur when we attach multiple instances of the same behavior to a DOM element and don't set their names. Because their names will be the same calculated value (i.e., NumberOnlyTextBox), we won't be able find one or more of them through the Sys.UI.getBehaviorByName method.

Attaching the multiple instances of the same behavior to a single DOM element might be a rarer case than most, but it can occur. Listing 3.22 shows how we're only able to find one of the NumberOnlyTextBox behaviors attached to our textbox.

LISTING 3.22 Problems Finding Behaviors by Name

```
<html>
<head runat="server">
  <title>Behavior Testing!</title>
</head>
<body>
  <form id="form1" runat="server">
  <asp:ScriptManager ID="SM1" runat="server" />

  // NumberOnlyTextBox omitted for brevity

  <asp:TextBox ID="txtBox1" runat="server" Width="150px" />

  <script type="text/javascript">
    $create(
      NumberOnlyTextBox,
      {id: "Behavior1"},
      null,
      null,
      $get("txtBox1")
    );

    $create(
      NumberOnlyTextBox,
      {id: "Behavior2"},
      null,
      null,
      $get("txtBox1")
    );

    var beh = Sys.UI.Behavior.getBehaviorByName
      ($get("txtBox1"), " NumberOnlyTextBox ");

    alert (beh.get_name());

    var behaviorsAssignedToDom =
      Sys.UI.Behavior.getBehaviors($get("txtBox1"));

    var behaviors = '';
```

LISTING 3.22 continued

```
      for (var i=0; i<behaviorsAssignedToDom.length; i++) {
        behaviors += behaviorsAssignedToDom[i].get_name() + " ";
      }

      // alerts NumberOnlyTextBox NumberOnlyTextBox because
      // there are two behaviors of that name
      alert (behaviors);

    </script>

    </form>
  </body>
  </html>
```

To correct this problem we need to explicitly set the name of any behaviors we create.

To conclude this section on problems with creating behaviors, although an error won't be thrown if a behavior doesn't have its id/name set when it's created, it's clearly better to do so to avoid some of the rarer problems with behaviors. Therefore, we suggest that you always set the id and name of a behavior whenever you create an instance of one. Listing 3.23 shows this pattern.

LISTING 3.23 Assigning ids and names to Behavior Instances

```
  <script type="text/javascript">
    $create(
      NumberOnlyTextBox,
      {id: "Behavior1",
       name: "Behavior1"},
      null,
      null,
      $get("txtBox1")
    );

    $create(
      NumberOnlyTextBox,
      {id: "Behavior2",
       name: "Behavior2"},
      null,
      null,
      $get("txtBox1")
    );
  </script>
```

Wrapping Up Behaviors

Behaviors are not too different from their base component type. The main difference is that a behavior must be associated to a DOM element, whereas a component must not be. The main difference between a control and a behavior is that a DOM element can have only one control associated to it, whereas a DOM element can have multiple behaviors.

SUMMARY

In this chapter, we examined components, controls, and behaviors. We looked at how the base component type contains commonly used objects and how controls and behaviors extend components to include a reference to a DOM element. We also looked at how you can build them by hand and how they're created using the $create function.

In the next chapter, we cover Sys.Application, which is the manager object for all components, controls, and behaviors. After we examine Sys.Application, we begin to tie the Microsoft AJAX Library into the server portion of ASP.NET AJAX with a chapter on how to create components, controls, and behaviors through .NET code. Finally, we wrap up components, controls, and behaviors with an in-depth look on how to localize them and how they react to being placed inside an UpdatePanel.

4

Sys.Application

IN CHAPTER 2, "MICROSOFT AJAX Library Programming," we explored the new programming constructs that the Microsoft AJAX Library provides. In Chapter 3, "Components," we used the skills we learned in Chapter 2 to create components, derived types, controls, and behaviors.

The next step is to learn about `Sys.Application` and how it acts as a JavaScript client runtime and how it works with components. In this chapter, we cover the three functional pieces of `Sys.Application`: how it manages components, how it goes through an initialization routine, and how it goes through a disposal routine. When we've covered these three pieces, you'll have learned everything you need to know about how to properly build new client components using the Microsoft AJAX Library and how to create instances of them so that they participate properly in the client runtime.

Background Information

Before we jump into `Sys.Application`'s three areas of functionality, let's first go over some background information.

Creating Sys.Application

Sys.Application is a global variable of type Sys._Application. The global variable is automatically created when MicrosoftAjax.js is parsed.

Sys.Application = new Sys._Application();

> ### ■ NOTE   Sys.Application versus Sys._Application
>
> Because Sys.Application is an instance of Sys._Application, all the type information we're providing in this section really applies to Sys._Application and not Sys.Application. But, because everybody else refers to Sys.Application as a quasi-type, we do, too, just so we don't confuse you. But remember, Sys.Application is an instance of Sys._Application.
>
> Also note that the Application in Sys._Application is prefixed with an underscore. As we covered in Chapter 2, an underscore indicates the private assessor level. This means that Sys._Application is not intended to be accessed by your code. You should never create an instance of Sys._Application yourself. Rather the global Sys.Application object should be used.
>
> Creating another instance of Sys._Application wouldn't be disastrous unless you reassigned Sys.Application to the new instance, but it still should not be done because of its intended privacy.

In Sys.Application's constructor, two important things take place.

First, all the internal members detailed in Table 4.1 are defined and initialized.

TABLE 4.1 Sys.Application Internal Members

Member	Type	Purpose
_components	Object	A list of components currently managed by the application. It's an object rather than an array, so components can easily and efficiently be accessed by an id rather than an array position.
_disposableObjects	Array	A list of objects that dispose should be called on when Sys.Application is disposed.
_createdComponents	Array	A list of components that have been created during the current component creation process. This list is important because the list of created components is an event argument to the load event.
_secondPassComponents	Array	A list of components that require their references to be processed after all components have been created.
_creatingComponents	Boolean	Indicates whether components are in the process of being created.
_disposing	Boolean	Indicates whether the dispose method has been entered.

We cover these internal members in more detail as we cover how each functional component is implemented.

Second, event handlers are created and attached to the window's load and unload events. The event handler attached to the window's load event is used to trigger Sys.Application's initialization routine, and the event handler attached to the window's unload event is used to trigger the unload routine. Listing 4.1 displays Sys.Application's full constructor.

LISTING 4.1 Sys.Application Constructor

```
Sys._Application = function Sys$_Application() {
    Sys._Application.initializeBase(this);

    this._disposableObjects = [];
```

Listing 4.1 continued

```
    this._components = {};
    this._createdComponents = [];
    this._secondPassComponents = [];

    this._unloadHandlerDelegate =
      Function.createDelegate(this, this._unloadHandler);
    this._loadHandlerDelegate =
      Function.createDelegate(this, this._loadHandler);

    Sys.UI.DOMEvent.addHandler
      (window, "unload", this._unloadHandlerDelegate);
    Sys.UI.DOMEvent.addHandler
      (window, "load", this._loadHandlerDelegate);
}
```

Attaching event handlers to the window is an important step because this couples `Sys.Application` to the DOM's window object. When the window loads, it starts up `Sys.Application`'s initialization routine, and when the window unloads it starts up `Sys.Application`'s unload routine. This coupling gives `Sys.Application` a runtime-like feel.

Type Information

`Sys.Application` inherits from `Sys.Component`. Inheriting from `Sys.Component` provides it with all the members and methods available to components, including the event handler list, the `disposing` event, and the `propertyChanged` event.

`Sys.Application` also implements the interface `Sys.IContainer`, which provides the methods `addComponent`, `removeComponent`, `getComponents`, and `findComponent`. The `Sys.IContainer` methods are used to implement the component manager functionality of `Sys.Application`, which we cover in detail in the "Component Manager" section later in this chapter.

Method Information

To provide the three pieces of functionality that we've described, `Sys.Application` uses the internal members detailed in Table 4.1 and the methods described in Table 4.2.

TABLE 4.2 Sys.Application Methods

Method Name	Description	Syntax
get_isCreatingComponents	Returns _creatingComponents internal member.	Sys.Application.get_isCreatingComponents()
beginCreateComponents	Sets the _creatingComponents value to true.	Sys.Application.beginCreateComponents();
endCreateComponents	Iterates through the list of _secondPassComponents, calling _setReferences on each object in the list. Clears the list of _secondPassComponents. Sets _creatingComponents to false.	Sys.Application.endCreateComponents();
add_load	Adds the event handler to the load event.	Sys.Application.add_load(*fn*);
remove_load	Removes the event handler from the load event.	Sys.Application.remove_load(*fn*);
raiseLoad	Raises the load event. Calls the global pageLoad method if it's present.	Sys.Application.raiseLoad();
add_init	Adds the event handler to the init event.	Sys.Application.add_init(*fn*);
remove_init	Removes the event handler from the init event.	Sys.Application.remove_init(*fn*);
add_unload	Adds the event handler to the unload event.	Sys.Application.add_unload(*fn*);
remove_unload	Removes the event handler from the unload event.	Sys.Application.remove_unload(*fn*);
addComponent	Adds a component to the managed components.	Sys.Application.addComponent(*comp*);
removeComponent	Removes a component from Sys.Application managed component's object.	Sys.Application.removeComponent(*comp*);

TABLE 4.2 continued

Method Name	Description	Syntax
findComponent	Finds a managed component.	Sys.Application. findComponent (*parent, componentId*);
getComponents	Copies the managed components into an array and returns the array.	Sys.Application. getComponents();
initialize	Sets the _initialization internal member to true. Calls _doInitialize.	Sys.Application. initialize();
dispose	Called when the page is destroyed. Raises the unload event. Iterates over the list of disposable objects and calls dispose on each object. Calls dispose on the ScriptLoading object. Calls base class dispose.	Sys.Application. dispose();
notifyScriptLoaded	Calls the ScriptLoader's notifyScriptLoaded so that it knows that the currently processing script is done.	Sys.Application. notifyScriptLoaded();
registerDisposableObject	Registers an object to have dispose called on it when Sys.Application is disposed.	Sys.Application. registerDisposableObject (*object*);

Method Name	Description	Syntax
unregisterDisposableObject	Removes an object from the list of objects that need to have dispose called on them when the Sys.Application is disposed.	Sys.Application. unregister DisposableObject (object);
_addComponentToSecondPass	Registers a component as needing to have its references set after all components have been created.	Private method
_doInitialize	Internal method that fires the init and load events. Responsible for creating components.	Private method
_loadHandler	Event handler for the window's load event.	Private method
_unloadHandler	Event handler for the window's unload event. Calls the dispose method.	Private method

Sys.Application has access to all the methods defined in Sys. Component and those that are detailed in Table 4.2. Because Sys. Application is a global variable versus a type, all the method calls are prefixed with Sys.Application.

Now that we've covered how Sys.Application is created and what members and methods are available to it, let's examine how it uses those members and methods to provide you with a client runtime you can interact with.

> **NOTE   Sys.Application.notifyScriptLoaded**
>
> We do not cover `Sys.Application.notifyScriptLoaded` in this chapter. Instead, we cover it in Chapter 7, "Control Development in a Partial Postback Environment," because its purpose is to instruct the script loader during a partial postback to move on to the next file.

Component Manager

One of `Sys.Application`'s main features is that of a component manager. As a component manager, it maintains an internal collection of components and provides functionality to add, remove, and find components.

> **NOTE   Why Use a Central Location to Manage Components?**
>
> Having a central location to manage components serves two purposes.
>
> First, if we want to ensure that all components have a unique `id`, it would be difficult if not impossible to do so if we didn't have a central location that maintained the list of already used `id`s. You could debate that having a unique `id` for a component might not be necessary, but it is a requirement for the Microsoft AJAX Library.
>
> Second, by having a central location to manage components and providing methods to retrieve a component by `id`, you eliminate the need to maintain global variables that point to the components. Instead, only the `id` of a component is needed to retrieve a variable that points to a component on demand. It's like having a key hook. Instead of having keys spread throughout the house, I place them all in one place. When I need my car key, I don't have to look all over the place for it; I just go to the key hook. I still need to know that I want my car key and not my house key, however.

To manage components, `Sys.Application` uses the internal member `_components`, which is of type `Object`, to maintain the collection of components. Using the associative array property of objects, components are stored in the `_components` member using the component's `id` as the key and the component as the value. Storing the components this way provides for the fastest possible lookups. Listing 4.2 demonstrates how Sys.Application adds components to its managed list.

LISTING 4.2 Adding a Component to the _components Object

```
this._components["MyComponentId"] = MyComponent;
this._components["SomeOtherComponentId"] = SomeOtherComponent;
```

The _component member is the underlying storage mechanism, but rather than allow outside code to manipulate it directly, Sys.Application exposes methods to interact with it. These methods are addComponent, removeComponent, findComponent, and getComponents.

> ### ■ NOTE   Sys.IContainer
>
> Coincidentally, these are the methods that are required by the Sys.IContainer interface, which Sys.Application implements. We guess that these methods are what Microsoft defines as container behavior.

Adding a Component

Adding a component to Sys.Application's collection of managed components is done through the addComponent method. We used the add Component method once before in a Chapter 3 example, so let's import the source code from that example. The code is redisplayed in Listing 4.3

LISTING 4.3 Using the addComponent Method

```
var newComponent =
  Sys.Component.create(
    MyComponent,
    null,
    null,
    null,
    null);

newComponent.set_id("MyNewComponent");
Sys.Application.addComponent(newComponent);
```

In this example, we created a new component, but didn't provide a component id. Because we failed to provide an id, addComponent *is not* automatically called by the Sys.Component.create method, and our component is just an object assigned to a variable, rather than a component managed by Sys.Application. We can manually add it to Sys.Application's managed components collection by setting the id through the set_id method and then calling the addComponent method using the component as the method call's parameter.

The addComponent method does two things before it adds the component to the managed component collection. First, it makes sure that id is set. If it isn't, an invalidOperation error is thrown stating the component's id is missing. The error causing code is shown in Listing 4.4.

LISTING 4.4 Component id Is Missing

```
var newComponent =
  Sys.Component.create(
    MyComponent,
    null,
    null,
    null,
    null);

// causes an invalidOperation error.
Sys.Application.addComponent(newComponent);
```

Second, if the id is set, but a component is already registered with the same id, an invalidOperation error is thrown stating a component is already registered with that id, as shown in Listing 4.5.

LISTING 4.5 Component id Is Already Defined

```
var newComponent =
  $create(
    MyComponent,
    null,
    null,
    null,
    null);

newComponent.set_id("MyNewComponent");
Sys.Application.addComponent(newComponent);

var myOtherComponent =
```

```
Sys.Component.create(
  MyComponent,
  null,
  null,
  null,
  null);

myOtherComponent.set_id("MyNewComponent");

// causes an invalidOperation error.
Sys.Application.addComponent(myOtherComponent);
```

If the ID is set and another component is not already registered using that ID, the component is added to the internal _components member.

> ■ **TIP**   **Delaying the Addition of a Component to Sys.Application's Managed Components**
>
> Every once in a while, you'll come across a situation where you don't want the component to be added to Sys.Application's list of managed components right away. For whatever reason, you want to create a component, manipulate it or use it in some way, and then add it to Sys.Application's list of managed components. By not setting the component's ID when you create it, you can cause the component to not be added to Sys.Application's object of managed components automatically. Then, whenever you're ready you can set its ID and add it to the component's list through addComponent. This process, unfortunately, does not work for controls or behaviors because their component ID is automatically determined based upon their associated element's ID.

Finding a Component

After we have registered a component, we can use the findComponent method to retrieve it so that a method can be called on it, so that it can be removed from the application, or for some other application-specific reason. Listing 4.6 demonstrates a findComponent call.

LISTING 4.6 findComponent Call

```
$create(
  MyComponent,
  {id: "MyNewComponent"},
  null,
  null,
  null);

var myNewComponent = Sys.Application.findComponent("MyNewComponent");
alert (myComponent.get_id());
```

> **▪ NOTE $find**
>
> Because finding a component by ID is so common, the Microsoft AJAX Library provides a shortcut method name, $find, which points to Sys.Application.findComponent. We'll use $find almost exclusively.

Finding a component is done by passing the component's ID into the find method. If the component is found, it is returned by the method; if it isn't found, null is returned.

Alternative Uses of $find

In all the code examples to this point, we've used the $find method to find a component registered within Sys.Application. Although this is by far the most common usage, the $find method can be used in two other ways.

The first alternative use is to find a component within any object that implements the Sys.IContainer interface. This is similar to how we've used the $find method already, except that rather than default to finding a component within Sys.Application, which implements Sys.IContainer, we specify a different parent object that implements Sys.IContainer. We can do this by passing in a second parameter to our $find method call. The following code details how we might use the $find method in this way:

```
SimpleContainer = function() {
  SimpleContainer.initializeBase(this);
  this._components = {};
};

SimpleContainer.prototype = {
  addComponent: function(component) {
    this._components[component.get_id()] = component;
  },

  removeComponent: function(component) {
    this._components[component.get_id()] = null;
  },

  findComponent: function(componentId) {
    return this._components[componentId];
  },

  getComponents: function() {
    var compArr = [];
    for (var compName in components) {
      compArr[compArr.length] = components[compName];
    }

    return compArr;
  }
}

SimpleContainer.registerClass("SimpleContainer",
  null , Sys.IContainer);

var simpleContainer = new SimpleContainer();

NewObject = function() {
  this._id = null;
};

NewObject.prototype = {
  set_id: function(value) {
    this._id = value;
  },
  get_id: function() {
    return this._id;
  }
};

// create a new component
var myNewObject = new NewObject();
```

```
myNewObject.set_id("MyNewObject");

simpleContainer.addComponent(myNewObject);

// wipe out what myNewObject points to
// for demonstration purposes.
myNewObject = null;

// retrieve myNewObject from simpleContainer
myNewObject = $find("MyNewObject", simpleContainer);
```

In this example, we first declare a new type, SimpleContainer. SimpleContainer implements the Sys.IContainer interface and provides implementations for the required methods. Next, we create an instance of the SimpleContainer type and assign to the variable simpleContainer. Next, we define a new object, NewObject, and add the set_id and get_id methods to its prototype. We then create an instance of NewObject and add it to SimpleContainer using SimpleContainer's addComponent method. After the MyNewObject has been added to SimpleContainer, we retrieve it using the $find method, passing in the ID MyNewObject and simpleContainer as the parent container to search in.

When the $find method begins to execute, it determines that the parent parameter is present and that it implements the Sys.IContainer interface. After it determines this, it executes the findComponent method on the parent parameter, passing in the id of the component to look for. It's then up to the implementation of the findComponent method to return the correct object.

Because Sys.Application implements Sys.IContainer, we can also pass it in as the parent parameter and have the same effect as not passing in a parent parameter at all.

```
var simpleContainer =
  $find("SimpleContainer", Sys.Application);
```

One thing to note about the Sys.IContainer interface is that although the method names all reference components (addComponent, find Component, and so on), there's nothing that prohibits noncomponents from being stored in an object that implements the Sys.IContainer interface. This is actually what we did in the previous example. To us, it seems like the method names on this interface are poorly named and should not refer to components at all.

The second alternative use of the $find method is to find a value of a property that is attached to an object.

If an ID and a parent are supplied to the $find method and the parent doesn't implement the Sys.IContainer interface, the ID is used as a property name on the parent, and the value assigned to that property is returned. The following listing demonstrates this idea:

```
var someObject = { name: "MyName" };
var objectsName = $find("name", someObject);

// alerts "MyName"
alert (objectsName);
```

This alternative use of the $find method is simple and relies on the associative array property of objects. For our code example above, the executed code that returns the property's value is equivalent to the following:

```
var id = "name"
return someObject[id];
```

These are the two alternative uses of the $find method.

Removing a Component

After we have a component registered, we can remove it using the remove Component method. This is done by passing in the component we want to remove to the method call, as shown in Listing 4.7.

LISTING 4.7 Using removeComponent

```
$create(
  MyComponent,
  {id: "MyNewComponent"},
  null,
  null,
  null);

var foundComponent = $find("MyNewComponent");
alert (foundComponent.get_id());

Sys.Application.removeComponent(foundComponent);
```

LISTING 4.7 continued

```
foundComponent = $find("MyNewComponent");

if (foundComponent !== null) {
  alert ("Found Component");
}
else {
  alert ("Didn't find Component");
}
```

A common reason we'll want to remove a component is that we're done with it and are ready to remove it from memory. Cleaning up unneeded components from Sys.Application is a good way to keep your application running smoothly and to keep its memory footprint small.

Getting Components

Because the components are stored in an object versus an array, getting a list of the currently registered components requires a for...in loop. Sys.Application provides a method, getComponents, which executes the for...in loop for us, which we can use to retrieve an array of the currently registered components. Listing 4.8 shows an example using this method.

LISTING 4.8 Using getComponents

```
$create(
  MyComponent,
  {id: "MyNewComponent"},
  null,
  null,
  null);

$create(
  MyComponent,
  {id: "MyOtherComponent"},
  null,
  null,
  null);

var registeredComponents =
```

```
    Sys.Application.getComponents();

alert ("Number of Components Registered: " +
    registeredComponents.length);
```

If we need a list of all registered components, such as for debugging purposes, using the getComponents method is much easier than trying to find a component using the for...in loop.

Initialization Routine

As we stated in the "Background Information" section, when the window raises its load event, Sys.Application's initialization routine starts (this is only partially true, see the following sidebar "Starting the Initialization Routine"). The initialization routine is primarily responsible for marking Sys.Application as initialized, creating components, and raising the load event. The routine starts with a call to Sys.Application's initialize method, which is shown in Listing 4.9.

LISTING 4.9 Sys.Application's initialize Method

```
initialize: function() {
  if(!this._initialized && !this._initializing) {
    this._initializing = true;
    window.setTimeout(
      Function.createDelegate(this, this._doInitialize), 0);
  }
}
```

The initialize method prevents the initialization routine from being executed twice by ensuring that two internal members, _initialized and _initializing, are both false before continuing. If it determines that Sys.Application is not initialized and it's not in the process of initializing, it calls the _doInitialize method using a timeout with a wait value of 0. (We'll see why we use a timeout in the "The init Event" section later in the chapter.)

Starting the Initialization Routine

The Client Framework is set up to enter the initialization routine through a call to Sys.Application.initialize. However, there are two different ways that initialize can be called.

The first way is through the method that is wired to the window's load event. The following code shows the code that's attached to the window's load event:

```
_loadHandler: function() {
  if(this._loadHandlerDelegate) {
    Sys.UI.DOMEvent.removeHandler
      (window, "load", this._loadHandlerDelegate);
    this._loadHandlerDelegate = null;
  }
  this.initialize();
}
```

The second way is through an explicit call that the ScriptManager control automatically includes in the page markup. Listed here is the code from the Render method of ScriptManager:

```
protected internal override void Render
  (HtmlTextWriter writer)
{
    this.PageRequestManager.Render(writer);
    if (!this.IsInAsyncPostBack)
    {
      this.IPage.ClientScript.RegisterStartupScript(
        typeof(ScriptManager), "AppInitialize",
        "Sys.Application.initialize();\r\n", true);
    }
    base.Render(writer);
}
```

At first glance, having two different ways of executing Sys.Application.initialize might seem unnecessary, but they are both necessary for different reasons.

The first method, calling it from the load event handler, is necessary because the Microsoft AJAX Library is supposed to be a stand-alone library that does not require the server portion of ASP.NET AJAX to work properly. If the library didn't contain code for executing Sys.Application.initialize when the window's load event occurred and the developer wasn't using the `ScriptManager` server control to register the library with the page, the developer would be responsible for figuring out when to call `Sys.Application.initialize`, which the developer may or may not do correctly. So, because Microsoft wanted to ensure that the library could stand alone without the server portion, they wired the `Sys.Application.initialize` call to the window's `load` event to ensure that it was called once the window loaded.

The second method, using the `ScriptManager` to emit a call to `initialize`, is necessary because calling `Sys.Application.initialize` earlier than waiting for the window's `load` event to fire is significantly better performing. Because the `ScriptManager` control will almost always be used to register the library with the page, emitting this call gives the best performance to the majority of the users.

So now that you know that both methods are used for different reasons, which one will be called when using the `ScriptManager` server control?

In the case where you are using the `ScriptManager` server control to register the library with the page, the explicit `Sys.Application.initialize` call always wins because the window's `load` event fires only after the page is done loading. *Done loading* means the page's entire HTML has been parsed and all binary data has been downloaded. The first part of that phrase, "the page's entire HTML has been parsed," includes JavaScript being parsed and executed. If the call to `Sys.Application.initialize()` is included on the page, and it always is when using the `ScriptManager` control, it will be executed when it's parsed, which will always occur before the window's `load` event is reached. Therefore, the `initialize` method call attached to the window's `load` event will never execute before the explicit call to `Sys.Application.initialize()`.

You might be wondering why the explicit call is even necessary. Why shouldn't the application wait for the window's `load` event to fire and then execute the `initialize` method? There are actually two reasons why we shouldn't wait for the `load` event to fire before calling the `initialize` method. The first reason is to ensure proper functionality across all browsers in all situations, and the second reason is performance.

The situation where the explicit call is necessary to ensure proper functionality is when the browser doesn't raise the window's load event as expected. An example of this is that older versions of Opera don't fire the load event when the user presses the Back or Forward buttons. Because of this, if a page is loaded because the user navigated to a previously visited page, Sys.Application does not initialize based on the window's load event firing; hence, the explicit call ensures proper functionality.

The reason the explicit call is necessary for best possible performance is we want to execute our initialize method as soon as the DOM is ready (i.e., all HTML is parsed and elements are created) to provide the best possible experience to the user. As previously stated, the window's load event fires only after the page's entire HTML has been parsed and *all binary data has been downloaded*. That binary data download could take a long time if the page is image heavy or has other binary elements such as Silverlight or Flash objects. While the binary data downloads, the page appears to be ready to use, but the window's load event is waiting to fire. It's possible and actually very likely that the user will be able to read the screen and attempt to execute functionality on the screen before all binary data has been loaded. If that happens, and the functionality the user is trying to execute requires some sort of library functionality that gets attached only after Sys.Application.initialize executes, the functionality is not available (if initialization didn't occur) until the window's load event fires. Because we want Sys.Application to be initialized as soon as legally possible, the explicit call provides the best way of ensuring that initialization doesn't wait until all binary data is downloaded.

■ NOTE DOMContentLoaded?

Some browsers supply another event, DOMContentLoaded, which is raised after all the DOM elements have been created but before the binary data download begins. Unfortunately, the event is not standard yet, and not all browsers support it, so it can't be relied on.

When the timeout expires, which happens right away, and the JavaScript execution engine transfers control to the timeout's callback, which in this case is the _doInitialize method shown in Listing 4.10, the method execution begins.

LISTING 4.10 Sys.Application's _doInitialize Method

```
_doInitialize: function() {
  Sys._Application.callBaseMethod(this, 'initialize');

  var handler = this.get_events().getHandler("init");
  if (handler) {
    this.beginCreateComponents();
    handler(this, Sys.EventArgs.Empty);
    this.endCreateComponents();
  }
  this.raiseLoad();
  this._initializing = false;
}
```

When the _doInitialize method is entered, the base class's, which is Sys.Component, initialize method is executed. This call marks the component as initialized. From there, the handler for the init event is retrieved. If the handler for the init event is found, the component creation process begins.

Component Creation Process

The component creation process is the portion of the initialization routine dedicated to creating components. The process consists of three steps: executing the beginCreateComponents method, executing the init handler, and executing the endCreateComponents method.

The first step in the process is the execution of the beginCreate Components method. The only thing this method does is set the _creating Components member to true. This might not seem like much, but it has an effect on how the actual creation of components occurs, which we cover later in this section.

The next step is the execution of the init event handler. The init event, like other .NET-style events, executes functions that have been added to it through the add_init method. In the init event's case, it is intended that functions containing $create method calls have been added to it. Let's take a closer look at the init event and detail what it does and how it works.

The init Event

With the init event, we've reached the first point in the initialization routine where outside code can execute. As you might have deduced from the methods that are called before and after the init handler is executed, beginCreateComponents and endCreateComponents, respectively, and from the fact that we're inside the component creation portion of this chapter, the init event's purpose is to create components.

It is the init event's purpose to create components because it is raised at a point when we're ensured that it is safe to alter the DOM. Altering the DOM, creating new DOM elements, moving existing DOM elements, and so on, are actions a component or its derived types control and behavior may do when they are initialized and if done too early may cause unrecoverable browser errors.

We know that when we reach the init event it is safe to modify the DOM because the method we're in, _doInitialize, was executed as a timeout's callback, and this ensured that the JavaScript execution engine transferred control back to the DOM creation call stack before calling the _doInitialize method. Therefore, the DOM has had a chance to fully create itself.

> **■ NOTE**   Timeouts and Call Stacks
>
> See the "Delayed Code Execution Using Timeouts and Intervals" section in Chapter 1, "Programming with JavaScript" for more information on how timeouts actually work.

To further explain this point, Listing 4.11 demonstrates code that causes an operation aborted error in Internet Explorer because our component modifies the DOM at an unsafe point.

LISTING 4.11 Code Causing an Operation Aborted Error

```
<html>
<head>
 <title>Operation Aborted</title>
</head>
<body>
 <form id="form1" runat="server">
 <asp:ScriptManager ID="ScriptManager1" runat="server" />
 <script type="text/javascript">

   MyDivComponent = function() {
     this._newDiv = null;
   };

   MyDivComponent.prototype = {
     initialize: function() {
       this._newDiv = document.createElement("div");
       document.body.appendChild(this._newDiv);
       this._newDiv.style.backgroundColor = "#2af5ea";
     }
   };

   MyDivComponent.registerClass("MyDivComponent", Sys.Component);

   $create(
     MyDivComponent,
     {id:"MyDivComponent"},
     null,
     null,
     null
   );
 </script>

</form>
</body>
</html>
```

This code caused an operation aborted error because our component appended a new element to the DOM before the DOM was fully created. For more information about when it is safe and unsafe to modify the DOM, see the following sidebar "Illegally Modifying the DOM."

Illegally Modifying the DOM

There is one main culprit in illegally modifying the DOM: modifying a parent DOM element from within a child element before the child element has been closed. The following code performs this illegal operation using an innerHTML replace. (We can also perform this illegal operation using DOM manipulation methods such as appendChild.)

```
<html>
<head>
</head>
<body>
  <div>
    <script type="text/JavaScript">
      document.body.innerHTML +=
        "invalid operation!";
    </script>
  </div>
</body>
</html>
```

This code tries to modify the innerHTML of the body tag from within a child tag before the body tag has closed. This can lead to the page failing to load and the error message displayed in Figure 4.1.

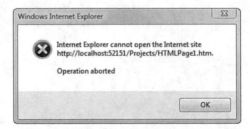

FIGURE 4.1 The Operation Aborted error in Internet Explorer

■ NOTE   Not All Browsers Are Equal

Not all browsers treat illegal DOM manipulations the same. Internet Explorer in particular is problematic with modifying a DOM element illegally, and this error applies to Internet Explorer 5.5, 6, and 7. Firefox seems to be okay with this type of manipulation, but there is no guarantee that other browsers and future versions of Firefox will successfully process this command.

There are a few ways to rectify this mistake.

1. Modify the DOM element from within itself, not within a child element:

```html
<html>
<body>
  <div>
  </div>
  <script type="text/JavaScript">
    document.body.innerHTML +=
        "invalid operation!";
  </script>
</body>
</html>
```

2. Modify the DOM element after it's been closed:

```html
<html>
<body>
  <p id='myParagraph'>
  </p>
  <script type="text/JavaScript">
    document.getElementById
      ('myParagraph').innerHTML +=
        "invalid operation!";
  </script>
</body>
</html>
```

3. Attach the code that manipulates the DOM element to the window's load event:

```html
<html>
<body onload=
  " document.getElementById
      ('myParagraph').innerHTML +=
        'invalid operation!';"
  <p id='myParagraph'>
  </p>
</body>
</html>
```

All methods of fixing this problem are available for us to use, but the third method, attaching the code to the window's load event, is the safest and most consistent. Using ASP.NET AJAX, we do something like the third method when we attach our JavaScript code to Sys.Application's init method.

To correct this error, we need to make sure that our component is not created until the DOM is fully created. To do this, we add our $create method call to Sys.Application's init event, which we know will be raised only after it is safe to modify the DOM. Listing 4.12 shows the corrected code.

LISTING 4.12 Using add_init to Create a Component

```html
<html>
<head runat="server">
  <title>Using the Init Event</title>
</head>
<body>
  <form id="form1" runat="server">
  <asp:ScriptManager ID="ScriptManager1" runat="server" />

  <script type="text/javascript">

    MyDivComponent = function() {
      this._newDiv = null;
    };

    MyDivComponent.prototype = {
      initialize: function() {
        this._newDiv = document.createElement("div");
        document.body.appendChild(this._newDiv);
        this._newDiv.style.backgroundColor = "#2af5ea";
        this._newDiv.style.width = "100px";
        this._newDiv.style.height = "100px";
      }
    };

    MyDivComponent.registerClass("MyDivComponent", Sys.Component);

    Sys.Application.add_init(
      function() {
        $create(
          MyDivComponent,
          {id:"MyDivComponent"},
          null,
          null,
          null
        )
      }
    );
  </script>

  </form>
</body>
</html>
```

As the highlighted code in Listing 4.12 shows, we wrapped the `$create` method call in an anonymous function and added it to the `init` event. By doing this, we delayed the `$create` method's execution until the `init` event is raised, which we know is done at a safe point.

So as a rule, we *always* create components by wrapping the `$create` method call in an anonymous function and passing it into `Sys.Applciation`'s `add_init` method.

We follow this rule even after `Sys.Application` has been through its initialization routine because the `add_init` method works differently than other add event handler methods. Listing 4.13 shows `add_init`'s body.

LISTING 4.13 Sys.Application's add_init Method

```
add_init: function(handler) {
  if (this._initialized) {
    handler(this, Sys.EventArgs.Empty);
  }
  else {
    this.get_events().addHandler("init", handler);
  }
}
```

As the code shows, `add_init` works differently if `Sys.Application` is already initialized. If it is initialized, it immediately executes the handler. If the handler contains a `$create` statement, this has the effect of executing the `$create` method right away when the anonymous function containing it is passed into the `add_init` method. If `Sys.Application` isn't initialized, the `add_init` method works like other add event handler methods, adding the handler to the `init` event.

> ■ **NOTE**   Sys.Application and Partial Postbacks
>
> It's important to note that during a partial postback caused by an `UpdatePanel`, `Sys.Application` is not destroyed and re-created because the window isn't unloaded and loaded again. This might seem obvious, but it means that during a partial postback `Sys.Application`'s initialization routine isn't re-executed. However, because `add_init` isn't adding event handlers to the `init` event due to `Sys.Application` being already initialized, `$create` statements should still be wrapped in an anonymous function and passed to `Sys.Application`'s `add_init` method. That way, if the `$create` statements happen to be executed when `Sys.Application` isn't already initialized, they'll still work properly.

Setting References

Now that we've covered the init event, let's talk about the effect that setting _creatingComponents to true, which happens in the beginCreate Components method, has on creating components.

In Chapter 3, when we covered the $create method, we discussed how the references parameter allows one component to be assigned to another component as a reference. We stated that for a component to be successfully assigned, the component must exist before the assignment occurs. This process is straightforward if you can guarantee the order in which components will be created. If we're writing $create statements by hand in a web page or in a JavaScript file, we can pretty much control the order that the $create statements are executed and therefore ensure that Component A is created before Component B and that Component A is available to be assigned as a reference to Component B.

However, as we discuss in Chapter 5, "Adding Client Capabilities to Server Controls," it's possible to create components through server code. With this capability, we can no longer ensure that Component A will be created before Component B because we really don't know in what order the server will emit the $create statements.

Given that we can no longer guarantee the order that the $create statements will be executed and their related components created, it becomes problematic to assign a component as a reference to another component.

However, the component creation process provides a workaround for this problem. It does this by setting _creatingComponents to true when the component creation process begins. When this value is set to true, the $create method performs differently with regard to references. Rather than process the references parameter and assign references to the creating component, an object is created containing the current component and the references it wants to be assigned. This object is then added to the _secondPassComponents object maintained by Sys.Application. The $create method then moves on without calling endUpdate, which as you might remember triggers the initialize method on the component.

After all the components have been created, the _secondPass Components objects are processed by the endCreateComponents method. It is safe to do so now because all components will be available as references to other components, and the order they were created in no longer matters.

The endCreateComponents method iterates over the secondPass Components member and calls the global _setReferences method we described in Chapter 3 using the object that contains the component and the references it wants to be assigned as the method call's parameters.

When the _setReferences method completes, endUpdate is called on the component, triggering the component's initialize method.

Listing 4.14 demonstrates this idea in action by creating a component that references another component that is created after it. However, because they utilize the Sys.Application's init event, the reference is assigned successfully.

LISTING 4.14 Setting a Forward Reference

```
<html>
<head>
  <title>Forward References</title>
</head>
<body>
  <form id="form1" runat="server">
  <asp:ScriptManager ID="ScriptManager1" runat="server" />

  <script type="text/javascript">

    MyReferencedComponent = function() { };
    MyReferencedComponent.registerClass
      ("MyReferencedComponent", Sys.Component);

    MyOtherComponent = function() {
      this._referencedComponent = null;
    };

    MyOtherComponent.prototype = {
      get_referencedComponent: function() {
        return this._referencedComponent;
      },
      set_referencedComponent: function(value) {
        this._referencedComponent = value;
      }
    };
    MyOtherComponent.registerClass
      ("MyOtherComponent", Sys.Component);

    Sys.Application.add_init(
```

LISTING 4.14 continued

```
        function() {
          $create(
            MyOtherComponent,
            {id:"MyOtherComponent"},
            null,
            {referencedComponent: "MyReferencedComponent" },
            null
          )
        }
      );

      Sys.Application.add_init(
        function() {
          $create(
            MyReferencedComponent,
            {id:"MyReferencedComponent"},
            null,
            null,
            null
          )
        }
      );

      Sys.Application.add_load(
        function(sender, args) {
          var myOtherComponent = $find("MyOtherComponent");
          alert (myOtherComponent.get_referencedComponent().get_id());
        }
      );

    </script>
    </form>
  </body>
  </html>
```

So, as Listing 4.14 demonstrates, forward references to components are allowed if we use the init event.

Load Event

When the component creation process concludes, the _doInitialize method continues and raises the load event. The load event is important because it is the first time we have the ability to interact with the initialization routine after all the components that were to be created by the init event have been created.

Like all other .NET-style events, the first argument in a `load` event handler is the sender or the object that raised the event. In this case, the sender is `Sys.Application`. However, unlike most of the other events that we've seen so far, the `load` event does not use the empty event argument type, `Sys.EventArgs.Empty`, as the second parameter. Instead, it uses the event arguments type, `Sys.ApplicationLoadEventArgs`, as the second parameter.

Table 4.3 details `Sys.ApplicationLoadEventArgs` members.

TABLE 4.3 Sys.ApplicationLoadEventArgs Members

Member Name	Type	Purpose
_components	Array	Contains the components that were created during the most recent component creation process
_isPartialLoad	boolean	Value indicating whether the most recent component creation process occurred due to a partial postback (i.e., UpdatePanels)

Using `Sys.ApplicationLoadEventArgs` as the second parameter provides information to the event handler. It provides a list of the components that were created during the component creation process and a `boolean` value indicating whether the component creation process was kicked off due to a partial-postback.

> ■ **NOTE** raiseLoad
>
> The `load` event is raised through the helper function `raiseLoad`. This is done so that other objects can raise the `load` event without having access to `Sys.Application`'s internals.

We used the `load` event in the Listing 4.14 in a simple manner, but Listing 4.15 expands on this example and uses the custom event arguments to extract other information.

LISTING 4.15 Using the load Event

```
<html>
<head>
  <title>Forward References</title>
</head>
<body>
  <form id="form1" runat="server">
  <asp:ScriptManager ID="ScriptManager1" runat="server" />

  <script type="text/javascript">
    MyReferencedComponent = function() { };
    MyReferencedComponent.registerClass
      ("MyReferencedComponent", Sys.Component);

    MyOtherComponent = function() {
      this._referencedComponent = null;
    };

    MyOtherComponent.prototype = {
      get_referencedComponent: function() {
        return this._referencedComponent;
      },
      set_referencedComponent: function(value) {
        this._referencedComponent = value;
      }
    };
    MyOtherComponent.registerClass
      ("MyOtherComponent", Sys.Component);

    Sys.Application.add_init(
      function() {
        $create(
          MyOtherComponent,
          {id:"MyOtherComponent"},
          null,
          {referencedComponent: "MyReferencedComponent" },
          null
        )
      }
    );

    Sys.Application.add_init(
      function() {
        $create(
          MyReferencedComponent,
          {id:"MyReferencedComponent"},
          null,
          null,
          null
```

```
        )
      }
    );

    Sys.Application.add_load(
      function(sender, args) {
        var createdComponents = args.get_components();
        if (createdComponents !== null) {
          for (var i=0; i<createdComponents.length; i++) {
            alert (
              "Component #" +
              (i+1) +
              ": " +
              createdComponents[i].get_id()
            );
          }
        }
      }
    );
  </script>
  </form>
</body>
</html>
```

After the load event is raised, the raiseLoad method looks for a global method called pageLoad. pageLoad is a kind of default event handler for the load event that you can create to handle the load event. Listing 4.16 demonstrates how you can use it.

LISTING 4.16 Using window.pageLoad

```
<html>
<head runat="server">
  <title>Forward References</title>
</head>
<body>
  <form id="form1" runat="server">
  <asp:ScriptManager ID="ScriptManager1" runat="server" />

  <script type="text/javascript">

    MyReferencedComponent = function() { };
    MyReferencedComponent.registerClass
      ("MyReferencedComponent", Sys.Component);

    MyOtherComponent = function() {
      this._referencedComponent = null;
    };
```

LISTING 4.16 continued

```
MyOtherComponent.prototype = {
  get_referencedComponent: function() {
    return this._referencedComponent;
  },
  set_referencedComponent: function(value) {
    this._referencedComponent = value;
  }
};
MyOtherComponent.registerClass
  ("MyOtherComponent", Sys.Component);

Sys.Application.add_init(
  function() {
    $create(
      MyOtherComponent,
      {id:"MyOtherComponent"},
      null,
      {referencedComponent: "MyReferencedComponent" },
      null
    )
  }
);

Sys.Application.add_init(
  function() {
    $create(
      MyReferencedComponent,
      {id:"MyReferencedComponent"},
      null,
      null,
      null
    )
  }
);

function pageLoad(sender, args) {
  var createdComponents = args.get_components();
  if (createdComponents !== null) {
    for (var i=0; i<createdComponents.length; i++) {
      alert (
        "Component #" +
        (i+1) +
        ": " +
        createdComponents[i].get_id()
      );
    }
  }
}
```

```
    </script>
    </form>
  </body>
  </html>
```

Frankly, we don't think that you should ever use it and that you should attach to the `load` event instead. It might be good for an initial test of what the `load` event arguments look like, but it becomes pointless in a real application's architecture.

Finally, when the `load` event is done executing, the `_initializing` flag is set back to `false`, and the initialization routine concludes.

The Unload Routine

The final piece of functionality that `Sys.Application` provides is an unload routine triggered when the window's `unload` event is raised. As it turns out, the `Sys.Application.dispose` method contains all the code that is executes in the unload routine.

Sys.Application.dispose

`Sys.Application.dispose` is responsible for ensuring that everything is cleaned up as the page is destroyed. Because you might want to write code that gets triggered when the page is disposing, the `dispose` method provides two ways of executing custom code.

First, like the global `window.pageLoad` method that is called during initialization if it is present, `dispose` calls the global `window.pageUnload` method if it's found. If we implement the method as shown in Listing 4.17, we can write code that gets executed when `dispose` starts.

LISTING 4.17 window.pageUnload

```
window.pageUnload = function(sender, args) {
  alert ("Sys.Application is being destroyed!");
}
```

However, rather than use the global `pageUnload` method, if you want to be notified of when `Sys.Application` is unloading, you should add an event handler to the `Sys.Application.unload` event. This event is raised from within the dispose method right after the pageUnload method is executed. An example of wiring up to the unload event is shown in Listing 4.18.

LISTING 4.18 Wiring to the unload Event

```
function unloadHandler(sender, args) {
  alert ("Sys.Application is being destroyed!");
}


Sys.Application.add_unload(unloadHandler);
```

Common uses of registering your own code for the dispose method are if you have noncomponent objects that need to be destroyed or global timers that need to be stopped.

Besides providing the unload event, dispose calls dispose on all disposable objects. Disposable objects are normally components, but they can be any object that implements the Sys.IDisposable interface, which guarantees the object has a dispose method to call.

We can manually add and remove from the list of disposable objects through two methods attached to Sys.Application: registerDisposable Object and unregisterDisposableObject.

registerDisposableObject

registerDisposableObject takes one parameter, the disposable object to add. Listing 4.19 shows a call to the registerDisposableObject method.

LISTING 4.19 Registering a Disposable Object

```
MyObject = function() {};

MyObject.prototype = {
  dispose: function() {
    alert ("My Object was disposed.");
  }
};
MyObject.registerClass("MyObject", null, Sys.IDisposable);

var myObject = new MyObject();
Sys.Application.registerDisposableObject(myObject);
```

> **■ NOTE**   Checking for Sys.IDisposable
>
> The `registerDisposableObject` and `unregisterDisposableObject` methods expect a parameter that implements `Sys.IDisposable`.

Now, with `myObject` registered as a disposable object, `dispose` will automatically be executed on our `myObject` instance.

unregisterDisposableObject

Just as we add to the list of disposable objects, we can remove from the list using the `unregisterDisposableObject` method. Listing 4.20 shows a call to the `unregisterDisposableObject` method.

LISTING 4.20 Unregistering a Disposable Object

```
MyObject = function() {};

MyObject.prototype = {
  dispose: function() {
    alert ("My Object was disposed.");
  }
};
MyObject.registerClass("MyObject", null, Sys.IDisposable);

var myObject = new MyObject();
Sys.Application.registerDisposableObject(myObject);

// unregister myObject
Sys.Application.unRegisterDisposableObject(myObject);
```

For the most part, you probably won't manually add or remove disposable objects from the list of disposable objects. Instead, you will automatically add to this list whenever you create an instance of a new component, because adding to the list of disposable objects is built in to `Sys.Component`'s constructor. `Sys.Component`'s constructor is shown in Listing 4.21, and the highlighted code is the call to register the component as a disposable object.

LISTING 4.21 Sys.Component's Automatic Registration as a Disposable Object

```
Sys.Component = function Sys$Component() {
  if (Sys.Application)
    Sys.Application.registerDisposableObject(this);
}
```

By automatically registering as a disposable object, a component is set up to be disposed of when the window is unloaded.

After the disposable object list has been iterated over and `dispose` has been called on each of the disposable objects, the `dispose` method continues.

The next step the `dispose` method performs is to unwire `Sys.Application` from the window. It does this by destroying the handlers that are attached to the window's `load` and `unload` events.

Finally, the `dispose` method calls the base class's `dispose` method, which is `Sys.Component`. If any event handlers have been registered for its disposing event, they are executed.

SUMMARY

In this chapter, we covered `Sys.Application`, the client runtime of the Microsoft AJAX Library. We started with how it can be used to manage components in an organized manner. We then covered how it provides an initialization routine with which we can interact to execute our own code in a safe manner. Finally, we covered how it provides an unload routine with which we can interact and register our own disposable objects.

■ 5 ■

Adding Client Capabilities to Server Controls

T HE POWER OF ASP.NET development has always been the development approach of using an event model that mirrors that of Windows Forms. This meant you did the majority of your development by dragging server controls onto the designer surface, setting properties of server controls, creating event handlers in code behind to handle postback events, and writing code to access a data source of some kind. This model of server-centric development has worked well for a long time, but increasingly users are demanding a richer UI experience that does not rely on postbacks and the slow response they tend to have. This presents an interesting dilemma for developers who have spent the majority of their development career working in the backend and have little experience writing JavaScript code. Then, to make matters worse, each browser tends to behave a little differently, and a tangled mess of `StringBuilder`-based JavaScript code turns your development experience into a nightmare. ASP.NET 2.0 AJAX Extensions make a lot of this easier now by providing a nice framework to work with to add browser-independent JavaScript code to your controls. In this chapter, we look at how to add client-side functionality to our server-based controls using ASP.NET 2.0 AJAX Extensions and how the framework provides many new features that make this easier than before.

Script-Generation Architecture

In Chapter 3, "Components," we looked at creating component-based behaviors and controls and how they can add new functionality to an existing DOM element using JavaScript and the Microsoft AJAX Library. As we turn our attention to building server-based controls that contain JavaScript functionality, there is a need to merge the client-centric JavaScript-based programming model with the server-centric .NET-based programming model. We need a way to be able to assign values to our server controls and have those values flow down to the client, influencing the client capabilities of our control on the client. This is where the script-generation architecture of ASP.NET 2.0 AJAX Extensions comes into play. The ASP.NET 2.0 AJAX Extensions provide a rich code-generation model for initializing behaviors and controls in the `ScriptBehaviorDescriptor` class and the `Script ControlDescriptor` class, respectively. These classes provide all the functionality needed to initialize the behavior and control classes with .NET-based data captured during the control development process. The `ScriptBehaviorDescriptor` and `ScriptControlDescriptor` classes actually work in conjunction with the `ScriptManager` control, which is responsible for managing all ASP.NET AJAX-related resources on a page. As we will shortly see, this control is the central figure in managing all script-related resources for a page, including but not limited to downloading Microsoft AJAX Library scripts to the client, generating web service JavaScript proxies, and registering controls that support `IExtenderControl` and `IScriptControl` interfaces so that the `ScriptBehaviorDescriptor`- and `ScriptControlDescriptor`-based information contained in them can be used to generate script initialization code.

Behavior and Control Script Generation

The focus of the `ScriptBehaviorDescriptor` and `ScriptControlDescriptor` classes is to generate the `$create` statement that initializes the `Sys.UI.Behavior` and `Sys.UI.Control` JavaScript classes on the client. The `$create` statement, as mentioned in Chapter 3, is responsible for assigning initial property values, adding event handlers to events, assigning other components as references, and associating a DOM element to a `Sys.UI.`

Component-based class. During the development of our server controls, we use these classes to add data that we have captured to be included in the `$create` statement generation. If we take a look at Figure 5.1, we can see a class hierarchy for the script-generation classes anchored by the `Script Descriptor` abstract class and the inherited `ScriptComponentDescriptor` class. It is the `ScriptComponentDescriptor` class that contains much of the functionality for the script generation, and the `ScriptBehaviorDescriptor` and `ScriptControlDescriptor` classes utilize this functionality to provide unique classes for their respective JavaScript counterparts.

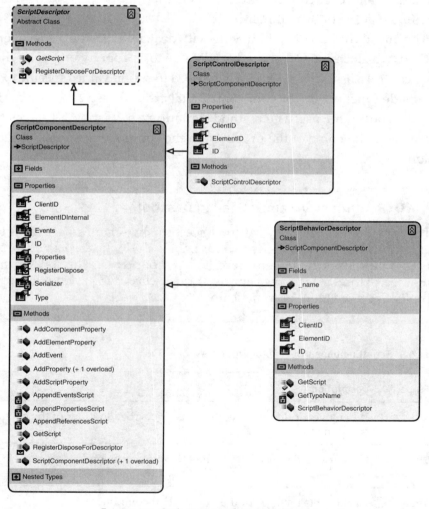

FIGURE 5.1 Script-generation class structure

ScriptComponentDescriptor

The `ScriptComponentDescriptor` class, which inherits from the `Script Descriptor` abstract class, provides most of the functionality for its inherited classes `ScriptBehaviorDescriptor` and `ScriptControlDescriptor`. The goal of this class is to merge the server-based .NET world with the JavaScript-based client world by providing properties, see Table 5.1, that identify the component and its type and methods, see Table 5.2, that create lists of properties, events, component references, DOM references, and JavaScript fragments and then use those lists to build up a complete `Sys.Component.Create` `$create` statement used to initialize a `Sys.UI.Behavior` or `Sys.UI.Control`.

The most common method you will deal with is the `AddProperty` method, which assigns an object-based value to a property on your behavior or control class. This method will be used to assign values specific to the client-side functionality of your control that are gathered as a user configures the control for use. The method signature, see Listing 5.1, takes two parameters: the name of the property on the component and the value to assign.

> ### ■ NOTE Property Names Used in Descriptors
>
> Throughout this chapter, you will see property names used during assignments. The names used should not include the associated `get_` or `set_` prefixes that were describe in Chapter 3. The `GetScript` method of the `ScriptComponentDescriptor` class will append the `set_` prefix to these values automatically.

TABLE 5.1 ScriptComponentDescriptor Properties

Property	Description
`ClientID`	When overridden in a derived class, gets the identifier of the client component
`ID`	Gets or sets the ID of the current ScriptComponentDescriptor instance
`Type`	Gets or sets the type of the target client component

TABLE 5.2 ScriptComponentDescriptor Methods

Method	Description
AddComponentProperty	Adds the specified property and associates that property with the specified component
AddElementProperty	Adds the specified property and associates that property with the specified element
AddEvent	Adds the specified event and handler
AddProperty	Adds the specified property and value
AddScriptProperty	Adds the specified property and associates the property with the specified script

LISTING 5.1 ScriptComponent Method Signatures

```
AddProperty(string PropertyName, object MyControl.Property);
AddComponent(string PropertyName, string JavaScriptComponentID);
AddElement(string PropertyName, string DomElementID);
AddEvent(string EventName, string JavaScriptFunctionName);
AddScriptProperty(string PropertyName, string JavaScriptCodeFragment);
```

The next two methods, AddComponentProperty and AddElement Property, are what we call reference-setting methods. These set a property to a component or element reference. The AddComponentProperty method takes the component ID that you pass in and on the client sets the property to a reference of the component using the $find shortcut method to get a reference to a component object that has been registered with the application through the addComponent method of the Sys.Application class. The AddElementProperty method takes the element ID that you pass in and on the client sets the property to a reference of a DOM element using the $get shortcut method to get a reference to a DOM element through the getElementById method of the Sys.UI.DomElement class.

The AddEvent method is used to attach an external JavaScript event handler to your component. The ability to attach events comes in handy when you have a control that needs to provide client-side events to the consumer of your control. The added ability that the Microsoft AJAX Library provides with the Sys.EventArgs and Sys.CancelEventArgs that are passed to each event handler brings a level of programming that matches what we have become used to in .NET development. The name of the event passed in to this method will correspond to the event on the component, and the JavaScript function name is the name of an external handler that will be called when the event occurs.

■ NOTE   Event Names Used in Descriptors

Throughout this chapter, you will see event names used during assignments. The names used should not include the associated add_ or remove_ prefixes that were describe in Chapter 3. The GetScript method of the ScriptComponentDescriptor class will append the add_ prefix to these values automatically.

The AddScriptProperty method provides an interesting feature in those hard-to-fit situations where the value assigned to the property needs to be evaluated on the client by the JavaScript eval method. In these cases, the value assigned to the property will be the result of an eval being applied to the contents of the second parameter before it is assigned to the property on the client. This can be helpful in situations where normal property assignment using the AddProperty method starts to break down, like when the data passed in is too complex for the JavaScriptSerializer or the value assigned is a combination of many different types that are brought together in an array.

The end result of all these values being assigned to various internal collections is a $create statement returned from the GetScript method, which is called by the ScriptManager during page processing. This abstract way of building up the component initialization code is much simpler than creating a big string using the StringBuilder class and hoping that everything gets created correctly.

GetScript Internals

You probably won't be surprised to see just what is going on under the hood with the GetScript method. It's surprising that no matter how far we get we still have to build up script one way or another. The calls to Append PropertiesScript, AppendEventScript, and AppendReference Script just loop through the internal collections of the properties, events, and references entries we added, converting the data types into JSON, where appropriate, and assigning them to the $create statement that is built up using the StringBuilder:

```
protected internal override string GetScript()
{
  if (!string.IsNullOrEmpty(this.ID))
  {
    this.AddProperty("id", this.ID);
  }
  StringBuilder builder = new StringBuilder();
  builder.Append("$create(");
  builder.Append(this.Type);
  builder.Append(", ");
  this.AppendPropertiesScript(builder);
  builder.Append(", ");
  this.AppendEventsScript(builder);
  builder.Append(", ");
  this.AppendReferencesScript(builder);
  if (this.ElementIDInternal != null)
  {
    builder.Append(", ");
    builder.Append("$get(\"");
    builder.Append(
    JavaScriptString.QuoteString(
      this.ElementIDInternal));
    builder.Append("\")");
  }
  builder.Append(");");
  return builder.ToString();
}
```

ScriptBehaviorDescriptor

The ScriptBehaviorDescriptor class is designed to generate a $create statement for use with a Sys.UI.Behavior class. The constructor, see Listing 5.2, takes the namespace and class name of the Sys.UI.Behavior class and the ID of the current associated control. The class is primarily used when creating controls that support the IExtenderControl interface or inherit from the ExtenderControl class. These types of controls are designed to allow adding client-side behavior to existing server controls and use the ScriptBehaviorDescriptor class to gather information used in the initialization of their corresponding behavior class.

LISTING 5.2 ScriptBehaviorDescriptor Constructor

```
ScriptBehaviorDescriptor("Namespace.Class", ID)
```

ScriptControlDescriptor

The ScriptControlDescriptor class is designed to generate a $create statement for use with a Sys.UI.Control class. The constructor, see Listing 5.3, takes the namespace and class name of the Sys.UI.Control class and the ID of the current associated control. The class is primarily used when creating controls that support the IScriptControl interface or inherit from the ScriptControl class. These types of controls are designed to allow adding client-side functionality internally to the controls and use the ScriptControlDescriptor class to gather information used in the initialization of their corresponding control class.

LISTING 5.3 ScriptComponentDescriptor Constructor

```
ScriptComponentDescriptor ("Namespace.Class", ID)
```

Script Resources

ASP.NET 2.0 introduced the ability for external resources to be embedded within web applications and controls and then accessed through the WebResource.axd URL. This functionality opened the door for developers to embed images, JavaScript files, and CSS files into the assembly, eliminating the need to have these files located on the file system. ASP.NET 2.0 AJAX Extensions rely heavily on this feature to deliver the various JavaScript files embedded in the System.Web.Extensions DLL that contains all its functionality.

Adding Script Resources

The process to add script resources to your project is relatively simple. The only requirement is that your project compile to a DLL. This limits the possibilities to web applications, which are the default in Visual Studio 2008, and control libraries. To properly configure a script resource, you must complete these two steps:

1. Make the JavaScript file a resource.
2. Add the WebResource attribute to the assembly.

Embedding a JavaScript File

To make a script file an embedded resource is a simple process that entails selecting the script file, selecting the properties for the file, and changing the build action to Embedded Resource (see Figure 5.2).

FIGURE 5.2 Selecting the Embedded Resource option of the build action

Using the WebResource Attribute

The WebResource attribute is used to identify an embedded resource that can be used as a web resource. The first parameter specifies the name of the resource, and should be named using the pattern RootNamespace.PathTo JavaScriptFile, with the root namespace being the namespace of the project and path to JavaScript file being the full path, including folder names if not in the root of the project. In the sample in Listing 5.4, the Image Rotator.js file is contained in a project called ImageRotatorExtender, and the file is at the root of the project. If the file were below, for instance, the Scripts folder, the entry would be ImageRotatorExtender.Scripts.Image Rotator.js instead. The second parameter specifies the MIME type to be used. In our case, we are referring to JavaScript files, so a content type of text/javascript is used.

LISTING 5.4 WebResource Attribute Usage

```
[assembly: WebResource("ImageRotatorExtender.ImageRotator.js",
    "text/javascript")]
```

ScriptReference

The ScriptReference class is designed to contain information about a script resource that is intended to be registered with the ScriptManager. The class contains a rich set of properties, as shown in Table 5.3, that provide a wealth of information about the script file and its intended use. Some of the entries are similar to the entries used in the WebResource attribute and, in fact, if the script file to be used is an embedded resource, it must have a corresponding WebResource attribute entry so that the Script Manager can find the resource during page processing. The constructor takes the name of the JavaScript file in the same format as the WebResource attribute and the type that contains the resource. In the case of Listing 5.5, the ImageRotator.js file we used in the WebResource is used, and the type for the current project's assembly is used as the type.

There are a few properties that are of interest as you work with the ScriptReferences class. The NotifyScriptLoaded property is used to add the notifyScriptLoaded method to the end of a script file and is used to notify the Sys.Application that the script has loaded. The Microsoft AJAX

Library uses this to ensure that scripts are loaded in the correct order when dependent scripts are used. If you have a script file that already contains this method, the property should be set to `false`; otherwise, a value of true will instruct the `ScriptManager` to append the `notifyScriptLoaded` method to the end of the script file. The `ScriptMode` property indicates whether to use the debug or release version of the script. The naming convention of ScriptFile.debug.js is used to indicate that a script file is the debug version.

TABLE 5.3 ScriptReference Properties

Property	Description
Assembly	Gets or sets the name of the assembly that contains the client script file as an embedded resource
IgnoreScriptPath	Gets or sets a value that indicates whether the `Script Path` property is included in the URL when you register a client script file from a resource
Name	Gets or sets the name of the embedded resource that contains the client script file
NotifyScriptLoaded	Gets or sets a value that indicates whether the `Script ResourceHandler` object automatically adds code at the end of the ECMAScript (JavaScript) file to call the `notifyScriptLoaded` method of the `Sys.Application` class
Path	Gets or sets the path of the referenced client script file, relative to the web page
ResourceUICultures	Gets or sets a comma-delimited list of UI cultures that are supported by the `Path` property
ScriptMode	Gets or sets the version of the client script file (release or debug) to use

LISTING 5.5 ScriptReference Constructor

```
ScriptReference("ImageRotatorExtender.ImageRotator.js",
    this.GetType().Assembly.FullName)
```

ScriptManager

The ScriptManager control is the central figure in the server-side functionality of ASP.NET 2.0 AJAX Extensions. The control provides functionality for registering scripts compatible with partial page updates, registering web services and application services, and scripts associated with server controls that implement the IExtenderControl and IScriptControl interfaces.

In this chapter, we cover setting up the ScriptManager and the core script-generation features. In Chapter 6, "ASP.NET AJAX Localization," we cover localization. In Chapter 7 "Control Development in a Partial Postback Environment" we cover how the ScriptManager participates in partial page rendering. In Chapter 8, "ASP.NET AJAX Communication Architecture," we cover the support for web services and in Chapter 9, "Application Services," we cover working with the application services.

Configuring the ScriptManager

The ScriptManager control is required on all pages that will support ASP.NET AJAX functionality. The default configuration shown in Listing 5.6 enables downloading of the core Microsoft AJAX Library scripts and scripts that are registered in server controls that implement the IExtender Control and IScript interfaces to the browser.

LISTING 5.6 ScriptManager Registration

```
<asp:ScriptManager ID="ScriptManager1" runat="server">
</asp:ScriptManager>
```

Master Pages, Controls, and the ScriptManagerProxy

In cases where you register the ScriptManager in a master page or a parent page that contains user controls, these lower-level controls in the control hierarchy can't have an additional ScriptManager, which can present a problem with content pages and user controls that are contained in a master page scenario. In cases such as this, the ScriptManagerProxy control shown in Listing 5.7 can be used to configure additional functionality at the content page or user control level. The use of this control also provides an additional level of abstraction in configuring functionality at these levels. It enables you to do things such as register web services used in a specific user control in the user control itself without requiring users of the control to know what the web service dependencies are and requiring their registration in the `ScriptManager` control on the parent.

> **■ NOTE   Default Behavior**
>
> Unlike the `ScriptManager` control, there is no default behavior of the `ScriptManagerProxy` control, so adding one to a content page or user control without adding additional configuration entries won't do anything.

LISTING 5.7 ScriptManagerProxy Registration

```
<asp:ScriptManagerProxy ID="ScriptManagerProxy1" runat="server">
</asp:ScriptManagerProxy>
```

Working with Scripts

One of the areas most utilized by the `ScriptManager` is its capability to generate script and script registration entries. In the case of script generation, the `ScriptManager` enables you to generate JavaScript proxy classes for registered web services and to generate `$create` statements for server controls that implement the `IExtenderControl` and `IScriptControl` interfaces. In the case of script registration, the `ScriptManager` is responsible for adding script source entries and script block entries into the associated page so that they are available on the client.

The `ScriptManager` control contains a `ScriptReferenceCollection` that contains `ScriptReference` entries for scripts that will be included on the page. The markup in Listing 5.8 shows how to add a script reference to `ScriptManager`. The addition of these script files enables the `Script Manager` to create a script source entry on the page that then accesses the script file through the ScriptResource.axd URL and associated HTTP handler that processes the request. It is through this process that the script files are downloaded to the browser and made available for use.

> **■ NOTE**   Processing ScriptResource.axd Requests
>
> In Chapter 8, we cover in detail how script requests are processed when we discuss the ASP.NET AJAX communication architecture.

LISTING 5.8 Script Registration

```
<asp:ScriptManager ID="ScriptManager1" runat="server">
    <Scripts>
        <asp:ScriptReference Path="~/MyScript.js" />
    </Scripts>
</asp:ScriptManager>
```

Adding Client-Side Behavior Using the ExtenderControl

Extender controls help maintain a server-centric development experience by enabling ASP.NET 2.0 developers to add client-side functionality to an existing server control. In this section, we cover how to create extender controls, the techniques for adding client-side functionality, and how to use existing server control development techniques to provide a rich development experience for a developer using your extender control.

> **■ NOTE**   ASP.NET AJAX Control Toolkit
>
> The ASP.NET AJAX Control Toolkit also provides a framework for creating extender controls and script controls. The difference between the two is that extender control and script control development using ASP.NET 2.0 Extensions directly provides the greatest amount of flexibility without the added need of additional binaries but at the cost of a slightly longer development cycle. If a more controlled and rapid development experience is what you are looking for, you might want to look at the ASP.NET AJAX Control Toolkit, which is covered in Chapter 10, "ASP.NET AJAX Control Toolkit Architecture," and Chapter 11, "Adding Client Capabilities to Server Controls Using the ASP.NET AJAX Control Toolkit."

ExtenderControl Overview

The `ExtenderControl` class enables you to add AJAX functionality to a server control using the server-centric model that developers have become accustomed to. In Figure 5.3, we can see that the `System.Web.UI.ExtenderControl` class gets its start by extending the functionality provided by the `System.Web.UI.Control` class. This is important because the `Control` class is the basis for all server controls in ASP.NET 2.0. By inheriting from the `Control` class, the extender control gains all the functionality we have come to rely on when using server controls such as data binding, control state, view state, design-time support, smart tags, and integration with the Properties window. The `ExtenderControl` also implements the `System.Web.UI.IExtenderControl` interface, which provides the hooks the `ExtenderControl` needs to integrate with ASP.NET 2.0 AJAX Extensions and to provide client-side script. The `GetScriptDescriptor` and `GetScript References` methods are called by the `ScriptManager` as the extender control is created, returning the behavior initialization script and script references, respectively, that are needed to ensure the client-side behavior of the control is properly configured.

Creating an Extender Control

The extender control we build is designed to work with an image control and provides the added behavior of looping through an additional set of images, adding image rotation behavior to the standard ASP.NET image control. The process of creating the extender control consists of four main tasks.

1. Creating the template classes
2. Providing implementation for the inherited extender control class
3. Providing implementation for the `Sys.UI.Behavior`-based JavaScript class
4. Attaching the extender control to an existing server control

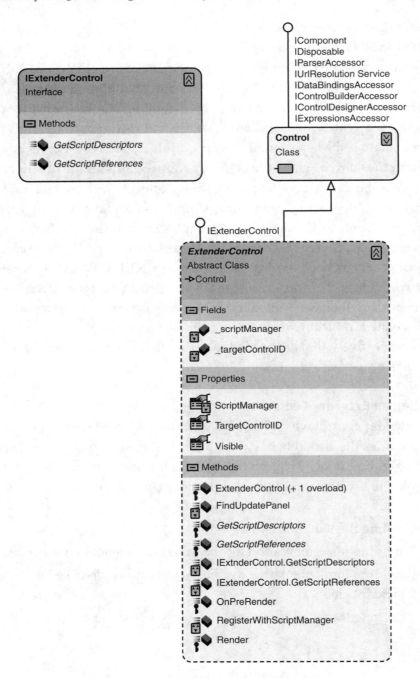

FIGURE 5.3 ExtenderControl class hierarchy

Visual Studio 2008 Extender Control Library Template

The new extender control library template shown in Figure 5.4 provides a great start to creating an extender control. The template creates a library project, see Figure 5.5, with an `ExtenderControl` class, a client behavior JavaScript class, and a resource file. The template also adds a `WebResource` entry and `ScriptResource` entry for the embedded client behavior script file so that it is available on the client.

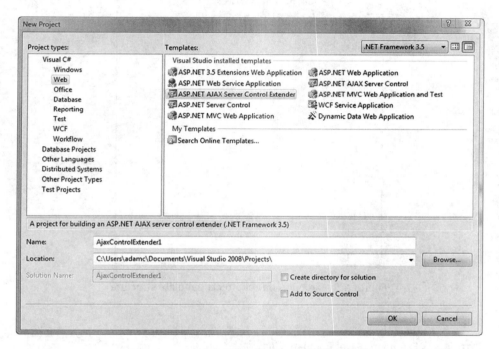

FIGURE 5.4 ExtenderControl project template

The `ExtenderControl` class that is generated, see Listing 5.9, contains a few entries we need to cover. The `System.Web.UI.TargetControl` attribute that is on the `ExtenderControl` class is used to limit the types of server controls the extender can be associated with. The use of the `Control` type in the template allows the extender control to be associated with any control because `Control` is the base class for all server controls. In our example, you will see that we change this value to a more specific type, which is recommended when creating your control. The template also creates overrides for the `GetScriptDescriptors` and `GetScriptReferences` methods (which we describe in more detail shortly).

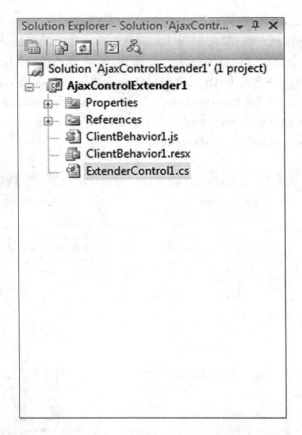

FIGURE 5.5 ExtenderControl project template structure

LISTING 5.9 ExtenderControl Template Class

```
[TargetControlType(typeof(Control))]
public class ExtenderControl1 : ExtenderControl
{
  public ExtenderControl1()
  {
  }
  protected override IEnumerable<ScriptDescriptor>
    GetScriptDescriptors(System.Web.UI.Control targetControl)
  {
    ScriptBehaviorDescriptor descriptor =
      new ScriptBehaviorDescriptor(
        "AjaxControlExtender5.ClientBehavior1",
       targetControl.ClientID);
        yield return descriptor;
  }
```

```
// Generate the script reference
protected override IEnumerable<ScriptReference>
  GetScriptReferences()
{
  yield return new ScriptReference(
    "AjaxControlExtender5.ClientBehavior1.js",
   this.GetType().Assembly.FullName);
}
}
```

> **■ NOTE**   Using the yield Keyword
>
> The yield keyword is used to return an enumerated value as a code block performs a custom iteration over an array or collection. In the case of the GetScriptDescriptors method, the yield statement is used as a shortcut to return the descriptor as an enumerated value.

The ClientBehavior JavaScript class shown in Listing 5.10 contains the basic elements of a behavior class, including a namespace registration, constructor, prototype, class registration, and notifyScriptLoaded call. The constructor is a bare-bones implementation that consists of an intialize Base call and requires additional coding for things such as member variable declaration. The prototype is also a bare-bones implementation with a call to callBaseMethod to initialize the behavior base class and a dispose function with a call to callBaseMethod and will also require additional coding for any properties, methods, or events that your behavior will implement.

LISTING 5.10 Sys.UI.Behavior Template Class

```
/// <reference name="MicrosoftAjax.js"/>

Type.registerNamespace("AjaxControlExtender5");

AjaxControlExtender5.ClientBehavior1 = function(element) {
  AjaxControlExtender5.ClientBehavior1.initializeBase(
    this, [element]);
}

AjaxControlExtender5.ClientBehavior1.prototype = {
  initialize: function() {
    AjaxControlExtender5.ClientBehavior1.callBaseMethod(
      this, 'initialize');
```

LISTING 5.10 continued

```
      // Add custom initialization here
  },
  dispose: function() {
    //Add custom dispose actions here
    AjaxControlExtender5.ClientBehavior1.callBaseMethod(
      this, 'dispose');
  }
}
AjaxControlExtender5.ClientBehavior1.registerClass(
  'AjaxControlExtender5.ClientBehavior1',
  Sys.UI.Behavior);

if (typeof(Sys) !== 'undefined') Sys.Application.notifyScriptLoaded();
```

Inheriting from the ExtenderControl-Based Class

The `ImageRotator` class, shown in Listing 5.11, is an extender control that provides the added behavior of looping through an additional set of images, adding image rotation capabilities to the standard ASP.NET image control. The class inherits from the `ExtenderControl` base class, which provides the ability to add client-side behavior to the attached control. The type of control the extender control supports is important in determining the client-side behavior, and the `TargetControlType` attribute should be used to ensure consumers of the extender control attach to a control of the proper type. In the `ImageRotator` extender, the `TargetControlType` of `Image` is used to ensure the extender is attached only to `Image` controls that the extender is designed to support.

> **■ NOTE**　Target Type and Client-Side Behavior
>
> When selecting a type to use, consider the properties and events of the HTML element it represents to ensure that the behavior will support them and any additional properties or events of any inherited type. The use of this attribute will provide you a compile-time check that can ensure you are associating your extender control with the correct type of control.

As you approach the development of an extender control, you need to consider the experience consumers of your control will have as they develop. The control should be easy to configure and should cleanly integrate with the behavior class that will provide the client-side functionality. The `ImageRotator` extender contains two main properties, `Rotation Interval` and `ImageList`. These provide configuration points for the control. The `ImageRotator` property determines the interval in seconds that the images in the `Image` control will be swapped out, and the `ImageList` property contains the images used during the swapping process. When creating properties, remember that the properties will be accessible in the Properties window during design time, so special attention should be paid to the data types used to ensure their compatibility with the Properties window. The `System.ComponentModel` and `System.ComponentModel.Designer` namespaces can come in handy when working with some data types, providing attributes and designers that can be applied to a property and thus ensuring a richer design-time experience for users of the extender control. An example of a `ComponentModel` attribute is the `DefaultValue` attribute used on the `RotationInterval` property to inform the designer that the default value of 3 should be used. The use of defaults can help ensure that the default implementation of your extender control has a desirable effect for users who might want an attach-and-run experience.

The information gathered from the properties is used by the `GetScript Descriptors` method and the `ScriptBehaviorDescriptor` class that is created inside it. The `ScriptBehaviorDescriptor` class contains all the elements needed to compose the `$create` statement used to initialize the behavior class for the extender control. The class contains the name of the behavior class, the control `id` of the attached control, and a collection of property assignments for the `RotationInterval` and `ImageList` values that were collected by the extender control. As the page is processing, the `Script Manager` control looks for child controls that implement the `IExtender Control` interface and calls the `GetScriptDescriptors` method on them, extracting out the `$create` statement that the descriptor contains and embedding it onto the page. This ability to assign property values on an extender control and have them participate in the client experience is what makes extender controls so appealing.

The GetScriptReference method creates a ScriptReference class designed to register the script file for use on an ASP.NET page. The class takes the full name of the client behavior file and the full name of the assembly and uses this information to register the script file. Because the Extender Control implements the IExtenderControl interface, the ScriptManager calls the GetScriptReferences method and adds the ScriptReference class to the ScriptReferenceCollection so that it is included on the page.

LISTING 5.11 ImageRotator ExtenderControl-Based Class

```
[TargetControlType(typeof(Image))]
public class ImageRotator : ExtenderControl
{
  public ImageRotator(){ }
  int _rotationInterval = 0;
  [DefaultValue(3), DisplayName("RotationInterval(seconds))")]
  public int RotationInterval
  {
    get
    {
      if (_rotationInterval == 0)
      {
        //set the default
        _rotationInterval = 3;
        return _rotationInterval;
      }
      else
      {
        return _rotationInterval;
      }
    }
    set
    {
      _rotationInterval = value;
    }
  }

  public string ImageList { get; set; }

  private string CreateImageListArray()
  {
    string[] imageList = ImageList.Split(',');
    if (imageList.Length == 0)
      return "";

    StringBuilder arrayList = new StringBuilder();
```

```csharp
    bool first = true;
    arrayList.Append("new Array(");
    foreach (string value in imageList)
    {
      if (first)
      {
        first = false;
      }
      else
      {
        arrayList.Append(",");
      }
      arrayList.Append("'");
      arrayList.Append(value);
      arrayList.Append("'");
    }
    arrayList.Append(")");
    return arrayList.ToString();
  }

  protected override IEnumerable<ScriptDescriptor>
    GetScriptDescriptors(System.Web.UI.Control targetControl)
  {
    ScriptBehaviorDescriptor descriptor = new
      ScriptBehaviorDescriptor(
        "ImageRotatorExtender.ImageRotator",
        targetControl.ClientID);
    descriptor.AddProperty("rotationInterval", RotationInterval);
    if (!string.IsNullOrEmpty(ImageList))
    {
      descriptor.AddProperty("imageList",ImageList.Split(','));
    }
    yield return descriptor;
  }

  // Generate the script reference
  protected override IEnumerable<ScriptReference>
    GetScriptReferences()
  {
    yield return new ScriptReference(
      "ImageRotatorExtender.ImageRotator.js",
      this.GetType().Assembly.FullName);
  }
}
```

Creating the Sys.UI.Behavior Class

The client behavior of the extender control is represented by the
Sys.UI.Behavior-based ImageRotator class shown in Listing 5.12. This

class adds the behavior to the Image of switching the image source periodically through an internal list of images.

> ■ **NOTE**   Detailed Explanation of the Behavior Class
>
> The makeup of the behavior class was covered in Chapter 3, so we concentrate only on the functionality as it relates to our example as we move forward.

The class contains the RotationInterval and ImageList properties that were part of the ScriptBehaviorDescriptor class and an internal _set Rotation method that sets up the behavior to call back into itself using the window.setInterval method to rotate the image. Notice that we are building up the JavaScript expression to be called by the setInterval method. This is required due to the source of the this value when calling methods. As you recall from Chapter 3, the behavior is actually a property of the element itself, so the code builds up a method call directly to the behavior by getting the element id and constructing an expression that calls the rotateImage method, ensuring we have the correct this context as the method is executed. Inside the rotateImage method, we access the image element and change to image source, and thus ensure the functionality we need to rotate the images.

LISTING 5.12 ImageRotator Sys.UI.Behavior-based Class

```
/// <reference name="MicrosoftAjax.js"/>


Type.registerNamespace("ImageRotatorExtender");

ImageRotatorExtender.ImageRotator = function(element) {
  ImageRotatorExtender.ImageRotator.initializeBase(this, [element]);
  this._imageIndex = 0;
  this._imageList = null;
  this._rotationInterval = 3;
}

ImageRotatorExtender.ImageRotator.prototype = {
  initialize: function() {
    ImageRotatorExtender.ImageRotator.callBaseMethod(this,'initialize');
    this._setupRotation();
```

```
    },
    dispose: function() {
      ImageRotatorExtender.ImageRotator.callBaseMethod(this, 'dispose');
    },
    get_rotationInterval: function(){
      return this._rotationInterval;
    },
    set_rotationInterval: function(value){
      this._rotationInterval = value;
    },
    get_imageList: function(){
      return this._imageList;
    },
    set_imageList: function(value){
      this._imageList = value;
    },
    _setupRotation: function(){
      var expression = "$get('" + this.get_element().id +
        "').ImageRotator._rotateImage()";
      setInterval(expression,this.get_rotationInterval()*1000);
    },
    _rotateImage: function(){
      var element = this.get_element();
      if(element)
      {
        element.src = this._imageList[this._imageIndex++];
        if(this._imageIndex > this._imageList.length - 1)
          this._imageIndex = 0;
      }
    }
  }
}
ImageRotatorExtender.ImageRotator.registerClass(
  'ImageRotatorExtender.ImageRotator', Sys.UI.Behavior);

if (typeof(Sys) !== 'undefined') Sys.Application.notifyScriptLoaded();
```

Attaching the Extender to a Control

With the creation of the extender control library completed, it is now time
to cover the design-time experience of using our ImageRotator extender
control. The first thing we want to talk about is the new Extender Control
Wizard, shown in Figure 5.6, that comes with Visual Studio 2008. The
Extender Control Wizard is used to automate the assignment of an extender control to a server control. The wizard is used when a page is in design
mode and is accessible from the smart tag Extender Wizard option on the
controls on a page. The wizard displays a list of available extender controls

from which you can select and name the extender control before the wizard creates the HTML markup that attaches the extender control to the current control. After the extender control has been attached, it is easy to move to the Properties window and fill in the appropriate entries, easily customizing the extender control for any particular situation. The HTML markup in Listing 5.13 shows a configured `ImageRotator` extender that was attached to an image control using the Extender Control Wizard, and Figure 5.7 shows the complete page.

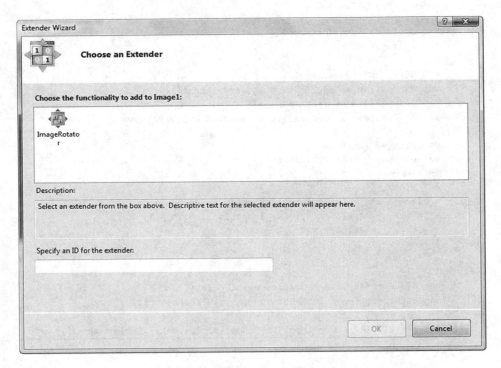

FIGURE 5.6 Extender Control Wizard

LISTING 5.13 Sample Web Page with an Image Control and Associated ImageRotator Control

```
...
<%@ Register assembly="ImageRotatorExtender"
        namespace="ImageRotatorExtender" tagprefix="cc1" %>
...
<asp:ScriptManager ID="ScriptManager1" runat="server">
</asp:ScriptManager>
<h3>Pictures of Florence provided by <asp:Image ID="Image2" runat="server"
```

```
ImageUrl="~/images/freeDigitalPhotoslogo.gif" /></h3>
<div>
  <asp:Image ID="Image1" runat="server" ImageUrl="~/images/1.jpg" />
  <cc1:ImageRotator ID="Image1_ImageRotator" runat="server"
    ImageList="images/1.jpg,images/2.jpg,images/3.jpg,images/4.jpg"
    TargetControlID="Image1" />
</div>
  ...
```

FIGURE 5.7 ImageRotator sample page

Adding Client-Side Functionality Using the ScriptControl

The need to add client-side functionality to server controls has been around since the early days of ASP.NET and has been accomplished in many ways. The combined use of the `ClientScriptManager` class and the `String Builder` class to build up dynamic JavaScript code worked, but the inconsistencies among the various browsers led to code that intermittently worked and was hard to debug. ASP.NET 2.0 AJAX Extensions and the Microsoft AJAX Library provide a much better way to add browser-independent client-side functionality to server controls by utilizing the `ScriptControl` and the `Sys.UI.Control` classes. In this section, we look at how we can create server controls that are built on these frameworks that can provide a browser-independent rich user experience on the client.

ScriptControl Overview

The `ScriptControl` class, shown in Figure 5.8, is an abstract class designed for use by developers who are creating server controls that require client-side functionality. If we look back at extender controls, the idea behind them was to add client-side behavior to an already existing server control without modifying that control. With the `ScriptControl`, we are interested in creating a completely contained control that provides a server-side design-time experience with integrated client-side functionality.

WebControl Class

The `WebControl` class builds on the functionality provided by the `Control` class and is the class of choice for building controls that provide UI and styling. The `WebControl` class adds the rendering and styling features needed by most server controls, providing a full service abstract class to build server controls from. In our discussion of the `WebControl` class to follow, we concentrate on the styling and rendering concepts needed to understand how to create a `ScriptControl`-based control.

The `WebControl` class provides a type-safe way of adding styles to your control by either setting a limited set of CSS attributes or by creating your own style class and exposing its properties. Some of the more common style properties of the `WebControl` class, see Listing 5.14, are `BackColor`, `Border Color`, `BorderStyle`, `BorderWidth`, `CssClass`, `Font`, `ForeColor`, `Height`, and `Width`. These are normally used to set the style of the control in a type-safe way. If these properties expose too few CSS attributes, the `WebControl` class can be extended to add additional CSS attributes based on custom style classes that expose all the attributes you need.

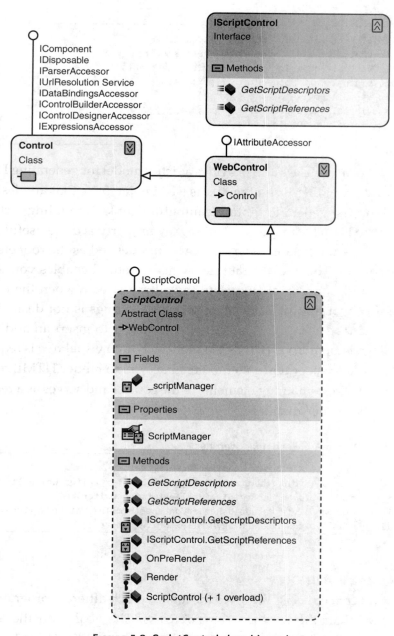

FIGURE 5.8 ScriptControl class hierarchy

LISTING 5.14 WebControl Style Properties

```
public virtual Color BackColor { get; set; }
public virtual Color BorderColor { get; set; }
public virtual BorderStyle BorderStyle { get; set; }
public virtual Unit BorderWidth { get; set; }
public virtual FontInfo Font { get; }
public virtual Color ForeColor { get; set; }
public virtual Unit Height { get; set; }
public virtual Unit Width { get; set; }
```

The WebControl class also provides a richer model for generating HTML content by providing virtual methods, see Listing 5.15, that are designed to break up the generation into meaningful chunks, providing a cleaner approach to HTML generation. The TagKey property is quite useful in situations where the default span element is not desired as the root element for the control. The AddAttributesToRender method enables you to add both CSS and non-CSS attributes to the output stream when the normal behavior of working with the style property settings is not desired. The RenderBeginTag and RederEndTab work as a pair to insert an additional containing element in cases where a more elaborate visual tree is required. Finally, the RenderContents method enables you to render HTML content that is inside the containing element for the control and serves as a replacement for the Render method.

LISTING 5.15 WebControl Rendering Overrides

```
protected virtual HtmlTextWriterTag TagKey { get; }
protected virtual void AddAttributesToRender(HtmlTextWriter writer);
public virtual void RenderBeginTag(HtmlTextWriter writer);
protected internal virtual void RenderContents(HtmlTextWriter writer);
public virtual void RenderEndTag(HtmlTextWriter writer);
```

ScriptControl Details

The ScriptControl class brings to the table a much different programming experience than the ExtenderControl class. The goal with the Script Control is to build HTML content and the supported client-side functionality that goes with it while keeping the user experience during design time the same as the extender control. The ScriptControl class brings to the table the same JavaScript-related functionality as the ExtenderControl abstract class, except the `GetScriptDescriptors` method deals with the `ScriptControlDescriptor` class rather than the `ScriptExtenderDescriptor` class. The difference between descriptor classes is the type of JavaScript class they are designed to work with. The `ScriptControlDescriptor` is designed to work with a class based on `Sys.UI.Control`, which is the type of class needed to provide client-side functionality to our `ScriptControl`. The `ScriptControl` class is also geared toward generating HTML with functionality it inherits from the `WebControl` class and should be used as a replacement to the `WebControl` when developing ASP.NET 2.0 AJAX Extensions controls that generate HTML content.

Creating a Script Control

The script control we build provides help support for an associated textbox. When a user clicks the help icon, an alert is shown containing contextual information about the textbox entry. The control contains a textbox and a help icon that is associated with the textbox and provides support for pre-filling the textbox value, setting the help text, and selecting the help icon. The process of creating the script control consists of four main tasks.

1. Creating the template classes
2. Providing implementation for the inherited script control class
3. Providing implementation for the `Sys.UI.Control`-based JavaScript class
4. Adding the control to a web page

Visual Studio 2008 Server Control Library Template

The new server control library template, shown in Figure 5.9, provides a great start to creating a script control. The template creates a library project, see Figure 5.10, with a `ScriptControl` class, a client control JavaScript class, and a resource file. The template also adds a `WebResource` entry and `ScriptResource` entry for the embedded client control script file so that it is available on the client.

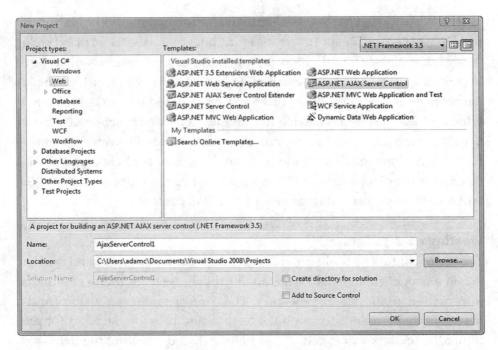

FIGURE 5.9 ScriptControl project template

The ScriptControl class that is generated contains the template code needed to get started in creating a script control (see Listing 5.16). The template makes no assumptions about how the control will be developed, provides no default overrides for the WebControl methods we discussed earlier, and will require at a minimum overriding the RenderContents method. The GetScriptDescriptors and GetScriptReferences methods we have discussed before, so we do not cover them again in this section.

LISTING 5.16 ScriptControl Template Class

```csharp
public class ServerControl1 : ScriptControl
{
  public ServerControl1()
  {
  }
  protected override IEnumerable<ScriptDescriptor>
    GetScriptDescriptors()
  {
    ScriptControlDescriptor descriptor = new
      ScriptControlDescriptor("AjaxServerControl1.ClientControl1",
        this.ClientID);
      yield return descriptor;
```

```
    }

    // Generate the script reference
    protected override IEnumerable<ScriptReference>
      GetScriptReferences()
    {
      yield return new
        ScriptReference("AjaxServerControl1.ClientControl1.js",
          this.GetType().Assembly.FullName);
    }
  }
```

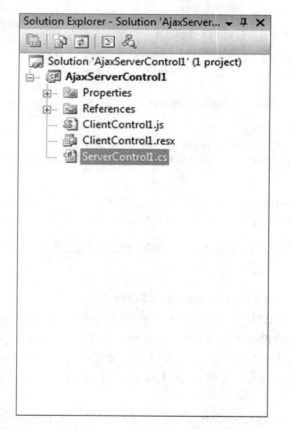

FIGURE 5.10 ScriptControl project template structure

The control's JavaScript class, shown in Listing 5.17, contains the basic elements of a Sys.UI.Control class, including a namespace registration, constructor, prototype, class registration, and notifyScriptLoaded call,

and will need implementation added to them just as the extender control
JavaScript file did.

LISTING 5.17 Sys.UI.Control Template Class

```
/// <reference name="MicrosoftAjax.js"/>

Type.registerNamespace("AjaxServerControl1");

AjaxServerControl1.ClientControl1 = function(element) {
  AjaxServerControl1.ClientControl1.initializeBase(this, [element]);
}

AjaxServerControl1.ClientControl1.prototype = {
  initialize: function() {
    AjaxServerControl1.ClientControl1.callBaseMethod(this,
      'initialize');

    // Add custom initialization here
  },
  dispose: function() {
    //Add custom dispose actions here
    AjaxServerControl1.ClientControl1.callBaseMethod(this, 'dispose');
  }
}
AjaxServerControl1.ClientControl1.registerClass(
  'AjaxServerControl1.ClientControl1', Sys.UI.Control);

if (typeof(Sys) !== 'undefined') Sys.Application.notifyScriptLoaded();
```

Inheriting from the ScriptControl-Based Class

The TextBoxInfo class, shown in Listing 5.18, is the control that provides
the textbox and associated help functionality for our sample control. The
creation of the control consists of many of the development tasks we performed for the extender control with the addition of drawing the UI
elements.

We begin our discussion of the TextBoxInfo control with the subject of
HTML rendering and the role of the TagKey property and the Render
Contents method. The TagKey property was overridden in the control to
provide support for a table root element rather than a span. The use of
a table provided a more flexible layout approach than working with the
span, and the ability to override the TagKey property made it simple to

implement this change. The `RenderContents` method was also overridden to draw the table rows and columns and the textbox and image HTML elements. The method utilizes the `HtmlTextWriterTag` and `HtmlTextWrite Attribute` classes to emit the HTML content to the `HtmlTextWriter`, which represents the output stream of the control. This implementation uses normal HTML tags, but you can also insert ASP.NET Server controls.

> **▪ NOTE   HTML Generation**
>
> The subject of HTML generation has been around since ASP.NET 2.0 and prior knowledge of the mechanics involved are assumed. For a more detailed explanation of building HTML content inside a `WebControl`-based class, see "Developing Custom Server Control" on the MSDN web site at http://msdn2.microsoft.com/en-us/library/ zt27tfhy.aspx.

The `InformationText`, `Text`, and `ImageUrl` properties of this control enable you to configure the control using the Properties window during design time and in code and markup. The `InformationText` property holds the value that is displayed to users when they select the help icon. The `Text` property provides a way to prepopulate the textbox value on the server. And the `ImageUrl` property enables consumers of the control to add any image they choose. The `ImageUrl` property provides some additional design features that offer another example of how to add a richer design-time experience to your controls. The control utilizes the `ImageUrlEditor` and the `UrlProperty` attributes to provide design-time support when adding the image URL for the help icon. The `ImageUrlEditor`, see Figure 5.11, provides the user with a clean way to find an image that is located in a web application and to assign the value to a property that accepts a URL. The `UrlProperty` attribute provides a filter that identifies specific file types that can be used to filter against the `ImageUrl` property. The use of these two items greatly enhances the design-time experience of assigning a URL to the `ImageUrl` property field and is something that is easy to do.

FIGURE 5.11 ImageURL Editor

The ScriptControl class provides the same hooks into the script-generation process as the ExtenderControl. The support for the IScript Control interface and the GetScriptDescriptors method allows a control built on this class to be included in the list of controls the ScriptManager will extract script information from as script entries are bound to the page. The ScriptControl relies on the ScriptControlDescriptor to gather information for the $create statement generation. This class is designed to emit a $create statement that initializes a Sys.UI.Control class and requires the name of the control class, the control id of the associated control, and a collection of property assignments for the InformationText, Text element, and Image element properties. The GetScriptReference method structure and behavior is the same as in the extender control.

> **■ NOTE** Order of Property Assignment in the $create Statement
>
> The decision to add the Text and ImageUrl properties to the HTML elements directly was due to an assignment order condition that could occur in this configuration. When the ScriptManager builds up the $create statement, the order of the entries can't be controlled. In the case of our control class, see Listing 5.19, if the element entries for the TextBox and Image were not added before the property assignments for the element references, the member values would be undefined as the get_ assignments are made.

LISTING 5.18 TextBoxInfo ScriptControl-Based Class

```
public class TextBoxInfo : ScriptControl
{
  private const string TextBoxId = "DataEntryTextBox";
  private const string ImageId = "InformationImageButton";

  public TextBoxInfo(){ }

  public string Text { get; set; }

  public string InformationText { get; set; }
  [Editor("System.Web.UI.Design.ImageUrlEditor, System.Design,
    Version=2.0.0.0, Culture=neutral, PublicKeyToken=b03f5f7f11d50a3a",
    typeof(UITypeEditor)), UrlProperty]
  public string ImageUrl { get; set; }

  protected override HtmlTextWriterTag TagKey
  {
    get
    {
      return HtmlTextWriterTag.Table;
    }
  }

  protected override void RenderContents(HtmlTextWriter writer)
  {
    writer.RenderBeginTag(HtmlTextWriterTag.Tr);
    writer.RenderBeginTag(HtmlTextWriterTag.Td);
    writer.AddAttribute(HtmlTextWriterAttribute.Id, TextBoxId);
    writer.AddAttribute(HtmlTextWriterAttribute.Type, "text");
    writer.AddAttribute(HtmlTextWriterAttribute.Value, Text);
    writer.RenderBeginTag(HtmlTextWriterTag.Input);
    writer.RenderEndTag();
```

LISTING 5.18 continued

```
        writer.RenderEndTag();
        writer.RenderBeginTag(HtmlTextWriterTag.Td);
        writer.AddAttribute(HtmlTextWriterAttribute.Id, ImageId);
        writer.AddAttribute(HtmlTextWriterAttribute.Src, ImageUrl);
        writer.RenderBeginTag(HtmlTextWriterTag.Img);
        writer.RenderEndTag();
        writer.RenderEndTag();
        writer.RenderEndTag();
    }

    protected override IEnumerable<ScriptDescriptor>
      GetScriptDescriptors()
    {
      ScriptControlDescriptor descriptor = new
        ScriptControlDescriptor("TextBoxInfoControl.TextBoxInfo",
        this.ClientID);
      descriptor.AddElementProperty("textBoxElement", TextBoxId);
      descriptor.AddElementProperty("imageElement", ImageId);
      descriptor.AddProperty("informationText", InformationText);
      yield return descriptor;
    }

    // Generate the script reference
    protected override IEnumerable<ScriptReference>
      GetScriptReferences()
    {
      yield return new
        ScriptReference("TextBoxInfoControl.TextBoxInfo.js",
        this.GetType().Assembly.FullName);
    }
  }
```

Sys.UI.Control Class

The TextBoxInfo JavaScript class in Listing 5.19 inherits from Sys.UI.
Control to provide the client-side functionality for our server control. The
class is made up of four properties, an event handler, and initialization code
that attaches the image element's click event to the event handler.

The goal in creating the control class should be to provide all the functionality needed to work with the associated HTML elements. In the initialization code of the control class, we are attaching an internal handler to
the click event of the button, which follows a common pattern of associating event handlers during initialization. The get_text method is provided to access the value of the textbox element on the control, providing

a clean way to access the contents of the textbox without directly accessing the element. As you develop your control classes, think of the user interaction on the client and how the control will be used and try to provide all the necessary properties and methods needed to work with the control in JavaScript.

LISTING 5.19 TextBoxInfo Sys.UI.Control-Based Class

```
/// <reference name="MicrosoftAjax.js"/>

Type.registerNamespace("TextBoxInfoControl");

TextBoxInfoControl.TextBoxInfo = function(element) {
  TextBoxInfoControl.TextBoxInfo.initializeBase(this, [element]);
  this._textBoxElement;
  this._imageElement;
  this._informationText;
}

TextBoxInfoControl.TextBoxInfo.prototype = {
  initialize: function() {
    TextBoxInfoControl.TextBoxInfo.callBaseMethod(this, 'initialize');
    $addHandlers(this._imageElement,
      {"click":this._imageElementClickHandler},this);
  },
  get_informationText: function(){
    return this._informationText;
  },
  set_informationText: function(value){
    this._informationText = value;
  },
  get_textBoxElement: function(){
    return this._textBoxElement;
  },
  set_textBoxElement: function(value){
    this._textBoxElement = value;
  },
  get_imageElement: function(){
    return this._imageElement;
  },
  set_imageElement: function(value){
    this._imageElement = value;
  },
  _imageElementClickHandler: function(e){
    alert(this._informationText);
  },
  get_text: function(){
    if(this._textBoxElement === "undefined")
```

LISTING 5.19 continued

```
        return "";
      else
        return this._textBoxElement;
    },
    set_text: function(value){
      if(this._textBoxElement !== "undefined")
        this._textBoxElement = value;
    },
    dispose: function() {
      //Add custom dispose actions here
      TextBoxInfoControl.TextBoxInfo.callBaseMethod(this, 'dispose');
    }
  }
}
TextBoxInfoControl.TextBoxInfo.registerClass('TextBoxInfoControl.TextBoxInfo
', Sys.UI.Control);

if (typeof(Sys) !== 'undefined') Sys.Application.notifyScriptLoaded();
```

Add the Control to a Page

Adding the control to a page is the same as adding any other ASP.NET server control. Your design-time experience will consist of dragging the control onto the designer surface and then adding an ImageUrl entry for the help icon and then adding your custom InformationText value to be displayed to the user. The complete page shows the textbox and help icon (see Figure 5.12). Figure 5.13 shows the simple alert that displays with the information text.

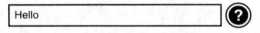

FIGURE 5.12 TextBoxInfo control

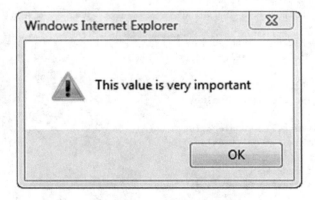

FIGURE 5.13 TextBoxInfo control help alert

Adding Client-Side Functionality to Composite Controls Using the IScriptControl Interface

One more scenario warrants discussion when we talk about adding client-side functionality to a server control: composite controls. These are controls that contain other ASP.NET server controls and build on the containment model to provide a server control. In this section, we cover creating a composite control version of our `TextBoxInfo` class that is developed using ASP.NET server controls rather than HTML elements. To create a control that supports adding server controls, we will use the `System.Web.UI.Web Controls.CompositeControl` class and a base and implement the `IScript Control` interface to provide the client-side functionality hooks needed for us to get the script onto the browser.

> **▪ NOTE** Composite Control Details
>
> There is an assumed level of knowledge of the `CompositeControl` in this section. If it has been a while since you worked with one or if you are new to composite controls, refer to "Developing a Composite Control" at http://msdn2.microsoft.com/en-us/library/aa719968. aspx for more information.

Composite Control Overview

The `CompositeControl` class was introduced in ASP.NET 2.0 and provides functionality that most composite controls will need. The class is designed to contain ASP.NET server controls and uses them to generate HTML content. This control is the base class for many controls in ASP.NET, including the `Wizard`, `Login,` and `LoginStatus` controls that were introduced in ASP.NET 2.0. The `TextBoxInfo ScriptControl` example from earlier in this chapter shows that in the `RenderContents` method we had to code quite a few lines just to render the textbox and image HTML elements. Later in this section, you will see that by basing our server control on the `Composite Control` class we can reduce the code size required to generate a control with similar functionality.

Looking at the class hierarchy in Figure 5.14, it will come as no surprise how familiar this class is to work with. Recall that the `WebControl` class is the one that provided us with all the rendering methods that simplified emitting HTML to the client. The `CompositeControl` class builds on this model by implementing the `INamingContainer` interface that provides a naming container for us to create our child controls in. The naming container is what ensures that the ASP.NET server control we create inside the composite control will have unique IDs throughout the page and will not collide with other controls. The `CompositeControl` class also provides functionality that you need when working with embedded controls, such as ensuring that child controls are created before they are accessed and in binding situations ensuring that all controls have been created before they are bound to a data source. There is more to cover with the `Composite Control` class when we get into the source code for our example, so let's talk about the `IScriptControl` interface quickly before we get into some code.

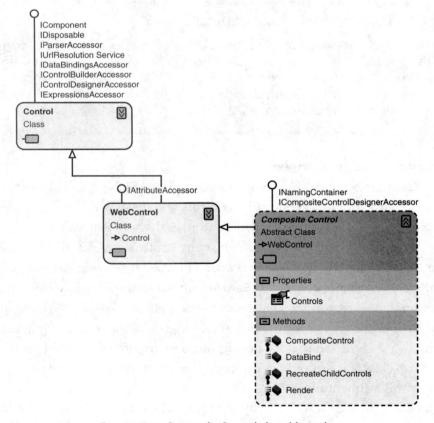

FIGURE 5.14 CompositeControl class hierarchy

Naming Container

In a web application, each page contains a hierarchy of controls that are both visible and nonvisible. The naming container for a given control is the parent control above it in the hierarchy that implements the INaming Container interface. A server control that implements this interface creates a unique namespace for the ID property values of its child server controls. This feature comes in handy when you bind data against some of the list controls, such as the Repeater and DataList controls. In these cases, when multiple entries in the data source create multiple instances of a server control inside these list controls, we need to ensure that each control has a unique ID and won't conflict with another control. This is what the naming container concept brings to the table and why it is so important.

IScriptControl Interface

The GetScriptDescriptors and GetScriptReferences methods on the ScriptControl class were provided by the IScriptControl interface and implemented by the ScriptControl. This pattern is the same when working with the CompositeControl class, but some other functionality that was buried in the internal implementation of the OnPreRender and Render override methods of these classes is not. When working directly with the IScriptControl interface, you need to ensure that the class itself is registered with the ScriptManager and that the script descriptors are extracted from your class and processed property. This requires overriding the default implementation of the OnPreRender and Render methods and provides functionality to properly register the control with the ScriptManager.

Creating the Composite Control

The TextBoxInfo class inherits from CompositeControl and implements the IScriptControl interface, creating a server control that provides the same functionality that we saw in the ScriptControl version earlier in this chapter.

The first thing we look at with this control is how we create the internal server controls and how we ensure they are created before we access them. The CompositeControl class has a virtual method AddChildControls that is responsible for creating all your internal ASP.NET server controls. In our example, see Listing 5.20, we have three internal controls (Table, TextBox, and Image) that will need to be created in this method. The first thing you do when implementing this method is to clear out the internal controls collection to reset the controls in the collection to ensure only the controls you want are created. Next, you create the Table, TextBox, and Image controls, assign them IDs, add them to the internal control collection, and set the internal ChildControlsCreated flag to true to indicate that the controls have been created. At this point, the controls are created and are ready to be accessed. If you take a look at the Text and ImageUrl properties, you will notice that their implementation calls the EnsureChildControls method before any of the controls they work with are accessed. This is a pattern you must follow when working inside a CompositeControl-based class to ensure that your controls are created before you access them. Now let's move to the next thing on our list, rendering of the contents.

LISTING 5.20 Creating Internal Controls

```
public class TextBoxInfo : CompositeControl, IScriptControl
{
  ScriptManager scriptManager;
  TextBox dataEntryTextBox;
  Image informationImageButton;
  Table pageLayoutTable;

  public TextBoxInfo()
  {
  }

  public string Text
  {
    get { EnsureChildControls(); return dataEntryTextBox.Text; }
    set { EnsureChildControls(); dataEntryTextBox.Text = value; }
  }

  public string ImageUrl
  {
    get { EnsureChildControls();
          return informationImageButton.ImageUrl;   }
    set { EnsureChildControls(); informationImageButton.ImageUrl =
      value; }
  }
```

```
    public string InformationText { get; set; }

    protected override HtmlTextWriterTag TagKey
    {
      get
      {
        return HtmlTextWriterTag.Div;
      }
    }

    protected override void CreateChildControls()
    {
      Controls.Clear();

      pageLayoutTable = new Table();
      pageLayoutTable.ID = "pageLayoutTable";
      Controls.Add(pageLayoutTable);

      dataEntryTextBox = new TextBox();
      dataEntryTextBox.ID = "DataEntryTextBox";
      Controls.Add(dataEntryTextBox);

      informationImageButton = new Image();
      informationImageButton.ID = "HelpIconImageButton";
      Controls.Add(informationImageButton);

      ChildControlsCreated = true;
    }
    ...
}
```

In the WebControl-based version of this control, we added code to the RenderContents method to create the HTML content that would be sent to the browser. In the case of our CompositeControl-based class, see Listing 5.21, we do the same thing but render our Table, TextBox, and Image controls a little differently. When working the ASP.NET server controls, rendering is as simple as calling the RenderControl method on the control itself and passing the HtmlTextWriter as a parameter. This delegates the responsibility of adding the control to the output stream to the control, simplifying the task of generating that HTML content. In our example, we build up the table that will contain the textbox and image controls, assign the controls to the controls collection of the table, and then render the table with all its contents.

LISTING 5.21 Internal Control Rendering

```
public class TextBoxInfo : CompositeControl, IScriptControl
{
  ...
  protected override void RenderContents(HtmlTextWriter writer)
  {
    TableRow row = new TableRow();
    TableCell textBoxCell = new TableCell();
    textBoxCell.Controls.Add(dataEntryTextBox);
    TableCell informationImageCell = new TableCell();
    informationImageCell.Controls.Add(informationImageButton);
    row.Cells.Add(textBoxCell);
    row.Cells.Add(informationImageCell);
    pageLayoutTable.Rows.Add(row);
    pageLayoutTable.RenderControl(writer);
  }
  ...
}
```

When we discussed the IScriptControl interface earlier, we covered the need to override the OnPreRender and Render methods to ensure our control is properly registered with the ScriptManager and our ScriptControl Descriptor entries are included in the script-generation process. If we take a look at the OnPreRender method, see Listing 5.22, we are registering the control with the ScriptManager using the RenderScriptControl generic method of the ScriptManager. This method takes your control as the generic type with a reference to your control as a parameter. This call registers the control with the ScriptManager so that the ScriptManager can call back into our control and get the ScriptDescriptors and ScriptReferences. It is the actual call to the RegisterScriptDescriptors method on the Script Manager in the Render method that triggers the call to GetScript Descriptors, enabling the JavaScript generation to be performed.

LISTING 5.22 IScriptControl Support

```
public class TextBoxInfo : CompositeControl, IScriptControl
{
  ...

  #region IScriptControl CompositeControl Overrides

  protected override void OnPreRender(EventArgs e)
  {
    if (!DesignMode)
```

```csharp
    {
      scriptManager = ScriptManager.GetCurrent(Page);

      if (scriptManager == null)
        throw new HttpException("ScriptManager must be on the page for
          the TextBoxInfo control to work properly");

        scriptManager.RegisterScriptControl<TextBoxInfo>(this);
    }

    base.OnPreRender(e);
  }

  protected override void Render(HtmlTextWriter writer)
  {
    if (!base.DesignMode)
      scriptManager.RegisterScriptDescriptors(this);

    base.Render(writer);
  }

  #endregion


  #region IScriptControl Members

  IEnumerable<ScriptDescriptor> IScriptControl.GetScriptDescriptors()
  {
    ScriptControlDescriptor descriptor = new
      ScriptControlDescriptor("TextBoxInfoCompositeControl.TextBoxInfo",
      this.ClientID);
    descriptor.AddElementProperty("textBoxElement",
      dataEntryTextBox.ClientID);
    descriptor.AddElementProperty("imageElement",
      informationImageButton.ClientID);
    descriptor.AddProperty("informationText", InformationText);
    yield return descriptor;
  }

  IEnumerable<ScriptReference> IScriptControl.GetScriptReferences()
  {
    yield return new ScriptReference(
      "TextBoxInfoCompositeControl.TextBoxInfo.js",
      this.GetType().Assembly.FullName);
  }

  #endregion
}
```

We leave out the JavaScript class because it so similar to the Script Control counterpart, using the same properties and event handler. If we reflect back on this particular control, we can see that the use of internal ASP.NET server controls can make things easier and enables you to build up some really complex controls that can provide a rich client-side experience.

SUMMARY

In this chapter, we covered three ways to add client-side functionality to server controls. The ExtenderControl approach was the most evasive of all by providing a way to alter the client behavior of a server control without changing its internal workings. The second approach we looked at builds on the longstanding WebControl approach, which enables you to build complex server controls using an HTML generation pattern that has been around for a while combined with new functionality provided by the ASP.NET AJAX framework. Finally, we looked an approach that builds on the ASP.NET server model that promotes encapsulation of server controls while providing client functionality to the control as a whole.

■ 6 ■
ASP.NET AJAX Localization

I N THE PREVIOUS CHAPTERS, we covered how to build a server control that corresponds to a client control. In this coverage, we also discussed how to embed JavaScript files in our server control using web resources so that our control's functionality was fully encapsulated.

In this chapter, we cover ASP.NET AJAX's localization capabilities. Because localization in ASP.NET AJAX works in coordination with localization in ASP.NET, we start with localization in ASP.NET and work our way into localization in ASP.NET AJAX.

We start with JavaScript's limited localization capabilities, and then we cover ASP.NET AJAX's new JavaScript features that fill the holes left by JavaScript.

From there, we walk through an example where we utilize ASP.NET AJAX's localization capabilities by developing a new ASP.NET AJAX control, the CurrencyTextBox. Finally, we update the page we localized in the first part of the chapter to include our new CurrencyTextBox control, and we show how we can add client localizable features at the page level.

Localization in ASP.NET

So what is localization? Localization is the process of making an application usable by different cultures. In .NET, a culture is a defined by the combination of a language and country or region. For instance, the en-US culture represents the English language and United States. Another example is the es-MX culture, which represents the Spanish language and Mexico.

> **■ TIP** Cultures
>
> In this chapter, when we refer to a specific culture, we list the language first and then the country or region in parentheses. For instance, es-MX is equivalent to Spanish (Mexico).

There are also noncountry or region-specific cultures called neutral cultures. Examples of these are en for English, it for Italian, and fr for French.

In .NET, each culture has a language associated to it; a set of formatting rules for common things such as numbers, currencies, and dates; and rules on how things are sorted.

When we localize an application, we want to apply a culture to it. We want the dates formatted properly, currencies to use the proper symbol and number formatting, and strings to be presented in the correct language. We accomplish this by following the three general steps of internationalization.

1. Determining what needs to be localized
2. Getting your application to run under a particular culture
3. Localizing displayed values

Let's walk through these steps.

> **■ NOTE** Internationalization Compared with Localization
>
> There is some debate on what internationalization is and what localization is. In our opinion, internationalization is the process of altering your application to accept a culture. This means removing hard-coded strings, telling dates and numbers to format accordingly, and also setting your application up to select a particular culture to run under.
>
> In contrast, localization is a particular culture's translated strings and formatted dates and numbers. You only internationalize an application once, but you localize many times.

Determining What Needs to Be Localized

Determining what needs to be localized is a straightforward process. With regard to a web page, anything that you would want to change when the culture changes needs to be localizable. Normally, this includes currencies, dates and times, numbers, strings, and graphics, but can also include other things such as what files are available to download and the overall layout of the page.

Let's take a look at an example web page and see what on it needs to be localized. Figure 6.1 shows our example web page, Transactions.aspx, with the items needing to be localized circled.

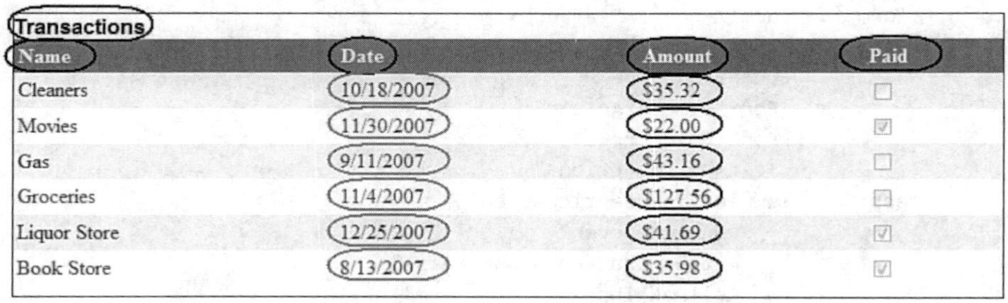

FIGURE 6.1 The Transactions page with what needs to be localized circled

In our Transactions page, we've circled the table's title; the table's headers: Name, Date, Amount, and Paid; and the date and dollar amounts. That covers almost the entire page!

> ■ **NOTE** Transaction Names
>
> We're not going to localize the transaction's name because most likely the transaction name is data driven, and if we wanted to localize the name, the translated name would come from a data source containing all the possible values.

Listing 6.1 shows Transactions.aspx's markup.

LISTING 6.1 Transactions.aspx Markup

```
<%@ Page Language="C#"
        AutoEventWireup="true"
        CodeBehind="Transactions.aspx.cs"
        Inherits="Localization.Transactions" %>


<html>
<head id="Head1" runat="server">
    <title>Transactions</title>
</head>
<body>
    <form id="form1" runat="server">
    <asp:Label ID="TransactionGridLabel"
               runat="server"
               Font-Names="Arial"
               Font-Bold="true"
               Text="Transactions" />
    <asp:GridView ID="TransactionsView"
                  runat="server"
                  AutoGenerateColumns="False"
                  CellPadding="4"
                  ForeColor="#333333"
                  GridLines="None"
                  Width="748px"
                  DataSourceID="TransactionDataSource">
        <Columns>
            <asp:BoundField
              HeaderText="Name"
              DataField="Name" />
            <asp:BoundField
              HeaderText="Date"
              DataField="Date"
              DataFormatString="{0:d}" />
            <asp:BoundField
              HeaderText="Amount"
              DataField="Amount"
              DataFormatString="{0:c}" />
            <asp:CheckBoxField
              DataField="Paid"
              HeaderText="Paid"
              ReadOnly="True" />
        </Columns>
    </asp:GridView>
    <asp:ObjectDataSource
      ID="TransactionDataSource"
      runat="server"
```

```
          SelectMethod="GetTransactions"
          TypeName="Localization.Transaction" />
      </form>
  </body>
</html>
```

Because we're going to be modifying this code to localize it, let's take a closer look at the markup.

After the normal page and form declarations, the first thing we do is add a label to the page and set its text to "Transactions", as shown in Listing 6.2.

LISTING 6.2 Transaction Label

```
<asp:Label
  ID="TransactionGridLabel"
  runat="server"
  Font-Names="Arial"
  Font-Bold="true"
  Text="Transactions" />
```

Next, we declare the `GridView` control, shown in Listing 6.3, which will display the table of transactions.

LISTING 6.3 Transactions GridView

```
<asp:GridView ID="TransactionsView"
              runat="server"
              AutoGenerateColumns="False"
              CellPadding="4"
              ForeColor="#333333"
              GridLines="None"
              Width="748px"
              DataSourceID="TransactionDataSource">
    <Columns>
      <asp:BoundField
        HeaderText="Name"
        DataField="Name" />
      <asp:BoundField
        HeaderText="Date"
        DataField="Date"
        DataFormatString="{0:d}" />
      <asp:BoundField
        HeaderText="Amount"
        DataField="Amount"
        DataFormatString="{0:c}" />
      <asp:CheckBoxField
```

LISTING 6.3 continued

```
            DataField="Paid"
            HeaderText="Paid"
            ReadOnly="True" />
    </Columns>
  </asp:GridView>
```

In the GridView's declaration, we declare four columns: Name, Date, Amount, and Paid. The columns are all bound to data contained in the data source identified by the data source id TransactionDataSource. Important to recognize is that we apply a DataFormatString to the Date and Amount columns so that the information is formatted to display a short date and a currency, respectively.

Finally, we define our ObjectDataSource named TransactionData Source that will provide the grid with its data, as shown in Listing 6.4.

LISTING 6.4 Transactions ObjectDataSource

```
<asp:ObjectDataSource
  ID="TransactionDataSource"
  runat="server"
  SelectMethod="GetTransactions"
  TypeName="Localization.Transaction" />
```

The TransactionDataSource uses the GetTransactions method that is available on the Localization.Transaction type. Listing 6.5 shows the Localization.Transaction type and its static GetTransactions method.

LISTING 6.5 Transaction Class

```
using System;
using System.Collections.Generic;

namespace Localization
{
  public class Transaction
  {
    public string Name { get; set; }
    public DateTime Date { get; set; }
    public decimal Amount { get; set; }
    public bool Paid { get; set; }

    public static List<Transaction> GetTransactions()
    {
      List<Transaction> transactions = new List<Transaction>{
```

```
            new Transaction
              { Name = "Cleaners",
                Amount = 35.32M,
                Date = new DateTime(2007, 10, 18),
                Paid = false },
            new Transaction
              { Name = "Movies",
                Amount = 22.00M,
                Date = new DateTime(2007, 11, 30),
                Paid = true },
            new Transaction
              { Name = "Gas",
                Amount = 43.16M,
                Date = new DateTime(2007, 9, 11),
                Paid = false },
            new Transaction
              { Name = "Groceries",
                Amount = 127.56M,
                Date = new DateTime(2007, 11, 04),
                Paid = false },
            new Transaction
              { Name = "Liquor Store",
                Amount = 41.69M,
                Date = new DateTime(2007, 12, 25),
                Paid = true },
            new Transaction
              { Name = "Book Store",
                Amount = 35.98M,
                Date = new DateTime(2007, 8, 13),
                Paid = true }
        };
        return transactions;
    }
}
```

As you can see from the listing, a `Transaction` contains four properties—`Name`, `Amount`, `Date`, and `Paid`—and the `GetTransactions` method returns six hard-coded transactions.

Now that we've shown the Transactions page markup and shown what we're going to localize, let's go over how to get your application to run under different cultures.

Running under a Particular Culture

So, in ASP.NET terms, what does it mean to run under a particular culture? It means that the thread that the current request is running on has its

CurrentCulture/CurrentUICulture properties assigned to the System. Globalization.CultureInfo instance that corresponds to a particular culture. Setting these values can occur in one of two ways: implicitly or explicitly.

Implicitly Setting the Current Culture

Implicitly setting the current culture means that ASP.NET uses a value passed in by the browser to automatically set the current culture. The browser passes in the languages it supports using the Accept-Language header, as shown in Figure 6.2.

FIGURE 6.2 Fiddler view of a request's Accept-Language header

In a default browser installation, the Accept-Language header value is set based on the installation language you choose or the language your operating system is running under. However, you also have the option of modifying it manually by altering the language preference within the browser. Altering the language preference within the browser will change which values are passed in with the Accept-Language header. Figure 6.3 shows the Accept-Language header for our request after we altered our browser's language setting to use English (Other Culture) [en-OC], a fictitious culture we're using as an example, English (Great Britain) [en-GB], and Arabic (Oman) [ar-OM].

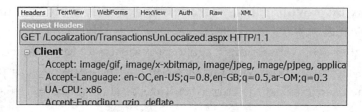

FIGURE 6.3 Fiddler's view of a request's Accept-Language header with multiple languages specified

When we provide multiple languages in the `Accept-Language` header, the browser sends along a quality value attached to each language. The quality values, indicated by the q= that proceeds each culture, can range from the high of 1 to the low of 0. The quality value tells the request receiver, in this case ASP.NET, which language to try first. In our example, the highest quality value is 1, which is associated to the en-OC culture (a blank quality value indicates 1), so this is the culture that ASP.NET will try first. If ASP.NET fails to create a `CultureInfo` object based on that value because it either isn't supported, which is the case because en-OC is a fictitious culture, or for some other reason, it moves on to the next culture based on the quality value. In our case, this is en-US, which has the quality value .8. If that culture fails, too, ASP.NET tries en-GB and then ar-OM. If all cultures fail, ASP.NET defaults to the server's culture.

> **■ NOTE   Setting the Language Preference**
>
> Setting the browser's language preference is different with each browser, but in most of them the preference is available under an options screen.

Explicitly Setting the Current Culture

In most applications, we want to provide a way for the user to override the implicit culture defined by the user's browser language preference. We do this because our users may want to run our application under a different culture, but not have that culture applied to every website they visit, which is what would happen if they alter their browser's settings. We can provide this ability by providing a way for users to explicitly set the culture of just our application.

Let's alter our Transactions page to provide a way to set the culture the request is running under. We start by adding a drop-down to our page that allows the user to select the current culture, as shown in Figure 6.4.

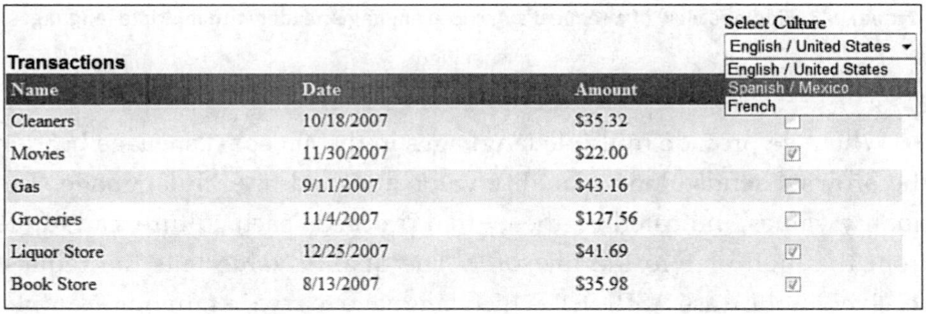

FIGURE 6.4 Transactions page with culture selector

Whereas our culture drop-down displays friendly values, the values corresponding to each drop-down item are the actual culture codes. The markup that specifies the drop-down's list items is displayed in Listing 6.6.

LISTING 6.6 Select Culture Drop-Down

```
...
<form id="form1" runat="server">
  <div id="CultureSelector"
      style="position: absolute; left: 610px;">
    <asp:Label
      ID="SelectCultureLabel"
      runat="server"
      Text="Select Culture" />
    <br />
    <asp:DropDownList
      ID="CultureSelectorDropDown"
      runat="server"
      AutoPostBack="True">
        <asp:ListItem
          Text="English / United States"
          Value="en-us" />
        <asp:ListItem
          Text="Spanish / Mexico"
          Value="es-mx" />
```

```
      <asp:ListItem
        Text="French"
        Value="fr" />
    </asp:DropDownList>
  </div>
  <div id="TransactionPanel"
      style="position: absolute; top: 50px;">
  …
```

Now that we have our drop-down on the page, we need to change the thread's current culture based on the drop-down's selected value. In our example, we do this by overriding the page's `InitializeCulture` method, as shown in Listing 6.7.

LISTING 6.7 InitializeCulture Method Override

```
protected override void InitializeCulture()
{
  base.InitializeCulture();
  if (Request.Form["CultureSelectorDropDown"] != null)
  {
    CultureInfo newCulture =
    CultureInfo.CreateSpecificCulture(
      Request.Form["CultureSelectorDropDown"]
    );

    // enables different culture info
    //(date formats, currency formats)
    Thread.CurrentThread.CurrentCulture = newCulture;

    // enables different resource files
    // (i.e. resources.es-mx.resx)
    Thread.CurrentThread.CurrentUICulture = newCulture;
  }
}
```

In this `InitializeCulture` override, we pull the value posted back by the drop-down out of the request's form collection and create a new `CultureInfo` object based on the value. We then take our new `CultureInfo` object and assign it to the current thread's `CurrentCulture` and `Current UICulture` properties, effectively changing the culture the thread is running on.

> **NOTE**   CurrentCulture and CurrentUICulture
>
> The reasons and history for having both `CurrentCulture` and `Current UICulture` are beyond the scope of this book. Leaving their history for another book, we will say, however, that `CurrentCulture` provides culture-specific formatting for dates and numbers, and `CurrentUI Culture` provides the ability for the `ResourceManager` to access resources related to a particular culture. Having two different properties gives us the option of using resources from one culture and formatting dates and numbers using a different one. An English (U.S.) speaking user running an application that needs to display a cost in euros is a common application of assigning different `CultureInfo` objects to the `CurrentUICulture` and `CurrentCulture` properties.

InitializeCulture

There are a couple points worth noting regarding the `InitializeCulture` method.

First, it executes early in the page's lifecycle. It's called early in the lifecycle so that the correct culture can be set before any controls are created in case a control needs to be localized. Because it's called before any controls are created, we can't access `CultureSelectorDropDown`'s current value because the control doesn't exist yet. Because the control doesn't exist, we can only access the value posted back by our drop-down by pulling it out of the form's parameter collection.

Second, overriding the page's `InitializeCulture` method is only one way of setting the thread's current culture. It would be tedious to do this on every page. If your application consistently uses a few master pages, maybe you would put it into the master page's code, but this could grow out of hand. A more scalable solution is to use an `HttpModule`'s `PreRequest HandlerExecute` event or an application's `global.asax Application_ BeginRequest` method. If you set the culture in either of those places, you have to code it only once.

Now that we've shown how to get our application to run under different cultures, let's go back and localize our Transactions page.

Localizing Displayed Values

As Figure 6.1 showed, we need to localize the table title, its column headers, its date column values, and its amount column values. We've also added a way to change the culture using a drop-down, so we add to our localization list the drop-down title and its display values.

To localize these parts of our page, we use two difference mechanisms. First, we use .NET's built-in formatting capabilities to automatically format the date and amount values. Second, we use local resources to translate the strings to the correct language.

Date and Amount

With the date and amount values, we don't have to do anything for our displayed values to be localized other than set the `CurrentCulture` property, as we did in Listing 6.7. Because we're using a `DataFormatString` for each column, our values will automatically be localized for us by .NET's built-in formatting capabilities. We get this for free because by default .NET applies the current culture to all its string formatting expressions. When our `GridView` is data bound, the underlying code that .NET automatically executes to create the date values looks something like what is displayed in Listing 6.8.

LISTING 6.8 Example Code for Applying a DataFormatString to a BoundField

```
DateTime date1 = new DateTime(2007, 10, 18);
string dateString1 = string.Format("{0:d}", date1);
```

When `string.Format` executes, it takes into account the current culture and automatically applies formatting rules based on the formatting expression. For instance, Listing 6.3 uses the `"{0:d}"` format expression. In using this expression, .NET automatically applies the formatting rule stored in `Thread.CurrentThread.CurrentCulture.DateTimeFormat.ShortDate Pattern` to the `DateTime` object `date1`, thus creating the string `10/18/2007`.

> ■ **NOTE** Formatting the Amount Field
>
> The same type of formatting occurs for the amount field except that the formatting rule is stored in `Thread.CurrentThread.CurrentCulture.NumberFormat`.

String Display

To localize our Transactions page's strings, we're going to provide the strings that .NET should use in place of our hard-coded values and then have .NET automatically apply those strings for us whenever we switch cultures. We do this using ASP.NET's local resource feature.

Local Resources

We apply the local resource feature through two tasks:

1. Create individual local resource files for our page and each culture.

2. Update our page markup to automatically use the resources.

.NET comes with a handy tool to apply the local resource feature, so we're going to use it and then talk about what it did.

To access the tool, we first need to open our `Transactions.aspx` page in either markup or design mode. Once the page is open, we can access the Generate Local Resource tool from Visual Studio's Tool menu, as shown in Figure 6.5.

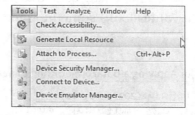

FIGURE 6.5 Accessing Visual Studio 2008's Generate Local Resource tool

After we select the Generate Local Resource tool, Visual Studio inspects our page for us and does two things. First, it generates a default local resources file, named Transactions.aspx.resx, and places it in the special `App_LocalResources` folder, as shown in Figure 6.6. Second, it adds `meta:resourcekey` attributes to all the page controls. Listing 6.9 shows the modified markup with the new `meta:resourcekey` tags highlighted.

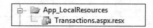

FIGURE 6.6 Newly Created Transactions.aspx.resx file in App_LocalResources

LISTING 6.9 meta:resourcekey Tags

```
<%@ Page Language="C#"
         AutoEventWireup="true"
         CodeBehind="Transactions.aspx.cs"
         Inherits="Localization.Transactions"
         meta:resourcekey="PageResource1" %>

<html>
<head id="Head1" runat="server">
  <title>Transactions</title>
</head>
<body>
  <form id="form1" runat="server">
  <div id="CultureSelector"
    style="position: absolute; left: 610px;">
      <asp:Label
        ID="SelectCultureLabel"
        runat="server"
        Text="Select Culture"
        meta:resourcekey="SelectCultureLabelResource" />
      <br />
      <asp:DropDownList
        ID="CultureSelectorDropDown"
        runat="server"
        AutoPostBack="True"
        meta:resourcekey="CultureSelectorDropDownResource1">
          <asp:ListItem
            Text="English / United States"
            Value="en-us"
            meta:resourcekey="ListItemResource1" />
          <asp:ListItem
            Text="Spanish / Mexico"
            Value="es-mx"
            meta:resourcekey="ListItemResource2" />
          <asp:ListItem
            Text="French"
            Value="fr"
            meta:resourcekey="ListItemResource3" />
      </asp:DropDownList>
  </div>
  <div
    id="TransactionPanel"
    style="position: absolute; top: 50px;">
```

LISTING 6.9 continued

```
<asp:Label
  ID="TransactionGridLabel"
  runat="server"
  Font-Names="Arial"
  Font-Bold="true"
  meta:resourcekey="TransactionGridLabelResource" />
<asp:GridView ID="TransactionsView"
              runat="server"
              AutoGenerateColumns="False"
              CellPadding="4"
              ForeColor="#333333"
              GridLines="None"
              Width="748px"
              DataSourceID="TransactionDataSource"
              meta:resourcekey="TransactionsViewResource1">
  <Columns>
    <asp:BoundField
      HeaderText="Name"
      DataField="Name"
      meta:resourcekey="BoundFieldResource1" />
    <asp:BoundField
      HeaderText="Date"
      DataField="Date"
      DataFormatString="{0:d}"
      meta:resourcekey="BoundFieldResource2" />
    <asp:BoundField
      HeaderText="Amount"
      DataField="Amount"
      DataFormatString="{0:c}"
      meta:resourcekey="BoundFieldResource3" />
    <asp:CheckBoxField
      DataField="Paid"
      HeaderText="Paid"
      ReadOnly="True"
      meta:resourcekey="CheckBoxFieldResource1" />
  </Columns>
</asp:GridView>
</div>
<asp:ObjectDataSource ID="TransactionDataSource"
                      runat="server"
                      SelectMethod="GetTransactions"
                      TypeName="Localization.Transaction" />
</form>
</body>
</html>
```

> **▪ NOTE   Localizing the Culture Selector Drop-Down**
>
> We're going to localize the Culture Selector drop-down we added in the previous section and the transaction grid we started out with initially. We'll localize its header and its list items.

Our Default Resource File

Opening up our new Transactions.aspx.resx resource file, shown in Figure 6.7, we see that Visual Studio has added a series of string resources and supplied values for some of them. What Visual Studio has done is go through each of the controls that are on our Transactions page and created a resource for all the localizable properties of that control. It has also automatically assigned the current value of the localizable property to the resource.

> **▪ NOTE   Localizable Properties**
>
> A property on a control is localizable if it is marked with the Localize attribute.

We can see this pattern more clearly by taking a closer look at the first three resources on our page, shown in Figure 6.7. In Figure 6.8, we see that each of the resource names begins with BoundFieldResource1, and then there is a dot followed by another string. Those appended strings that follow the dot operator are the localizable properties of the control to which BoundFieldResource1 is mapped.

In Figure 6.8, we see that the BoundFieldResource1.HeaderText resource has the value of Name. Name was automatically assigned to the resource because it was the current value of the mapped control's Header Text property.

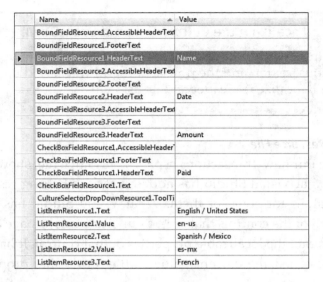

Name	Value
BoundFieldResource1.AccessibleHeaderText	
BoundFieldResource1.FooterText	
BoundFieldResource1.HeaderText	Name
BoundFieldResource2.AccessibleHeaderText	
BoundFieldResource2.FooterText	
BoundFieldResource2.HeaderText	Date
BoundFieldResource3.AccessibleHeaderText	
BoundFieldResource3.FooterText	
BoundFieldResource3.HeaderText	Amount
CheckBoxFieldResource1.AccessibleHeaderT	
CheckBoxFieldResource1.FooterText	
CheckBoxFieldResource1.HeaderText	Paid
CheckBoxFieldResource1.Text	
CultureSelectorDropDownResource1.ToolTi	
ListItemResource1.Text	English / United States
ListItemResource1.Value	en-us
ListItemResource2.Text	Spanish / Mexico
ListItemResource2.Value	es-mx
ListItemResource3.Text	French

FIGURE 6.7 Resources in Transactions.aspx.resx

BoundFieldResource1.AccessibleHeaderText	
BoundFieldResource1.FooterText	
BoundFieldResource1.HeaderText	Name

FIGURE 6.8 BoundFieldResource1 in Transactions.aspx.resx

The meta:resourcekey Tags

So, to which control is `BoundFieldResource1` mapped? It's mapped to the first `BoundField` in our `TransactionsView` `GridView` control. We know it's mapped to this control because the `BoundField` specifies the `meta:resourcekey="BoundFieldResource1"` in its markup. This `meta:resourcekey` attribute is what links the control to the resources in the local resource file.

Adding the `meta:resourcekey` to our `BoundField` is all we need to do for the `BoundFieldResource1` resources to be applied to our `BoundField`. Each of the individual `BoundFieldResource1` resources: `AccessibleHeaderText`, `FooterText`, and `HeaderText` will automatically be applied to our `Bound Field`.

Now, when we execute our page in the browser, the default resource file will automatically be applied to the page. The initial output looks exactly the same as it did in Figure 6.4 because our resource file contains the same values as the control's hard-coded values, but in the background .NET is using our Transactions.aspx.resx file to set the associated properties on our page's controls.

We can see that .NET is using the Transactions.aspx.resx file to set the associated properties by either removing the hard-coded value of one of our properties or changing the value of one of our resources. Listing 6.10 shows the `GridView`'s first `BoundField` without a `HeaderText` property specified, and Figure 6.9 shows the output of running the page. Of course, the page looks exactly the same as it did before.

LISTING 6.10 BoundField Using meta:resourcekey and No HeaderText

```
<asp:BoundField
  DataField="Name"
  meta:resourcekey="BoundFieldResource1" />
```

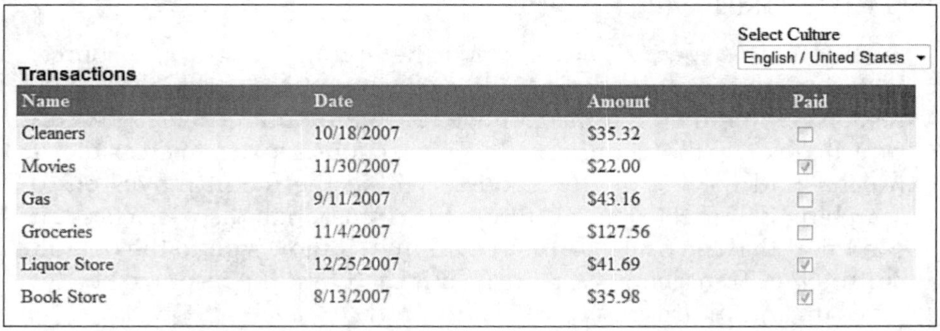

Transactions			Select Culture
			English / United States ▾
Name	**Date**	**Amount**	**Paid**
Cleaners	10/18/2007	$35.32	☐
Movies	11/30/2007	$22.00	☑
Gas	9/11/2007	$43.16	☐
Groceries	11/4/2007	$127.56	☐
Liquor Store	12/25/2007	$41.69	☑
Book Store	8/13/2007	$35.98	☑

FIGURE 6.9 Transactions page using Transactions.aspx.resx

Culture-Specific Resource Files

At this point, we've created the default local resource file for our Transactions page, but we still need to create our culture-specific resource files.

We start this process by copying our default resource file twice so that we have three copies of it. We then need to rename the copies to Transactions.aspx.fr.resx and Transactions.aspx.es-mx.resx. Figure 6.10 shows our solution explorer with the three local resource files created.

FIGURE 6.10 The three local resource files

As the specific filenames might suggest, .NET determines which local resource file to use through the resource file's name. The names follow a specific pattern:

`PageName.culture.resx`

In creating local resource files for our Transactions page, we use the Transactions.aspx as the *PageName,* and then replace the *culture* with the cultures we're supporting: es-MX and fr to end up with local resource files that support the Transactions page and the es-MX and fr cultures.

> **■ NOTE**   Resolving Resources
>
> .NET follows a specific pattern when attempting to resolve a resource. It starts with the most specific culture file it can find and looks for the resource value there. In the case we're running under the es-MX culture, it looks for the resource in the Transactions.aspx.es-mx.resx file. If it can't find the file or the resource within the file, it moves on to searching within the neutral culture file, Transactions.aspx.es.resx. If it can't find that file or the resource within it, it moves on to the default culture file, Transactions.aspx.resx. If it can't find the resource here, it gives up and returns null.

> **■ NOTE**   Missing en-US Local Resource File
>
> You might have noticed that we do not have a file named Transactions.aspx.en-us.resx for the English (United States) culture. We don't need to create this file because our default resource file is already translated to English, so we can just have .NET use that file for the en-US culture.

Now that we have our two new resource files the last step is to replace the English versions of the strings with their translated versions. Figure 6.11 and Figure 6.12 show the Spanish (Mexico) and French local resource files, respectively, after the English strings have been translated. (We've also removed the blank values.)

Name	Value
BoundFieldResource1.HeaderText	Nombre
BoundFieldResource2.HeaderText	Fecha
BoundFieldResource3.HeaderText	Cantidad
CheckBoxFieldResource1.HeaderText	Pagado
CurrencyRangeLabelResource1.Text	Filtro De la Cantidad
DateRangeLabelResource1.Text	Filtro De la Fecha
FilterButtonResource1.Text	Transacciones Del Filtro
FilterLabelResource1.Text	Filtros De la Transacción
ListItemResource1.Text	Inglés/Estados Unidos
ListItemResource1.Value	en-us
ListItemResource2.Text	Español/México
ListItemResource2.Value	es-mx
ListItemResource3.Text	Francés
ListItemResource3.Value	fr
PageResource1.Title	Transacciones
SelectCultureLabelResource.Text	Seleccione La Cultura
TransactionGridLabelResource.Text	Transacciones

FIGURE 6.11 The Spanish (Mexico) local resource file

Name	Value
BoundFieldResource1.HeaderText	Nom
BoundFieldResource2.HeaderText	Date
BoundFieldResource3.HeaderText	Quantité
CheckBoxFieldResource1.HeaderText	Payé
CurrencyRangeLabelResource1.Text	Filtre De Quantité
DateRangeLabelResource1.Text	Filtre De Date
FilterButtonResource1.Text	Transactions De Filtre
FilterLabelResource1.Text	Filtres De Transaction
ListItemResource1.Text	L'Anglais/Etats-Unis
ListItemResource1.Value	en-us
ListItemResource2.Text	Espagnol/Mexique
ListItemResource2.Value	es-mx
ListItemResource3.Text	Français
ListItemResource3.Value	fr
PageResource1.Title	Transactions
SelectCultureLabelResource.Text	Choisissez La Culture
TransactionGridLabelResource.Text	Transactions

FIGURE 6.12 The French local resource file

With the completion of our local resource files, our Transactions page is fully localized. Figure 6.13 and Figure 6.14 show what the Transactions page looks like after the current culture has been changed to Spanish (Mexico) and French, respectively.

		Seleccione La Cultura	
		Español/México ▾	
Transacciones			
Nombre	Fecha	Cantidad	Pagado
Cleaners	18/10/2007	$35.32	☐
Movies	30/11/2007	$22.00	☑
Gas	11/09/2007	$43.16	☐
Groceries	04/11/2007	$127.56	☐
Liquor Store	25/12/2007	$41.69	☑
Book Store	13/08/2007	$35.98	☑

FIGURE 6.13 The Transactions page under the Spanish (Mexico) culture

		Choisissez La Culture	
		Français ▾	
Transactions			
Nom	Date	Quantité	Payé
Cleaners	18/10/2007	35,32 €	☐
Movies	30/11/2007	22,00 €	☑
Gas	11/09/2007	43,16 €	☐
Groceries	04/11/2007	127,56 €	☐
Liquor Store	25/12/2007	41,69 €	☑
Book Store	13/08/2007	35,98 €	☑

FIGURE 6.14 The Transactions page under the French culture

A Few Final Words about Resources

We've only scratched the surface of what resource files can do for you. They can store not just strings but also files, audio clips, icons, images, and other items. Almost anything that should change based on the currently running culture can be stored in a resource file and automatically applied.

Besides the local resource feature that we walked through in localizing our Transactions page, .NET provides another type of resource file called global resources. These files aren't tied to a specific page, but float in the application's global space, available for any page or control to use them.

Finally, the resource features provided by default in ASP.NET are an implementation of the resource provider pattern. .NET supplies a set of interfaces that you can implement to provide your own resource management infrastructure. A common use of this pattern is to pull resources from the database rather than physical files. After all, if you're supporting 30 cultures, managing local resource files for each page and user control can be cumbersome.

Localization in ASP.NET AJAX

Now that we've walked through localization in ASP.NET, we're going to walk through the new localization capabilities ASP.NET AJAX provides.

The localization capabilities that ASP.NET AJAX provides all relate to the client, so all the new localization code we will be writing is going to be in JavaScript. However, the localization features completely rely on ASP.NET to work properly, so this isn't one of the client features that although contained within the Microsoft AJAX Library can work without the server counterpart.

The new localization features provided by ASP.NET AJAX are similar to the features provided by ASP.NET and revolve around dates, numbers, and strings.

Before we begin covering the new localization capabilities provided by ASP.NET AJAX, let's walk through the existing localization capabilities of normal JavaScript and point out some of its shortcomings.

JavaScript Localization Capabilities

JavaScript is not a culture-aware programming language. It almost never alters its behavior based on the operating system language or the browser's assigned languages. Furthermore, there isn't a consistent way to programmatically query the JavaScript runtime for any sort of culture information. The built-in `navigator` object provides some language information, but the availability and values of the language properties— `language`, `browser Language`, and `userLanguage`—are not uniform across browsers, so they can't be used reliably.

Not taking the browser's language or operating system's current culture into account causes problems when working with numbers and dates. These problems arise because different cultures have different ways of writing numbers and dates, and JavaScript just doesn't have the capabilities of understanding or outputting different formats.

> **■ NOTE**   English Formatting
>
> Although JavaScript understands some basic English formatting, it really doesn't even have the capabilities of understanding English-formatted numbers and dates consistently.

Numbers

The problem with numbers in JavaScript is that different cultures use different values for their decimal and number-group separators. For instance, in the French culture, the number six and thirty-six one-hundredths is written as 6,36 because they use a comma as the decimal separator. The same number written in English is 6.36. If we want to code a page to understand 6,36 as six and thirty-six one-hundredths, we have to write special parsing code to initially treat it as a string and then convert it into a number. However, 6.36 is automatically recognized as six and thirty-six one-hundredths because JavaScript understands that the decimal point is the decimal number separator.

A similar problem occurs with the number-group separator. In the French culture, they use a blank space, whereas in English they use a comma. The number four thousand three hundred and six is written 4 306 in the French culture, but 4,306 in the English culture. In this case, JavaScript doesn't understand either of the formatted numbers because it's expecting the number to be unformatted and written 4306. In this case, if the user entered either the English or French formatted number, we'd have to write special parsing code to convert it into a value understood by JavaScript.

As you can see, those wanting to write numbers in their own culture-specific format are limited because JavaScript only understands the English culture's decimal formatting and doesn't understand any culture's number separator.

JavaScript does provide the ability to format numbers based on the current culture, however. Using the toLocaleString method, a number object can be converted into a string according to the host environment's current culture. That is, if my machine is running under the French culture, Listing 6.11 would produce Figure 6.15.

LISTING 6.11 JavaScript Formatting Numbers Using toLocaleString

```
<script type="text/javascript">
  var num1 = 4305;
  alert(num1.toLocaleString());
</script>
```

FIGURE 6.15 The toLocaleString output of a number when the operating system is running in French

Dates

Just as we saw problems with JavaScript numbers, the same sort of problems appears with dates. The date December 26, 2007 is written as 12/26/2007 in the English culture, whereas it is written 26/12/2007 in the French culture. If we try to create dates from these strings using the code shown in Listing 6.12, only the English version would successfully create the date we were expecting. This is because the Date type doesn't take the current culture into account.

LISTING 6.12 Incorrectly Creating Dates in JavaScript

```
// successfully creates the date we expect
var date = new Date("12/26/2007");

// creates a date somewhere in 2009
var date2 = new Date("26/12/2007");
```

As with numbers, the one thing the Date type will do correctly according to the host environment's current culture is provide the ability to format the date and time according to the default format for the culture. In the Windows world, at least, this means that if my operating system is running under the French language and my system clock is set to the Pacific standard time (PST) time zone, a Date type created and displayed using the code listed in Listing 6.13 will output Figure 6.16.

LISTING 6.13 Formatting Dates in JavaScript Using toLocaleString

```
<script type="text/javascript">
  var d = new Date("12/26/2007 12:25PM");
  alert (d.toLocaleString());
</script>
```

FIGURE 6.16 The toLocaleString output of a date when the operating system is
running in French

The toLocaleString, toLocaleDateString, and toLocaleTimeString methods are better than nothing, but it doesn't do much for helping us turns strings written in a particular culture's format into Date objects. It also only uses the operating system's language setting and is not affected by the browser's language preferences.

That pretty much wraps it up for JavaScript's built-in capabilities for localizing dates and numbers.

ASP.NET AJAX Localization Capabilities

Now that we've walked through JavaScript's limited localization capabilities and seen its problems, let's cover what ASP.NET AJAX provides to supplement those localization capabilities.

ASP.NET AJAX splits localization into two sections: script globalization and script localization. Script globalization fixes the problems with

JavaScript's Date and Number types, and script localization provides an easy way to use translated versions of strings.

> **■ NOTE   Localization Feature Split**
>
> You can compare ASP.NET AJAX localization feature separation to how ASP.NET separates localization based on the CurrentCulture and CurrentUICulture properties of the executing thread. CurrentCulture provides date and number localization, and CurrentUICulture provides access to a specific culture's resource file.

Because we just went over JavaScript's Date and Number type shortcomings, let's start with script globalization, and then cover script localization.

Script Globalization

Script globalization adds capabilities to the Date and Number types so that date and number strings written in a specific culture's format can be converted into date and number objects. It also adds capabilities to the Date, Number, and String types so that dates and numbers can be formatted according to a particular culture's formatting rules.

Enabling these capabilities is a two-step process. First, we need to set the ScriptManager control's EnableScriptGlobalization property to true, as shown in Listing 6.14; it is set to false by default.

LISTING 6.14 Enabling Script Globalization

```
<asp:ScriptManager
  ID="ScriptManager"
  runat="server"
  EnableScriptGlobalization="True">
```

Second, we need to set the CurrentCulture property of the ASP.NET thread that is handling the request to the correct culture. Setting the CurrentCulture property to a particular CultureInfo object is the controlling factor of what culture will be available on the client and how dates and numbers are parsed and formatted. So, if we want the Number and Date

types' new capabilities to use the French culture's date and number formatting, we need to set the `CurrentCulture` property of the thread to the
French `CultureInfo` object. We've shown how to do this in previous examples, but Listing 6.15 shows how to set the current thread's `CurrentCulture`
property to the neutral French culture.

LISTING 6.15 Setting the Thread's CurrentCulture to the Neutral French Culture

```
CultureInfo newCulture = CultureInfo.CreateSpecificCulture("fr");
Thread.CurrentThread.CurrentCulture = newCulture;
```

Now that we've enabled script globalization on the `ScriptManager` control and set our thread's `CurrentCulture` property, ASP.NET AJAX is ready
to parse and format dates and numbers according to a specific culture. We
first walk through the new capabilities, and then give a brief explanation on
how it all works.

Numbers

ASP.NET AJAX provides four new functions to work with numbers. They are
the two static functions, `Number.parseInvariant` and `Number.parseLocale`,
and the two instance functions, *number*.`format` and *number*.`localeFormat`.
The methods' purpose, description, and syntax are detailed in Table 6.1.

TABLE 6.1 New Number Type Methods

Method Name	Description	Syntax
Number.parseInvariant	Attempts to convert the stringValue parameter into a number based on the Invariant culture's number formatting rules	var num = Number. parseInvariant (stringValue);
Number.parseLocale	Attempts to convert the stringValue parameter into a number based on the current culture's number formatting rules	var num = Number. parseLocale (stringValue);

Method Name	Description	Syntax
format	Formats the number using the Invariant culture's number formatting rules and the format string provided and returns a string	`var str = number.format("formatString");`
localeFormat	Formats the number using the current culture's number formatting rules and the format string provided and returns a string	`var str = number.localeFormat ("formatString");`

Listing 6.16 shows examples of the new methods' use, and Figure 6.17 and Figure 6.18 show the respective alert boxes.

> **■ NOTE   Using the French Culture**
>
> We're hard-coding our InitializeCulture method to set the Current Culture property to the French CultureInfo object.

LISTING 6.16 Using Number.parseLocale and Number.parseInvariant

```
<asp:ScriptManager ID="ScriptManager"
                   runat="server"
                   EnableScriptGlobalization="true" />

<script type="text/javascript">
  Number.parseLocaleFixed = function(value) {
    return Number.parseLocale(value.replace(" "," "));
  }

  // convert "4,305" into a number using the invariant culture
  var num1 = Number.parseInvariant("4,305");

  // convert "4 305" into a number using the local culture
  // (which is French)
  var num2 = Number.parseLocaleFixed("4 305");

  // format num1 as a currency using the local culture
```

LISTING 6.16 continued

```
alert(num1.localeFormat("c"));

// format num2 as a currency using the invariant culture
alert(num2.format("c"));
</script>
```

FIGURE 6.17 The localeFormat **output of a number when the operating system is running in French**

FIGURE 6.18 The format output of a number when the operating system is running in French

parseLocale Bug

As you can see from the code displayed in Listing 6.16, rather than call Number.parseLocale directly, we're using an intermediate function called Number.parseLocaleFixed. We're using this function because there's a bug in the provided French formatting information that the server passed down to the client, and because of it parseLocale fails to work properly when we're using the French culture information.

The parseLocale method works by attempting to convert the string into a number it understands. To do this, it strips away the number separators, in the English culture commas and in the French culture spaces, and replaces any decimal separator it finds with a decimal point. So, the first step in parseLocale is to change 4 305 into 4305. This is where the bug lies. The code fails to remove the space because it is looking for the wrong type of space.

If you or I type a space on the keyboard using the spacebar, we're actually telling the computer we want to enter ASCII code 0032. We can actually manually enter this code by holding down the Alt key and typing in 0032. If you do this and you're inside a text-editing program, you should see a space appear on the screen. This is the type of space that we normally use when we type out 4 305, and this is the space you would expect the parseLocale code to strip out.

However, because of a bug in how Microsoft generated the information that contains the character to strip out, the French culture number separator is not ASCII code 0032, but is rather ASCII code 0160, which is a nonbreaking space (in HTML). If we type Alt 0160, the space looks no different from a normal space, but it is actually a completely different character, and because it's a completely different character, parseLocale fails to work properly.

Understanding what the problem is, parseLocaleFixed goes ahead and replaces any ASCII code 0032 characters in the string with ASCII code 0160. Therefore, when the value is sent off to the parseLocale method, it is parsed successfully.

Caveat: We know the French culture has this problem, but we don't know whether any other cultures that use the space as the number separator also have this problem. If you're planning on using this method, investigate the cultures you're supporting to make sure that the parse methods work as expected.

Furthermore, when Microsoft fixes this bug, you will need to either change your code to call the parseLocale method directly or write a better parseLocaleFixed method that takes into consideration that it may have been fixed.

> **■ NOTE**   Invariant Culture
>
> The Invariant culture is a hard-coded culture definition. Using this hard-coded culture definition provides predictable results because it is the same across all computers using the same system. In this case, ASP.NET AJAX mostly uses English culture conventions in the Invariant culture.

Dates

ASP.NET AJAX provides four new functions to work with dates. They are the two static functions, Date.parseInvariant and Date.parseLocale, and the two instance functions, *date*.format and *date*.localeFormat. The methods' purpose, description, and syntax are detailed in Table 6.2.

TABLE 6.2 New Date Type Methods

Method Name	Description	Syntax
Date.parseInvariant	Attempts to convert the stringValue parameter into a date based on the Invariant culture's date formatting rules.	var date = Date. parseInvariant (*stringValue*);
Date.parseLocale	Attempts to convert the stringValue parameter into a date based on the current culture's date formatting rules. Can optionally take a date format string that overrides the current culture's date formatting rules and uses that string to try and create the date instead.	var date = Date. parseLocale (*stringValue*, *dateFormat*);
format	Formats the date using the Invariant culture's date formatting rules and the format string provided and returns a string.	var str = *date*. format("formatString");

Method Name	Description	Syntax
localeFormat	Formats the date using the current culture's date formatting rules and the format string provided and returns a string.	var str = *date*. localeFormat ("formatString");

Listing 6.17 shows examples of the new methods' use, and Figure 6.19 and Figure 6.20 show the respective alert boxes.

LISTING 6.17 Using Date.parseLocale and Date.parseInvariant

```
<asp:ScriptManager ID="ScriptManager"
                   runat="server"
                   EnableScriptGlobalization="true" />

<script type="text/javascript">
  // convert "12/22/2007" into a date using the invariant culture
  var date1 = Date.parseInvariant("12/22/2007");

  // convert "22/12/2007" into a date using the local culture
  var date2 = Date.parseLocale("22/12/2007");

  // format date1 as a short date using the local culture
  alert(date1.localeFormat("d"));

  // format date2 as a short date using the invariant culture
  alert(date2.format("d"));
</script>
```

FIGURE 6.19 The localeFormat output of a date when the operating system is running in French

FIGURE 6.20 The format output of a date when the operating system is running in French

Strings

The two new static methods that ASP.NET AJAX provides for the String type, format and localeFormat, mimic .NET's string.format method. They format strings using argument replacement. Listing 6.18 shows a basic string.format expression.

LISTING 6.18 Using String.format

```
for (var i=0; i<5; i++) {
  alert (string.format(
    "My current number {0} is greater than {1}",
    i, i-1));
}
```

■ **NOTE**   string.format overloading

.NET's string.format method was split into two methods because JavaScript lacks method overloading.

As you can see, the syntax is identical to .NET's. The format and localeFormat methods also allow us to provide data format strings just as we would in .NET. Listing 6.19 shows examples of these.

LISTING 6.19 Using Data Format Strings

```
var dateTime = Date.parseInvariant("SAT, 22 DEC 2007 12:15:00 GMT");

// alerts 12/22/2007
alert (String.format(
  "The current invariant formatted date is {0:d}", dateTime));

// alerts 12:15:00
```

```
alert (String.format("
  The current invariant formatted time is {0:T}", dateTime));

// alerts 22/12/2007
alert (String.localeFormat(
  "The current locale formatted date is {0:d}", dateTime));

// alerts 12:15:00
alert (String.localeFormat(
  "The current locale formatted time is {0:T}", dateTime));
```

> **■ TIP   Data Format Strings**
>
> The format strings that are appropriate are data type dependent just like they are in .NET. We're able to use d and T here because we're working with dates, but these format strings wouldn't be appropriate if our argument were a number object.
>
> The data format strings available for the Date and Number types in JavaScript are the same as those that are available in .NET for the Date Time and Double types.

Briefly, let's discuss how the formatting takes place. When the string is read, the format items (i.e., {0:d}) are parsed and processed. In the case of the String.format method, each argument's replacement variable, which is a Date, has format called on it passing in the data format string. So, when the first String.format method executes, the code listed here is executed to format the dateTime variable properly and replace the format item:

```
dateTime.format("d");
```

Likewise, when the String.localeFormat method executes, the localeFormat method is executed on the dateTime variable and the value replaces the format item:

```
dateTime.localeFormat("d");
```

This pattern can be used to create our own formattable objects. If we define a type that implements a format method or a localeFormat method, those methods will be executed whenever a String.format or a String.localeFormat call contains an object of that type. Listing 6.20 demonstrates this idea.

LISTING 6.20 Defining Our Own Formattable Object

```
MyObject = function(value) { this._value = value; };

MyObject.prototype = {
  format: function(argFormat) {
    if (argFormat === "abc") {
      return "You applied ABC to " + this._value;
    }
    return this._value;
  },
  localeFormat: function(argFormat) {
    if (argFormat = "123") {
    return "You applied 123 to " + this._value;
    }
    return this._value;
  }
};

var newObj = new MyObject(65);

// alerts "You applied ABC to 65"
alert (String.format("{0:abc}", newObj));

// alerts "You applied 123 to 65"
alert (String.localeFormat("{0:123}", newObj));
```

So that explains the new localization capabilities available with the Number, Date, and String types, but how does it all work? How does Number.parseLocale know that it should use a comma or a blank space as the number-group separator?

These new features rely on a special object called Sys.CultureInfo to provide information about the current and invariant cultures. Let's look at Sys.CultureInfo in a bit more detail.

Sys.CultureInfo

A Sys.CultureInfo object is equivalent to .NET's CultureInfo object. Like the .NET object, it contains properties that hold the culture's name, number formatting information, and date-time formatting information. Table 6.3 describes these properties.

TABLE 6.3 Sys.CultureInfo Properties

Property Name	Description
name	Contains the name of the culture. For instance, `"en-us"`, `"fr"`, or `"es-mx"`.
numberFormat	Contains information about how numbers should be format-ted. For instance, the number separator is a comma (`,`), a decimal point is a period (`.`), the currency symbol is `$`, and there should be two digits after the decimal point.
dateTimeFormat	Contains information about how dates should be formatted. For instance, the abbreviated month names are Jan, Feb, Mar… Dec; the default date format is m/d/yyyy, and the short time pattern is h:mm tt.

There are always two statically available `Sys.CultureInfo` objects available through expando properties on `Sys.CultureInfo`. The Invariant culture, which is accessed through `Sys.CultureInfo.InvariantCulture`, and the current culture, which is accessed through `Sys.CultureInfo.Current Culture`, are always available.

The `Sys.CultureInfo` object attached to the `Sys.CultureInfo.InvariantCulture` property never changes and is read-only. All ASP.NET AJAX implementations will have the same `Invariant` culture object.

The `Sys.CultureInfo` object attached to the `Sys.CultureInfo.Current Culture` property changes based on the `CultureInfo` object that is assigned to the `CurrentCulture` property of the executing .NET thread. This means that if you have enabled script globalization through the `ScriptManager`, ASP.NET AJAX's server code will read the `CultureInfo` object assigned to the currently executing thread's `CurrentCulture` property and automatically generate JavaScript code that mimics this `CultureInfo` object. Listing 6.21 is the extracted source code from `ScriptManager` that creates the client culture information.

LISTING 6.21 Registering Globalization Script Block in ScriptManager

```
private void RegisterGlobalizationScriptBlock()
{
  if (this.EnableScriptGlobalization)
  {
```

LISTING 6.21 continued

```
      string clientCultureScriptBlock =
        ClientCultureInfo.GetClientCultureScriptBlock(
        CultureInfo.CurrentCulture
      );
      if (clientCultureScriptBlock != null)
      {
        ScriptRegistrationManager.RegisterClientScriptBlock(
          this,
          typeof(ScriptManager),
          "CultureInfo",
          clientCultureScriptBlock,
          true
        );
      }
    }
  }
```

We can see the culture information being set by examining the rendered HTML of our Transactions page after the CurrentCulture has been set to France's CultureInfo object. Listing 6.22 shows part of this code. (We cut out most of the code due to length.)

LISTING 6.22 The Abbreviated __cultureInfo Declaration

```
<script type="text/javascript">
//<![CDATA[
var __cultureInfo = '{"name":"fr-
FR","numberFormat":{"CurrencyDecimalDigits":2,"CurrencyDecimalSeparator":",",
,"IsReadOnly":false,"CurrencyGroupSizes":[3],"NumberGroupSizes":[3],"Percent
GroupSizes":[3], … ,
"NativeDigits":["0","1","2","3","4","5","6","7","8","9"],"DigitSubstitution"
:1},"dateTimeFormat":{"AMDesignator":"","Calendar":{"MinSupportedDateTime":"
\/Date(-
62135568000000)\/","MaxSupportedDateTime":"\/Date(253402300799999)\/","Algor
ithmType":1,"CalendarType":1, … ,
"MonthGenitiveNames":["janvier","février","mars","avril","mai","juin","juill
et","août","septembre","octobre","novembre","décembre",""]}}';//]]>
</script>
```

■ **NOTE**   __cultureInfo

The __cultureInfo variable created here is automatically parsed by the Microsoft AJAX Library and assigned to the Sys.CultureInfo. CurrentCulture property.

> **NOTE   ASP.NET AJAX Script Globalization Requires ASP.NET**
>
> Because ASP.NET AJAX requires ASP.NET to emit the correct `Sys.CultureInfo` object based on the `CurrentCulture` assigned to the currently running .NET thread, ASP.NET AJAX script globalization is one of the few client features that is specifically tied to ASP.NET and cannot be used properly without it. `Number.parseLocale` and the other methods won't cause an error, but they also won't be able to parse anything but English (United States) either.

Now that we've walked through what `Sys.CultureInfo` contains and how the static property `Sys.CultureInfo.CurrentCulture` is set, we can begin to understand how the `Number`, `Date`, and `String` methods that parse strings or create formatted strings based on the current or `Invariant` culture do so by using the `Sys.CultureInfo` object.

Script Localization

Script localization is composed of two different features. The first provides a way to replace an entire script with a localized version. This is called the static-file model. The second provides a way to automatically generate a JavaScript object based on a resource file and have it combined with a script library to produce a localized library. This is called the embedded-resource model and works similarly to the resource manager feature provided by ASP.NET.

Unlike script globalization, script localization is enabled by default. It is controlled by the `EnableScriptLocalization` property on the `Script Manager` control, and that property is set to `true` by default. Listing 6.23 shows how to set the property explicitly.

LISTING 6.23 Enabling Script Localization Explicitly

```
<asp:ScriptManager ID="ScriptManager"
                   runat="server"
                   EnableScriptLocalization="true" />
```

Rather than explain the static and embedded resource models in an abstract manner, let's walk through an example, using our previously created Transactions page, that uses both models, and we explain as we go.

Filtering the Transactions Page

In this example, we add the ability to filter our Transactions by amount. (We're not actually going to implement the filtering part of the example, just the user interface portion.) Figure 6.21 shows our Transactions page with our amount filter added.

Name	Date	Amount	Paid
Cleaners	10/18/2007	$35.32	☐
Movies	11/30/2007	$22.00	☑
Gas	9/11/2007	$43.16	☐
Groceries	11/4/2007	$127.56	☐
Liquor Store	12/25/2007	$41.69	☑
Book Store	8/13/2007	$35.98	☑

Amount Filter
From: [   ] To: [   ] [Filter Transactions]   English / United States ▾

FIGURE 6.21 The Transactions page with the amount filter

The user will enter numbers into the two textboxes and then press the Filter Transactions button to submit the page with the intention of filtering the list of transactions based on the amounts entered. The page will check to make sure the numbers are valid and if not present the user with a useful error message (in the user's language of course) stating the problem. Example errors are shown in Figure 6.22 and Figure 6.23.

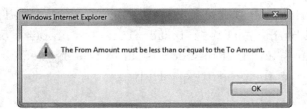

FIGURE 6.22 An English error message stating the amount values are invalid

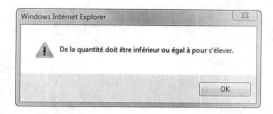

FIGURE 6.23 A French error message stating the amount values are invalid

Our currency filter is implemented using two instances of a new control: `CurrencyTextBox`. Its requirements are as follows:

1. Users can type numbers in their local format (i.e., 3,456 or 3 456) or without any formatting (3456).

2. When the textbox loses focus, the numbers convert to currency format. Figure 6.24 shows the textbox with focus, and Figure 6.25 shows the textbox after it loses focus.

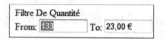

FIGURE 6.24 A focused and unformatted `CurrencyTextBox`

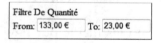

FIGURE 6.25 An unfocused and formatted `CurrencyTextBox`

3. When the textbox regains focus, the currency string is converted to a number in the original format the user typed it in (i.e., 3456, 3 456, or 3,456).

4. If the user enters an invalid number into the textbox, a JavaScript alert is displayed telling the user about the error. The message needs to be in the correct language. Figure 6.26 and Figure 6.27 demonstrate two of the possible alerts.

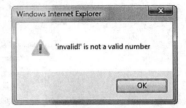

FIGURE 6.26 An English error message displayed after entering an invalid number

FIGURE 6.27 A French error message displayed after entering an invalid number

To develop this control we're going to use a new class project called Localization.Controls. After we get our project created and have deleted the initial Class.cs file, we need to create the three parts of our control.

1. A server control contained in a C# file
2. A client control contained in a JavaScript file
3. The resource files that contain the translated versions of our strings

Figure 6.28 shows the files inside our new class project in Visual Studio.

FIGURE 6.28 Our project's layout in Visual Studio

Localization.Controls.CurrencyTextBox Server Control

To start, let's create our new server control called `Localization.Controls.CurrencyTextBox` and place it in a C# file called CurrencyTextBox.cs. Its code is listed in Listing 6.24.

LISTING 6.24 CurrencyTextBox Server Control

```csharp
using System;
using System.Collections.Generic;
using System.Web.UI;
using System.Web.UI.WebControls;

namespace Localization.Controls
{
  public class CurrencyTextBox : TextBox, IScriptControl
  {
    private ScriptManager _scriptManager;
    protected ScriptManager PageScriptManager
    {
      get
      {
        if (_scriptManager == null)
        {
          _scriptManager = ScriptManager.GetCurrent(this.Page);
        }
        return _scriptManager;
      }
    }

    protected override void OnPreRender(EventArgs e)
    {
      base.OnPreRender(e);
      if (!DesignMode)
      {
        if (PageScriptManager == null)
        {
          throw new InvalidOperationException(
            "ScriptManager not present on page.");
        }
        PageScriptManager.RegisterScriptControl<CurrencyTextBox>(this);
      }
    }

    protected override void Render(HtmlTextWriter writer)
    {
      base.Render(writer);
      if (!DesignMode)
      {
```

LISTING 6.24 continued

```
        if (PageScriptManager == null)
        {
          throw new InvalidOperationException(
            "ScriptManager not present on page.");
        }
        PageScriptManager.RegisterScriptDescriptors(this);
    }
  }

  #region IScriptControl Members

  public IEnumerable<ScriptDescriptor> GetScriptDescriptors()
  {
    ScriptControlDescriptor scd =
      new ScriptControlDescriptor(
        "Localization.Controls.CurrencyTextBox",
        this.ClientID);

    if (!string.IsNullOrEmpty(this.Text))
    {
      scd.AddProperty("nonFormattedValue", this.Text);
    }
    yield return scd;
  }

  public IEnumerable<ScriptReference> GetScriptReferences()
  {
    yield return new
      ScriptReference(
        "Localization.Controls.ClientScript.CurrencyTextBox.js",
        typeof(CurrencyTextBox).Assembly.FullName);
  }

  #endregion
  }
}
```

Localization.Controls.CurrencyTextBox has three main features.

First, it inherits from System.Web.UI.WebControls.TextBox, so it will have the look and feel of a normal textbox.

Second, it implements IScriptControl. In the GetScriptDescriptors method, we return a ScriptControlDescriptor that will automatically create a new client control of type Localization.Controls.CurrencyTextBox. In the GetScriptReferences method, we return a ScriptReference that refers to the embedded JavaScript class that contains our Localization.Controls.CurrencyTextBox client type.

Finally, in the `OnPreRender` method, it registers itself with the `Script Manager` as a `ScriptControl`, and in the `Render` method, it registers itself with the `ScriptManager` as having `ScriptDescriptors`.

Localization.Controls.CurrencyTextBox Client Control

Next, let's create the client control, `Localization.Controls.Currency TextBox`, and place it in the new JavaScript file CurrencyTextBox.js. Listing 6.25 shows the skeleton of our new client control.

LISTING 6.25 CurrencyTextBox JavaScript Skeleton Declaration

```
/// <reference name="MicrosoftAjax.js">
Number.parseLocaleFixed = function(value) {
  return Number.parseLocale(value.replace(" "," "));
}
Type.registerNamespace("Localization.Controls");
Localization.Controls.CurrencyTextBox = function(element) {
  Localization.Controls.CurrencyTextBox.initializeBase
    (this, [element]);
};

Localization.Controls.CurrencyTextBox.prototype = {
  initialize: function() {
    Localization.Controls.CurrencyTextBox.callBaseMethod
      (this, 'initialize');
  },

  dispose: function() {
    Localization.Controls.CurrencyTextBox.callBaseMethod
    (this, 'dispose');
  },
};

Localization.Controls.CurrencyTextBox.registerClass(
  "Localization.Controls.CurrencyTextBox",
  Sys.UI.Control);
```

> ■ **NOTE** Number.parseLocaleFixed
>
> We're going to need `Number.parseLocaleFixed` again for this sample. See the sidebar "parseLocale Bug" earlier in the chapter for more information about the need for this method.

We need to add event handlers to the textbox's focus and blur events so that we can change the value from a formatted to an unformatted value and vice versa. To assist with these features, we're going to keep track of the unformatted version. Keeping track of the unformatted version also provides us the ability to set it from server code as the textbox's initial value. Listing 6.26 adds the private members to our JavaScript class and the unformatted value's getters and setters.

LISTING 6.26 Defining the Private Members and Properties

```
Localization.Controls.CurrencyTextBox = function(element)
{
  Localization.Controls.CurrencyTextBox.initializeBase
    (this, [element]);
  this._focusDelegate = null;
  this._blurDelegate = null;
  this._unFormattedValue = null;
};

Localization.Controls.CurrencyTextBox.prototype = {
  get_unFormattedValue: function() {
    return this._unFormattedValue;
  },

  set_unFormattedValue: function(value) {
    this._unFormattedValue = value;
  }
};
```

Our initialize method is responsible for wiring the event handler methods to the focus and blur events and formatting any initial unformatted value. Our dispose method is responsible for removing the event handlers from our textbox. Listing 6.27 shows the initialize and dispose methods.

LISTING 6.27 initialize and dispose Methods

```
… // prototype
initialize: function() {
  Localization.Controls.CurrencyTextBox.callBaseMethod
    (this, 'initialize');

  var elm = this.get_element();

  // set the formatted value to an initial value if provided.
```

```
        if (this._unFormattedValue !== null &&
            this._unFormattedValue !== "") {
                this._format(this._unFormattedValue, elm);
        }

        // create and wire the focus and blur delegates to the element.
        this._focusDelegate = Function.createDelegate(this, this._onFocus);
        this._blurDelegate = Function.createDelegate(this, this._onBlur);

        $addHandler(elm, "focus", this._focusDelegate);
        $addHandler(elm, "blur", this._blurDelegate);
    },

    dispose: function() {
      $clearHandlers(this.get_element());
      this._focusDelegate = null;
      this._blurDelegate = null;
      Localization.Controls.CurrencyTextBox.callBaseMethod
        (this, 'dispose');
    }
```

Our initialize method specifies three methods that we still need to define: _format, _onFocus, and _onBlur. These methods are responsible for converting our textbox's value to and from a formatted version and displaying an error message if we enter an invalid number into the textbox. Listing 6.28 displays the code for the _format method.

LISTING 6.28 _format Method

```
_format: function(value, elm) {
  var parsedNumber = Number.parseLocaleFixed(value);
  if (!isNaN(parsedNumber)) {
    elm.value = parsedNumber.localeFormat("c");
    return true;
  }
  return false;
}
```

The _format method replaces the textbox's value with a currency formatted version of the number and returns a boolean value indicating whether it was successful. It does this by first attempting to parse the value as a Number using the parseLocaleFixed method. If the parsedNumber is in fact a number, testing it using the built-in isNaN method, the number is formatted as a currency using the localeFormat method and assigned to the element's value. It then returns true to indicate success. If the parsed Number is not a number, the method returns false to indicate failure.

Listing 6.29 displays the code for the _onFocus method.

LISTING 6.29 _onFocus Method

```
_onFocus: function(args) {
  if (this._unFormattedValue !== null) {
    var elm = this.get_element();
    elm.value = this._unFormattedValue;
    elm.select();
  }
}
```

The _onFocus method simply takes the unFormattedValue and if it's not null assigns it to the element. It then selects the textbox's text using the select method.

Listing 6.30 displays the code for the _onBlur method.

LISTING 6.30 _onBlur Method

```
_onBlur: function(args) {
  var elm = this.get_element();
  var textBoxValue = elm.value;

  // update the non-formatted value.
  this._unFormattedValue = textBoxValue;

  if (textBoxValue !== null && textBoxValue !== "") {
    if (!this._format(textBoxValue, elm)) {
      alert (
        String.format(
          CurrencyTextBox.Res.InvalidNumberMessage,
          textBoxValue
        )
      );
    }
  }
}
```

The _onBlur method is responsible for taking the textbox's current value and replacing it with the currency formatted version of the value. If it fails to format the textbox's value, the method needs to display an error message stating that the value in the textbox is an invalid number. Listing 6.31 highlights the code that displays this alert.

LISTING 6.31 Displaying the Error Message Alert

```
alert (
  String.format(
    CurrencyTextBox.Res.InvalidNumberMessage,
    textBoxValue
  )
);
```

As the code shows, it uses the `String.format` method to build a string that contains the error message. It does this, however, using a string stored in `CurrencyTextBox.Res.InvalidNumberMessage`, an object we have yet to define. When `String.format` executes, it evaluates the string stored in `InvalidNumberMessage` and replaces its `{0}` argument with `textBoxValue`.

To understand the `CurrencyTextBox.Res.InvalidNumberMessage` object, we need to cover the JavaScript resources for the `CurrencyTextBox` and then cover how these resources become available on the client.

CurrencyTextBox Resources

Creating our `CurrencyTextBox` resources starts off by creating a new default resource file. Unlike with local resources in ASP.NET where the first part of the resource filename related the resource to the page, these resource filenames can be called whatever we want. But, for consistency, we name our resource file CurrencyTextBox.resx and place it in the ClientResources directory. Figure 6.29 shows our newly created file sitting in its directory.

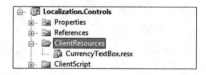

FIGURE 6.29 The CurrencyTextBox resource file

■ NOTE   Global Resources

JavaScript resource files act more like global resource files. We haven't covered them, but they're just resource files that aren't associated to a particular ASP.NET page.

Now that we have our resource file created, we need to add the `InvalidNumberMessage` to it as a string resource. We do this by opening up the resource file in design mode and adding a name-value pair. Figure 6.30 shows our resource file after we've added our `InvalidNumberMessage` resource.

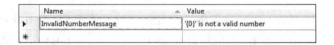

Name	Value
InvalidNumberMessage	'{0}' is not a valid number

FIGURE 6.30 The InvalidNumberMessage resource

Having the `InvalidNumberMessage` written in English is a start, but we need to support our other two cultures: es-MX and fr. To support these cultures, we need to create resource files that support those cultures. To do this, we just copy our resource file a couple of times, alter the filenames to reflect the associated culture, and update the `InvalidNumberMessage` with a translated version. Figure 6.31 shows Visual Studio with the three resource files, and Figure 6.32. and Figure 6.33 show the translated version of the files.

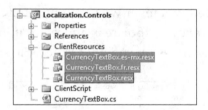

FIGURE 6.31 Visual Studio with the three resource files

Name	Value
InvalidNumberMessage	'{0}' no es un número válido

FIGURE 6.32 The CurrencyTextBox.es-mx.resx resource file

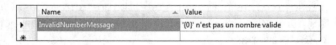

Name	Value
InvalidNumberMessage	'{0}' n'est pas un nombre valide

FIGURE 6.33 The CurrencyTextBox.fr.resx resource file

So, we've created our three resource files, one for each culture, but we still have a final step of associating them to a particular JavaScript. This final step takes place in AssemblyInfo.cs, where we use a `ScriptResource` attribute to associate the resource files with a JavaScript file and provide a type name. Figure 6.34 shows the IntelliSense for the `ScriptResource` attribute, and Listing 6.32 shows the `ScriptResource` attribute that associates our resource files with our JavaScript file.

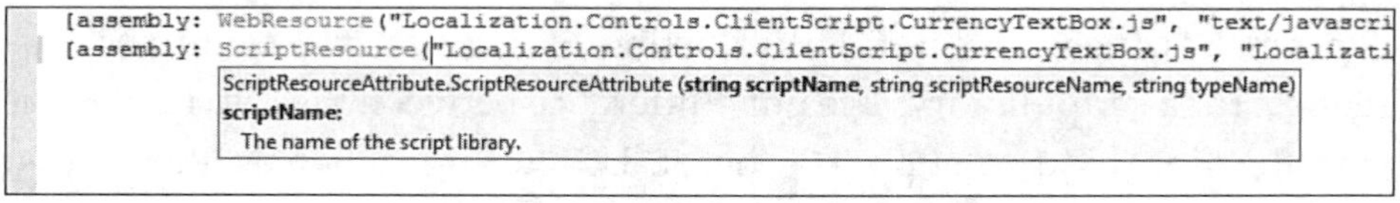

```
[assembly: WebResource("Localization.Controls.ClientScript.CurrencyTextBox.js", "text/javascri
[assembly: ScriptResource("Localization.Controls.ClientScript.CurrencyTextBox.js", "Localizati
              ScriptResourceAttribute.ScriptResourceAttribute (string scriptName, string scriptResourceName, string typeName)
              scriptName:
                 The name of the script library.
```

FIGURE 6.34 ScriptResource attribute in AssemblyInfo.cs

LISTING 6.32 ScriptResource Attribute in AssemblyInfo.cs

```
[assembly: ScriptResource(
  "Localization.Controls.ClientScript.CurrencyTextBox.js",
  "Localization.Controls.ClientResources.CurrencyTextBox",
  "CurrencyTextBox.Res")
]
```

The `ScriptResource` attribute takes three parameters. The first parameter is the name of the JavaScript file to which we want to associate the resources. The second is the unlocalized name of the resource file that contains the resources. It also doesn't contain the .resx extension. Finally, the final parameter is the client type name that we want to assign the resources to. You can pick anything you want for the final parameter, but this type name is the prefix for any of your resources when you want to access them on the client. In this example, we picked `CurrencyTextBox.Res` so when we want to access the `InvalidNumberMessage` resource on the client we access it as `CurrencyTextBox.Res.InvalidNumberMessage`.

So, that covers how we wire up our resources to our JavaScript file. What we still don't know, however, is how ASP.NET AJAX makes `Currency TextBox.Res.InvalidNumberMessage` available to us on the client.

Providing Localized Scripts

Providing the resource `CurrencyTextBox.Res.InvalidNumberMessage` to us on the client is a two-step process.

First, the correct ScriptResource.axd URL, which provides access to our embedded script, has to be built and placed on the client. The Script Resource.axd URL build process, which occurs in the `ScriptResource Handler`, determines what culture this URL supports by examining the `CurrentUICulture` property of the current thread. It then encodes the `CurrentUICulture` into the URL. Listing 6.33 gives two examples of a request for a script library. The only difference between the two requests is that the first request supports the en-US culture, whereas the second request supports the es-MX culture. The highlighted portions show how they are slightly different.

LISTING 6.33 ScriptResource.axd Paths for CurrencyTextBox.js with Different Cultures

```
http://joel-
pc/Localization/ScriptResource.axd?d=y0FpvlbR8rvCNIvjznmXr8afiNyFTtTqcbECtPx
EmFGxuSOO_5l5U-Vhi9JVx4FrLRqtsDHMoC136Aj-a1pckaLf79Lsrvmp9fe9QNdUekM1&amp;
t=ffffffff957fb73d


http://joel-pc/Localization/ScriptResource.axd?d=
y0FpvlbR8rvCNIvjznmXr8afiNyFTtTqcbECtPxEmFGxuSOO_5l5U-Vhi9JVx4FrLRqt
DHMoC136Aj-a1pckTA_GsG6CN_yvUOcVAEkIO81&amp;t=ffffffff957fb73d
```

> ■ **NOTE** Script Caching
>
> Because the ScriptResource.axd URL changes based on the `CurrentUI Culture`, each requested culture-specific script will have a cached copy on the client.

Now that we've covered that it's up the ScriptResource.axd URL build process to encode the `CurrentUICulture` information into the URL, we can look at the second step in the process.

The second step of the process is handling the HTTP request for the ScriptResource.axd URL. As was the case with building the ScriptResource. axd URL, `ScriptResourceHandler` handles the request.

> **■ TIP   ScriptResourceHandler**
>
> We're leaving out a lot of the details about how `ScriptResource`
> `Handler` works. It's a very important part of ASP.NET AJAX, and we
> cover it in depth in Chapter 8, "ASP.NET AJAX Communication
> Architecture," and Chapter 9, "Application Services."

`ScriptResourceHandler` starts by decrypting the request's parameters
and determining what file and what culture the request contains. After it
determines the culture, it reads the correct resource file and combines it
with the JavaScript file that was also specified in the request. What ends up
being emitted in the response is code like that shown in Listing 6.34.

LISTING 6.34 Embedded CurrencyTextBox.Res

```
/// <reference name="MicrosoftAjax.js">
Number.parseLocaleFixed = function(value) {
  return Number.parseLocale(value.replace(" "," "));
}

Type.registerNamespace("Localization.Controls");
Localization.Controls.CurrencyTextBox = function(element)
{
  Localization.Controls.CurrencyTextBox.initializeBase
    (this, [element]);

  this._focusDelegate = null;
  this._blurDelegate = null;
  this._unFormattedValue = null;
};

Localization.Controls.CurrencyTextBox.prototype = {
  … // PROTOTYPE BODY OMITTED FOR BREVITY
};

Localization.Controls.CurrencyTextBox.registerClass (
  "Localization.Controls.CurrencyTextBox",
  Sys.UI.Control
);
Type.registerNamespace('CurrencyTextBox');
CurrencyTextBox.Res={"InvalidNumberMessage":"\u0027{0}\u0027 n\u0027est
pas un nombre valide"};
if(typeof(Sys)!=='undefined')Sys.Application.notifyScriptLoaded();
```

As the highlighted portion of Listing 6.34 shows, ASP.NET AJAX automatically inserted the `CurrencyTextBox.Res` object with the `Invalid-NumberMessage` property and assigned it the value `\u0027{0}\u0027 n\u0027est pas un nombre valide`. This is how we're able to access `Currency TextBox.Res.InvalidNumberMessage`.

■ NOTE   \u0027

ASP.NET AJAX encoded the string's single quotations.

■ TIP   ASP.NET AJAX and ASP.NET Correlation

Just as script globalization used the thread's `CurrentCulture` property to create the correct `Sys.CultureInfo` object for the `Sys.Culture Info.CurrentCulture` property, script localization uses the thread's `CurrentUICulture` property to choose the correct resource file for the script library. This is functionally similar to how ASP.NET uses `CurrentCulture` to format dates and numbers and uses `CurrentUI Culture` to choose the correct resource file.

Adding the Filters to the Page

Now that we've walked through our `CurrencyTextBox` control, let's create our amount filter. Listing 6.35 shows the markup that adds two `Currency TextBox` controls and a Filter Transactions button to the page to build our amount filter.

LISTING 6.35 Defining the Amount Filter

```
<div id="FilterPanel"
    style="position: relative; top: 2px; left: 5px;">
  <div id="CurrencyFilterPanel"
      style="position: absolute;">
    <div id="CurrencyRangeFilterHeader"
        style="position: relative">
      <asp:Label ID="CurrencyRangeLabel"
                 runat="server"
                 Text="Amount Filter"
                 meta:resourcekey="CurrencyRangeLabelResource1" />
```

```
        </div>
        From:
        <cc1:CurrencyTextBox ID="FromCurrencyTextBox"
                             runat="server"
                             Width="75px"
                             Wrap="False" />
        To:
        <cc1:CurrencyTextBox ID="ToCurrencyTextBox"
                             runat="server"
                             Width="75px"
                             Wrap="False" />
        <asp:Button ID="FilterButton"
                    runat="server"
                    Text="Filter Transactions"
                    OnClientClick="return checkAmounts();"
                    meta:resourcekey="FilterButtonResource1" />
    </div>
    </div>
```

Our `CurrencyTextBoxes` are self-contained and will validate user input as the user leaves the textbox. However, we still need to do a little validation when the user presses the Filter Transactions button. We want to validate two things. First, because the user could have entered an invalid value in the textbox and not changed it to a valid value even after we've displayed the initial error message, we want to revalidate that the `Currency TextBoxes` contain valid values. Second, after their values have been validated, we want to make sure that the From `CurrencyTextBox` has a value less than or equal to that of the To `CurrencyTextBox`. Allowing the From value to be greater than the To value just doesn't make any sense.

If at any point the code finds a problem with the `CurrencyTextBox` values, a localized message should be displayed to the user stating the problem.

We apply our validation logic by creating a JavaScript method called `checkAmounts` and wiring it to the `OnClientClick` property of our Filter Transactions button. We're going to place our `checkAmounts` method inside its own JavaScript file called Filter.js. Figure 6.35 shows Visual Studio with the new JavaScript file added.

FIGURE 6.35 Our new Filter.js file

■ NOTE   OnClientClick

Wiring to the `OnClientClick` results in the `checkAmounts` function being applied to the input tag's `onclick` event.

We also need to add a `ScriptReference` to our page's `ScriptManager` control. Listing 6.36 shows the new `ScriptReference` inside our `Script Manager` control.

LISTING 6.36 Adding the Filter.js ScriptReference

```
<asp:ScriptManager ID="ScriptManager"
                   runat="server"
                   EnableScriptGlobalization="true"
                   EnableScriptLocalization="true">
  <Scripts>
    <asp:ScriptReference Path="~/ClientScript/Filter.js" />
  </Scripts>
</asp:ScriptManager>
```

Now that we've got our Filter.js file wired up to our `ScriptManager` control, we need to write the checkAmounts function. Listing 6.37 shows the full method body of checkAmounts.

LISTING 6.37 Defining checkAmounts

```
/// <reference name="MicrosoftAjax.js">
function checkAmounts() {
  var fromAmount = $find("FromCurrencyTextBox");
  var unFormattedFrom = fromAmount.get_unFormattedValue();
  var formattedFrom = null;

  if (unFormattedFrom !== null && unFormattedFrom !== "") {
    formattedFrom = Number.parseLocaleFixed(unFormattedFrom);
    if (isNaN(formattedFrom)) {
      alert (
```

```
            String.format(
              Filter.Res.InvalidCurrencyFilterMessage,
              Filter.Res.FromAmount
            )
          );
          return false;
      }
    }

    var toAmount = $find("ToCurrencyTextBox");
    var unFormattedTo = toAmount.get_unFormattedValue();
    var formattedTo = null;

    if (unFormattedTo !== null && unFormattedTo !== "") {
      formattedTo = Number.parseLocaleFixed(unFormattedTo);
      if (isNaN(formattedTo)) {
        alert (
          String.format(
            Filter.Res.InvalidCurrencyFilterMessage,
            Filter.Res.ToAmount
          )
        );
        return false;
      }
    }

    if (formattedFrom !== null && formattedTo !== null) {
      if (formattedFrom > formattedTo) {
        alert (Filter.Res.ToAmountGreaterThanFromAmountMessage);
        return false;
      }
    }

    return true;
}
```

The checkAmounts method performs three tasks.

First, it determines whether the value of the From CurrencyTextBox is valid. It does this by reparsing the unformatted value stored in the client control using parseLocaleFixed and testing it as a number using the isNaN method. If the value isn't a valid number, a message is alerted stating that the From amount is invalid and the method returns false.

The second task repeats the first step, but uses the To CurrencyTextBox instead.

The final task is to compare the values of the two CurrencyTextBoxes (if both have been set) and make sure that the From value is less than or equal to the To value. If this test fails, a message is alerted stating that the "From Amount must be less than or equal to the To amount," and the method returns `false`.

Finally, the method returns `true` if it passes all tests.

In Listing 6.37, we highlighted the code that produces the messages displayed to the user when the code finds a problem with one of the filters' values. We highlighted it because we use an object to store the strings rather than hard-code them directly into the code.

We store them in an object called `Filter.Res` that is also placed in our Filter.js file. Listing 6.38 shows the definition of `Filter.Res`.

LISTING 6.38 Defining Filter.Res

```
Type.registerNamespace("Filter");
Filter.Res = {
  FromAmount: "From Amount",
  InvalidCurrencyFilterMessage:
    "The filter can't be applied because
    the '{0}' is not a valid number.",
  ToAmount: "To Amount",
  FromAmountGreaterThanToAmountMessage:
    "The From Amount must be less
      than or equal to the To Amount."
};
```

`Filter.Res` is similar to the `CurrencyTextBox.Res` object we accessed from within our `CurrencyTextBox` client control. The main difference between the two is that we are declaring `Filter.Res` directly in our Filter.js file instead of using an external resource file and having ASP.NET AJAX generate the object and attach it to our rendered JavaScript. This is one of the main differences between the embedded resource model and the static file model.

Figure 6.36 shows our Transactions page with an error message displayed after we've clicked the Filter Transactions button.

The problem with the current state of our Transactions page with our new filter added is that no matter what culture we select using our Select Culture drop-down, the error messages produced by the Filter Transactions button are always in English. To fix this, we need to localize our Filter.js file. We do this by using ASP.NET AJAX's static file localization model.

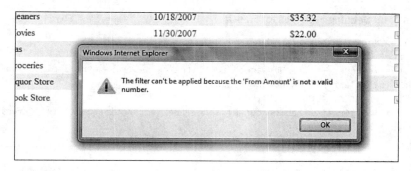

FIGURE 6.36 Transactions page with "Invalid From Amount" error message

We've already started the process by placing our error messages in the separate `Filter.Res` object. The next step is to create copies of the Filter.js file for each culture and to rename them accordingly. Figure 6.37 shows our `ClientScript` folder after we've created the two new Filter.js files.

FIGURE 6.37 Localized Filter.js files

As Figure 6.37 shows, the naming convention for the static files is *FileName.culture*.js.

As you might have deduced, changing the values stored in `Filter.Res` is how we're going to localize each Filter.js file for the Spanish (Mexico) and French cultures. Listing 6.39 and Listing 6.40 show the `Filter.Res` object in the Spanish (Mexico) and French Filter.js files.

LISTING 6.39 Defining Filter.Res for Spanish(Mexico)

```
Filter.Res = {
  FromAmount: "De Cantidad",
  InvalidCurrencyFilterMessage: "El filtro no puede ser aplicado porque '
{0} ' no es un número válido.",
  ToAmount: "A la Cantidad",
  FromAmountGreaterThanToAmountMessage: "De cantidad debe estar menos que o
el igual al a ascender."
};
```

LISTING 6.40 Defining Filter.Res for French

```
Filter.Res = {
  FromAmount: "De la Quantité",
  InvalidCurrencyFilterMessage: "Le filtre ne peut pas être appliqué parce
que '{0}' 'n'est pas un nombre valide.",
  ToAmount: "À la Quantité",
  FromAmountGreaterThanToAmountMessage: "De la quantité doit être inférieur
ou égal à pour s'élever."
};
```

Replacing `Filter.Res` values with localized versions isn't the last step in the static file model. We need to modify our `ScriptReference` to include information about what culture-specific versions of our static file exist. We do this by setting the `ResourceUICultures` property. Listing 6.41 shows how we set this property to support the es-MX and fr cultures.

LISTING 6.41 Setting ResourceUICultures on the Filter.js ScriptReference

```
<Scripts>
  <asp:ScriptReference Path="~/ClientScript/Filter.js"
    ResourceUICultures="es-mx, fr" />
</Scripts>
```

Now when we run our page, ASP.NET AJAX automatically substitutes the appropriate localized version of our Filter.js file. Figure 6.38 shows the Script Documents loaded by Internet Explorer when we navigate to our Transactions page and select the Spanish / Mexico value from the Select Culture drop-down.

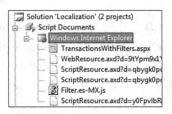

FIGURE 6.38 Script Documents showing Filter.es-mx.js file use

Having the actual Filter.es-mx.js file loaded into the Script Documents list means that there is an actual `script` tag on the page that points back to this file. Listing 6.42 shows an excerpt of our Transactions page's rendered HTML that holds this `script` tag.

LISTING 6.42 The Filter.es-MX.js script Tag

```
<script src="ClientScript/Filter.es-MX.js"
   type="text/javascript"></script>
```

> ## ◼ NOTE   Static File Localization Model
>
> With the static file model, replacing strings with translated versions is the most common use of the script localization capability, but we're not constrained to just replacing strings because we're replacing the entire file. We could alter the way our methods work based on which culture is being used, or we could have a completely different file body.

Finally, when we click our Filter Transactions button when the From value is greater than the To value, an error message in Spanish will display. Figure 6.39 shows this error message.

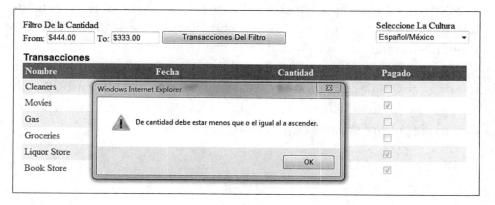

FIGURE 6.39 Our Spanish error message

> ## ◼ TIP   Missing Localized JavaScript File
>
> Suppose, for instance, that we deleted the Filter.es-MX.js file from the ClientScript directory, but left the es-MX value in the ResourceUI Cultures property of the Filter.js ScriptReference. If you changed the running culture to Spanish (Mexico), ASP.NET AJAX would still update the Filter.js script tag to use the Filter.es-mx.js file. At the point where ASP.NET AJAX makes a decision to use this file, it has no idea what static files are available, because they could be anywhere on the file system. Because of this, no Filter.js file would be loaded at all, and our checkAmounts function would not be available to us.

Now that we've updated our page to automatically load the localized version of our Filter.js file, we've successfully localized the ASP.NET AJAX portion of our now filter Transactions.aspx page.

SUMMARY

In this chapter, we covered ASP.NET AJAX localization. Because its inner workings rely heavily on regular ASP.NET localization, we started with one method of localization and localized an ASP.NET page using local resources.

We then moved on to ASP.NET AJAX's localization capabilities by covering what new JavaScript methods support localization in client code and how the server portion of ASP.NET AJAX supports these new JavaScript methods through the `Sys.CultureInfo` object.

We then developed a brand new ASP.NET AJAX control that used the new localized JavaScript methods and a new ability that enables us to modify embedded script files on-the-fly by associating a resource file to the script file through the new `ScriptResource` attribute.

Finally, we brought our new control to the page and used it to provide filtering capabilities. In addition to using our new localized control, the filtering capabilities relied on the ASP.NET AJAX static file localization model to provide culture-specific resources at the page level.

7

Control Development in a Partial Postback Environment

IN THE PRECEDING CHAPTERS, we covered how to create ASP.NET AJAX server controls that contain AJAX capabilities. We added AJAX capabilities to a server control by creating custom client components, behaviors, and controls that used and extended the Microsoft AJAX Library and then used a `ScriptDescriptor` to automatically create an instance of the client component, behavior, or control whenever that server control was added to a page.

Whenever we walked through an example, we always looked at how the server control worked during a full page load. We always fully replaced the content of the page with new content and discussed what the server control was doing. However, we're sure that you are aware that ASP.NET AJAX provides a way to partially update a page through the `UpdatePanel` server control. Using an `UpdatePanel` changes things a bit. Because we're replacing parts of the DOM, rather than fully replacing it with new content, our client components, controls, and behaviors can be disposed of and created during a partial postback. We might not have anticipated them being used this way, and they may have some unexpected problems when they are.

So, in this chapter, we talk about what happens when we place an ASP.NET AJAX server control inside an `UpdatePanel`.

We start with an overview of how an UpdatePanel behaves both on the client and the server and then move on to how a partial postback affects a component, control, or behavior.

From there, we cover how registering a client script changes in a partial postback environment, because this is a common task for control developers, and then we conclude with how Sys.Application reacts to a partial postback.

UpdatePanel Behavior

To understand how an ASP.NET AJAX server control is affected by placing it in an UpdatePanel and how our code might need to change to accommodate the partial postback environment, we need to first understand the general behavior of an UpdatePanel.

An UpdatePanel control is used to partially render portions of a page without the need to write any JavaScript code. The ease of adding AJAX capabilities to an application while still utilizing the server-based development skills developers already have has made the UpdatePanel the most rapidly adopted piece of ASP.NET AJAX.

> ■ **NOTE** Coverage of the UpdatePanel
>
> In this chapter, we focus on the UpdatePanel from the perspective of a control developer and not as a general page developer. This means that we do not go into a lot of detail about how to use the UpdatePanel but instead focus on how it affects the controls contained within it.
>
> The goal of this section is to give you just enough details on the inner workings of the UpdatePanel to explain how a component, behavior, or control can be affected by a partial postback.

The diagram in Figure 7.1 shows the high-level steps that occur on both the client and the server when a partial postback occurs.

A triggering event from the UpdatePanel begins the process that builds up a request and sends it to the server for processing. When the server receives the request, it is processed just like any other page request. The page lifecycle executes as it normally does with the page and its child controls rendering their contents to an appropriate `HtmlTextWriter`[1] and then sends the response back to the client.

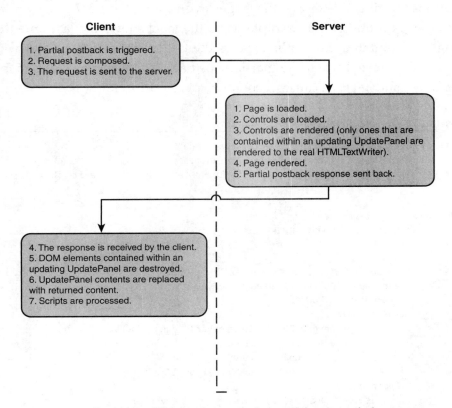

Client

1. Partial postback is triggered.
2. Request is composed.
3. The request is sent to the server.

Server

1. Page is loaded.
2. Controls are loaded.
3. Controls are rendered (only ones that are contained within an updating UpdatePanel are rendered to the real HTMLTextWriter).
4. Page rendered.
5. Partial postback response sent back.

4. The response is received by the client.
5. DOM elements contained within an updating UpdatePanel are destroyed.
6. UpdatePanel contents are replaced with returned content.
7. Scripts are processed.

FIGURE 7.1 High-level steps during partial page rendering

Upon receiving the response from the server, the client replaces the contents of the updating `UpdatePanels` with the response received from the server. In addition, any associated scripts that were part of the response are processed.

From this brief description, you can see that there are many steps that occur on both the client and the server to process a partial postback; and as you will learn, many factors have to be considered for ASP.NET AJAX controls contained within an `UpdatePanel` to work correctly.

---

[1] The main difference that occurs during a partial postback versus a normal postback is that when a control is not contained within an updating `UpdatePanel`, the `HtmlText Writer` that it renders to is not the one that is used to compose the response. Rather, it is a throw-away writer.

To demonstrate a little further how the UpdatePanel behaves, let's examine a simple page that contains an UpdatePanel, a label, a textbox, and two buttons. Listing 7.1 shows the page layout, and Figure 7.2 shows its browser output. On our example page, the label shows the last time the page was updated, the textbox shows the last time the UpdatePanel was updated, Button1 causes a partial postback and UpdatePanel1 to be updated, and Button2 causes a complete page postback.

LISTING 7.1 Sample UpdatePanel Page Markup

```
<%@ Page Language="C#" AutoEventWireup="true"
                CodeBehind="Default.aspx.cs"
                Inherits="SimpleUpdatePanelDemo._Default" %>

<html>
  <head runat="server">
    <title>Sample Update Page</title>
  </head>
  <body>
    <form id="form1" runat="server">
      <asp:Label ID="Label1" runat="server">
        <%=DateTime.Now %>
      </asp:Label>
      <asp:ScriptManager ID="ScriptManager1" runat="server" />
      <asp:UpdatePanel ID="UpdatePanel1"
                  runat="server"
                  UpdateMode="Conditional">
        <ContentTemplate>
          <asp:TextBox ID="TextBox1" runat="server" />
        </ContentTemplate>
        <Triggers>
          <asp:AsyncPostBackTrigger ControlID="Button1"
                            EventName="Click" />
        </Triggers>
      </asp:UpdatePanel>
      <div>
        <asp:Button ID="Button1"
                  runat="server"
                  Text="Update Panel Refresh" />
      </div>
      <div>
        <asp:Button ID="Button2"
                  runat="server"
                  Text="Complete Page Refresh" />
      </div>
    </form>
  </body>
</html>
```

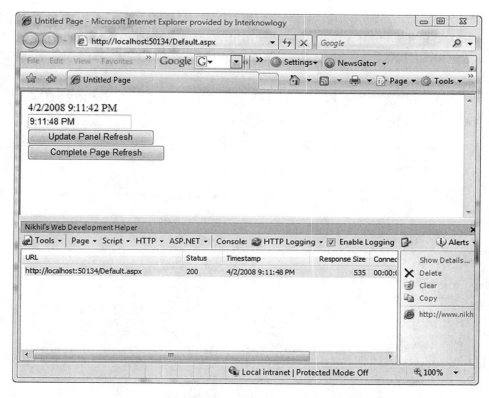

FIGURE 7.2 Sample UpdatePanel page browser display

When we press Button1, a partial postback occurs. Using Web Development Helper, Figure 7.3 shows the partial postback HTTP request and response. Looking at the information contained in the request, which is the top portion of Figure 7.3, we can see that the request includes TextBox1 and its value, the page's ViewState, Button1 and its value, the event validation information, which is used to ensure the validity of the controls' values on the server, and ScriptManager1 and its value, which has been updated to include the button's ID that caused the postback.

When the server processes the partial postback request, the page and controls are processed just as if we had initiated a normal postback. What this boils down to is that during a partial postback, the page's controls will be performing the same steps they did when our page was first created, essentially re-creating the controls from scratch again. The fact that all controls are reprocessed just as they were on the page's first load is an important consideration because, as you will see later in this chapter, some of our development practices that would work fine during a complete page refresh will not work anymore.

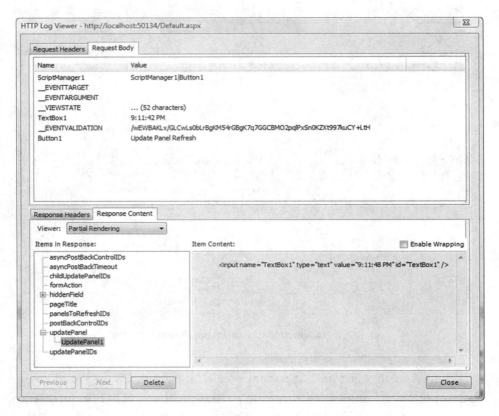

FIGURE 7.3 Web Development Helper view of a partial postback

∎ TIP ScriptControls and ExtenderControls

Recalling our earlier discussions about ExtenderControl and Script Control, the two base server types we use to create ASP.NET AJAX controls, we know that when these controls process they create ScriptDescriptor objects that will eventually be translated to client code and register as requiring certain script files by creating Script Reference objects.

After our controls have completed processing and the page has completed rendering, the response, shown in the bottom portion of Figure 7.4 in its text form, is sent back to the client for processing. The response's pipe-delimited format is specific to a partial postback and contains the information needed by the Microsoft AJAX Library to partially update the DOM tree.

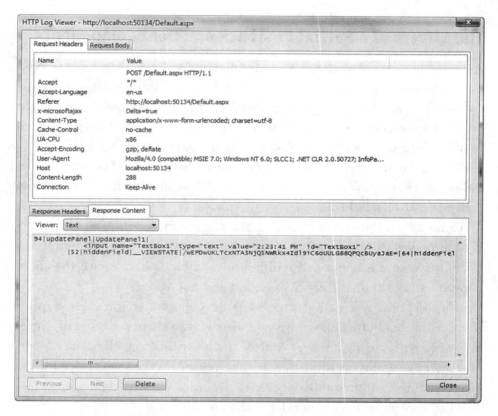

FIGURE 7.4 Web Development Helper view of a partial postback in text form

▪▪ NOTE   Missing Details

Yes, we're completely glossing over the details of how the partial postback response is actually created. The point we're trying to stress is that all server controls, whether they are contained within an updating UpdatePanel or not, are processed.

Using Web Development Helper to view the response in a formatted manner, shown in Figure 7.3, we can see the HTML content that will replace the `UpdatePanel1` leaf of the DOM tree as the response is processed. The other data contained within the response will also affect how the `UpdatePanel` behaves, but this replacing a DOM element's content with new HTML is essentially the main behavior of the `UpdatePanel`.

The Effects of a Partial Postback on Client Components

As stated earlier, we must be cognizant that our ASP.NET AJAX server controls can be placed inside an `UpdatePanel`. We need to understand how our controls will react when placed inside an `UpdatePanel` because there might be unexpected results when the server control's associated client component is disposed of and re-created during the partial postback.

To begin to understand how a client component can be affected by a partial postback, we first need to have a clear picture of what happens to them during a partial postback.

Generally, if the server control that a client component was created by is reprocessed during a partial postback *and* its output is sent down to the client because it is contained within an updating `UpdatePanel`, the client component is automatically disposed of and re-created.

The disposal re-creation process is best illustrated through a quick demonstration. In the following code, we define a client component, create an instance of it using a server control and a `ScriptComponentDescriptor`, and then place the control within an `UpdatePanel`. When we click a button also contained within our `UpdatePanel`, we'll see through debug messages that our component is disposed and then re-created.

■ **NOTE**   Components versus Behaviors and Controls

At this level of abstraction, it does not matter whether the client component is a true component inheriting directly from `Sys.Component` or whether it is a behavior or control. They are affected in much the same way by a partial postback.

Listing 7.2, Listing 7.3, and Listing 7.4 show the code pieces of our example.

LISTING 7.2 Component.js

```
/// <reference name="MicrosoftAjax.js" />
MyComponent = function() {
  MyComponent.initializeBase(this, null);
}
MyComponent.prototype = {
  initialize: function() {
    Sys.Debug.trace(
      String.format("Component: {0} initialized", this.get_id()));
    MyComponent.callBaseMethod(this, 'initialize');
  },
  dispose: function() {
    Sys.Debug.trace(
      String.format("Component: {0} disposed", this.get_id()));
    MyComponent.callBaseMethod(this, 'dispose');
  }
}
MyComponent.registerClass("MyComponent", Sys.Component);
```

> **NOTE Debug Messages**
>
> Notice that we output debug messages when our component goes through its `initialize` and `dispose` methods. These messages will appear in the Visual Studio output window.

LISTING 7.3 SimpleComponent.cs

```
using System.Web.UI;
using System.Collections.Generic;

[assembly: WebResource ("Controls.JavaScript.Component.js",
                        "text/javascript")]

namespace Controls
{
  public class SimpleComponent : ScriptControl
  {
    protected override IEnumerable<ScriptDescriptor>
      GetScriptDescriptors()
    {
      ScriptComponentDescriptor scd =
        new ScriptComponentDescriptor("MyComponent");
```

LISTING 7.3 continued

```
        scd.ID = "Comp 1";
        yield return scd;
    }

    protected override IEnumerable<ScriptReference>
      GetScriptReferences()
    {
      yield return
        new ScriptReference("Controls.JavaScript.Component.js", "Controls");
    }
  }
}
```

LISTING 7.4 SimpleComponent.aspx

```
<%@ Page Language="C#"
        AutoEventWireup="true"
        CodeBehind="SimpleComponent.aspx.cs"
        Inherits="Chapter_7.SimpleComponent" %>

<%@ Register Assembly="Controls"
        Namespace="Controls"
        TagPrefix="cc1" %>
<html>
<head runat="server">
  <title>Untitled Page</title>
</head>
<body>
  <form id="form1" runat="server">
  <asp:ScriptManager ID="SM1" runat="server" />
  <asp:UpdatePanel ID="UP1"
                   runat="server"
                   UpdateMode="Conditional">
    <ContentTemplate>
      <cc1:SimpleComponent ID="Component" runat="server" />
      <asp:Button ID="tstButton" Text="Update" runat="server" />
    </ContentTemplate>
  </asp:UpdatePanel>
  </form>
</body>
</html>
```

When we execute our page from within Visual Studio, we see the component's initialization message in the Visual Studio output window. Figure 7.5 shows the initialization message.

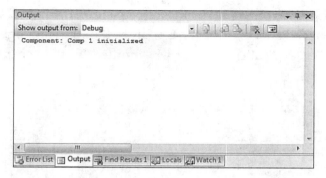

FIGURE 7.5 The initialization message in the Visual Studio Debug window

When we click the Update button, two more messages are appended to the Visual Studio output window, as shown in Figure 7.6.

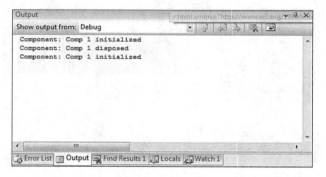

FIGURE 7.6 The dispose and second initialization messages in the Visual Studio Debug window

The second message in the window indicates that `dispose` was called on component `Comp 1`, and the third message indicates that `initialize` was called again. This output indicates that our component was disposed and re-created again when the partial postback response was received. If we repeatedly click the Update button, `Comp 1` will be repeatedly disposed and re-created, going through its initialization process each time.

`Comp 1` is re-created again when we click the Update button because, as covered in the "UpdatePanel Behavior" section, `Comp 1`'s owner server control, which in our example is the `SimpleComponent` control that was added to the page through markup, is processed again and therefore emits the same $create statement it did on the initial page load. Figure 7.7 shows the response received after clicking the Update button. The highlighted portion shows the $create statement that was emitted by the ScriptComponent Descriptor.

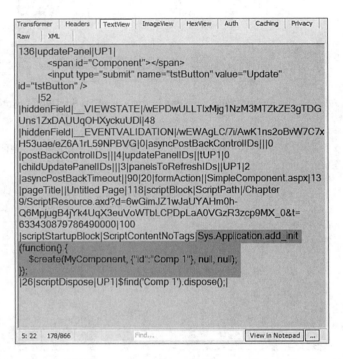

FIGURE 7.7 Re-creating Comp 1 during a partial postback

Whereas a client component is re-created in a partial postback when its containing server control is re-rendered and the control's Script Descriptors are processed, how a client component is automatically disposed differs depending on whether the component is truly a component, directly inheriting from Sys.Component, or whether it is a control or behavior. Because the disposal methods differ and because knowing how and when your client component is disposed allows you to correct disposing problems and tweak the disposal pattern, let's take a closer look at them. First, we focus on how controls and behaviors are automatically disposed, and then we focus on how components are automatically disposed.

Automatic Disposal of Behaviors and Controls

Automatic disposal of a behavior or control occurs during a partial postback when the behavior's or control's associated DOM element is destroyed. DOM elements are destroyed when they are contained within a section of the DOM tree that is being replaced by a partial postback response.

To illustrate this, we place an ASP.NET AJAX server control that creates a client behavior inside an UpdatePanel and then cause the UpdatePanel to update.

Listing 7.5, Listing 7.6, and Listing 7.7 highlight the code for our Simple Behavior test page and control.

LISTING 7.5 SimpleBehavior.js

```
SimpleBehavior = function(element) {
  SimpleBehavior.initializeBase(this, [element]);
};
SimpleBehavior.prototype = {
  dispose: function() {
    Sys.Debug.trace
      (String.format("Behavior: {0} disposed", this.get_id()));
    SimpleBehavior.callBaseMethod(this, 'dispose');
  }
};
SimpleBehavior.registerClass("SimpleBehavior", Sys.UI.Behavior);
```

LISTING 7.6 SimpleBehavior.cs

```
using System.Web.UI;
using System.Collections.Generic;

[assembly: WebResource ("Controls.JavaScript.SimpleBehavior.js",
                        "text/javascript")]

namespace Controls
{
  public class SimpleBehavior : ScriptControl
  {
    protected override IEnumerable<ScriptDescriptor>
      GetScriptDescriptors()
    {
      yield return
        new ScriptBehaviorDescriptor("SimpleBehavior", this.ClientID);
    }
```

LISTING 7.6 continued

```
      protected override IEnumerable<ScriptReference>
        GetScriptReferences()
    {
      yield return new
        ScriptReference(
          "Controls.JavaScript.SimpleBehavior.js",
          "Controls");
    }
  }
}
```

LISTING 7.7 SimpleBehavior.aspx

```
<%@ Page Language="C#"
        AutoEventWireup="true"
        CodeBehind="SimpleBehavior.aspx.cs"
        Inherits="Chapter_7.SimpleBehavior" %>

<%@ Register Assembly="Controls"
            Namespace="Controls"
            TagPrefix="cc1" %>

<html>
<head runat="server">
  <title>Simple Behavior</title>
</head>
<body>
  <form id="form1" runat="server">
  <asp:ScriptManager ID="SM1" runat="server" />
  <asp:UpdatePanel ID="UP1" runat="server" UpdateMode="Conditional">
    <ContentTemplate>
      <cc1:SimpleBehavior ID="Beh1" runat="server" />
      <asp:Button ID="tstButton" Text="Update" runat="server" />
    </ContentTemplate>
  </asp:UpdatePanel>
  </form>
</body>
</html>
```

Looking at Listing 7.8, which partially shows the HTML created when
the Simple Behavior page is first rendered, we can see that the UpdatePanel,
represented by the div tag with id="UP1", contains the span tag that represents the Beh1 instance of the SimpleBehavior server control. There is also

a `SimpleBehavior` behavior attached to that `span` tag by the highlighted `$create` statement.

LISTING 7.8 Rendered HTML from SimpleBehavior.aspx

```html
<html xmlns="http://www.w3.org/1999/xhtml" >
<head>
  <title>
      Simple Behavior
  </title>
</head>
<body>
  <form name="form1"
        method="post"
        action="SimpleBehavior.aspx"
        id="form1">
...
    <div id="UP1">
      <span id="Beh1"></span>
      <input type="submit"
             name="tstButton"
             value="Update"
             id="tstButton" />
    </div>
...
  <script type="text/javascript">
  //<![CDATA[
  Sys.Application.initialize();
  Sys.Application.add_init(function() {
    $create(SimpleBehavior, null, null, null, $get("Beh1"));
  });
  //]]>
  </script>
  </form>
</body>
</html>
```

When we click the Update button, `UpdatePanel` `UP1`'s content, which includes the `span` tag created for the `Beh1` `SimpleBehavior`, is going to be replaced with new content. We can see this by using Web Development Helper to capture the HTTP traffic. Figure 7.8 shows the captured response and highlights the portion that indicates that `UP1`'s content will be replaced.

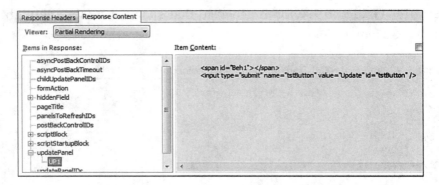

FIGURE 7.8 UpdatePanel UP1's content being replaced

Right before UP1's content is replaced with the new content, a method on the client PageRequestManager object called _destroyTree is executed. _destroyTree's responsibility is to find any behaviors or controls that are attached to any DOM element contained within UP1's DOM tree and call dispose on it. The method does this by recursively iterating through UP1's DOM tree and determining whether there is a control or behaviors attached to the current DOM element. It finds controls through the control expando property that will be attached to the DOM element if a control is attached, and it finds behaviors by using the static method Sys.UI.Behavior.get Behaviors, which returns all behaviors attached to a given DOM element. If it finds attached controls or attached behaviors, it calls dispose on each control or behavior and moves on.

This is how behaviors and controls are automatically disposed.

> ■ **NOTE**   PageRequestManager
>
> The client PageRequestManager object is the object that is responsible for handling UpdatePanels. It is contained within the MicrosoftWeb Forms.js file and is responsible for creating the partial postback request and for processing the partial postback response.

Problems with the ImageRotator Extender

Now that we understand how placing an ASP.NET AJAX server control inside an UpdatePanel affects when and how behaviors and controls will automatically be disposed and re-created, let's take a look at one of our previous examples, the ImageRotator extender that we created in Chapter 5, "Adding Client Capabilities to Server Controls," and see how it acts when we place it inside an UpdatePanel. Walking through this example will allow us to see how a common programming mistake hidden in a normal postback environment can have a drastic impact in a partial postback environment.

To start, Listing 7.9 shows the page with the ImageRotator extender inside an UpdatePanel.

LISTING 7.9 ImageRotator Extender in an UpdatePanel

```
<%@ Page Language="C#"
        AutoEventWireup="true"
        CodeBehind="Default.aspx.cs"
        Inherits="PartialPostBackWeb._Default" %>

<%@ Register assembly="ImageRotatorExtender"
             namespace="ImageRotatorExtender"
             tagprefix="cc1" %>

<html>
<head runat="server">
  <title>Image Rotator Update Panel Example</title>
</head>
<body>
  <form id="form1" runat="server">
    <h2>Pictures of Florence provided by
      <asp:Image ID="Image2"
                 runat="server"
                 ImageUrl="~/images/freeDigitalPhotoslogo.gif" />
    </h2>
    <h3> Page Last Updated:
      <asp:Label ID="Label1" runat="server"
        Text="Label" />
    </h3>
    <asp:ScriptManager ID="ScriptManager1" runat="server" />
    <asp:UpdatePanel ID="UpdatePanel1"
                     runat="server"
                     UpdateMode="Conditional">
      <ContentTemplate>
        <h4>Update Panel Last Updated <%=DateTime.Now %>
        </h4>
        <asp:Image ID="Image1"
                   runat="server"
                   ImageUrl="~/images/1.jpg" />
```

LISTING 7.9 continued

```
                <cc1:ImageRotator ID="Image1_ImageRotator"
                            runat="server"
                            ImageList="images/2.jpg,
                                    images/3.jpg,
                                    images/4.jpg,
                                    images/1.jpg"
            TargetControlID="Image1" />
        </ContentTemplate>
        <Triggers>
          <asp:AsyncPostBackTrigger
            ControlID="Button1"
            EventName="Click" />
        </Triggers>
    </asp:UpdatePanel>
    <div>
      <asp:Button ID="Button1"
                runat="server"
                Text="Post Back Update Panel" />
    </div>
    <div>
        <asp:Button ID="Button2"
                  runat="server"
                  Text="Post Back Page" />
    </div>
      <p>
        <a href="http://www.freedigitalphotos.net">Royalty free stock
        Photography</a> for websites, PowerPoint, newletters, forums,
        blogs, schools and homework - FreeDigitalPhotos. net
      </p>
    </div>
  </form>
</body>
</html>
```

When we cause the UpdatePanel to refresh multiple times by clicking Button1 (Postback Update Panel), we start to get some interesting results. Figure 7.9 shows the odd-looking image that we get after we've caused the UpdatePanel to refresh a few times.

We see this odd-looking image because whenever an instance of the ImageRotator is created, which occurs every time we cause the UpdatePanel to refresh, a new interval is attached to the window. Listing 7.10 highlights the code that creates the interval.

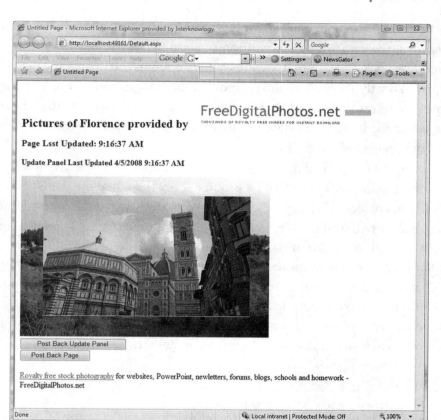

FIGURE 7.9 ImageRotator extender in an UpdatePanel

LISTING 7.10 Improperly Disposed Window.setInterval call

```
_setupRotation: function(){
  var expression = String.format("$get('{0}').
    ImageRotator._rotateImage()", this.get_element().id);

  window.setInterval(expression,this.get_rotationInterval()*1000);
}
```

> **NOTE**   Full Source Code
>
> Chapter 5 contains the full source code of the ImageRotator extender.

Because we do not clear the interval when the `ImageRotator` behavior disposes, we create a race condition of sorts between the different registered intervals. One interval expires, and it updates the image; the next one expires shortly thereafter, and it updates the image; and so on. The more times we refresh the `UpdatePanel`, the more intervals that get attached and the faster the image is updated. Cause the `UpdatePanel` to refresh enough and the image becomes a blur.

If we had not placed the `ImageRotator` extender in an `UpdatePanel`, not clearing the interval really isn't a problem because when the page unloads the `window` object is destroyed and therefore so are all of its registered intervals. But now that we are effectively causing our `ImageRotator` behavior to go through repeated initialize and dispose cycles without the page fully unloading, our programming mistake becomes obvious.

We can easily solve our interval problem by properly clearing the interval in the `dispose` method. The highlighted sections in Listing 7.11 show the changes needed to save the interval's ID and then use it in a `window.clearInterval` call in the `dispose` method.

LISTING 7.11 Clearing the Interval

```
/// <reference name="MicrosoftAjax.js"/>
Type.registerNamespace("ImageRotatorExtender");

ImageRotatorExtender.ImageRotator = function(element) {
  ImageRotatorExtender.ImageRotator.initializeBase(this, [element]);
  this._imageIndex = 0;
  this._imageList = null;
  this._rotationInterval = 3;
  this._intervalId = null;
}

ImageRotatorExtender.ImageRotator.prototype = {
...
  dispose: function() {
    this._imageList = null;
    if (this._intervalId !== null) {
      window.clearInterval(this._intervalId);
      this._intervalId = null;
    }
    ImageRotatorExtender.ImageRotator.callBaseMethod(this, 'dispose');
  },
...
  _setupRotation: function(){
```

```
var expression =
  String.format(
    "$get('{0}').ImageRotator._rotateImage()",
    this.get_element().id);
this._intervalId =
  window.setInterval(expression,this.get_rotationInterval()*1000);
},
...
}
...
```

Automatic Disposal of Components

As discussed in the "Automatic Disposal of Behaviors and Controls" section, behaviors and controls can be automatically disposed of during partial postback processing. This occurs when the DOM element the control or behavior is attached to is replaced by the results of the partial postback. Disposing of the behavior or control is a necessary step because it's possible, and actually very likely, that the server code that executes to generate the partial postback response will emit JavaScript statements to create the same controls and behaviors again, which will result in errors if the previous controls and behaviors haven't been destroyed.

But what about components? Because they aren't attached to a DOM element, how are they affected by a partial postback?

Like behaviors and controls, components can be automatically destroyed during a partial postback. They are destroyed if they were created by a *server control* whose output is contained within an updating UpdatePanel. Because a component is not associated to a DOM element, there's no way that a component can be disposed of due to a DOM element being destroyed (as happens for a behavior or control). Instead, a component is disposed through a mechanism called a dispose script.

Dispose Scripts

A dispose script is a JavaScript statement associated to an UpdatePanel such that when the UpdatePanel refreshes, it is automatically executed.

When we create an instance of a component using a ScriptComponent Descriptor and the associated server control has an UpdatePanel as a parent control, a dispose script that disposes the component is automatically created and attached to the parent `UpdatePanel`. Listing 7.12 shows the dispose script that is automatically emitted because of the `ScriptComponent Descriptor` in Listing 7.3.

LISTING 7.12 Comp 1's Dispose Script

```
<script type="text/javascript">
//<![CDATA[
Sys.Application.initialize();
Sys.WebForms.PageRequestManager.getInstance()._registerDisposeScript
  ("UP1", "$find(\u0027Comp 1\u0027).dispose();");
Sys.Application.add_init(function() {
  $create(MyComponent, {"id":"Comp 1"}, null, null);
});
//]]>
</script>
```

In Listing 7.12, the dispose script registration is highlighted. Using the `_registerDisposeScript` method available on the `PageRequestManager` object, the dispose script `$find(\u0027Comp 1\u0027).dispose();` is registered to execute when `UpdatePanel` `UP1` refreshes.

> ■ **NOTE** Escaped Quotes
>
> \u0027 is the escaped value for the single quote (').

It is important to understand that the dispose script shown in Listing 7.12 is registered with the `UpdatePanel` during the *initial* execution of the page and not when the partial postback response is received. When the partial postback response is received, the dispose scripts that were *previously* registered with an `UpdatePanel` are executed, cleared, and then new dispose scripts are registered. This makes sense because the previously created components need to be destroyed. Components that are to be created based on the partial postback response will register new dispose scripts that will be executed during the next partial postback.

To illustrate this point, we can modify Listing 7.3 to create a different component when the code is executing within a partial postback. Listing 7.13 shows the updated code.

LISTING 7.13 Creating Different Components Based on Partial Postback

```
protected override IEnumerable<ScriptDescriptor>
  GetScriptDescriptors()
{
  if (ScriptManager.GetCurrent(this.Page).IsInAsyncPostBack)
  {
    ScriptComponentDescriptor scd =
      new ScriptComponentDescriptor("MyComponent");
    scd.ID = "Partial Postback Component";
    yield return scd;
  }
  else
  {
    ScriptComponentDescriptor scd =
      new ScriptComponentDescriptor("MyComponent");
    scd.ID = "Non-Partial Postback Component";
    yield return scd;
  }
}
```

Now, when we click the Update button, the nonpartial postback component will be disposed, and the partial postback component will be created. Figure 7.10 shows the debug messages displayed in the Visual Studio output window when each component is initialized and disposed.

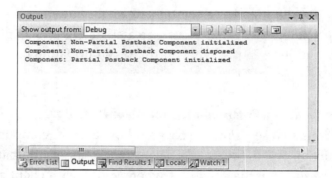

FIGURE 7.10 The disposal and initialization of each component

In addition to containing the code to create the partial postback component, the partial postback response contains a new dispose script that will dispose of the partial postback component the next time the UP1 UpdatePanel is refreshed. Figure 7.11 shows the partial postback response and highlights the dispose script registered to dispose the partial postback component.

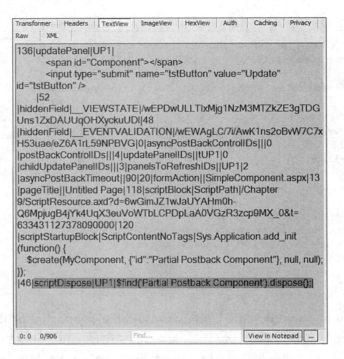

FIGURE 7.11 The dispose script for the partial postback component

Finally, just to summarize, a component will be automatically destroyed due to a partial postback if it was created using a `ScriptComponent Descriptor` and its owner server control has an updating `UpdatePanel` as an ancestor.

Manual Disposal of a Component, Control, or Behavior

In the previous two sections, we covered how a client component can be automatically disposed due to a partial postback. These automatic disposal patterns cover most of the situations where you'll use a client component, but sometimes you'll want manual control of the disposal.

These situations fall into one of two categories. Either the behavior or control isn't disposed automatically because of something that it does internally to itself or you want to prevent the automatic disposal in certain situations. When these situations arise, you must take manual control of the disposal process.

Manual Disposal of Control and Behaviors

The first situation that we cover is when automatic disposal of a behavior or control doesn't occur as expected because of something it does internally to itself. This primarily happens for one reason: The DOM element associated to the control or behavior was initially a child of an `UpdatePanel`, but was moved to a different part of the DOM tree. When the `UpdatePanel` updates, the automatic destruction code fails to find the DOM element and therefore fails to destroy the control or behavior. This can easily cause an error because a control or behavior with the same ID is going to be created and added to `Sys.Application`.

Let's walk through an example in which you need to move the DOM element to another location in the tree to get some functionality to work properly, and because of this you need to manually dispose of the behaviors and controls associated to the DOM element.

HoverCard

In this example, we want to create a draggable panel that displays information about a person. We'll call this draggable panel a `HoverCard`, and we want to encapsulate all the necessary functionality in a control so that we can reuse it as needed.

To start, let's take a look at the server control's code that we'll store in HoverCard.cs. Listing 7.14 shows the server control's code.

LISTING 7.14 HoverCard Server Control

```
public class HoverCard : ScriptControl
{
  private Panel _dragHandle = new Panel();

  protected override void OnInit(System.EventArgs e)
  {
    base.OnInit(e);
    _dragHandle.Width = Unit.Pixel(200);
    _dragHandle.Height = Unit.Pixel(30);
    _dragHandle.BackColor = Color.DarkSlateBlue;
  }

  protected override IEnumerable<ScriptDescriptor>
   GetScriptDescriptors()
  {
    yield return
```

LISTING 7.14 continued

```
      new ScriptControlDescriptor("HoverCard", this.ClientID);
    }

    protected override IEnumerable<ScriptReference>
      GetScriptReferences()
    {
      yield return new ScriptReference
        ("Controls.JavaScript.HoverCard.js", "Controls");
    }

    protected override HtmlTextWriterTag TagKey
    {
      get
      {
        return HtmlTextWriterTag.Div;
      }
    }

    protected override void AddAttributesToRender
      (HtmlTextWriter writer)
    {
      base.AddAttributesToRender(writer);
      writer.AddStyleAttribute
        (HtmlTextWriterStyle.Width, "200px");
      writer.AddStyleAttribute
        (HtmlTextWriterStyle.Height, "150px");
      writer.AddStyleAttribute
        (HtmlTextWriterStyle.BackgroundColor, "Gainsboro");
    }

    protected override void OnPreRender(System.EventArgs e)
    {
      base.OnPreRender(e);
      this.Controls.Add(this._dragHandle);
      DragPanelExtender dpe = new DragPanelExtender();
      dpe.ID = this.ID + "DragPanelExtender";
      dpe.DragHandleID = this._dragHandle.ClientID;
      dpe.TargetControlID = this.ClientID;
      this.Controls.Add(dpe);
    }
    protected override void RenderContents(HtmlTextWriter writer)
    {
      base.RenderContents(writer);
      writer.Write(@"
        <span>Name: Joel Rumerman</span>
        <br />
        <span>Hometown: Silver Spring, Md</span>
        <br />
```

```
  <span>Spouse: Stacey</span>
  <br />
  <span>Siblings: Keri</span>");
    }
  }
```

This server control does a few things. First, it renders output that looks something like Figure 7.12.

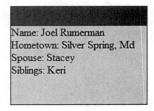

FIGURE 7.12 A HoverCard's visual output

It does this by hard coding some output values in the `Render` method and setting some of the control's attributes in the `AddAttributesToRender` method.

Second, it creates and wires up a `DragPanelExtender`, one of the extenders available in the AJAX Control Toolkit, to the control in the `OnPre Render` method. This gives the control its dragging capabilities by attaching a behavior to the DOM element.

Finally, it creates a client control of type `HoverCard` by registering a `ScriptReference` to the HoverCard.js JavaScript file, shown in Listing 7.15, and using a `ScriptControlDescriptor` to create an instance of the control.

LISTING 7.15 HoverCard Client Control

```
HoverCard = function(element) {
  HoverCard.initializeBase(this, [element]);
};
HoverCard.prototype = {
  initialize: function() {
    HoverCard.callBaseMethod(this, 'initialize');
  },
  dispose: function() {
    Sys.Debug.trace
      (String.format("Control: {0} disposed", this.get_id()));
    HoverCard.callBaseMethod(this, 'dispose');
  }
};
HoverCard.registerClass("HoverCard", Sys.UI.Control);
```

So far, so good. When we add a `HoverCard` to a test page, shown in Listing 7.16, it works as expected. We can drag it around by the title bar and it displays the information correctly.

LISTING 7.16 HoverCard Test Page

```
<%@ Page Language="C#"
        AutoEventWireup="true"
        CodeBehind="HoverCardTester.aspx.cs"
        Inherits="Chapter_7.HoverCardTester" %>

<%@ Register Assembly="Controls"
        Namespace="Controls"
        TagPrefix="cc1" %>

<html>
<head runat="server">
  <title>HoverCard Tester</title>
</head>
<body style="width:100%;height:750px">
  <form id="form1" runat="server">
  <asp:ScriptManager ID="SM1" runat="server" />
  <cc1:HoverCard ID="HC" runat="server" />
  </form>
</body>
</html>
```

Figure 7.13 shows the `HoverCard`'s initial position, and Figure 7.14 shows the `HoverCard`'s position after we've dragged it a bit to the right.

FIGURE 7.13 The HoverCard's initial location

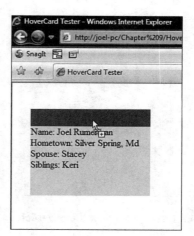

FIGURE 7.14 The HoverCard after we've dragged it a bit

However, problems start to occur when the HoverCard is placed within a div tag that is positioned somewhere on the page. The HoverCard's initial position seems to be offset by the div tag's position on the screen, and clicking its header causes the HoverCard to initially move by the same offset.

Listing 7.17 shows the modifications to our test page with the div tag.

LISTING 7.17 HoverCard Test Page with div Tag

```
<form id="form1" runat="server">
<asp:ScriptManager ID="SM1" runat="server" />
<div style="position: absolute;
            top: 50px;
            left: 50px;
            height: 200px;
            width: 200px;
            border: solid 1px black;">
  <cc1:HoverCard ID="HC" runat="server" />
</div>
</form>
```

Figure 7.15 shows the original position of the HoverCard, and Figure 7.16 shows the position of the HoverCard *right after* we clicked the HoverCard's header. Notice how the cursor is in one spot, but the HoverCard is not under it.

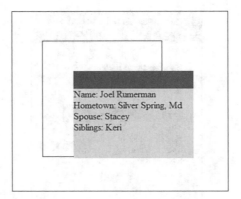

FIGURE 7.15   Initial position of the HoverCard in the div tag

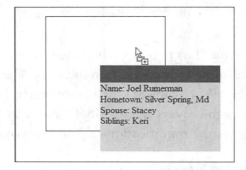

FIGURE 7.16   The HoverCard's position after we've clicked the header

This is obviously not good. If we play around with our div tag, we can make the problem even more pronounced.

> ■ **NOTE**   The Purpose of Wrapping the HoverCard in a div Tag
>
> Wrapping the HoverCard control in a div tag simulates it being contained within another control, a situation that is most likely going to come up.

Without delving into the causes of the positioning problems too deeply, we'll tell you two things. First, the cause of the problem is the DragPanel Extender. Second, if we move our HoverCard's associated DOM element so that it is a child of the body element rather than a child of the div tag, the problem is corrected.

■ NOTE   DragPanelExtender

We're not trying to pick on the DragPanelExtender with this example. We may be using it incorrectly, but it does help us elucidate the concept we're trying to cover very nicely.

In light of this knowledge, we're going to alter our HoverCard.js file a bit so that it automatically moves the HoverCard's associated DOM element to be a child of the body tag instead of where it was originally positioned in the DOM tree. Listing 7.18 highlights the changes needed to accomplish this.

LISTING 7.18 Altering HoverCard's initialize Method to Move the Element to the Body

```
initialize: function() {
  HoverCard.callBaseMethod(this, 'initialize');
  var elm = this.get_element();
  elm.parentNode.removeChild(elm);
  document.body.appendChild(elm);
},
```

Now when we view our test page, our HoverCard works as it did before and is positioned correctly.

But (there's always a *but,* isn't there?), we caused ourselves a hidden problem. We caused the problem by moving the HoverCard from its original DOM location and therefore it won't automatically be destroyed when it is contained within an updating UpdatePanel. Listing 7.19 sets up this situation by updating our page's markup and wrapping our HoverCard in an UpdatePanel.

LISTING 7.19 Placing Our HoverCard in an UpdatePanel

```
<asp:UpdatePanel ID="UP1"
                 runat="server"
                 UpdateMode="Conditional">
  <ContentTemplate>
    <div style="position: absolute;
                top: 50px;
                left: 50px;
                height: 200px;
                width: 200px;
                border: solid 1px black;">
      <cc1:HoverCard ID="HC" runat="server" />
    </div>
    <asp:Button ID="tstButton" Text="Update" runat="server" />
  </ContentTemplate>
</asp:UpdatePanel>
```

When we initially run the page, the HoverCard is displayed properly and we're able to move it about. Figure 7.17 displays the initial view of the page.

FIGURE 7.17 The initial view of the page wrapped in an UpdatePanel

However, when we cause the UpdatePanel to update by clicking the Update button, we receive a JavaScript error. Figure 7.18 shows the error that we received.

The error states that "Two components with the same id 'HCDrag PanelExtender' can't be added to the application." This is essentially telling us that there is a component with the ID HCDragPanelExtender already in Sys.Application's list of managed components and that we're trying to add a second one. Adding more than one component to Sys.Application with the same ID is illegal, as we covered in Chapter 4, "Sys.Application."

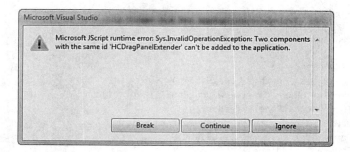

FIGURE 7.18 The JavaScript error after we clicked the Update button

If we click Continue on our Visual Studio JavaScript error prompt, we receive a second error, shown in Figure 7.19: "Two components with the same id 'HC' can't be added to the application." This second error messages indicates that we have another conflict.

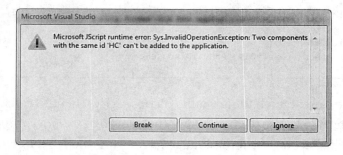

FIGURE 7.19 The second JavaScript error after we clicked the first error's Continue button

These errors occurred because when we moved the HoverCard's associated DOM element from its original location in the DOM tree to a child of the body element instead in the initialize method, we broke its capability to be automatically disposed when the containing UpdatePanel was updated.

However, by manually registering a dispose script with the UpdatePanel that disposes of the HoverCard, we can correct the problem. Listing 7.20 shows the code necessary to dispose of our HoverCard properly.

LISTING 7.20 Placing Our HoverCard in an UpdatePanel

```
protected override void OnPreRender(System.EventArgs e)
{
  base.OnPreRender(e);
  this.Controls.Add(this._dragHandle);
  DragPanelExtender dpe = new DragPanelExtender();
  dpe.ID = "HCDragPanelExtender";
  dpe.DragHandleID = this._dragHandle.ClientID;
  dpe.TargetControlID = this.ClientID;
  this.Controls.Add(dpe);

  ScriptManager sm = ScriptManager.GetCurrent(this.Page);
  string manualDisposeScript = string.Format(@"
    var elm = $get('{0}');
    if (elm !== null) {{
      elm.control.dispose();
      var behaviors = Sys.UI.Behavior.getBehaviors(elm);
      for (var i=0; i < behaviors.length; i++) {{
        behaviors[i].dispose();
      }}
      elm.parentNode.removeChild(elm);
    }}
  ", this.ClientID);
  sm.RegisterDispose(this, manualDisposeScript);
}
```

We take care of three things in the dispose script. First, we dispose of the control attached to the element using the control expando property that's attached to it. Second, we retrieve all behaviors attached to the element using the Sys.UI.Behavior.getBehaviors method and then iterate over them calling dispose on each behavior. Finally, we remove the element from the DOM tree so that we don't have the same HoverCard on the page more than once.

We register the dispose script using the RegisterDispose instance method available on the current ScriptManager. RegisterDispose takes two parameters. The first parameter is the control that we want to associate the dispose script to. The second is the script to execute.

> **■ TIP   RegisterDispose When Not Inside an UpdatePanel**
>
> Dispose scripts are useful only when the control is contained within an UpdatePanel. Executing the RegisterDispose method when the control is not contained within an UpdatePanel ends up having no effect. In fact, no JavaScript that represents the dispose script is emitted to the client even if we registered one on the server.

When our page renders, the dispose script is registered with the PageRequestManager, just as for a component. Listing 7.21 shows the dispose script being registered.

LISTING 7.21 The HoverCard's Dispose Script Registered with the PageRequestManager

```
Sys.WebForms.PageRequestManager.getInstance()._registerDisposeScript
("UP1", "var elm = $get(\u0027HC\u0027); if (elm !== null) {
elm.control.dispose(); var behaviors = Sys.UI.Behavior.getBehaviors(elm);
for (var i=0; i\u003cbehaviors.length; i++) { behaviors[i].dispose();}
elm.parentNode.removeChild(elm); }");
```

> **NOTE** Reformatted
>
> We reformatted Listing 7.21 to make it somewhat legible.

Now, when we click the Update button, the existing HoverCard is completely disposed, and when the partial postback response is received and a new HoverCard is created, there are no JavaScript errors.

Preventing Automatic Disposal of Components

As we covered so far in this chapter, there are two reasons your component, behavior, or control will automatically be disposed. One, it's contained within a portion of the DOM tree that is being replaced by a partial postback response. Two, the server control that created the component is contained within an UpdatePanel and that UpdatePanel is being updated.

Unfortunately, unless you move the associated DOM element to some other part of the DOM tree, there is no way to prevent the automatic disposal of a control or a behavior.

There is a way, however, to prevent the automatic disposal of a component. It might seem obvious after we cover it, but the way to prevent automatic disposal of a component is to not use a ScriptComponentDescriptor to create the component. Using the ScriptComponentDescriptor is what automatically registers a dispose script with the containing UpdatePanel. If we don't use a ScriptComponentDescriptor, but instead manually create our component by emitting our own JavaScript, we can leave the dispose script out altogether or create our own that works differently than the default.

ErrorHandler Component

A good example of when we'll want to do this is when we have a component represented by a server control that we intend to be global to the application. An example of this is the ErrorHandler component we created in Chapter 3, "Components." We intend that this component will be created once when the page initializes, will live throughout the page's life, and be disposed of when the page unloads. However, if the ErrorHandler component is created by a related server control, which internally uses a ScriptComponentDescriptor, and that control is placed within an UpdatePanel, every time that UpdatePanel updates, our ErrorHandler component will be disposed of and re-created. The re-creation of the ErrorHandler component won't cause errors itself, but if it's disposed of and then JavaScript code throws an error before it's re-created, the ErrorHandler component won't be around to handle that error. Also, disposing of and re-creating it is a waste of processing and resources.

To start, let's assume that we have the ErrorHandler component's code available to us in a JavaScript file. (Its full source is available in Appendix D, "Client Error Handling Code.") We create an instance of the component using a related server control, which uses a ScriptComponentDescriptor. Listing 7.22 shows the server control's code.

LISTING 7.22 The ErrorHandler Server Control

```
using System.Collections.Generic;
using System.Web.UI;
using System;

namespace ErrorHandlerLibrary
{
  public class ErrorHandler : ScriptControl
  {
    protected override IEnumerable<ScriptReference>
      GetScriptReferences()
    {
      yield return
        new ScriptReference("ErrorHandlerLibrary.ErrorHandler.js",
                            typeof(ErrorHandler).Assembly.FullName);
    }

    protected override IEnumerable<ScriptDescriptor>
      GetScriptDescriptors()
    {
```

```
    ScriptComponentDescriptor scd =
      new ScriptComponentDescriptor("ErrorHandler");
    scd.ID = "ErrorHandler";
    yield return scd;
  }
 }
}
```

> ■ **NOTE**   **Abbreviated Version**
>
> Appendix D has the full version of the ErrorHandler's server control.
> For brevity, we're just displaying the pertinent parts of it.

Next, we place our ErrorHandler server control inside an UpdatePanel,
as shown in Listing 7.23.

LISTING 7.23 The ErrorHandler Test Page

```
<%@ Page Language="C#"
        AutoEventWireup="true"
        CodeBehind="ErrorHandler.aspx.cs"
        Inherits="Chapter_7.ErrorHandler" %>

<%@ Register Assembly="Controls"
            Namespace="Controls"
            TagPrefix="cc1" %>
<html>
<head runat="server">
  <title>Error Handler Test Page</title>
</head>
<body>
  <form id="form1" runat="server">
    <asp:ScriptManager ID="SM1" runat="server" />
    <asp:UpdatePanel ID="UP1" runat="server" UpdateMode="Conditional">
      <ContentTemplate>
        <cc1:ErrorHandler ID="ErrorHandler" runat="server" />
        <asp:Button ID="tstButton" Text="Update" runat="server" />
      </ContentTemplate>
    </asp:UpdatePanel>
  </form>
</body>
</html>
```

As you might have guessed, every time we click the Update button, the ErrorHandler component is disposed of and re-created. Figure 7.20 shows the initialization and disposal debug messages in the Visual Studio output window.

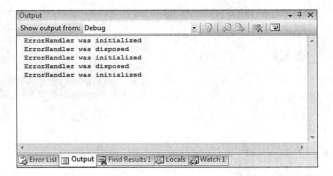

FIGURE 7.20 ErrorHandler's initialization and disposal messages

We can prevent this unwanted disposal and re-creation by not using a ScriptComponentDescriptor and emitting our own JavaScript component $create statement. Listing 7.24 shows how we can alter our ErrorHandler server control to control the disposal of the component.

LISTING 7.24 Updating ErrorHandler to Manually Create the ErrorHandler Component

```
protected override IEnumerable<ScriptDescriptor> GetScriptDescriptors()
{
  return null;
}

protected override void OnPreRender(EventArgs e)
{
  base.OnPreRender(e);
  string createErrorHandler = @"
    Sys.Application.add_init(
      function() {
        var errHandler = $find('ErrorHandler');
        if (errHandler === null) {
          $create(ErrorHandler, {id:'ErrorHandler'}, null, null, null);
        }
      }
    );";
  ScriptManager.RegisterStartupScript(
    this,
```

```
    typeof(ErrorHandler),
    "ErrorHandlerCreate",
    createErrorHandler,
    true);
}
```

The first thing we do in the server control is not use a `ScriptComponent Descriptor` to create the `ErrorHandler` component. Instead, we use the `OnPreRender` method to register a startup script that will create the `ErrorHandler` *if it does not already exist.*

Now, our component will be disposed of only when the page unloads, and it will be created only if it doesn't already exist. We can cause partial postbacks as many times as we want and our component will not be disposed of and re-created.

Loading of JavaScript Statements and Files

The way the `UpdatePanel` processes your scripts as they are returned from a partial page rendering can be a bit confusing at first. In many cases, some of the techniques you have used in the past for registering scripts no longer function correctly during a partial postback, and worse yet, some script registration techniques will work during the page's initial request and during a postback but will not work during a partial postback. The goal of this section is to understand why this is happening and how to adjust your coding approach to have a consistent client script registration experience during all these cases.

ScriptManager Registration Methods

The `ClientScriptManager`'s static `RegisterXXX` methods that we access through the page's `ClientScript` property have been the preferred way of registering scripts since the release of ASP.NET 2.0. However, with the new partial postback capabilities provided by ASP.NET AJAX, the `ClientScriptManager` and its `RegisterXXX` methods no longer work across all page-rendering situations. Specifically, the `ClientScriptManager`'s `RegisterXXX` methods do not work properly during a partial postback.

This is the case because the `UpdatePanel`, `ScriptManager`, and a private object of type `PageRequestManager` take over responsibility for generating a partial postback response, and those objects don't have access to the scripts that were registered using the `ClientScriptManager`. (The primary reason for this is because of the way `ClientScriptManager` was written and not anything that was programmed wrong in ASP.NET AJAX.)

Because of `ClientScriptManager`'s shortcomings, ASP.NET AJAX comes with a new way of registering client scripts that successfully registers scripts in all rendering environments (normal postback and partial postback): through `ScriptManager`'s static `RegisterXXX` methods.

Fortunately, it's pretty easy to learn the new `RegisterXXX` methods, detailed in Table 7.1, because they are direct replacements for the `ClientScriptManager` methods that we previously used to register scripts.

TABLE 7.1 ScriptManager Script Registration Methods

Method	Description
`RegisterArrayDeclaration`	Provides the ability to register a JavaScript array that will be properly registered when using an `UpdatePanel` and comes in handy when the client needs information that is obtainable only during runtime.
`RegisterClientScriptBlock`	Provides the ability to register a script block that is properly registered when using an `UpdatePanel` and provides the ability to have the script tags added automatically or be included in the script block for cases where you want to control the script tag attributes.
`RegisterClientScriptInclude`	Provides the ability to register a script file that is properly registered when using an `UpdatePanel`. The script file is registered using the `src` attribute on the `script` tag and must be in the web folder structure of your application, because this method of registration does not work with embedded resources.
`RegisterClientScriptResource`	Provides the ability to register a script file that is embedded in an assembly and needs to be properly registered when using an `UpdatePanel`. In cases of an `Extender Control` or `ScriptControl` registering with the `ScriptReference` class.

Method	Description
RegisterOnSubmitStatement	Provides the ability to register script fragments that will be included in the WebForm_OnSubmit method on a page. When you use this registration method, all script fragments that are registered will run when the page is partially updating or doing a full postback.
RegisterStartupScript	Provides the ability to register script fragments that will be run when the page is initially created or after a partial rendering has occurred.

In some cases, however, these new methods have a slightly different signature and behavior than the ClientScriptManager methods they replaced.

To demonstrate these differences, let's take a look at the three different ways we can register a client script block. Listing 7.25 shows the three method calls.

LISTING 7.25 ClientScriptManager versus ScriptManager Script Registration

```
this.ClientScript.RegisterClientScriptBlock
  (this.GetType(),
  "MyOriginalAlert",
  "alert('We are loaded with ClientScript.ClientScriptBlock');",
  true);

ScriptManager.RegisterClientScriptBlock(
  this,
  this.GetType(),
  "MyOriginalScriptManagerAlert",
  "alert('We are loaded with
          ScriptManager.RegisterClientScriptBlock');",
  true);

ScriptManager.RegisterClientScriptBlock(
  this.TextBox2,
  typeof(TextBox),
  "TextBox2Script",
  "alert('TextBox2 based script is here')",
  true);
```

The first method registers the script with the page using ASP.NET's `ClientScriptManager`. When the page is first created or when the page is posted back, the script will run; however, the script will not run in a partial postback.

The second method uses the new `ScriptManager` method of registering a script block. This script will run when the page is first loaded, during a normal postback, *and* during a partial postback.

The final method shows the power of the new methods and how they are specifically tuned to the `UpdatePanel`. In this case, we can associate the script to a control and run that script only when the control is part of the response. What this means is that when the page is first created and when the page is in a normal postback, the script will run. The script will also run when `TextBox2` is included in a partial postback response. This ability becomes handy when you have multiple `UpdatePanel` controls on a page and want to run a script only when the control is contained in an `UpdatePanel` that is being partially rendered.

> ■ **TIP** **Always Use the ScriptManager for Client Script Registration**
>
> Now that we're in a partial postback world, you should always use `ScriptManager` to register your scripts. Getting in this habit will allow your scripts to work seamlessly in both a normal rendering and in a partial rendering environment. The only catch to this rule is if you're a third-party control developer. In that case, you might want to confirm that ASP.NET AJAX is installed in the environment your code is executing in before using `ScriptManager` to register the scripts.

To get a better feel for how scripts are affected by a partial postback, let's walk through a quick example in which we register a couple of scripts using `ClientScriptManager` and `ScriptManager`. We start with the `UpdatePanel` sample page we used earlier in the chapter (redisplayed in Listing 7.26) and update its code behind to register the scripts in its `Page_Load` method. Listing 7.27 shows the updated code behind, and Figure 7.21 shows the page's visual output.

LISTING 7.26 Page-Rendering Markup

```
<%@ Page Language="C#"
        AutoEventWireup="true"
        CodeBehind="Default.aspx.cs"
        Inherits="SimpleUpdatePanelDemo._Default" %>


<html>
<head runat="server">
  <title>Untitled Page</title>
</head>
<body>
  <form id="form1" runat="server">
    <asp:Label ID="Label1" runat="server">
      <%=DateTime.Now %>
    </asp:Label>
    <asp:ScriptManager ID="ScriptManager1" runat="server" />
    <asp:UpdatePanel ID="UpdatePanel1"
                     runat="server"
                     UpdateMode="Conditional">
      <ContentTemplate>
        <asp:TextBox ID="TextBox1" runat="server" />
      </ContentTemplate>
      <Triggers>
        <asp:AsyncPostBackTrigger ControlID="Button1"
                                  EventName="Click" />
      </Triggers>
    </asp:UpdatePanel>
    <div>
      <asp:Button ID="Button1"
                  runat="server"
                  Text="Update Panel Refresh" />
    </div>
    <div>
      <asp:Button ID="Button2"
                  runat="server"
                  Text="Complete Page Refresh" />
    </div>
  </form>
</body>
</html>
```

LISTING 7.27 Script Registration Code Behind

```
public partial class _Default : System.Web.UI.Page
{
  protected void Page_Load(object sender, EventArgs e)
  {
    this.TextBox1.Text = DateTime.Now.ToLongTimeString();

    this.ClientScript.RegisterClientScriptBlock
     (this.GetType(),
      "MyOriginalAlert",
      "alert('We are loaded with ClientScript.ClientScriptBlock');",
      true);

    ScriptManager.RegisterClientScriptBlock
      (this,
       this.GetType(),
       "MyOriginalScriptManagerAlert",
       "alert('We are loaded with
               ScriptManager.RegisterClientScriptBlock');",
       true);

  }
}
```

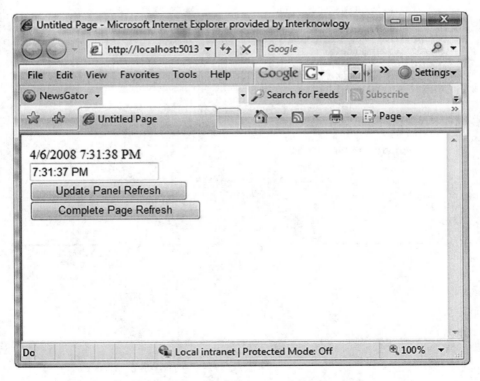

FIGURE 7.21 Partial page-rendering sample

During the page's initial execution both scripts run successfully and show the alerts shown in Figure 7.22 and Figure 7.23, respectively.

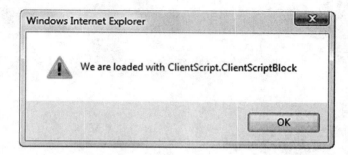

FIGURE 7.22 Alert from ClientScriptManager registration in page load

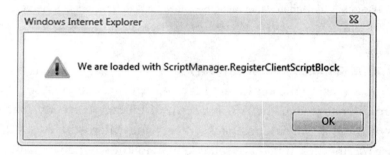

FIGURE 7.23 Alert from ScriptManager registration in page load

However, when we initiate a partial postback by clicking Button1, the script registered using the ScriptManager will execute successfully, redisplaying Figure 7.22, but the script registered using the ClientScriptManager will not. This is because scripts registered with the ClientScriptManager are not considered in the processing of the partial postback request and do not affect the response sent to the client.

Viewing the partial postback response in Web Development Helper, shown in Figure 7.24 we can clearly see that the script registered using the ScriptManager is included in the partial postback response and is treated as a ScriptContentNoTags script block.

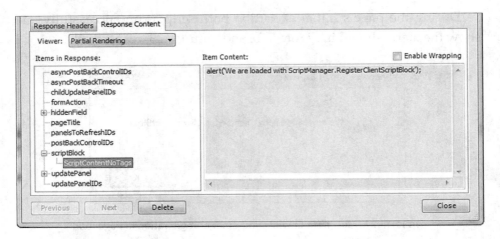

FIGURE 7.24 UpdatePanel response shown in Web Development Helper

Sys.Application.notifyScriptLoaded()

When you are using the `RegisterClientScriptInclude` method, take special care to ensure that the ASP.NET AJAX Library correctly loads your scripts during a partial postback. When the Microsoft AJAX Library processes script files, it needs a reliable way to know when a script file has completely loaded so that it can move on to the next one. Unfortunately, there is no cross-browser compliant way of knowing when a script file has completely loaded. Therefore, the Microsoft AJAX Library requires that when a script file is loaded during a partial postback it has a call to `Sys.Application.notifyScriptLoaded()`at the end of the script file. Executing this method at the end of the script file tells the script-loading object inside the Microsoft AJAX Library that the current script has completed loading and the next available script can start.

This method was briefly mentioned in Chapter 5 when we were discussing the `ScriptReference` class and how the `Sys.Application.notify`
`ScriptLoaded` method was used when you registered your behavior or control scripts. In those cases, the JavaScript files were embedded resources, and the `ScriptManager` automatically added the method call to the end of our scripts as they were downloaded to the client.

However, when we manually register a file using the `Register ClientScriptInclude` method, we need to manually add the call to `Sys.Application.notifyScriptLoaded` at the end of the script file for it to be loaded successfully during a partial postback.

If the `Sys.Application.notifyScriptLoaded` method is absent or more than one call to the method is within a single file, the Microsoft AJAX Library throws an error as it tries to load the script.

When using the `notifyScriptLoaded` method, always check for the presence of the Microsoft AJAX Library on the client (to prevent the call from failing). The check, done by detecting whether `Sys` is defined and shown in Listing 7.28, should be placed before the `Sys.Application.notifyScriptLoaded` call to ensure it will work correctly. This check is especially important when a script file may be used outside an ASP.NET AJAX-enabled application. In that case, if the check is not there, the script file will throw an error when one really should not be thrown.

LISTING 7.28 Check for Sys.Application

```
if (typeof(Sys) !== 'undefined')
   Sys.Application.notifyScriptLoaded();
```

Finally, as stated earlier, if more than one call to `Sys.Application.notifyScriptLoaded` is made by a single script file, an error will occur. This subtle issue can come up when you have a common script file that you are using that can be registered using both the `ScriptReference` class and the `RegisterClientScriptInclude` methods of registration. In this case, you must set the `NotifyScriptLoaded` property of the `ScriptReference` class to `false` to suppress the default injection of the `Sys.Application.notify ScriptLoaded` method into your script. Listing 7.29 shows an example of creating a `ScriptReference` where it won't inject the `Sys. Application.notifyScriptLoaded` call automatically.

LISTING 7.29 Turning Off the Automatic Sys.Application.notifyScriptLoaded Injection

```
protected override IEnumerable<ScriptReference> GetScriptReferences()
{
   ScriptReference sr = new ScriptReference("Common.js", "Controls");
   sr.NotifyScriptLoaded = false;
   yield return sr;
}
```

Sys.Application Events

One of common ways that we interact with Sys.Application is through its events. We register $create statements with the init event, we wire up handlers to the load event so that we can execute code after all components have been created, and we watch the unload event to execute custom cleanup code or to persist changes the user made during the course of using the page.

We covered the use of these events in Chapter 4, and we covered them under the presumption that Sys.Application was first initializing. We covered them under this presumption because with partial postbacks these events are used again and they act and work differently than when the page is first initializing. To be more precise, the init event works differently and the load event is re-raised. The unload event does not factor into the processing of a partial postback.

The init Event

In Chapter 4, when we covered the init event, we stated that the add_init method was different from other add_*eventName* methods. As you learned in that chapter, if Sys.Application was already initialized, the add_init method executed the *handler* parameter instead of adding it to the list of handlers to execute when the init event was raised. Listing 7.30 displays the body of the add_init method.

LISTING 7.30 Sys.Application's add_init Method

```
function Sys$_Application$add_init(handler) {
  var e = Function._validateParams(arguments,
            [{name: "handler", type: Function}]);
  if (e) throw e;
  if (this._initialized) {
    handler(this, Sys.EventArgs.Empty);
  }
  else {
    this.get_events().addHandler("init", handler);
  }
}
```

This change in behavior is important to understand when working within a partial postback environment. It's important because control developers often face this concern: If I use one of the `ScriptDescriptors` as the mechanism for creating client components, it will emit a `$create` statement that is added to the `init` event using the `add_init` method. If I know that the `init` event is not re-raised during a partial postback, my component will not be created during a partial postback, and I must handle the partial postback situation differently.

Because the `add_init` method takes into account whether the application is already initialized, which it will be if the method is executed during a partial postback, we do not need to alter how we create client components during a partial postback.

The load Event

As covered in Chapter 4, the `load` event is raised during `Sys.Application`'s initialization cycle after all components have been created. The event's arguments that it is raised with are of type `Sys.ApplicationLoadEventArgs` and contain an array of all the components that were created during the initialization cycle and a Boolean flag that indicates whether the event is being raised during a partial postback.

During a partial postback, the `load` event is raised again. However, this time the event argument parameter contains a list of the components that were created during the partial postback, and the `inPartialLoad` property is set to `true`.

To illustrate this, let's set up a simple example in which we watch the `load` event. Reusing our existing `HoverCard` control, Listing 7.31 sets up a test page where we have two `HoverCards`: one within an `UpdatePanel` and one outside it. We also add an event handler to `Sys.Application`'s `load` event where using `trace` statements we output the contents of the event arguments passed into the handler.

LISTING 7.31 The Load Event Test Page

```
<%@ Page Language="C#"
        AutoEventWireup="true"
        CodeBehind="LoadEvent.aspx.cs"
        Inherits="Chapter_7.LoadEvent" %>

<%@ Register Assembly="Controls"
            Namespace="Controls"
            TagPrefix="cc1" %>
```

LISTING 7.31 continued

```html
<html>
<head runat="server">
  <title>Load Event Test Page</title>
</head>
<body style="width: 1024px; height: 768px">
  <form id="form1" runat="server">
  <asp:ScriptManager ID="SM1" runat="server" />
  <asp:UpdatePanel ID="UP1" runat="server" UpdateMode="Conditional">
    <ContentTemplate>
      <div style="position:absolute;
                  top:100px;
                  left:225px">
        <cc1:HoverCard ID="InsideUpdatePanelHC" runat="server" />
      </div>
      <asp:Button ID="tstButton" Text="Update" runat="server" />
    </ContentTemplate>
  </asp:UpdatePanel>
  <cc1:HoverCard ID="OutsideUpdatePanelHC" runat="server" />
  </form>
</body>

<script type="text/javascript">
  function loadHandler(sender, args) {
    Sys.Debug.trace(String.format
      ("In partial postback: {0}", args.get_isPartialLoad()));
    var comps = args.get_components();
    for (var i=0; i<comps.length; i++) {
      Sys.Debug.trace(String.format
        ("Created Component: {0}", comps[i].get_id()));
    }
  }
  Sys.Application.add_load(loadHandler);
</script>
</html>
```

Figure 7.25 shows the Visual Studio output window after we load the page.

As Figure 7.25 shows, we are not in a partial load, and both HoverCard controls and their respective DragPanelExtenders are contained within the list of components that were created.

When we click the Update button and cause a partial postback, load Handler executes again because the load event is re-raised. Figure 7.26 shows the new messages that are appended to the Visual Studio output window.

FIGURE 7.25 The output of the loadHandler method

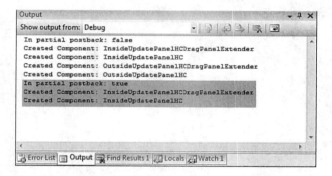

FIGURE 7.26 The output of the loadHandler method

As Figure 7.26 shows, we are in a partial load and only the `Inside UpdatePanelHC` and its respective `DragPanelExtender` were created during processing of the partial postback response.

SUMMARY

In this chapter, we covered how the partial postback environment affects our control development. Knowing how and when components are automatically disposed of and re-created due to a partial postback allows us to alter this pattern as needed to our advantage when we are working outside the default development situations.

We also covered the new script registration methods available from the `ScriptManager` and how they work during a partial postback. These enable us to register JavaScript that works during all rendering environments.

Finally, we covered how `Sys.Application`'s `load` and `init` events react to a partial postback and how we can use them to successfully attach code during a partial postback.

PART III
Communication

8

ASP.NET AJAX Communication Architecture

THE COMMUNICATION ARCHITECTURE of ASP.NET AJAX is a must know for any developer. The way the client communicates with the server can influence many of your design decisions during development and can be the difference between having an efficient and easily configurable communication channel or one that is slow and hard to work with.

The communication layer that ASP.NET AJAX provides enables you to easily communicate between the client and the server and includes features such as automatic proxy generation for web services and page methods; built-in proxies for working with the ASP.NET 2.0 application services such as the authentication service, profile service, and role service; and the ability to work with JavaScript Object Notation (JSON)-based data.

In this chapter, we cover the server-based ASP.NET 2.0 AJAX Extensions communication architecture and the client-based Microsoft AJAX Library communication architecture. We begin our discussions with the ASP.NET 2.0 AJAX Extensions, describing the new Window Communication Foundation (WCF) web services features, page methods, JSON serialization, and the server framework components that provide the underlying functionality for communication on the server. Then, we move on to the Microsoft AJAX Library and discuss service proxies, JSON serialization, and the web request core components.

New Communication Paradigm

The method of communication in ASP.NET AJAX is a paradigm shift from the standard postback model of ASP.NET 2.0. That model consisted of server-side event handlers processing requests that originated on the client. In ASP.NET AJAX, the focus is on fine-grain communication that can accomplish a specific task using a lightweight call to the server that does not require a postback. This model of the client calling back to the server is similar in a lot of ways to how client/server programming works, where the client makes a call to the server for data and then processes the data locally. This emphasis on client-side functionality is why we spent the first part of this book covering JavaScript and the Microsoft AJAX Library, so we would have a solid foundation of client-side programming. The first instinct most people have when hearing of this new approach to development is to completely rewrite their application to be client-centric. This is not what we are proposing. In our experience, you will see a combination of these two models during development, with ASP.NET 2.0 AJAX Extensions and the Microsoft AJAX Library providing the foundation for smaller request types such as dynamic data population and data validation, and ASP.NET 2.0 providing the foundation for working with postbacks and page transitions. As we think about these lightweight calls that ASP.NET AJAX relies on, we can't help but discuss the REST architectural pattern that is the guiding principal for this type of communication.

> **▪ NOTE   The Meaning of Postback**
>
> The term *postback* in our case means calling back to the page and running through a complete page lifecycle. This page lifecycle incurs a huge cost on small page requests because ASP.NET loads up view state, the control tree, and fires event handlers that cause the page to call back to the server. Calling a web service using ASP.NET AJAX does not do this and is therefore a much more efficient way to call back to the server without incurring a complete page lifecycle.

Representational State Transfer (REST) is an architectural pattern used in the World Wide Web and can be loosely described as a pattern that relies on resources to expose an addressable interface, enabling you to transmit data over HTTP without the need of an additional layer. The term *REST* originated in Roy Fielding's[1] doctoral dissertation about the web and has become a widely adopted pattern used by many web developers. The exact implementation of REST can vary, so to appeal to the purists we discuss REST as it relates to ASP.NET AJAX. After all, this is the implementation that we really care about in this book.

REST is used heavily in ASP.NET AJAX to support calling web services, page methods, and application services. The key to this type of communication is exposing functionality through unique URLs that represent a unique resource on the server. In the case of a REST-based web service call, your request header might look like Listing 8.1, where the HTTP verb is POST, the URL is /WCFAjaxService.svc/Echo, and the content type is application/json.

LISTING 8.1 REST-Based Web Service Header

```
POST /WCFAjaxService.svc/Echo HTTP/1.1
Accept: */*
Accept-Language: en-us
Referer: http://localhost:1472/Default.aspx
Content-Type: application/json; charset=utf-8
UA-CPU: x86
Accept-Encoding: gzip, deflate
User-Agent: Mozilla/4.0 (compatible; MSIE 7.0; Windows NT 6.0; SLCC1; .NET
CLR 2.0.50727; InfoPath.2; MS-RTC LM 8; .NET CLR 3.5.21022; .NET CLR
3.0.04506)
Host: localhost:1472
Content-Length: 17
Connection: Keep-Alive
Cache-Control: no-cache

{"value":"Hello"}
```

So, what makes this call RESTful? The first characteristic is that the URL is distinct. If we were to call another REST-based web service, we would have to change our URL by replacing the /Echo ending with another one. The next characteristic is the use of a constrained set of well-defined operations. In ASP.NET AJAX, you can use the HTTP GET or POST verb, both part of the HTTP protocol, to make requests to the server. The final characteristic is a constrained set of content types that must be used. ASP.NET AJAX supports the JSON and XML content types and distinguishes between them

---

[1] Roy Fielding's doctoral dissertation can be found at www.ics.uci.edu/~fielding/pubs/dissertation/top.htm.

by using the Content-Type HTTP header. In cases of JSON, the content type is `application/json`, for XML returned from an ASMX-style web service the content type is `text/xml`, and for WCF-style web services the content type is `application/xml`.

The influence that REST has on both the server and client communication stacks will be evident as we discuss web services, page methods, and the client proxy classes. The focus during our discussions in these areas is on lightweight calls consisting of JSON content, with the subject of SOAP excluded from our discussion not only for RESTful reasons but also due to a lack of support for it in the Microsoft AJAX Library.

ASP.NET AJAX 2.0 Extensions Communication Architecture

The server communication architecture of ASP.NET 2.0 AJAX Extensions encompasses many layers that provide various services to the request as it is processed. The diagram in Figure 8.1 shows the different layers that make up the communication stack on the server. The web service, page method, and application services serve as the three main ways of interacting with the server and provide varying levels of interaction. The serialization layer provides support for converting .NET data types to and from JSON. The HTTP Modules and Handlers layer provides the underlying support that makes all this happen and builds on the services of ASP.NET 2.0 to provide support for the REST-based communication paradigm of ASP.NET AJAX.

> **■ NOTE** Application Services Covered Later
>
> In our discussion to follow, we will leave the subject of application services for our next chapter, where we cover the Authentication Service, Profile Service, and Role Service, along with creating a custom application service.

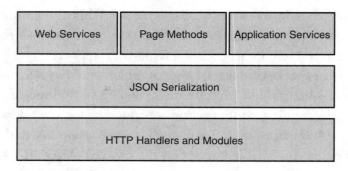

FIGURE 8.1 ASP.NET AJAX server communication architecture

With Figure 8.1 as our guide, let's take a look at the various layers and their respective components with a goal of understanding web services and page methods, serialization, and the underlying technologies that comprise the server communication stack.

Web Services

The big news in ASP.NET 2.0 AJAX Extensions is the support for WCF and the new enhancements it contains for creating RESTful web services. The ability to call web services from a JavaScript client without the overhead of SOAP and the ability to work with JSON-based data have opened the door for WCF-based web services to be consumed by ASP.NET AJAX, just as their ASMX counterparts were in the previous version. Because WCF is a new technology, we should start our discussion with a description of what it is and what it was designed to accomplish.

What Is Windows Communication Foundation?

The story of WCF and what it provides goes way beyond the normal client/server usage you will encounter in ASP.NET AJAX. However, an overview will help you understand the importance of the technology in the enterprise and why you should create services using it.

With regard to how we communicated between processes and machines in the past, we had quite a few choices, including web services, .NET remoting, and sockets, each resulting in a different programming experience. The goal of WCF is to consolidate the programming experience associated with these various technologies into one application programming interface (API), allowing us to code the same way no matter what the communication mechanism is. This approach of one API is a huge advantage over ASMX, which was designed to work only with web services. This consistent programming experience would then be supplemented by a flexible configuration model that would provide the ability to communicate in various ways just by changing configuration information for the endpoint. This "code-once configure for many" approach is what makes WCF so appealing to developers and why it is supported in ASP.NET AJAX. If we take this approach of flexible configuration to the enterprise, we can conceivably change the configuration information for any service and have that service communicate with an ASP.NET AJAX client using JSON with no code changes to the service.

Anatomy of a Web Service

A service is composed of a contract, address, binding, and behavior that come together to represent an endpoint. It is through this endpoint that all communication with the service occurs and client access to the functionality is provided. The contract for the endpoint identifies the operations that are supported, the address indicates where the endpoint can be found, the binding specifies how the client communicates with the endpoint, and the behavior specifies implementation details. To better understand the composition of an endpoint, let's take a look at these pieces individually. The following subsections describe the functionality they provide and how they integrate with each other.

Contracts

There are two types of contracts you will deal with in WCF: One is a service contract, and the other is a data contract. The service contract describes the operations supported by the web service, and the data contract describes the data the web service works with.

Service Contracts

A service contract is composed of two components: a contract and an implementation of that contract. The contract is normally represented by an interface, and the implementation is provided by a class that implements the methods of the interface.

An interface contains the method signatures that make up the operations the web service will support. The `IService1` interface in Listing 8.2 is a simple interface that we will use to describe a typical contract interface. The first thing to notice about this interface is the `ServiceContract` attribute applied to it. The `ServiceContract` attribute is used to indicate that the interface defines a service contract and contains methods that will be exposed by the contract. The second thing to notice is the `OperationContract` attribute applied to the `EchoNumber` method. The `OperationContract` attribute is used to indicate that a method is part of the service contract and should be placed on all methods that are part of the service contract. As far as the interface goes, this is all you have to do to enable an interface to be a service contract.

LISTING 8.2 Service Contract Interface

```
[ServiceContract]
public interface IService1
{
  [OperationContract]
  string EchoNumber(int value);

}
```

A service class contains the implementation details for the method signatures of the service contract it is associated with. If we refer to the service class in Listing 8.3, we can see the beauty of this design. The `Service1` class contains pure implementation code without the need for any WCF-specific attributes, which greatly simplifies the service class and cleanly separates the contract from the implementation. If there were a need to create an additional service class that provided a different implementation to the same method signature, it would be as simple as creating another service class that implements the `IService1` interface.

LISTING 8.3 Service Implementation Class

```
public class Service1 : IService1
{
  public string EchoNumber(int value)
  {
    return string.Format("You entered: {0}", value);
  }
}
```

In the beginning of the section, we made the statement that the contract is normally represented by an interface. However, there is actually another way to create a service contract that combines the contract with the implementation. The `Service2` class in Listing 8.4 combines the contract with the implementation by using the `ServiceContract` and `OperationContract` attributes directly on the service class. This more compact version of a service resembles the ASMX approach to web services and might be a good alternative to someone who is more familiar with that style of programming.

LISTING 8.4 Combines Contract and Implementation Class

```
[ServiceContract]
public class Service2
{
  [OperationContract]
  public string EchoNumber(int value)
  {
    return string.Format("You entered: {0}", value);
  }
}
```

Using Classes or Interfaces

The question of whether to combine your services contract (interface) and implementation (service class) into a single class or follow the practice of separating the contract from the implementation is a subjective one. A good rule of thumb is if the service will be used by clients other than ASP.NET AJAX, the approach of separating the interface from the implementation will give you much more flexibility in the long run. If the goal is to create a single service similar to an ASMX service that will be used only by ASP.NET AJAX, however, an all-in-one approach is an option. In fact, as you will see later, this is what the templates in Visual Studio 2008 do when creating AJAX-enabled WCF web services.

Data Contracts

The service contract in Listing 8.2 used simple data types that WCF can handle natively as the message is serialized into JSON. When more complex data types are used, however, WCF needs some help in determining how to serialize the data. This is where data contracts are used. A data contract is used by WCF to determine the format of data as it is serialized and deserialized during normal message processing. The data contract itself is defined by adding the `DataContract` and `DataMember` attributes to a class, structure, or enumeration.

The `DataContract` attribute is used to specify that a class, structure, or enumeration defines or implements a data contract and is capable of being serialized. A simple implementation of this attribute can be seen in Listing 8.5, where the `Address` class uses the `DataContract` attribute to inform WCF that this class is a data contract. By using this attribute, WCF knows that this class contains items that can be serialized. The `DataContract` attribute is only part of the serialization story and requires a `DataMember` attribute to identity fields and properties that will be part of the complete data contract to be serialized. This method of explicit opt-in is in stark contrast to the `BinaryFormatter` and the `XmlSerializer` we have used in the past. In the case of the `BinaryFormatter`, all public and private fields of a type were included during serialization. And in the case of the `XmlSerializer`, all public fields and properties of a type were included during serialization. In Listing 8.5, we see that all the properties have the `DataMember` attribute applied to them, so all the properties will be serialized. If we were to remove the `DataMember` attribute from, say, the `Zip` property, for example, we would see that this property would not be included in the serialization process and therefore would not be part of the object post serialization.

LISTING 8.5 Simple Data Class

```
[DataContract]
public class Address
{
   [DataMember]
   public int Id { get; set; }
   [DataMember]
   public string Street { get; set; }
   [DataMember]
   public string City { get; set; }
   [DataMember]
   public string State { get; set; }
   [DataMember]
   public string Zip { get; set; }
}
```

Address

All endpoints have an address associated with them that is used to locate and identify the endpoint. This address consists primarily of a Uniform Resource Identifier (URI), which specifies the location of the endpoint. In the case of WCF and ASP.NET 2.0 AJAX Extensions, the endpoint is hosted by ASP.NET, which fixes the address to your web application and eliminates the need to specify an address.

Binding

We previously talked about how WCF separates how a web service is written from how it communicates with a client. A binding is one of the ways this separation is achieved. A binding is used to specify how to communicate with an endpoint and consists of protocol, transport, and message encoding elements that define how WCF channels are built up to provide the required communication features for an endpoint. The protocol elements determine the security and reliability of the communication with the endpoint. The transport elements determine whether TCP, HTTP, or HTTPS is used. And message encoding determines whether JSON or Plain Old XML (POX) is used by the endpoint.

Behavior

Behaviors provide the ability to alter the service, contract, endpoint, and operational behavior of the WCF runtime and provide another way to configure how a WCF service works. The service behaviors provide the ability to change the entire WCF service runtime, including transaction support, authorization support, metadata publishing support, and throughput throttling support. The contract behaviors provide the ability to set the queuing requirements a binding must meet and whether the binding supports ordered messaging. The endpoint behaviors provide the ability to specify debugging support, support for callbacks when working with duplex clients, and optimization of receiving messages that are transactional, to name a few. The operation behaviors provide the ability to specify the behavior of serialization and whether to accept incoming transactions from a client.

Implementing Services

Now that you understand the ABCs (address, binding, and contract) of WCF web services, it is time to create an AJAX-enabled WCF service. The AJAX-enabled WCF service we create provides the ability to look up a product number and return the details of the product that can then be used to populate entries on a web form. An application using a service to dynamically populate the UI is a pattern you will see many times when working with ASP.NET AJAX. This surgical use of web services is what makes the technology so appealing and enables you to provide a rich experience to your users.

As we describe how to implement the service, we focus on the server-side aspects only and leave the client-side portion for the second half of this chapter, where we discuss the Microsoft AJAX Library communication features.

The construction of a service follows three main steps that build on what you have learned so far:

1. Create the service contract.
2. Create the data contract.
3. Configure the service.

Creating a Service Contract

The product service class, shown in Listing 8.6, is designed to return product information based on a single product number or a `SearchCriteria` class that potentially contains values for product number, description, and price. The service itself is decorated with the `ServiceContract` attribute with the namespace property set to `ajaxbooksamples.com`, which is used to distinguish our product service from another one with the same name. The method signatures are decorated with the `OperationContract` attribute, which designates they are part of the contract for the service and consumable by the client. When creating a combined service such as this, remember that only methods marked with the `OperationContract` attribute will be included in the contract. This means that if you have additional methods that help support the service, they are by default not included in the service contract.

> ### ■ NOTE AJAX-Enabled WCF Service Template
>
> The good news about creating an AJAX-enabled WCF service is that Visual Studio 2008 comes with the AJAX-enabled WCF Service template, shown in Figure 8.2, which makes creating them easy. The template, which is available when adding a new item to the project, is designed to create a single class service, which is similar to the ASMX approach.

> ### ■ NOTE AspNetCompatibilityRequirements Attribute
>
> You many notice the use of the AspNetCompatabilityRequirements attribute on the service class. This is added by the template and is required by all services that are to participate in AJAX-enabled web service calls.

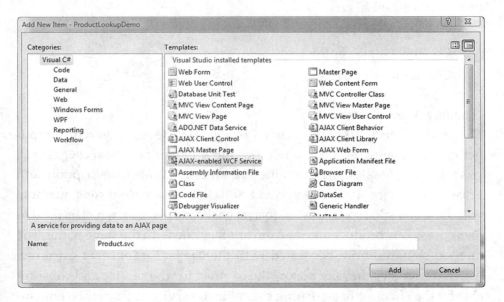

FIGURE 8.2 AJAX-enabled WCF service template

LISTING 8.6 Product Service Class

```
[ServiceContract(Namespace = "http://ajaxbooksamples.com")]
[AspNetCompatibilityRequirements(
   RequirementsMode = AspNetCompatibilityRequirementsMode.Allowed)]
public class Product
{
  [OperationContract]
  public ProductDetail Lookup(string productNumber)
  {
    if (string.IsNullOrEmpty(productNumber))
      throw new ArgumentNullException("productNumber");

      return ProductSearch.Lookup(productNumber);
  }

  [OperationContract]
  public ProductDetail AdvancedLookup(SearchCriteria criteria)
  {
    if (criteria == null)
      throw new ArgumentNullException("criteria");

      return ProductSearch.Lookup(criteria.ProductNumber);
  }
}
```

Creating a Data Contract

The ProductDetail and SearchCriteria classes used by our product service
need to be decorated with the DataContract and DataMember attributes to
ensure proper serialization as the service processes requests. The Product
Detail class in Listing 8.7 demonstrates how to do this and must be dupli-
cated on the SearchCriteria class before the types can be used.

LISTING 8.7 ProductDetail Data Class

```
[DataContract]
public class ProductDetail
{
  public ProductDetail() { }
  public ProductDetail(string productNumber, string description,
    decimal price)
  {
    ProductNumber = productNumber;
    Description = description;
    Price = price;
  }
```

LISTING 8.7 continued

```
    [DataMember]
    public string ProductNumber { get; set; }
    [DataMember]
    public string Description { get; set; }
    [DataMember]
    public decimal Price { get; set; }
}
```

Configuring the Service

To properly configure an AJAX-enabled WCF service, you have to register the service with ASP.NET 2.0 AJAX Extensions, ASP.NET, and IIS. The registration with ASP.NET 2.0 AJAX Extensions is required to ensure the client has a proxy to use when calling the service from JavaScript. The registration with ASP.NET and IIS ensures the endpoint is properly configured and the web service is accessible by the client.

Registering the Service with the ScriptManager

We talked about the `ScriptManager` in Chapter 5, "Adding Client Capabilities to Server Controls." In that chapter, we covered the role that the `ScriptManager` plays in managing all ASP.NET AJAX resources on a page, but deferred the topic of web service registration until now.

The role of the `ScriptManager` when working with web services is to generate the JavaScript proxy class that the client uses to interact with the service. To register your web service with the `ScriptManager`, you must create a `ServiceReference` class that represents your web service and add it to the Services collection of the `ScriptManager`. The `ServiceReference` class comes with two properties that are used to identify the location of the service and indicate how the script is generated (see Table 8.1). In Listing 8.8, we see that the product service is declaratively registered with the `ScriptManager`, which creates a script reference for the proxy class.

TABLE 8.1 Properties of the ServiceReference Class

Method	Description
InlineScript	Gets or sets a value that indicates whether the proxy-generation script is included in the page as an inline script block or is obtained by a separate request
Path	Gets or sets the path of the referenced web service

NOTE   InlineScript Property Usage

The ServiceReference class contains the InlineScript property used to determine how the proxy script is generated. If you look in the SDK, you will see that you can have either the proxy referenced on the page in a script block or by a script reference on the server. When using WCF, you should use the default setting of InlineScript=false, which references the proxy using a script reference on the server.

LISTING 8.8 Service Registration with the ScriptManager

```
<form id="form1" runat="server">
  <asp:ScriptManager ID="ScriptManager1" runat="server">
    <Services>
      <asp:ServiceReference Path="~/Product.svc" />
    </Services>
  </asp:ScriptManager>
  ...
</form>
```

Registering the Service with ASP.NET and IIS

In the previous sections on service binding and behavior, we discussed the ability to configure a service to work with any varying number of clients. In ASP.NET 2.0 AJAX Extensions, this configuration is done in the web. config file or your web application. If you use the AJAX-enabled WCF service template, the configuration settings for the service will be created for you automatically. However, knowing what the entries do is still important, especially when you start modifying the template-generated code.

In Listing 8.9 the System.ServiceModel element contains the behavior and service configuration information for our product service. The behavior information is contained in the behaviors element, and the service bindings are contained in the services element. The behaviors of a service influence the WCF runtime characteristic of the service. In our case, the enableWebScript behavior makes it possible for the web service to be consumed from an ASP.NET AJAX page. The service address, binding, and contract influence how the client communicates with the service. Setting the binding to webHttpBinding enables the service to communicate using HTTP requests using the REST-based communication pattern. And setting the contract to the ProductLookupDemo.Product class specifies that this class contains the contract for our service.

LISTING 8.9 Product Service Configuration Settings

```
<system.serviceModel>
  <behaviors>
    <endpointBehaviors>
      <behavior name="ProductLookupDemo.ProductAspNetAjaxBehavior">
        <enableWebScript />
      </behavior>
    </endpointBehaviors>
  </behaviors>
  <serviceHostingEnvironment aspNetCompatibilityEnabled="true" />
  <services>
    <service name="ProductLookupDemo.Product">
      <endpoint address=""
        behaviorConfiguration="ProductLookupDemo.
        ProductAspNetAjaxBehavior"
        binding="webHttpBinding"
        contract="ProductLookupDemo.Product" />
    </service>
  </services>
</system.serviceModel> is
```

Page Methods

The use of page methods in ASP.NET 2.0 AJAX Extensions can be thought of as a special type of web service that enables you to create a method on an ASP.NET 2.0 page and expose it as a REST resource. The appeal of page methods is that they provide a familiar coding experience to developers used to programming ASP.NET pages and allow them to call back to the server without creating a web service and, more important, without incurring the overhead of the page lifecycle.

> ■ **NOTE**   **Page Method Issues**
>
> As we begin our discussion about page methods, you should keep a few things in mind. First, page methods work only on pages and are not supported in controls. Second, the underlying serialization technology used by page methods is being replaced by the WCF JSON serializer. If you plan to use page methods, you should use types that are easy to serialize and avoid using complex types that require additional coding to serialize properly.

The implementation of page methods is simple, requiring the method to be declared as static and the `System.Web.Services.WebMethod` attribute to be applied. The code in Listing 8.10 shows the declaration for the `Product Lookup` and `AdvancedProductLookup` page methods that provide the same functionality as their AJAX-enabled WCF service counterparts.

LISTING 8.10 Page Method Declaration

```
[WebMethod]
public static ProductDetail ProductLookup(string productNumber)
{
  if (string.IsNullOrEmpty(productNumber))
    throw new ArgumentNullException("productNumber");

  return ProductSearch.Lookup(productNumber);
}

[WebMethod]
public static ProductDetail AdvancedProductLookup(SearchCriteria criteria)
{
  if (criteria == null)
    throw new ArgumentNullException("criteria");

  return ProductSearch.Lookup(criteria.ProductNumber);
}
```

As with web services, registration with the `ScriptManager` is required to generate the proxy class needed to call the page methods from the client.

The registration process, as seen in Listing 8.11, is simple and only requires setting the EnablePageMethods property to true to get all page methods on the page to be callable.

LISTING 8.11 ScriptManager Setting for Page Methods

```
<asp:ScriptManager ID="ScriptManager1" runat="server"
EnablePageMethods="true">
</asp:ScriptManager>
```

Serialization

The support for serialization in ASP.NET 2.0 AJAX Extensions spans not only web services but also into many of the supporting classes responsible for transmitting proxy and initialization data to the client. In most cases, the serialization of objects happens automatically. In more complex scenarios, however, some additional work is required to properly convert data to and from JSON. In this section, we cover the complex subject of serialization and how ASP.NET 2.0 AJAX Extensions support working with JSON data of varying complexities.

JavaScript Object Notation

Before we go into how to serialize JSON, it might be wise to talk about what JSON is. JSON, JavaScript Object Notation, is a lightweight data interchange format that is both easy to read and compact. The composition of JSON data follows two patterns:

1. Name and value pairs of data in the format of name:value inside a left brace, {, and right brace, }, and separated by commas
2. Arrays containing comma-separated data inside a left bracket, [, and right bracket,]

To get a better feel for how an object is composed in JSON, let's take a look at the ProductDetail class from earlier. The JSON representation of the ProductDetail class, shown in Listing 8.12, uses name:value pairs to represent the ProductNumber, Description, and Price values of the object. What makes working with JSON so appealing is its tight integration with JavaScript and how it leverages the object notation that is natively supported, making it easy to turn JSON data into an object by applying the JavaScript eval operator to the data.

LISTING 8.12 JSON Representation of the ProductDetail Class

```
{"ProductNumber":"200","Description":"Black XBox Controller","Price":50}
```

DataContractJsonSerializer

The `DataContractJsonSerializer` provides services to serialize and deserialize JSON data and is the replacement for the `JavaScriptSerializer` used in previous versions. The move to the `DataContractJsonSerializer` in ASP.NET 2.0 AJAX Extensions centralizes all the serialization services to a common platform contained in the `System.Runtime.Serialization` namespace, thus providing a consistent method of serialization shared between services and internal classes.

JavaScriptSerializer Usage Internally by ASP.NET AJAX Extensions

The use of the `JavaScriptSerializer` has been deprecated in this new version, but internally some areas of ASP.NET 2.0 AJAX Extensions are still using the serializer. Examples include the `ScriptComponentDescriptor`, `ScriptBehaviorDescriptor`, `ScriptControlDescriptor`, and page methods, which can lead to additional serialization work if you work with types that are shared between web services, behaviors, and controls. A good rule of thumb is to limit your usage of types that need custom serialization to web services and leave property assignments in behaviors and controls to simple types or types that can easily be serialized.

To demonstrate how to work with the serializer, we take a string representation of our `ProductDetail` class and convert it into a `ProductDetail` instance, as shown in Listing 8.13, and then convert it back into a JSON string, as shown in Listing 8.14, illustrating the steps required to serialize and desterilize JSON data using the `DataContractJsonSerializer`. The `productDetailJSON` is a JSON string that represents our `ProductDetail` class. The escape sequences embedded in the string are required to ensure the values are formatted correctly for the serializer. The interesting thing about the `DataContractJsonSerializer` is that it works with a memory stream rather than strings and therefore requires our string data to be converted into a memory stream before we can begin the serialization process.

LISTING 8.13 Reading JSON Data

```
string productDetailJson =
"{\"ProductNumber\":\"200\",\"Description\":\"Xbox Live
360\",\"Price\":\"50\"}";

//read from JSON string
byte[] stream = System.Text.Encoding.GetEncoding(
            "iso-8859-1").GetBytes(productDetailJson);
MemoryStream memoryStream = new MemoryStream(stream);
DataContractJsonSerializer jsonSerializer = new
DataContractJsonSerializer(typeof(ProductDetail));
ProductDetail productDetail = (ProductDetail)jsonSerializer.ReadObject
(memoryStream);
```

The DataContractJsonSerializer comes with over nine constructors. The two you will use most frequently when working with JSON are in Table 8.2. The first constructor is designed to initialize the serializer to work with a single type and is used when you have an object to serialize that is relatively simple. The second constructor takes not only a type but also a collection of known types that may be present during serialization. This constructor is useful when your data type is more complex in nature and requires some help in determining how to serialize the data. In Listing 8.14, we are using the single constructor to create an instance of the serializer that is set up to work with the ProductDetail class.

TABLE 8.2 Constructors of the DataContractJsonSerializer

Constructor	Description
DataContractJsonSerializer(Type)	Deserializes JSON data and returns the deserialized object
DataContractJsonSerializer(Type, IEnumerable<(Of <(Type)>)>)	Initializes a new instance of the DataContractJsonSerializer class to serialize or deserialize an object of the specified type, with a collection of known types that may be present in the object graph

The next step in our process is to deserialize, or read in `DataContract JsonSerializer` speak, the memory stream into a `ProductDetail` class instance. This is performed by the `ReadObject` method, which reads in the memory stream, providing an output capable of being cast to an instance of a `ProductDetail` type (see Table 8.3). At this point, you can work with the `productDetail` variable in its .NET data form.

TABLE 8.3 Subset of Methods of the DataContractJsonSerializer

Method	Description
ReadObject	Deserializes JSON data and returns the deserialized object
WriteObject	Serializes an object to a JSON document

Now that we have the data in a .NET data type, we will walk through the steps to convert it back to JSON. The use of memory streams is continued during the serialization process when the serializer writes, in `Data ContractJsonSerializer` speak, the `ProductDetail` type to a JSON string. The process entails writing the .NET type to a memory stream and then encoding a byte array into a string. The encoding class in the `System.Text` namespace comes in handy during this step, providing the ability to encode the memory stream to an ISO-based string. So at this point, we have now successfully converted a JSON representation of the `ProductDetail` class into an object and then back into JSON.

LISTING 8.14 Writing JSON Data

```
//write from object back to string
memoryStream = new MemoryStream();
jsonSerializer.WriteObject(memoryStream, productDetail);
string productDetailJSON2 = Encoding.GetEncoding(
"iso-8859-1").GetString(memoryStream.ToArray());
```

Complex Data and Serialization

So far, we have worked with a scenario that is simple, and the `Data ContractJsonSerializer` can easily determine the type we are working with. However, this is not always the case. Consider, for instance, the

BusinessEntity class in Listing 8.15. It contains one property, Entities, that is of type ArrayList, which stores items as objects. If we were passed a JSON string that contains items of varying types in this ArrayList, the DataContractJsonSerializer would have a hard time determining the true data types of these entries because there is no type information associated with JSON. This is where the concept of known types comes into play to help the serializer figure out the true data types of these JSON strings.

> **■ NOTE   Type Information in JSON**
>
> We just made a statement that type information is not in JSON. In the true sense of things, it is not. However, Microsoft does include type information in JSON that is passed between the client and the server. The ASP.NET AJAX Extensions and Microsoft AJAX Library use this information to assist in the serialization process.

The KnownType attribute, when applied to a class, assists the serializer in determining the types that could be involved during the serialization process. When the serializer starts the deserialization process, it looks for CLR types that implement the data contract passed in and uses a list of known types to figure out the correct type to use. By applying the KnownType attribute to your class, you are adding types to this known type list, letting the serializer know that these particular types should be considered during serialization. In Listing 8.16, we can see that the KnownType attribute has been applied to the BusinessEntities class, adding the Vendor and Customer types to the list of known types. Now when the serializer encounters a type in the ArrayList, it uses these types to help determine the correct type to be serialized.

LISTING 8.15 BusinessEntities Class

```
public class BusinessEntities
{
  public BusinessEntities() { Entities = new ArrayList(); }

  [DataMember]
  public ArrayList Entities { get; set; }
}
```

LISTING 8.16 BusinessEntity Class with KnownType Attribute

```
[DataContract]
[KnownType(typeof(Customer))]
[KnownType(typeof(Vendor))]
public class BusinessEntities
{
  public VariousEntities() { Entities = new ArrayList(); }

  [DataMember]
  public ArrayList Entities { get; set; }
}
```

In some cases, applying the KnownType attribute to a class is not possible or desired (for example, when the data classes are already created and they can't be modified). In this case, you have two options, depending on the usage of the data. If the DataContractJsonSerializer is natively being used, as in our previous examples, adding the known types to a collection and passing them into the overloaded constructor of the DataContract JsonSerializer will enable the serializer to use these types during the serialization process. If the types are being used in web services, modifying the web.config file is the best approach.

The web.config file approach adds entries of known types to the data ContractSerializer element, making them available during the serialization process. The configuration entries shown in Listing 8.17 declare the BusinessEntities type and then add the Customer and Vendor as known types for it. An entry of a declared type and associated known types would be added for each data type that requires known types to be correctly serialized.

LISTING 8.17 DataContractSerializer Configuration Option

```
<system.runtime.serialization>
  <dataContractSerializer>
    <declaredTypes>
      <add type="ServiceData.Complex.BusinessEntities,
        ServiceData, Version = 1.0.0.0, Culture = neutral,
        PublicKeyToken=null">
        <knownType type="ServiceData.Complex.Business,
          ServiceData, Version = 1.0.0.0, Culture = neutral,
          PublicKeyToken=null" />
        <knownType type="ServiceData.Complex.Customer,
          ServiceData, Version = 1.0.0.0, Culture = neutral,
          PublicKeyToken=null" />
```

LISTING 8.17 continued

```
        <knownType type="ServiceData.Complex.VendorEntity,
            ServiceData, Version = 1.0.0.0, Culture = neutral,
            PublicKeyToken=null" />
        </add>
      </declaredTypes>
    </dataContractSerializer>
  </system.runtime.serialization>
```

Server Framework Components

ASP.NET 2.0 AJAX Extensions provide a series of HTTP handlers and modules designed to assist in the communication between the client and the server. These handlers and modules provide services such as processing web requests, processing application service requests, returning dynamically generated web service JavaScript proxy classes, and returning script resources that are embedded in assemblies. In the sections to follow, we look at how these handlers and modules work in conjunction with ASP.NET to process incoming requests and thus additional functionality needed by ASP.NET 2.0 AJAX Extensions. We begin our discussion by reviewing how the ASP.NET 2.0 application lifecycle works. This overview will help you better understand where handlers and modules fit into the overall request processing cycle. The discussion then transitions to the handlers and modules and the functionality they provide.

ASP.NET Application Lifecycle

The application lifecycle that ASP.NET 2.0 goes through when processing a request consists of quite of few layers. As you can see in Figure 8.3, the flow of a request from a client starts with the request coming into IIS and logic being applied to determine whether the ASP.NET runtime will be processing the request. If the file extension of the request ends with .aspx, .ascx, .ashx, .asmx, or .svc, the ASP.NET 2.0 runtime handles the request, and the Application Manager creates an application domain for the request. This application domain is used to provide isolation between the various web applications in IIS and allows each web application to be managed separately. The byproduct of creating an application domain is the creation of the HTTP runtime, which consists of the HttpContext, HttpRequest,

`HttpResponse`, and `HttpApplication` objects that work together to process the request. The `HttpContext` class contains objects specific to the current application request, such as the `HttpRequest` and `HttpResponse` objects. The `HttpRequest` object contains information about the current request, including cookies and browser information. The `HttpResponse` object contains the response sent to the client, including all rendered output and cookies. It is the `HttpApplication` pipeline contained in the `HttpApplication` object that is of most interest to us, because the pipeline is responsible for the instantiation of the HTTP handlers and modules for the ASP.NET 2.0 AJAX Extensions framework.

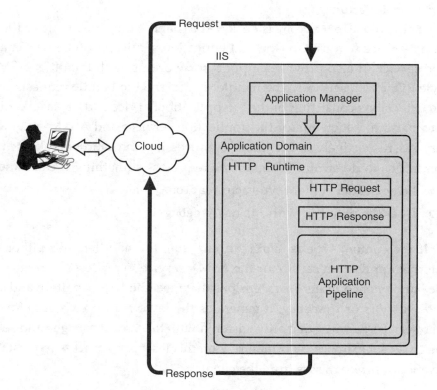

FIGURE 8.3 ASP.NET application lifecycle

■ **NOTE** More Information about HTTP Handlers and Modules

For a more detailed explanation about HTTP handlers and modules that are discussed in the next sections, see Appendix C, "ASP.NET Handlers and Modules."

HTTP Handlers

In their simplest form, HTTP handlers run in response to a request into an ASP.NET application and are part of the `HttpApplication` pipeline illustrated in Figure 8.3. In the course of processing the request, the `HttpApplication` pipeline loads the specific handler based on the file extension of the request and uses it to process the request. It is during this processing that the ASP.NET 2.0 AJAX Extensions handlers provide added functionality to the request, providing support for handling REST-based web services, application services, and script resource requests.

ScriptHandlerFactory

The `ScriptHandlerFactory` is designed to handle the entire suite of REST-based service requests for the authentication service, profile service, and role service. It also provides support for working with the older ASMX-style REST web services. The handler is designed to handle requests with file extensions consisting of the *_ApplicationService.axd or *.asmx wildcard pattern, which are for the application services and ASXM-style web services, respectively. In the course of processing, the handler looks for two conditions to determine whether the request is something it can handle:

1. Is the header content type `application/json`?
2. Does the path end with `/js` or `/jsdebug`?

If the content type is `application/json`, the handler calls either the internal application service or the ASMX service to process the request. If the handler encounters file extensions that meet the *.asmx pattern and also end with `/js` or `/jsdebug`, it generates the JavaScript proxy class for the web service. Services that are registered with the `ScriptManager` and select the `InlineScript=false` option rely on this feature to process requests for JavaScript proxy classes from the client.

ScriptResourceHandler

The `ScriptResourceHandler` is used by ASP.NET 2.0 AJAX Extensions to process requests for script resources that contain the ScriptResource.axd filename. Scripts that are embedded assembly resources and are registered with the `ScriptManager` rely on this handler to get loaded onto the page.

In fact, this is how the framework JavaScript files MicrosoftAjax.js, MicrosoftAjaxWebForms.js, and MicrosoftAjaxTimer.js are delivered to the client. How the requests are formatted and how the handler processes the requests is interesting.

If you look at the source of your pages, you will see a script reference like the one in Listing 8.18 that the handler is designed to work with. As the handler processes the request, it first decrypts the d parameter, which contains information such as whether the script file should be GZip compressed, the name of the assembly that contains the embedded JavaScript resource, and whether the handler should add a call to Sys.Application. notifyScriptLoaded at the end of the script block to notify the application that the script has been loaded. The handler then uses this information to create an instance of the type that contains the script resource, composes the output, compresses the output if needed, and then returns the final result to the client.

LISTING 8.18 Page Script Reference

```
<script src="/ScriptResource.axd?d=Sl3Kr-
7xWWkkjj5ukGgAiCB2QH_y5ShPnuPcE9X_hwycHPq4qQVE6dFU6GXJ5Y7fD5xllEai_EA_iwv2nk
JkNWtIXT-SnVWidtzFxWE8roE1&amp;t=633127670283933053"
type="text/javascript"></script>
```

System.ServiceModel.Activation.HttpHandler

The System.ServiceModel.Activation.HttpHandler is the WCF counterpart to the ScriptHandlerFactory handler. This handler is designed to process both REST-based requests and standard SOAP-based requests for files with the *.svc wildcard pattern. The handler processes two types of requests with respect to AJAX-enabled WCF services:

1. Requests that contain the application/json header content type
2. Requests with file extensions that end in /js or /jsdebug

As with the ScriptHandlerFactory, requests with the application/ json are handled as REST-based requests, using the DataContractJson Serializer to serialize and deserialize the message. Requests that end with

/js or /jsdebug return the JavaScript proxy class for the web service. If any of these conditions are not met, the handler processes the request as a standard WCF SOAP-based request.

HTTP Modules

An HTTP module is similar in concept to the HTTP handler in the sense that it runs in response to a request into an ASP.NET application. In the case of a module, however, it runs with every request regardless of the HTTP verb or the path of the URL. The HTTP module works with the Http Application pipeline as it goes through the various events that occur during processing, providing extensibility points as events occur, much like an event handler.

ScriptModule

The ScriptModule module works with three HttpApplication events that are of importance to ASP.NET 2.0 AJAX Extensions: PreSend RequestHeader, PostAcquireRequestState, and AuthenticateRequest. The PreSendRequestHeaders event is used in cases where the UpdatePanel is posting back to the server. When this event occurs, the module rewrites the HTTP headers and formats the content posted back into a pipe-delimited format that the client-side code uses to redraw the invalidated region with the new content. The PostAcquireRequestState event is used to handle page method calls to the server. When this event occurs, the module first verifies the request by ensuring the file extension is .aspx and the content type is application/json, and then processes the request using the same internal code the ScriptHandlerFactory uses to process a request. The AuthenticateRequest event is used to set the SkipAuthorization property of the HttpContext in situations where a script resource is being requested or in cases where the authentication service is being called.

Configuration

The configuration of an ASP.NET AJAX web application is automatic in Visual Studio 2008 because all web applications are ASP.NET AJAX enabled by default. This makes working with web applications a lot easier in this version and eliminates the need to add ASP.NET 2.0 AJAX Extensions configuration entries by hand. In this section, we show how the handler and modules are registered in ASP.NET AJAX, closing the loop on the server framework components.

The configuration of ASP.NET 2.0 AJAX Extensions, see Listing 8.19, is contained in two sections of the web.config file: `ConfigSections` and `System.Web`. The `ConfigSection` defines the various subsections that contain ASP.NET AJAX-specific information such as the authentication service, profile service, and role service information for the application services. The `System.Web` section contains the handler and module registration for the `ScriptHandlerFactory`, `ScriptResourceHandler`, and the `Script Module`. If we take a look at the handlers section inside the `System.Web` element, we can see that the default handler for all ASMX files is removed. This is how `ScriptHandlerFactory` can override the default implementation for these file types and either process the REST-based requests or pass them back to the default handler. The next thing to note in this section is the registration of the `ScriptHandlerFactory` for the ASMX web application services. By registering the file paths with ASP.NET, these handlers are now responsible for processing requests that match these extensions. The last entry in this element is the registration of the `ScriptResourceHandler` for the files with the ScriptResource.axd path name. The last item to talk about in the web.config is the `httpmodules` element, which contains the registration of the `ScriptModule`, which provides implementation for the `PreSend RequestHeader`, `PostAcquireRequestState`, and `AuthenticateRequest` events of the `HttpApplication`.

■ **NOTE** **Where Is the WCF Handler?**

The one item you will see missing in the `System.Web` section is the `System.ServiceModel.Activation.HttpHandler` for WCF. This handler is actually registered in the master web.config file, which the web.config file builds on.

LISTING 8.19 ASP.NET AJAX Configuration

```xml
<?xml version="1.0"?>
<configuration>
 ...
<configSections>
  <sectionGroup name="system.web.extensions" ...>
    <sectionGroup name="scripting" ...>
      <section name="scriptResourceHandler" .../>
        <sectionGroup name="webServices" ...>
          <section name="jsonSerialization" .../>
          <section name="profileService" ... />
          <section name="authenticationService" .../>
          <section name="roleService" ... />
        </sectionGroup>
      </sectionGroup>
  </sectionGroup>
</configSections>
<system.web>
  <httpHandlers>
    <remove verb="*" path="*.asmx"/>
    <add verb="*" path="*.asmx" validate="false"
       type="System.Web.Script.Services.ScriptHandlerFactory,
       System.Web.Extensions, Version=3.5.0.0,
       Culture=neutral, PublicKeyToken=31BF3856AD364E35"/>
    <add verb="*" path="*_AppService.axd" validate="false"
       type="System.Web.Script.Services.ScriptHandlerFactory,
       System.Web.Extensions, Version=3.5.0.0,
       Culture=neutral, PublicKeyToken=31BF3856AD364E35"/>
    <add verb="GET,HEAD" path="ScriptResource.axd"
       type="System.Web.Handlers.ScriptResourceHandler,
       System.Web.Extensions, Version=3.5.0.0,
       Culture=neutral, PublicKeyToken=31BF3856AD364E35"
       validate="false"/>
  </httpHandlers>
  <httpModules>
    <add name="ScriptModule"
       type="System.Web.Handlers.ScriptModule,
       System.Web.Extensions,
       Version=3.5.0.0, Culture=neutral,
       PublicKeyToken=31BF3856AD364E35"/>
  </httpModules>
 </system.web>
 ...
</configuration>
```

Microsoft AJAX Library Communication Architecture

The Microsoft AJAX Library communication architecture builds on a layered approach, just like the ASP.NET 2.0 AJAX Extensions communication architecture, to provide various services to the client as it integrates with the server. The diagram in Figure 8.4 shows the different layers that make up the communication stack on the client. The service proxy layer provides a browser-independent way to access web services, application services, and page methods. The serialization layer provides support for converting JavaScript types to and from JSON. And web request core components provide the underlying support that makes all this happen.

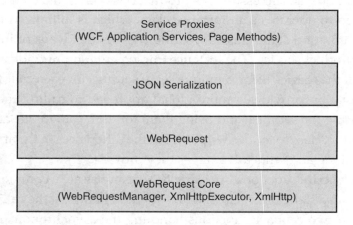

FIGURE 8.4 Microsoft AJAX Library communication architecture

With Figure 8.4 as our guide, let's take a look at the various layers and their respective components with a goal of understanding service proxies, JSON serialization, and the web request core components that comprise the client communication stack.

Service Proxies

The Microsoft AJAX Library provides proxy services for WCF, application services, and page methods, providing functionality for the client to call into all these server-side services in a browser-independent way. In this section, we explore how these proxy services work and how to interact with them.

> **■ NOTE** Application Services
>
> The subject of application services is the topic of the next chapter, so they are not covered here.

Using the Product Service Proxy

The product class provides the method signatures and data type declarations for the product service we covered earlier. This proxy class is similar in concept to the web service proxy class generated when working with web services in .NET and provides many of the abstractions that have made that model so successful. The product class generated by the server is constructed to operate as an instance class, which is initialized using the new operator, or a static class providing two distinct ways of interacting with the product service. The instance implementation provides a flexible way to call the service using a unique set of settings for each call. The static implementation provides a more global approach to calling the service, consolidating the settings, and using them for each call. In our discussion of the product class to follow, we point out the differences in the approaches as we go along and what advantages they provide.

The JavaScript functions in Listing 8.20 demonstrate a common pattern when calling a static proxy class, with a method handling the calling of the service and two callback functions handling the asynchronous response. The first thing to understand when working with the product class is where the namespace comes from. The namespace that all proxy classes will use is dictated by the Namespace property of the ServiceContract attribute applied to the service class. In our case, we are using ajaxbooksample.com, which is the name we used when creating our AJAX-enabled WCF service.

During proxy generation, a method is created on the proxy class for each operation that is exposed by the service. The method itself consists of a slightly different signature from the one on the server, which is due in part to the underlying services of the WebServiceProxy class that our product class derives from. In the case of our Lookup method, we have an additional set of parameters, including an optional success callback function pointer, an optional failed callback function pointer, and an optional user context parameter. The two callback functions are used by the proxy class to call back into our JavaScript code as the asynchronous request completes. The user context parameter provides a way to pass user-defined data to the asynchronous call and have it available when the call completes. This comes in handy when you have a common callback function that processes requests for all service operations and you need additional context information to successfully wrap up the call.

The `onSuccess` callback function is called when the web service request is successful and is passed the JavaScript object representation of the JSON deserialized result, the user context value, and the name of the web service method called. The `onFailed` callback function is called when the web service request has failed and is passed an instance of the `WebServiceError` object, the user context value, and the name of the web service method called. The `WebServiceError` object that is passed in contains a flag indicating whether the request has timed out, the error message, the stack trace, the exception type, and the status code of the request (see Table 8.4). These values can then be used to help determine the type of error that occurred during transmission. When processing requests that contain errors, the status code will be the most beneficial in determining the type of error that occurred. A status code in the 400 range is a client-centric error status and can be anything from the request timing out (408) to an unsupported media type (415) for a message that is in the incorrect format. A status code in the 500 range is a server-centric error status and can be anything from an internal server error (500) to a service unavailable (503), which can occur when the server is to busy or shut down.

TABLE 8.4 Properties of the WebServiceError Class

Method	Description
exception	Gets the exception type of the error
message	Gets the error message returned by the error
statusCode	Gets the status code for the HTTP response
stackTrace	Gets the stack trace returned by the server
timedOut	Gets a value that indicates whether the web service failed because it timed out

> ### ■ NOTE   Properties in Classes
>
> In Chapter 3, "Components," we discussed that the Microsoft AJAX Library uses get_ and set_ prefixes for properties to provide the same effect of a property setter and getter in .NET. In the properties above and throughout this section, we just designate the name of the property with the assumption that the prefixes are the understood access method.

The example of the product class in Listing 8.20 provides one way to implement a static calling pattern. As we stated earlier, however, there are a few ways we can implement this class. The proxy class comes with a few properties that enable us to configure some of the behavioral aspects of the class (see Table 8.5). In Listing 8.21, the product class has been set up in the page load to use a global calling pattern with the onSuccess and onFailed callbacks being set up globally. Then, our calling method simply passes in the data to be sent using those default values. Not to confuse the matter more, but it is possible to provide an override to the configuration in Listing 8.21 by calling the product class in the manner shown in Listing 8.20, which overrides any of the onSuccess and onFailed settings that were globally set. The final pattern we talk about is the instance pattern, which is demonstrated in Listing 8.22, where the product service is being called by creating a new instance of the product class.

TABLE 8.5 Proxy Class Properties

Property	Description
defaultFailedCallback	Gets or sets the default failed callback function for the service
defaultSucceededCallback	Gets or sets the default succeeded callback function for the service
path	Gets or sets the path to the service
timeout	Gets or sets the timeout in milliseconds for the service

> **■ NOTE   Path of Service**
>
> The path of the service in all these samples defaults to the path set by the proxy-generation code on the server.

Request Timeouts

The proxy class supports the ability to set the timeout of a request using the set_timeout property. In the default static implementation of the proxy, the value is a global setting and will be used by all requests. If a per-incidence setting is needed, you must create a new instance of the proxy class and call the request through that instance. Setting the timeout is not the hardest part of the equation. What value to use, and what to do when the request times out, is. There is no hard and fast rule for setting timeout values, and each situation will differ. However, you should consider some things when approaching how to handle timeouts, such as whether the request should automatically resend or whether the user should be required to do this manually. If the request is re-sent, how many times should this happen, and do you inform the user? If the user is required to manually resend, what information do you provide, and is it appropriate to interrupt the use case such as when a request is made as a user leaves a textbox to do an automatic lookup that prepopulates form fields?

LISTING 8.20 Product Service JavaScript Proxy Calling Functions

```
function LookupProduct()
{
  var criteria = new ProductLookupDemo.SearchCriteria();
  criteria.ProductNumber = $get("productNumber").value;
  ajaxbooksamples.com.product.AdvancedLookup(criteria,
    onSuccess,onFailed);
}

function onSuccess(result, userContext, methodName )
{
  $get("productDescription").value = result.Description;
  $get("productPrice").value = result.Price;
}
```

LISTING 8.20 continued

```
function onFailed(result, userContext, methodName)
{
  alert("An error occured \n"  + result.get_message());
}
```

LISTING 8.21 Product Service Global Setup Calling Pattern

```
function pageLoad()
{
  ajaxbooksamples.com.product.set_defaultSucceededCallback(onSuccess);
  ajaxbooksamples.com.product.set_defaultFailedCallback(onFailed);
}

function LookupProduct()
{
  var criteria = new ProductLookupDemo.SearchCriteria();
  criteria.ProductNumber = $get("productNumber").value;
  jaxbooksamples.com.product.AdvancedLookup(criteria);

}
...
```

LISTING 8.22 Product Service Instance Calling Pattern

```
function LookupProduct()
{
  var criteria = new ProductLookupDemo.SearchCriteria();
  criteria.ProductNumber = $get("productNumber").value;
  ajaxbooksamples.com.product.AdvancedLookup(criteria);

}
...
```

Product Service Proxy Class Details

The proxy class generated for our product service class is the same type of
class we discussed in Chapter 3 and uses many of the features of the client-
side framework such as namespaces, type declaration, inheritance, and
type registration. As we begin this section, you might be wondering why
we would cover this class. After all, the proxy is automatically generated,
and its use is simple. In our experience, we have seen that a solid understanding of the proxy class structure is a valuable asset when it comes time

to troubleshoot communication errors. Being able to step through the proxy class as it is processing the request and understanding what is going on can help in those tough situations where your web service calls are failing. In our discussions of the product service class to follow, we begin with the registration of the class, and then move on to the methods and properties of the class, which are declared in the class's prototype, and finally consider the static representation of the proxy.

The namespace and type declaration of the class are shown in Listing 8.23. The namespace that the proxy uses comes directly from the Service Contract attribute's Namespace property assigned to each service class. In the case of our product service class, refer to Listing 8.6, the namespace value is ajaxbooksamples.com and is what the proxy class uses when registering the namespace. The type declaration for the class initializes the timeout, userContext, succeeded and failed properties inherits from the System.Net.WebServiceProxy class, which the proxy class derives from.

> **■ NOTE   Changing Namespace in ServiceContract**
>
> It will not be uncommon during development to change the namespace on the web service as a final name is decided on. When this is done, you need to go back to your JavaScript code and change the namespace used to call the proxy class.

LISTING 8.23 Product Service Namespace Registration and Proxy Initialization

```
Type.registerNamespace('ajaxbooksamples.com');

ajaxbooksamples.com.product=function() {
ajaxbooksamples.com.product.initializeBase(this);
this._timeout = 0;
this._userContext = null;
this._succeeded = null;
this._failed = null;
}
```

The proxy class's prototype, shown in Listing 8.24, is composed of all operations of the web service that are decorated with the Operation Contract attribute. In the case of our product service, we have two operations declared in the proxy class's prototype: Lookup and AdvancedLookup.

These methods use the functionality of the `WebServiceProxy` base class to invoke the service, passing in the path of the service, the name of the operation to call, the parameters for the call, a succeed callback function reference, a failed callback function reference, and the user context. The path of the service is dynamically generated using the web application as the base and is assigned during later stages of the proxy class initialization using the `set_path` property setter. The name of the method to call comes directly from the name of the web service operation and is also used by the generator to create the method stub in the proxy. The parameters for the method will match entry for entry with the operation on the web service. The generation process actually combines these values into an object initialization string that is then used as a parameter into the `invoke` method. The remaining parameters are the optional callback and user context parameters, which can either be provided on a per-call basis or added globally to the static representation of the proxy, which we talk about shortly.

> ■ **NOTE**   Changing Operation Names
>
> The names of the web service operations are tightly tied to the proxy class, and any changes in the web service operation require a change in your code that implements the proxy class.

LISTING 8.24 Product Service Proxy Prototype

```
ajaxbooksamples.com.product.prototype={
  _get_path:function(){
    var p = this.get_path();
    if (p)
      return p;
    else
      return ajaxbooksamples.com.product._staticInstance.get_path();
  },

  Lookup:function(productNumber,succeededCallback, failedCallback,
    userContext){
      return this._invoke(this._get_path(),
        'Lookup',false,{productNumber:productNumber},
        succeededCallback,failedCallback,userContext);
    },
  AdvancedLookup:function(criteria,succeededCallback, failedCallback,
    userContext){
```

```
    return this._invoke(this._get_path(),
      'AdvancedLookup',false,{criteria:criteria},
      succeededCallback,failedCallback,userContext);
  }
}
```

The proxy class registration, shown in Listing 8.25, registers the product service class and associates it with the WebServiceProxy class it inherits from. To reduce the number of proxy class instances created and to simplify use, the proxy generator provides a static reference of the proxy class with overrides to the standard WebServiceProxy properties that call back into this static reference. It is through these static properties that the global callback function pointers and user context values are assigned.

LISTING 8.25 Product Class Registration

```
ajaxbooksamples.com.product.registerClass('ajaxbooksamples.com.product',Sys.
Net.WebServiceProxy);

ajaxbooksamples.com.product._staticInstance =
  new ajaxbooksamples.com.product();

ajaxbooksamples.com.product.set_path = function(value) {
  ajaxbooksamples.com.product._staticInstance.set_path(value);
}

ajaxbooksamples.com.product.get_path = function() {
  return ajaxbooksamples.com.product._staticInstance.get_path();
}

ajaxbooksamples.com.product.set_timeout = function(value) {
  ajaxbooksamples.com.product._staticInstance.set_timeout(value);
}

ajaxbooksamples.com.product.get_timeout = function() {
  return ajaxbooksamples.com.product._staticInstance.get_timeout(); }

ajaxbooksamples.com.product.set_defaultUserContext = function(value) {
  ajaxbooksamples.com.product._staticInstance.set_defaultUserContext(
    value);
}

ajaxbooksamples.com.product.get_defaultUserContext = function() {
  return
ajaxbooksamples.com.product._staticInstance.get_defaultUserContext();
}
```

LISTING 8.25 Continued

```
ajaxbooksamples.com.product.set_defaultSucceededCallback = function(value){

ajaxbooksamples.com.product._staticInstance.set_defaultSucceededCallback(val
ue);
}

ajaxbooksamples.com.product.get_defaultSucceededCallback = function() {
    return
ajaxbooksamples.com.product._staticInstance.get_defaultSucceededCallback();
}

ajaxbooksamples.com.product.set_defaultFailedCallback = function(value)
{
ajaxbooksamples.com.product._staticInstance.set_defaultFailedCallback(
value);
}
ajaxbooksamples.com.product.get_defaultFailedCallback = function() {
return
ajaxbooksamples.com.product._staticInstance.get_defaultFailedCallback();
}
ajaxbooksamples.com.product.set_path("/Product.svc");

ajaxbooksamples.com.product.Lookup=
    function(productNumber,onSuccess,onFailed,userContext) {
  ajaxbooksamples.com.product._staticInstance.Lookup(
    productNumber, onSuccess,onFailed,userContext);
}
```

The proxy class also registers all the data types that are part of the web service interface, providing the client-side types for use in JavaScript. In Listing 8.26 we see that the ProductDetail and SearchCriteria types from our product service are registered with their .NET-specific namespace information. This registration provides the type information that Microsoft AJAX uses when serializing or deserializing the JSON data as it is passed between the client and the server.

> **■ NOTE**　**JSON Type Information**
>
> This added type information was the subject of our "Type Information in JSON" note in the "Complex Data and Serialization" section earlier in the chapter.

LISTING 8.26 Product Service Data Type Registration

```
var gtc = Sys.Net.WebServiceProxy._generateTypedConstructor;

Type.registerNamespace('ProductLookupDemo');

if (typeof(ProductLookupDemo.ProductDetail) === 'undefined') {
  ProductLookupDemo.ProductDetail=gtc(
    "ProductDetail:http://schemas.datacontract.org/2004/07/
    ProductLookupDemo");

ProductLookupDemo.ProductDetail.registerClass(
  'ProductLookupDemo.ProductDetail');
}

if (typeof(ProductLookupDemo.SearchCriteria) === 'undefined') {
  ProductLookupDemo.SearchCriteria=gtc(
    "SearchCriteria:http://schemas.datacontract.org/2004/07/
    ProductLookupDemo");

ProductLookupDemo.SearchCriteria.registerClass(
  'ProductLookupDemo.SearchCriteria');
}
```

The format of the JSON data passed between the client and the server depends on the direction of the request. In the case of outbound requests, the JSON format looks like Listing 8.27, with the criteria parameter signifying the parameter name on the web service operation that will be receiving the data, and the remaining portion detailing the data type and content sent. The type is declared using the type information that was generated by the proxy generation on the server, shown in Listing 8.26, using the format __type as the property and SearchCriteria:http://schemas.datacontract. org/2004/07/ProductLookupDemo as the value of the __type property. The format of the type value follows the pattern of an XML namespace, which the WCF service expects as its processing the parameter. The remaining portion of the JSON value contains the name:value pairs that represent the SearchCriteria object. In the case of incoming requests, the JSON format looks like Listing 8.28, with the d parameter signifying the overall data that was received, and the remaining portion detailing the data type and content. The type is declared using the format __type as the property and Type:#Namespace as the value of the __type property. The format Type#Namespace consists of the server-based .NET type of the object and the namespace that the type resides in. The remaining values of the JSON string contain the `name:value` pairs for the properties of the `ProductDetail` object and their values.

■ NOTE   Inconsistencies in Type Format

The inconsistency in type formatting between requests and responses is a little confusing at first because it's hard to understand why this would have been done. I guess since the WCF team owns the web service portion of things now, they can dictate what they want.

■ NOTE   Changing Type Information

One common practice performed during development is refactoring, where you modify your code as you go along, making small tweaks that enhance the maintainability and readability of the code. During these times, classes can change names and namespaces. Be sure to keep in mind that any changes performed on the server that affect the data types on the client could warrant changing your proxy calling code.

LISTING 8.27 Type-Based JSON

```
{"criteria":{"__type":"SearchCriteria:http://schemas.datacontract.org/2004/0
7/ProductLookupDemo","ProductNumber":"200"}}
```

LISTING 8.28 Type-Based JSON

```
{"d":{"__type":"ProductDetail:#ProductLookupDemo","Description":"Black XBox
Controller","Price":50,"ProductNumber":"200"}}
```

Known Type and Proxy Type Registration

The `KnownType` attribute that we discussed in the "Complex Data and Serialization" section earlier in the chapter also comes into play when types are generated for the proxy class. The use of the `KnownType` attribute adds that type to the registered types in the proxy. In Listing 8.29, we can see that not only is the `BusinessEntities` type registered, but also the `Customer` and `Vendor` types, even though they are not directly used by any of the methods on the web service. The inclusion of known types in the proxy class assists the JSON serializer in determining the data type to use when converting the data before it is sent back to the server and then on the server when the `Data ContractJsonSerializer` attempts to convert the JSON to a .NET data type.

LISTING 8.29 KnownType Type Declarations

```
var gtc = Sys.Net.WebServiceProxy._generateTypedConstructor;

Type.registerNamespace('AjaxServiceDemo');

if (typeof(AjaxServiceDemo.BusinessEntities) === 'undefined') {
  AjaxServiceDemo.BusinessEntity=gtc(
   "BusinessEntities:http://schemas.datacontract.org/2004/07/
   AjaxServiceDemo");
  AjaxServiceDemo.BusinessEntities.registerClass(
    'AjaxServiceDemo.BusinessEntities');
}

if (typeof(AjaxServiceDemo.Customer) === 'undefined') {
  AjaxServiceDemo.Customer=gtc(
    "Customer:http://schemas.datacontract.org/2004/07/
    AjaxServiceDemo");
  AjaxServiceDemo.Customer.registerClass(
    'AjaxServiceDemo.Customer');
}
if (typeof(AjaxServiceDemo.Vendor) === 'undefined') {
  AjaxServiceDemo.Vendor=gtc(
    "Vendor:http://schemas.datacontract.org/2004/07/
    AjaxServiceDemo");
  AjaxServiceDemo.Vendor.registerClass(
    'AjaxServiceDemo.Vendor');
}
```

Using the Page Method Proxy Class

The page methods proxy class provides the method signatures and data type declarations for the `ProductLookup` and `AdvancedProductLookup` page methods we covered earlier. The generation of this proxy class follows the same pattern as the web service proxy class, including a static representation and the reliance of the `WebServiceProxy` class to provide the underlying request and response functionality.

In Listing 8.30, we can see that the calling pattern is similar to the web service proxy class and uses a similar static class approach to methods. The name of the proxy class when using page methods will always be `PageMethods`, and the methods to call will always match the method names on the page. The use of callbacks and user context is the same as in our web service proxy class, and so is the ability to set these values globally. The one thing that page method proxy classes do not provide is a varying implementation approach using both instance and static representations. The default static usage is all that is supported.

LISTING 8.30 Page Method JavaScript Proxy Calling Functions

```
function PageMethodLookupProduct()
{
  criteria.ProductNumber = $get("productNumber").value;
  PageMethods.AdvancedLookupProduct(criteria,onSuccess,onFailed);

}

function onSuccess(result, userContext, methodName)
{
  $get("productDescription").value = result.Description;
  $get("productPrice").value = result.Price;
}

function onFailed(result, userContext, methodName)
{
  alert("An error occured \n"  + result.get_message());
}
```

WebServiceProxy Class

The `Sys.Net.WebServiceProxy` class is the base class used for proxies generated by the `ScriptManager` and provides the web service request and response functionality for inherited classes. The class contains properties to set the path of the service to call, the timeout for each request, the default user context data passed through the request call and made available to the callback functions, the default success callback function, and the default failure callback function (see Table 8.6). The class also contains an `invoke` method that calls the specified web service dependent on the path and handles all the pre- and post-processing that occurs during the call (see Table 8.7).

TABLE 8.6 WebServiceProxy Class Properties

Property	Description
defaultFailedCallback	Gets or sets the default failed callback function for the service
defaultSucceededCallback	Gets or sets the default succeeded callback function for the service
path	Gets or sets the path to the service
timeout	Gets or sets the timeout in milliseconds for the service

TABLE 8.7 WebServiceProxy Class Methods

Method	Description
invoke	Calls the specified web service method

If we refer back to the product proxy class prototype in Listing 8.24, the _invoke method that provides the functionality for the Lookup method is actually a reference to the invoke method of the WebServiceProxy class. The product class uses this method to call the service, using the pre- and post-processing that the invoke method provides, including setting the content type, serializing the parameter data to JSON, submitting the response, handling the response from the asynchronous request, and calling the registered succeeded and failed callback functions.

The abstraction to the underlying HTTP transport that the WebService Proxy class provides makes it a great class to not only inherit from but to directly use when you need to communicate with a web service in a customized way.

Serialization

The Sys.Serialization.JavaScriptSerializer provides JSON serialization services to the Microsoft AJAX Library. This JavaScript-based serializer is a much simpler type of serializer than the .NET-based `DataContract` `JsonSerializer` on the server and is designed to work with JavaScript `Objects`, `Dates`, `Numbers`, `Booleans`, and `String` values. The serializer has two static methods, `serialize` and `deserialize`, that are used to serialize and deserialize JavaScript types to and from JSON strings. The sample in Listing 8.31 demonstrates how to use the serializer, taking the `Product` `Detail` class from our product service and converting it to JSON. The output of the serializer, which should look familiar by now, contains the type of the object and the `name:value` pairs representing the properties.

> ## ■ NOTE   Prototype Classes and Serialization
>
> The Microsoft AJAX classes you create using the prototype model do not serialize by default using the `JavaScriptSerializer`. The reason for this is the serializer is designed to use the expando properties of an object to extract the property names and values to be serialized (see Chapter 3). In the Prototype Model, the properties are set up using the `get_` and `set_` naming convention and do not follow the expando pattern. One way to get around this is to create a method on the Microsoft AJAX class that can return an expando version of your class and pass that to the `JavaScriptSerializer`.

LISTING 8.31 Serializing JavaScript Objects

```
//create product detail using type from proxy
var productDetail = new ProductLookupDemo.ProductDetail();
productDetail.ProductNumber = "200";
productDetail.Description = "Black XBox Controller";
productDetail.Price = 50;

//serialize to JSON string
var productDetailJSON =
Sys.Serialization.JavaScriptSerializer.serialize(productDetail);

//send to output
Sys.Debug.trace(productDetailJSON);

//Results from Sys.Debug.trace window
{"__type":"ProductDetail:http://schemas.datacontract.org/2004/07/Product
LookupDemo","ProductNumber":"200","Description":"Black XBox
Controller","Price":50}
```

WebRequest

The `Sys.Net.WebRequest` class provides browser-independent asynchronous communication support to the Microsoft AJAX Library. In most cases, you will not use this class directly. Instead, you will use its services when calling the web service proxy classes that are automatically generated for you. Sometimes, however, its direct use is required (for example, when you need to make network requests that are not simple web service calls, when you need to set HTTP request properties directly, or when you need to use a custom executor).

> ■ **NOTE**   Custom Executor
>
> The Microsoft AJAX Library provides a plug-in model that enables developers to create custom asynchronous executors that provide request and response services to the `WebRequest` class. The `XMLHttp Executor` class is an example of a custom executor that uses the services of the browser's `XMLHttp` object to make calls to the server.

The `WebRequest` class comes with properties that expose the various parts of a request. The properties in Table 8.8 represent such items as the request body, the headers of the request, the HTTP verb, and the URL of the request. The class also comes with a set of methods, shown in Table 8.9, that enable the registration of completion handler and provide the ability to invoke the request. To get a feel for how different coding directly against the `WebRequest` object is, let's re-create the call to the `AdvancedLookup` operation on our product service.

TABLE 8.8 WebRequest Class Properties

Property	Description
body	Gets or sets the HTTP body of the web request
executor	Gets or sets the executor of the associated web request instance
headers	Gets the HTTP headers for the web request

TABLE 8.8 continued

Property	Description
httpVerb	Gets or sets the web request HTTP verb used to issue the web request
timeout	Gets or sets the timeout value for the web request instance
url	Gets or sets the URL of the web request instance
userContext	Gets or sets the user context associated with the web request instance

TABLE 8.9 WebRequest Class Methods

Method	Description
add_completed	Registers an event handler to associate with the web request instance
completed	Raises the completed event for the associated Sys.Net.WebRequest instance
getResolvedUrl	Gets the resolved URL of the web request instance
invoke	Issues a network call for the web request instance
remove_completed	Removes the event handler associated with the web request instance

In Listing 8.32, we can see what is required to create the AdvancedLookup request to the product service. The web service proxy class did quite a bit for us, including serializing the parameters to JSON, setting the content type header, setting the URL of the service, composing the request body, determining the HTTP verb to use for the request, invoking the request, and handling the post-processing of the request before it was sent to the onSuccess or onFailed callback functions. In the case of the WebRequest class, we will have to perform all these things by hand.

The majority of the items in the code in Listing 8.32 are self-explanatory based on knowledge you have gained throughout this chapter, but there are a few things that require a more detailed explanation. The JSON data that is placed into the body of the request requires a certain format. The data must be in the format of parameterName:ParameterData, with the parameter name being the name of the of the parameter in the web service operation, and the parameter data being the JSON representation of the data expected.

The role of the onCompleted callback function and the parameters passed into it is a new concept introduced with this class and a sign of how close we are getting to the executor that handles the request. The onComplete function takes two arguments: an executor and event arguments. The executor is of most interest to us because it contains all the information about the request that was made. The executor, unless overridden, will be the default XML HttpExecutor class, which handles calling the XMLHttp object directly. This class contains a rich set of properties that contain a wealth of information about the request including the status of the request, whether it timed out or was aborted, and the response data, just to name a few (see Table 8.10). The amount of work required to properly process a request is substantial, with the majority of the work devoted to figuring out what the response really is. The fact that a result was returned does not mean the result is actually valid. Checks to determine whether the header contains a jsonerror entry, if the status code returned is in a valid range, and whether the request timed out or was aborted are needed to ensure the request is processed correctly. If we are successful and get a result that was converted to JSON correctly by calling the get_object method on the executor, we can work with the result to populate the form. The one catch to the result is the format it is in. If you recall from Listing 8.28, the JSON returned is composed of a d parameter that contains the JSON data from the web service. When assigning values to the form, we have to drill into the ProductDetail properties, which are contained in the d parameter.

LISTING 8.32 WebRequest Version of the AdvancedLookup Web Service Call

```
// Call WebRequest
CallServiceWithWebRequest();

// WebRequest Wrapper
function CallServiceWithWebRequest()
{

  var searchCriteria = new ProductLookupDemo.SearchCriteria();
  searchCriteria.ProductNumber = "200";
  searchCriteria.Description = "Black XBox Controller";
  searchCriteria.Price = 50;

  var searchCriteriaJSON =
    Sys.Serialization.JavaScriptSerializer.serialize(
    searchCriteria);

  var request = new Sys.Net.WebRequest();
  request.get_headers()['Content-Type'] = 'application/json;
    charset=utf-8';
  request.set_url("Product.svc/AdvancedLookup");
  request.set_body("{\"criteria\":" + searchCriteriaJSON + "}");
  request.set_httpVerb("POST");
  request.add_completed(onCompleted);
  request.invoke();
}

// Completion Handler
function onCompleted(executor, eventArgs)
{
 if (executor.get_responseAvailable())
 {
   var statusCode = executor.get_statusCode();
   var result = null;
   try
   {
     result = executor.get_object();
   }
   catch (ex) {}
    var error = executor.getResponseHeader("jsonerror");
    var errorObj = (error === "true");
    if (errorObj)
    {
      //display error
      var errorMessage = String.format("An error occurred with a message
        of {0} with a stact trace of {1} and an execption type of
        {2}",result.Message, result.StackTrace, result.ExceptionType);
        alert(errorMessage);
    }
    if (((statusCode < 200) || (statusCode >= 300)) || errorObj)
```

```
    {
      var error;
      if (result && errorObj)
      {
        //display error
        var errorMessage = String.format("An error of type {0} occurred
          with a message of {1}",result.get_exceptionType(),
          result.get_message());
        alert(errorMessage);
      }
      else
      {
        //display error
        alert(executor.get_responseData());
      }
    }
    else
    {

      //update the UI
      $get("productDescription").value = result.d.Description;
      $get("productPrice").value = result.d.Price;

    }
  }
  else
  {
    var errorMessage;
    if (executor.get_timedOut())
    {
      //display error
      errorMessage = "Request timed out";
    }
    else if(executor.get_aborted())
    {
      errorMessage = "Request was aborted";
    }
    else
    {
      //display error
      errorMessage = "Error occurred no result returned";
    }
  }
}
```

Web Request Core

The web request core components make up the underlying plumbing that
supports the asynchronous communication model in the Microsoft AJAX

Library. The components provide services such as abstracting the interaction with the XMLHttpExecutor, providing low-level network support for calling web services, and selecting the XMLHttp object for a specific browser.

WebRequestManager

The Sys.Net.WebRequestManager class provides an abstraction above the low-level Sys.Net.WebRequestExecutor-based class that performs the actual interaction with the network stack. In a typical case, this class is used by the WebRequest class in its invoke method to call the Sys.Net. xmlhttpexecutor class to process the request. In this scenario, the executor calls the web service and on completion calls the registered completion handler in the WebRequest class to process the response. The real work of processing the request is done by the executor and the WebRequest object, with the WebRequestManager acting as a broker between these two classes.

XMLHttpExecutor

The Sys.Net.XMLHttpExecutor class is the default executor in the Microsoft AJAX Library and provides access to the browser's underlying XMLHttp object. This class is responsible for composing the raw HTTP request and calling the proper XMLHttp object to send the request to the server. The class comes with properties that provide all kinds of information, including whether a response is available, the response data, the JSON representation of the response, and whether it timed out (see Table 8.10). The class also comes with methods that support an asynchronous calling model, providing the ability to execute a request by calling the executeRequest method and then aborting the request if needed by calling the abort method (see Table 8.11). As the request is processing, the started and aborted properties can be used to determine processing status.

TABLE 8.10 XMLHttpExecutor Class Properties

Property	Description
aborted	Returns a value that indicates whether the executor was aborted
responseAvailable	Returns a value that indicates whether the network request returned without being aborted or timing out

Property	Description
responseData	Gets the text representation of the response body
started	Returns a value that indicates whether the executor has forwarded the request to the browser's XMLHTTP object
statusCode	Gets the status code of the browser's XMLHTTP object
statusText	Gets the status text from the browser's XMLHTTP object
timedOut	Returns a value that indicates whether the executor timed out
object	Gets the JSON-evaluated object from the response
xml	Returns an XMLDOM object that contains the XML response from the browser's XMLHTTP object

TABLE 8.11 XMLHttpExecutor Class Methods

Method	Description
abort	Stops the pending network request issued by the executor
executeRequest	Executes a network request as specified in the associated WebRequest instance
getAllResponseHeaders	Returns the response headers
getResponseHeader	Gets the value of a specified response header

XmlHttp

The XMLHTTP object has been around since Internet Explorer 5.0, where it was first introduced as a mechanism to perform out-of-bound HTTP request to the web server. Over the years, various other browsers have provided the same support, implementing it in various ways. The renewed interest in this object came about with the advent of AJAX and the need to provide a rich user experience. In the Microsoft AJAX Library, the usage of this underlying object is now provided in a browser-agnostic way, enabling the platform to provide a rich user experience on a number of popular browsers.

SUMMARY

The communication architecture of ASP.NET 2.0 AJAX Extensions and the Microsoft AJAX Library is enormous, providing a wide array of services, from web services support, JSON serialization, and custom processing on the server side to proxy classes, JSON serialization, and browser-independent access to web services on the client. This rich communication infrastructure provides the services needed to create the rich REST-based communication between the client and the server, which is paramount to creating a rich user experience on the web.

◼ 9 ◼

Application Services

A SP.NET 2.0 MEMBERSHIP, ROLE, and user profile services and their companion ASP.NET AJAX application services provide a complete membership, role, and profiles offering on both the client and the server. The addition of the application services and the supporting proxy classes contained in the Microsoft AJAX Library extend the ability to work with these server-based technologies onto the client, providing a much needed lightweight alternative to an otherwise heavy server control–based experience. In this chapter, we look at the ASP.NET 2.0 membership, role, and user profile services and what they provide from a server perspective, with a goal of understanding at a high level how these features work. We then move on to the ASP.NET AJAX application services, detailing how they work and integrate with their server counterparts. In the final section of this chapter, we show how to create custom application services and the benefits they provide.

ASP.NET 2.0 Membership, Role, and User Profile Services

ASP.NET 2.0 membership, role, and user profile services are built on many different technologies that come together to provide a unified approach to working the authentication, authorization, and user-specific data. In this section, we cover many of the components that make up these offerings, including Forms authentication, the ASP.NET Provider Model, and the Web Site Administration Tool, along with membership, role, and user profile services.

Forms Authentication

Before we consider ASP.NET 2.0 membership, role, and user profile services, we need to talk about authentication, and in particular Forms authentication. Windows authentication, Passport authentication, and Forms authentication are the three types of authentication modes supported in ASP.NET 2.0. Windows authentication makes use of the local Windows users and groups to store user credentials, which are then used to authenticate users during page requests. Passport, or Windows Live ID, is the Microsoft initiative for a single authentication point and is used on sites such as Hotmail and MSN. Forms authentication is a cookie-based authentication model that relies on a membership-based provider to store and authenticate users during page requests. In ASP.NET 2.0, it is Forms authentication that ASP.NET membership uses to authenticate users during page requests; we focus on this technique when discussing authentication with ASP.NET 2.0 membership.

Forms authentication works by issuing a cookie and using that cookie to validate a user as that user navigates through a site. If a request is made and a cookie does not exist or is invalid, the user is redirected to a configured login page to provide a username and password verifiable against the membership provider–based user store. After the user has been authenticated, the user is redirected back to the originally requested page, from which the user can continue navigating through the site.

If we look at the request processing a little closer, we will see it's actually IIS and ASP.NET that work together to determine access to your site. The IIS side of things uses the settings in the IIS metabase to determine its authentication mode, which will be the first that is applied to the request. With Forms authentication, you should set IIS to use anonymous access as the authentication mode, which delegates the authentication to ASP.NET and Forms authentication instead. The ASP.NET side of things then uses Forms authentication to authenticate the request and determine whether the user is valid. To enable Forms authentication, you must add the configuration entry shown in Listing 9.1 to your web.config file. The authentication element sets the mode to Forms, and the forms element is used to configure the authentication behavior. The forms element comes with quite a few entries that control things such as the URL that contains the login page, the name of the cookie on the client, a default URL to send users to after successful login, and many more (see Table 9.1).

LISTING 9.1 Forms Authentication Configuration

```
<system.web>
  <authentication mode="Forms">
    <forms loginUrl="Login.aspx"
           protection="All"
           timeout="30"
           name=".ASPXAUTH"
           path="/"
           requireSSL="false"
           slidingExpiration="true"
           defaultUrl="default.aspx"
           cookieless="UseDeviceProfile"
           enableCrossAppRedirects="false" />
  </authentication>
</system.web>
```

TABLE 9.1 Forms Authentication Elements

Element	Description
loginUrl	Points to your application's custom login page. You should place the login page in a folder that requires Secure Sockets Layer (SSL) to help ensure the integrity of the credentials when they are passed from the browser to the web server.
protection	Specifies the type of encryption, if any, to use for cookies. Valid values are All, Encryption, None, and Validation. All specifies that the application uses both data validation and encryption to help protect the cookie.
timeout	Specifies the time, in integer minutes, after which the cookie expires.

TABLE 9.1 continued

Element	Description
name	Specifies the HTTP cookie to use for authentication. The default is ".ASPXAUTH".
path	Specifies the path for cookies that are issued by the application. The default is a slash (/), because most browsers are case sensitive and will not send cookies back if there is a path case mismatch.
requireSSL	Specifies whether an SSL connection is required to transmit the authentication cookie.
slidingExpiration	Specifies whether sliding expiration is enabled.
defaultUrl	Defines the default URL that is used for redirection after authentication.
cookieless	Defines whether cookies are used and their behavior. Valid values are UseCookies, UseUri, AutoDetect, and UseDeviceProfile. The default is UseDeviceProfile.
enableCrossAppRedirects	Indicates whether authenticated users are redirected to URLs in other web applications.

The default behavior of the preceding configuration is to allow any anonymous user to access the site, which, as you can tell, is not what we would want for Forms authentication. This is where the companion web.config entry of authorization comes into play. The authorization element, see Listing 9.2 and Table 9.2, enables us to map authorization to web resources using the allow and deny subelements and thus limit the access of users, roles, and HTTP verbs to all web resources. This element, in combination with the authentication and forms elements, is what makes Forms authentication possible.

LISTING 9.2 Authorization Element Configuration

```
<system.web>
  <authorization>
    <deny users="?" />
  </authorization>
</system.web>
```

TABLE 9.2 Deny and Allow Element Entries

Element	Description
users	A comma-separated list of usernames that are denied access to the resource. A question mark (?) denies anonymous users, and an asterisk (*) indicates that all user accounts are denied access.
roles	A comma-separated list of roles that are denied access.
verbs	A comma-separated list of HTTP transmission methods that are granted access to the resource. Verbs that are registered to ASP.NET are GET, HEAD, POST, and DEBUG.

ASP.NET 2.0 Provider Model

The ASP.NET 2.0 Provider Model provides a uniform way for the membership, role, and profile services to provide common functionality regardless of the underlying system providing the services. This uniform approach enables developers to easily exchange out backend systems that provide the underlying services without having to change the calling APIs. This type of functionality enables the membership provider to be switched from the default SQL membership provider to a provider that works with Active Directory or Oracle, without any modifications to the web application. ASP.NET comes with a default set of SQL providers that provide support for working with a SQL database to store the membership, role, and profile information for your web site (see Table 9.3). These providers are configured in the machine.config file, as shown in Listing 9.3, and are shared across all web applications. These providers by default are configured to work with the LocalSqlServer connection string entry, which points to a SQLExpress database. If you want to use a standard SQL database, just override the LocalSqlServer connection string entry in your web.config file, as shown in Listing 9.4, to point to a SQL database server of your choice. The database that you use must contain a predefined set of tables and stored procedures, and the aspnet_reqsql.exe application is used to initialize the database with this information. The application works either as a command-line application or as a wizard and simply creates the tables and stored procedures used by the services to store and retrieve data.

TABLE 9.3 Provider Services and Default Classes

Provider Service	Default Provider Class
Membership	System.Web.Security.SqlMembershipProvider
Role	System.Web.Security.SqlRoleProvider
Profile	System.Web.Profile.SqlProfileProvider

LISTING 9.3 Default Provider Registration and Configuration

```
<configuration>
...
  <connectionStrings>
    <add name="LocalSqlServer"
      connectionString="data source=.\SQLEXPRESS;Integrated
      Security=SSPI;AttachDBFilename=|DataDirectory|aspnetdb.mdf;User
      Instance=true" providerName="System.Data.SqlClient" />
  </connectionStrings>
  <system.web>
    <membership>
      <providers>
        <add name="AspNetSqlMembershipProvider"
          type="System.Web.Security.SqlMembershipProvider, System.Web,
          Version=2.0.0.0, Culture=neutral,
          PublicKeyToken=b03f5f7f11d50a3a"
          connectionStringName="LocalSqlServer"
          enablePasswordRetrieval="false" enablePasswordReset="true"
          requiresQuestionAndAnswer="true" applicationName="/"
          requiresUniqueEmail="false" passwordFormat="Hashed"
          maxInvalidPasswordAttempts="5" minRequiredPasswordLength="7"
          minRequiredNonalphanumericCharacters="1"
          passwordAttemptWindow="10"
          passwordStrengthRegularExpression="" />
      </providers>
    </membership>
    <profile>
      <providers>
        <add name="AspNetSqlProfileProvider"
          connectionStringName="LocalSqlServer" applicationName="/"
          type="System.Web.Profile.SqlProfileProvider, System.Web,
          Version=2.0.0.0, Culture=neutral,
          PublicKeyToken=b03f5f7f11d50a3a" />
      </providers>
    </profile>
    <roleManager>
```

```
        <providers>
          <add name="AspNetSqlRoleProvider"
            connectionStringName="LocalSqlServer" applicationName="/"
            type="System.Web.Security.SqlRoleProvider, System.Web,
            Version=2.0.0.0, Culture=neutral,
            PublicKeyToken=b03f5f7f11d50a3a" />
          <add name="AspNetWindowsTokenRoleProvider" applicationName="/"

type="System.Web.Security.WindowsTokenRoleProvider,System.Web,
            Version=2.0.0.0, Culture=neutral,
            PublicKeyToken=b03f5f7f11d50a3a" />
        </providers>
      </roleManager>
    </system.web>
  ...
</configuration>
```

LISTING 9.4 Default LocalSqlServer Override in web.config

```
<connectionStrings>
  <remove name="LocalSqlServer"/>
  <add name="LocalSqlServer" connectionString="DataSource=localhost;
    Initial Catalog=aspnetdb;Integrated Security=True"
    providerName="System.Data.SqlClient"/>
</connectionStrings>
```

Web Site Administration Tool

The Web Site Administration Tool provides an easy way to manage your web site configuration without having to edit the web.config file manually. You can access the tool off the Project menu by selecting the ASP.NET Configuration menu option, which will open the Web Site Administration Tool page, shown in Figure 9.1, providing a Forms-based way to edit configuration information about your site. The tool contains three main tabs that provide specific UIs for managing entries in each of these areas: Security, Application, and Provider. The Security tab, shown in Figure 9.2, enables you to manage all the security settings for your application, including setting up users and passwords, creating roles, and creating access rules for the various web resources in your application. The Application tab is focused on managing application settings and SMTP settings, configuring debugging and tracing, and managing whether the application is online or offline. The Provider tab enables you to select from a list of configured providers and select the global provider that will be used on your site or individually select a specific provider for membership or roles. The Security tab will be of most interest to us as we cover working with membership and roles because it contains all the UIs needed to manage entries of this type.

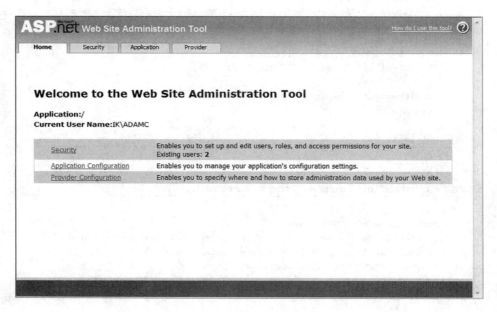

FIGURE 9.1 Web Site Administration Tool

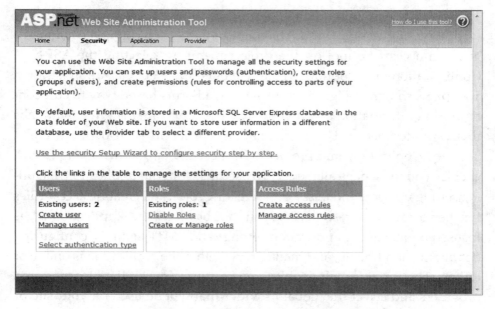

FIGURE 9.2 Web Site Administration Tool Security tab

Membership

ASP.NET membership was introduced in ASP.NET 2.0 and provides services that work in conjunction with Forms authentication to manage and authenticate users using either a rich API or a set of built-in server controls that connect to a provider-based data store. The use of membership either with the APIs or with the built-in server controls enables you to create new users, manage user-related information such as username and password, authenticate users as they access your site, integrate membership with roles and profiles, and use a custom membership provider.

The Membership static class is the foundation for the membership services in ASP.NET and provides a wealth of properties shown in Table 9.4 and methods shown in Table 9.5 that provide all you need to manage users. The class provides all the functionality needed to validate users and handle all the maintenance tasks such as creating, updating, and deleting users. You can also enhance the user authentication experience in this class; you can set password length, maximum number of invalid login attempts, whether the user is able to reset a password, and many more. The page in Figure 9.3 is a sample login screen that shows the two methods of logging in a user. The API version is what we talk about now and consists of capturing the usernames and passwords for users and whether the users want to set a cookie to remember them. The Login button has some companion code, shown in Listing 9.5, that shows the steps needed to authenticate the user, set the Forms authentication cookie, and redirect back to the calling page. The configuration of Forms authentication ensures that this page will be called whenever an anonymous user accesses the site. The ReturnUrl parameter in the query string contains the page the user tried to access while not logged in.

TABLE 9.4 Common Membership Class Properties

Property	Description
EnablePasswordReset	Gets a value indicating whether the current membership provider is configured to allow users to reset their passwords

TABLE 9.4 continued

Property	Description
EnablePasswordRetrieval	Gets a value indicating whether the current membership provider is configured to allow users to retrieve their passwords
MaxInvalidPasswordAttempts	Gets the number of invalid password or password-answer attempts allowed before the membership user is locked out
MinRequiredNonAlphanumericCharacters	Gets the minimum number of special characters that must be present in a valid password
MinRequiredPasswordLength	Gets the minimum length required for a password
PasswordAttemptWindow	Gets the time window between which consecutive failed attempts to provide a valid password or password answer are tracked
RequiresQuestionAndAnswer	Gets a value indicating whether the default membership provider requires the user to answer a password question for password reset and retrieval
UserIsOnlineTimeWindow	Specifies the number of minutes after the last-activity date/time stamp for a user during which the user is considered online

TABLE 9.5 Common Membership Class Methods

Method	Description
CreateUser	Overloaded. Adds a new user to the data store.
DeleteUser	Overloaded. Deletes a user from the database.

Method	Description
FindUsersByName	Overloaded. Gets a collection of membership users where the username contains the specified username to match.
GetUser	Overloaded. Gets the information for a membership user from the data source.
UpdateUser	Updates the database with the information for the specified user.
ValidateUser	Verifies that the supplied username and password are valid.

Membership also comes with a rich set of server controls that perform many of the same tasks as the APIs and provide a user interface to accomplish these tasks (see Table 9.6). The Login control, shown at the bottom of the Login page in Figure 9.3, provides the exact same functionality as the API version above it but requires no coding. To use the control, you just drag and drop it onto the designer and you are ready to go. The nice thing about using many of these controls is that they support templates that enable you to customize the look and feel of the controls.

TABLE 9.6 Membership Controls

Control	Description
Login	Provides UI elements for logging in to a website
LoginView	Displays the appropriate content template for a given user, based on the user's authentication status and role membership
PasswordRecovery	Provides UI elements that enable a user to recover or reset a lost password and receive it in e-mail
LoginStatus	Detects the user's authentication state and toggles the state of a link to log in to or log out of a web site
LoginName	Displays the value of the System.Web.UI.Page.User.Identity.Name property

TABLE 9.6 continued

Control	Description
CreateUserWizard	Provides a user interface for creating new web site user accounts
ChangePassword	Provides a user interface that enable users to change their website password

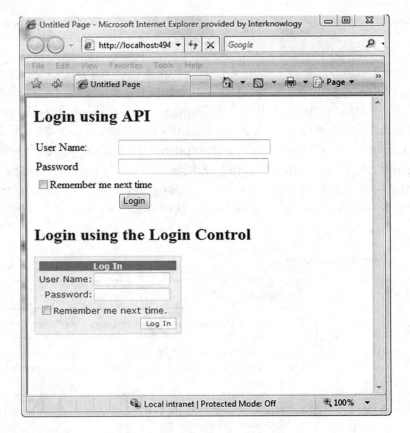

FIGURE 9.3 Membership login sample screen

LISTING 9.5 Login Using Membership API

```
public partial class login : System.Web.UI.Page
{
  protected void Page_Load(object sender, EventArgs e)  { }
```

```
protected void ButtonLogin_Click(object sender, EventArgs e)
{
    if (Membership.ValidateUser(TextBoxUserName.Text,
        TextBoxPassword.Text))
    {
        FormsAuthentication.SetAuthCookie(TextBoxUserName.Text,
            CheckBoxRememberMe.Checked);
        Response.Redirect(Request.Params["ReturnUrl"].ToString());
    }
    else
    {
        LabelInvalidLogin.Visible = true;
    }
}
}
```

The Web Site Administration Tool provides a complete no-code solution to managing users and comes in handy when user administration will not be an exposed feature of your site. The Create User screen shown in Figure 9.4 enables you to add users to the site and assign roles at the same time. The Manage User screen shown in Figure 9.5 enables you to search for users and optionally edit them using the Edit User screen in Figure 9.6. This out-of-the-box type functionality can come in handy when full-blown management screens using the server controls and API are not possible.

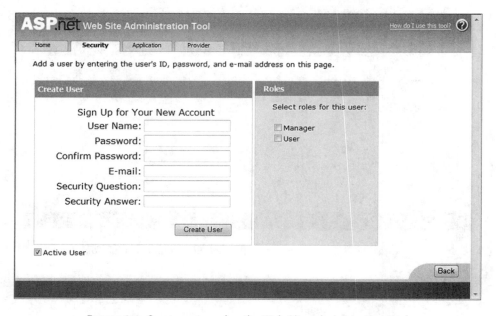

FIGURE 9.4 Create users using the Web Site Administration Tool

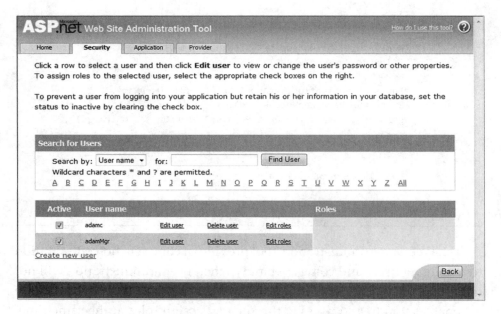

FIGURE 9.5 Managing users using the Web Site Administration Tool

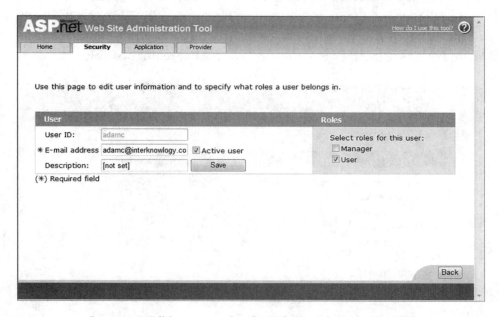

FIGURE 9.6 Editing users using the Web Site Administration Tool

Roles

The section on membership was all about authenticating users and ensuring their identity. Roles, on the other hand, are about authorization and the act of authorizing a valid user to access a resource. Role management enables you to specify access rights to groups (roles) and then assign users to those groups. Roles typically have names such as manager, supervisor, and administrator, and relate to functions a user will perform on a site. It is then through roles that you manage access to resources on your web site, restricting access based on a role and not a specific user. In some cases, a user can perform many roles in a web site, and role management supports this by enabling users to be in more than one role at a time.

To begin working with roles, you must add the `roleManager` element to the web.config file, as shown in Listing 9.6. This entry turns on roles and uses the default provider to interact with the data store. After roles have been turned on, you have to add entries to the `authorization` element, as shown in Listing 9.7, to limit access to web resources. These entries follow the same `allow` and `deny` pattern as Forms authentication, but take a role name. As you can imagine, adding entries by hand into the web.config file can be tedious, and this is where the Web Site Administration Tool comes in handy.

The Web Site Administration Tool is another option you can use to add `authorization` entries and follows a more graphical approach. The management of roles can be accessed on the Security tab by clicking any of the links under Roles or Access Rules (refer to Figure 9.2). The Role Management screen shown in Figure 9.7 makes it easy to add roles and manage users in roles. The Manage Access Rules screen shown in Figure 9.8 enables you to manage access to web resources by folder. This screen is used along with the Add New Access Rule screen to set permissions on folders and manage access to all resources in the folder (see Figure 9.9). As you add restrictions to folders, a separate web.config entry following the same pattern as Listing 9.7 is added to the affected folder. The ordering of roles is important during evaluation, with the first match being the one that is processed, and the move up and move down buttons provide an easy way to set the correct evaluation order of the roles entered.

> ## ■ NOTE   Access Rights to Folders and Web Service Proxies
>
> The access rules you apply to folders that contain web services can limit your ability to load the client-side proxies. This type of situation occurs when a user is in a role that does not have permission to a supporting service that is contained in a separate folder. In this case the web service proxy will not be brought down to the client and when the application tries to access the proxy the object will not be set.

LISTING 9.6 Configuring Roles

```
<roleManager
    enabled="true"
</roleManager>
```

LISTING 9.7 Configuring Role Access

```
<configuration>
  <location path="Managers">
    <system.web>
      <authorization>
        <allow roles="Manager" />
        <deny users="*" />
      </authorization>
    </system.web>
  </location>
<configuration>
```

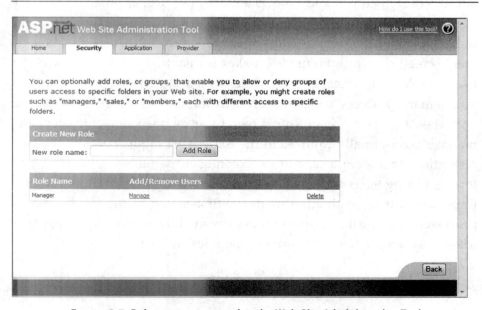

FIGURE 9.7 Role management using the Web Site Administration Tool

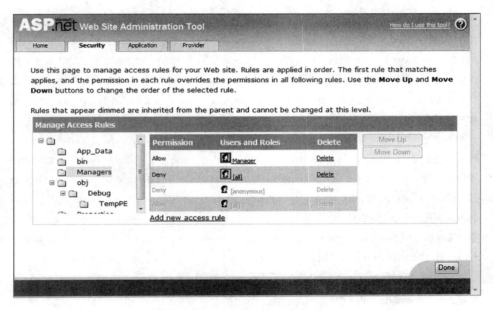

FIGURE 9.8 Managing access using roles

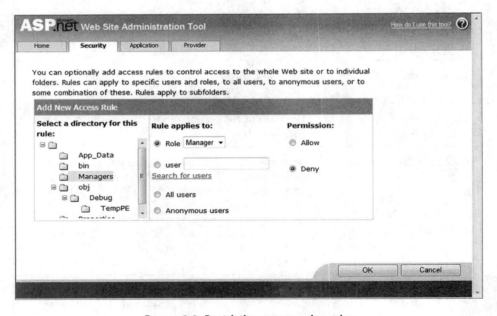

FIGURE 9.9 Restricting access using roles

The Role class, which is the center of all this functionality, contains many properties and methods that will be used as you interact with roles. The access rules you can create with the Web Site Administration Tool will only go so far before you have to work with the Roles class directly to perform addition logic. The properties shown in Table 9.7 center on configuring roles, enabling you to specify the cookie name, set a sliding expiration for the cookie, and set the cookie timeout, to name a few. In a typical situation, all these values use the defaults. If you need to modify any of them, however, just add them to the roleManager element, as shown in Listing 9.6. The methods shown in Table 9.8 are used more frequently and enable you to manage roles and validate membership in a role and check whether a role exists. The page code in Listing 9.8 demonstrates a common use for roles in limiting user access to page content. In this example, users are restricted from adding a discount to an order if they are not in the Managers role. The SetSecurityMessage function demonstrates how to show the roles users are in so that in a case like this they can ask to be added if appropriate.

TABLE 9.7 Common Roles Class Properties

Property	Description
CacheRolesInCookie	Gets a value indicating whether the current user's roles are cached in a cookie.
CookieName	The name of the cookie where role names are cached. The default is .ASPXROLES.
CookiePath	The path of the cookie where role names are cached. The default is /.
CookieProtectionValue	One of the CookieProtection enumeration values indicating how role names that are cached in a cookie are protected. The default is All (validation and encryption).
CookieRequireSSL	true if SSL is required to return the role names cookie to the server; otherwise, false. The default is false.
CookieSlidingExpiration	true if the role names cookie expiration date and time will be reset periodically; otherwise, false. The default is true.
CookieTimeout	An integer specifying the number of minutes before the roles cookie expires. The default is 30 minutes.
MaxCachedResults	The maximum number of role names to be cached for a user. The default is 25.

TABLE 9.8 Common Roles Class Methods

Method	Description
AddUserToRole	Adds the specified user to the specified role.
CreateRole	Adds a new role to the data source.
DeleteCookie	Deletes the cookie where role names are cached.
DeleteRole	Overloaded. Removes a role from the data source.
FindUsersInRole	Gets a list of users in a specified role where the username contains the specified username to match.
GetAllRoles	Gets a list of all the roles for the application.
GetRolesForUser	Overloaded. Gets a list of the roles that a user is in.
GetUsersInRole	Gets a list of users in the specified role.
IsUserInRole	Overloaded. Gets a value indicating whether a user is in the specified role.
RemoveUserFromRole	Removes the specified user from the specified role.
RoleExists	Gets a value indicating whether the specified role name already exists in the role data source.

LISTING 9.8 Using the Role API

```
public partial class OrderEntry : System.Web.UI.Page
{
  protected void Page_Load(object sender, EventArgs e)
  {
    if (User.IsInRole("Managers"))
    {
      DropDownListDiscount.Enabled = true;
      LinkButtonManagerEnable.Visible = false;
    }
    else
    {
      DropDownListDiscount.Enabled = false;
      SetSecurityMessage();
    }
  }
}
```

LISTING 9.8 continued

```
private void SetSecurityMessage()
{
  string[] roles = Roles.GetRolesForUser();
  StringBuilder securityMessage = new StringBuilder();
  securityMessage.Append("You are not in the Managers role and
    therefore your usage of this page is limited. ");

  securityMessage.Append("You are currently in the following
    roles: ");

  int roleCount = roles.Length;

  if (roleCount == 0)
  {
    securityMessage.Append("None");
  }
  else
  {
    foreach (string role in roles)
    {
      securityMessage.Append(role);
      if (óroleCount != 0)
      {
        securityMessage.Append(", ");
      }
    }
  }

  LabelSecurityMessage.Text = securityMessage.ToString();
}
}
```

Profiles

The need to store user-specific information is a common one that occurs often when creating sites. To implement a solution to achieve this might require creating a database table, a series of store procedures, and a data class that can be called from your pages to work with the information gathered. Then, add to this the need to store this information about a per-user basis and the solution becomes even more complex. This is where profiles come in and provide a clean way to work with user-specific data.

> **■ NOTE** Profiles in Visual Studio 2008
>
> The Web Application Project Model is the only model supported by Visual Studio 2008 using .NET 3.5, which precludes it from dynamically generating the `Profile` class based on web.config entries. In this section, we deal with this by creating our own `ProfileBase`-based class and using it to represent our profile data.

Profiles are used with membership to maintain user-specific information persisted between requests by the profile provider. As you interact with your profile information, the provider takes care of saving and retrieving your user-based data through the services provided by the `ProfileBase` class, eliminating the need to directly interact with the data store.

To start working with profiles, you need to create a class that inherits from `ProfileBase`, which provides all the base services for working with profiles. The `UserProfile` class shown in Listing 9.9 inherits from `Profile Base` to provide a series of both simple and complex properties that represent user information. The `FavoriteColor`, `PetsName`, and `HomePage Settings` properties comprise the information our `UserProfile` class will work with. They rely on the services provided by the base class for storing, retrieving, and saving property information. The static `GetUserProfile` method is how you get a reference to the profile data and start working with the profile data. This method uses membership to get the current user's name, which is used when accessing the profile data. After the profile data class has been created you can enable profiles and associate your new class with the profile service by adding the profile configuration entry to the web.config file and assigning the `UserProfile` class as the inherits class attribute, as shown in Listing 9.10. This configuration entry enables profiles and sets the data type used to store and retrieve data to the `User Profile` type.

The interface that the `UserProfile` class provides makes it easy to work with profile information. The Profile Maintenance page shown in Figure 9.10 and the companion code shown in Listing 9.11 demonstrates how to work with the `UserProfile` class. This page is used to manage user profiles. It provides a simple UI that enables users to manipulate entries and have them saved for later use.

LISTING 9.9 UserProfile Class

```
public class UserProfile : ProfileBase
{
  public static UserProfile GetUserProfile()
  {
    return Create(Membership.GetUser().UserName) as UserProfile;
  }

  [SettingsAllowAnonymous(false)]
  public string FavoriteColor
  {
    get { return base["FavoriteColor"] as string; }
    set { base["FavoriteColor"] = value; }
  }
  [SettingsAllowAnonymous(false)]
  public string PetsName
  {
    get { return base["PetsName"] as string; }
    set { base["PetsName"] = value; }
  }
  [SettingsAllowAnonymous(false)]
  public HomePageSettings HomePageSettings
  {
    get
    {
      HomePageSettings pageSettings = base["HomePageSettings"] as
        HomePageSettings;
      if (pageSettings == null)
      {
        pageSettings = new HomePageSettings();
        base["HomePageSettings"] = pageSettings;
      }
      return pageSettings;
    }

    set { base["HomePageSettings"] = value; }
  }
}

public class HomePageSettings
{
    public string News { get; set; }
    public string Weather { get; set; }
    public string Sports { get; set; }
}
```

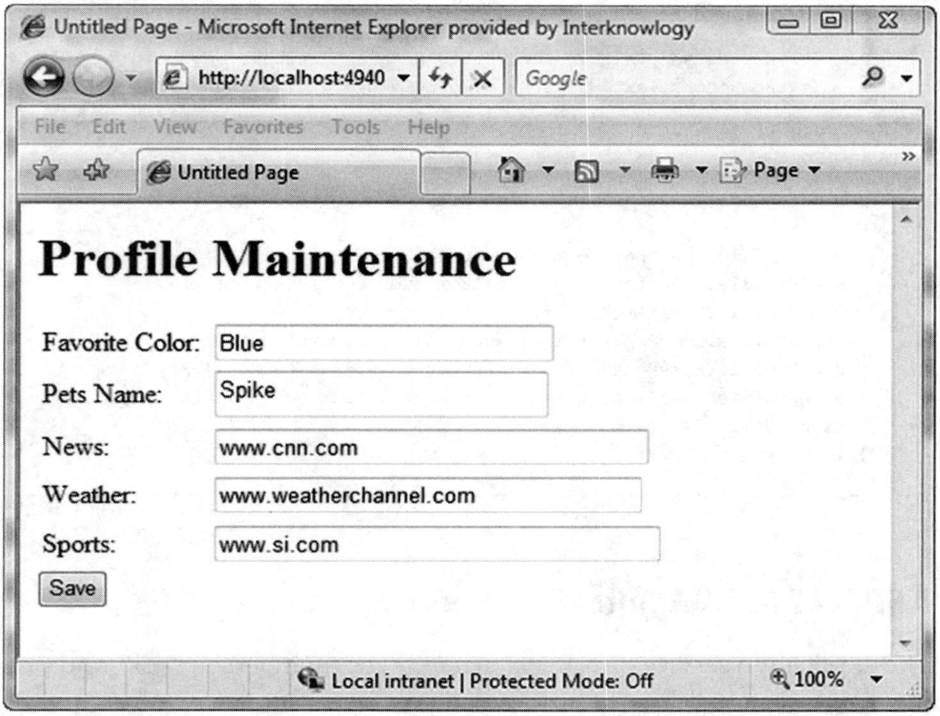

FIGURE 9.10 Profile Maintenance page

LISTING 9.10 Profile Configuration

```
<profile
  enabled="true"
  inherits="ApplicationServicesDemo.UserProfile"/>
```

LISTING 9.11 Using the UserProfile Class

```
public partial class ProfileMaintenance : System.Web.UI.Page
{
  protected void Page_Load(object sender, EventArgs e)
  {
    if (!Page.IsPostBack)
    {
      UserProfile userProfile = UserProfile.GetUserProfile();
      TextBoxFavoriteColor.Text = userProfile.FavoriteColor;
      TextBoxPetsName.Text = userProfile.PetsName;
      TextBoxNews.Text = userProfile.HomePageSettings.News;
```

LISTING 9.11 continued

```
        TextBoxWeather.Text = userProfile.HomePageSettings.Weather;
        TextBoxSports.Text = userProfile.HomePageSettings.Sports;
    }
}

    protected void ButtonSaveClick(object sender, EventArgs e)
    {
        UserProfile userProfile = UserProfile.GetUserProfile();
        userProfile.FavoriteColor = TextBoxFavoriteColor.Text;
        userProfile.PetsName = TextBoxPetsName.Text;
        userProfile.HomePageSettings.News = TextBoxNews.Text;
        userProfile.HomePageSettings.Weather = TextBoxWeather.Text;
        userProfile.HomePageSettings.Sports = TextBoxSports.Text;
        userProfile.Save();
    }
}
```

ASP.NET AJAX Application Services

The application services are an extension of the membership, role, and profile services previously discussed. These application services provide access into membership, roles, and profiles using a client-side API. The power of these services is their tight integration and the reliance on the same server-based APIs that membership, roles, and profiles rely on. Often working on an application, you will need to verify a user's role or temporarily log a user in to perform some task. This was all possible before, but required a postback that made the effort much slower. With application services, we can now perform these tasks without a postback; we just use the client-side proxies that come with the Microsoft AJAX Library.

Authentication Service

The authentication service is an extension of ASP.NET membership on the client and provides a limited subset of the functionality of its server counterpart. The functionality provided concentrates on logging a user in to and out of the site and determining whether the current user is logged in.

Configuration

By default, the authentication service is not enabled and must be configured. As discussed in Chapter 8, "ASP.NET AJAX Communication Architecture," all the services are already there and part of your standard

ASP.NET AJAX application and just need to be activated. The web.config entries shown in Listing 9.12 are needed to configure authentication services. The authentication, role, and profile services are all configured in the `system.web.extensions` element. In the case of the authentication service, we need to add the `authenticationService` element and set its `enabled` attribute to `true`.

LISTING 9.12 Authentication Service Configuration

```
<system.web.extensions>
  <scripting>
    <webServices>
      <authenticationService enabled="true" />
    </webServices>
  </scripting>
</system.web.extensions>
```

The Sys.Services.AuthenticationService Class

The `Sys.Services.AuthenticationService` class is a proxy class contained in the MicrosoftAjax.js file. This class is a static class that inherits from the `Sys.Net.WebProxy` class covered in Chapter 8 and exhibits the same static behavior. The properties are listed in Table 9.9 and provide support for adding callback functions and validating whether a user is logged in. The methods are listed in Table 9.10 and provide the limited ability to log in and log out.

TABLE 9.9 AuthenticationService Properties

Property	Description
`defaultLoginCompletedCallback`	The default handler that will be called when the login attempt is completed. Once set, this handler will be called for each request.
`defaultLogoutCompletedCallback`	The default handler that will be called when the logout attempt is completed. This handler will be called for each request.
`isLoggedIn`	Returns `true` or `false` based on whether the user is logged in.

TABLE 9.10 AuthenticationService Methods

Method	Description
login	Used to log in to membership
logout	Used to log out of membership

Using the Authentication Service

In most applications that are using membership, there are additional features that would be nice to have on the client. The ability to change the logged-in user without causing a postback is one of them. Often in business applications, there is a need to have a manager override entries made in a data-entry screen by a user of limited rights. The ability to switch user context using the authentication service without causing a postback would provide a nice alternative to the longer process of switching users via the membership controls.

To demonstrate this, we look at an order-entry screen that provides the ability to add a discount. In most cases, you would not want just any employee to do this. Therefore, we need a manager override to accomplish this. This is where the ability to log in on the client comes into play. In this case, we enable a manager to log in to the application, make a change, and then log out, thus resetting the credentials to the user. The order-entry screen shown in Figure 9.11 contains a Discount drop-down, access to which requires a user with manager rights. The Enable link next to the drop-down brings up the Login screen shown in Figure 9.12, which enables a user to log in with manager credentials, enabling the drop-down and enabling the user to discount the order. The call to the authentication service is shown in Listing 9.13. It passes in the username and password provided by the user and attempts to log the user in. A successful login validates the user and enables the drop-down. One thing that we are not checking for in this case is the role that the newly logged-in user is in. This will be the topic of the next section, as we cover more of what the application services provide on the client.

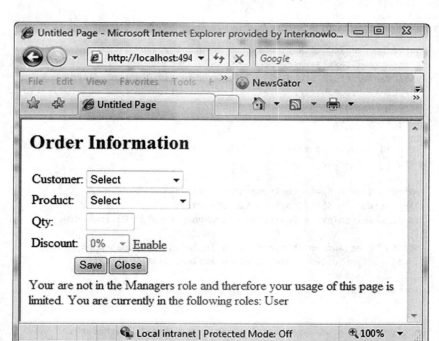

FIGURE 9.11   Order entry screen

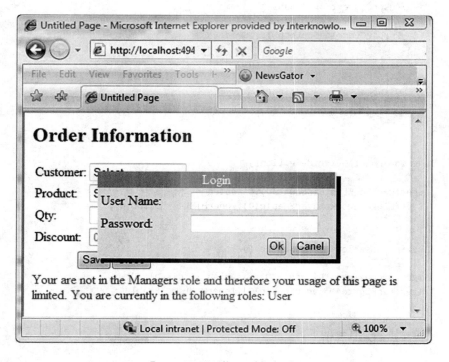

FIGURE 9.12   Client-side login

LISTING 9.13 Authentication Service Call

```
//Server Control Constant code from OrderEntry.aspx
<script type="text/javascript">
  var DropDownListDiscountID = "<%= DropDownListDiscount.ClientID %>";
  var LinkButtonManagerEnableID = "<%=LinkButtonManagerEnable.ClientID
    %>";
</script>

//code in javascript file
function ManagerLogin()
{
  var userName = $get("LoginUserName").value
  var password = $get("LoginPassword").value
  var linkButtonText = $get(LinkButtonManagerEnableID).innerHTML;

  Sys.Services.AuthenticationService.login(userName,password,false,
    null,null,onSuccessManagerLogin,onFailed,linkButtonText);

  ResetLogin()
}

function onSuccessManagerLogin(result, userContext, methodName )
{
  if(result == true)
  {
    if(userContext == "Enable")
    {
      EnableOverrideSection();
    }
    else
    {
      DisableOverrideSection();
    }
  }
}

function EnableOverrideSection()
{
  $get(DropDownListDiscountID).disabled = "";
  $get(LinkButtonManagerEnableID).innerHTML = "Disable";
}

function DisableOverrideSection()
{
  $get(DropDownListDiscountID).disabled = "disabled";
  $get(LinkButtonManagerEnableID).innerHTML = "Enable";
}

function ResetLogin()
```

```
{
   $get("LoginUserName").value = "";
   $get("LoginPassword").value = "";
}

function onFailed(result, userContext, methodName)
{
   alert("An error occurred \n"  + result.get_message());
}
```

Role Service

The role service provides a client-side subset of the functionality provided by the ASP.NET Roles class. The primary focus of roles on the client is viewing and verifying the roles of the current logged-in user.

Configuration

Because all the application services are not enabled by default, the same process of enabling the service as we did with the authentication service is needed here. The roleService entry shown in Listing 9.14 must be added to the System.Web.Extensions element and the enabled attribute set to true. This will now enable the service and allow communication with the client.

LISTING 9.14 Role Service Configuration

```
<system.web.extensions>
  <scripting>
    <webServices>
      <roleService enabled="true" />
    </webServices>
  </scripting>
</system.web.extensions>
```

The Sys.Services.RoleService Class

The Sys.Services.RoleService class is a proxy class just like the Authentication class and is contained in the MicrosoftAjax.js file. Just like the Authentication class, this class is a static class that inherits from the Sys.Net.WebProxy class. The properties listed in Table 9.11 provide support for adding callback functions and viewing the roles the currently logged-in user is a member of. The methods listed in Table 9.12 enable you to load all the roles a user is a member of and verify that a user is in a specific role.

TABLE 9.11 RoleService Properties

Property	Description
defaultLoadCompletedCallback	The default handler that will be called when the call to load is completed. Once set, this handler will be called for each request.
roles	Returns an array of roles the user is in.

TABLE 9.12 RoleService Methods

Method	Description
isUserInRole	Determines whether the user is in the role passed in
load	Gets the roles for the current user

Using the Role Service

In our authentication example, we noticed a huge hole in our implementation. After we logged a user in, we failed to validate the role the user was in before allowing the user to apply a discount to the order. Now we add some additional validation, using the role service to validate that the user is in the correct role. The new version of our manager override is shown in Listing 9.15, with the common code removed for brevity. In this new version, after we have successfully logged in to the application, we use the role service to load up the available roles for the user. The call to the load method actually loads the available roles into the static `RoleService` class, where they are available to the `isUserInRole` method used to validate that a user is in the specified role. We use this method to verify that our newly logged-in user is actually a member of the Managers role before we enable the discount drop-down.

LISTING 9.15 Role Service Call

```
function onSuccessManagerLogin(result, userContext, methodName )
{
   if(result == true)
   {
      GetRoles("Enable");
   }
}

function GetRoles(callingContext)
{
   Sys.Services.RoleService.load(onSuccessGetRoles,
      onFailed,callingContext);
}

function onSuccessGetRoles(result, userContext, methodName )
{
   if(userContext == "Enable")
   {
      if(Sys.Services.RoleService.isUserInRole("Manager"))
      {
         EnableOverrideSection();
      }
      else
      {
         alert("User does not have manager rights");
      }
   }
   else
   {
      DisableOverrideSection();
   }
}
```

Profile Service

The profile service builds on the functionality we used on the server to provide client-side access to the profile properties. The nice thing about working with profiles is that we can actually modify the values on the client, something we could not do with the other services.

Configuration

The profile service configuration is probably the most problematic of all service configurations due to the fine detail that needs to be addressed during configuration. The addition of the profileService element to the System.Web.Extensions section shown in Listing 9.16 not only requires setting the enabled attribute to true, it also requires all the properties you will work with to be registered as being readable and optionally writable. This double entry can make things a little difficult if you have a lot of properties.

LISTING 9.16 Profile Service Configuration

```
<system.web.extensions>
  <scripting>
    <webServices>
      <profileService enabled="true"
        writeAccessProperties="FavoriteColor,PetsName,
          HomePageSettings/>
    </webServices>
  </scripting>
</system.web.extensions>
```

The Sys.Services.ProfileService Class

The Sys.Services.ProfileService class is a proxy class just like the Authentication and Role class and is contained in the MicrosoftAjax.js file. Just like the other classes, this class is a static class that inherits from the Sys.Net.WebProxy class. The properties listed in Table 9.13 enable you to add callback functions and interact with the profile properties via the properties property. The methods listed in Table 9.14 enable you to load and save the specified profile properties that are associated with the currently logged-in user.

TABLE 9.13 ProfileService Properties

Property	Description
defaultLoadCompletedCallback	The default handler that will be called when the load attempt is completed. Once set, this handler will be called for each request.
defaultSaveCompletedCallback	The default handler that will be called when the save attempt is completed. This handler will be called for each request.
properties	Preloaded properties from the LoadProperties setting using the ScriptManager.

TABLE 9.14 ProfileService Methods

Method	Description
load	Calls to the server to get the property names passed in. The result parameter on the loadCompleted handler contains the entries for the properties.
save	Saves the properties passed in to the server.

Using the Profile Service

The AJAX Profile Maintenance page shown in Figure 9.13 is the ASP.NET AJAX version of the Profile Maintenance page we created earlier. The page starts up with no profile information and enables you to get profiles and save profiles based on the logged-in user. The profile service works with the profile properties by downloading and uploading specific values based on the property array passed into the load and save method. This method of working with profile properties is a little different from on the server, where the values are always there, so pay special attention to the properties you currently have downloaded to ensure they are there. The profile service calls are shown in Listing 9.17, where we first bring down the profiles and assign them to the textbox entries and then send them back when we have completed modifying them.

One more option is available when bringing down profile properties. The ScriptManager provides a LoadProperties attribute off the Profile Service entry that enables you to bring down a select list of profile properties when the page is loaded (see Listing 9.18).

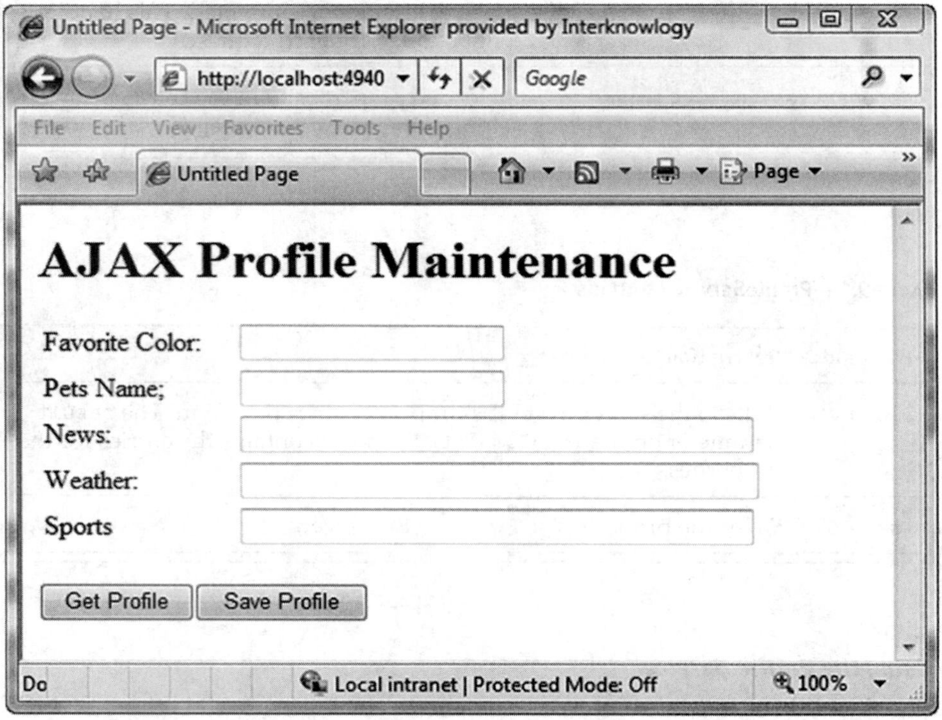

FIGURE 9.13 AJAX Profile Maintenance page

LISTING 9.17 Profile Service Calls

```
function ButtonGetProfile_onclick()
{
  Sys.Services.ProfileService.load(["FavoriteColor","PetsName",
    "HomePageSettings"],onSuccess,onFailed,"gettingData");
}

function ButtonSaveProfile_onclick()
```

```
{
  Sys.Services.ProfileService.properties.FavoriteColor =
    $get("TextFavoriteColor").value;
  Sys.Services.ProfileService.properties.PetsName =
    $get("TextPetsName").value;
  Sys.Services.ProfileService.properties.HomePageSettings.News =
    $get("TextNews").value;
  Sys.Services.ProfileService.properties.HomePageSettings.Weather =
    $get("TextWeather").value;
  Sys.Services.ProfileService.properties.HomePageSettings.Sports =
    $get("TextSports").value;

  Sys.Services.ProfileService.save(["FavoriteColor","PetsName",
    "HomePageSettings"],onSuccess,onFailed,"savingData");

}

function onSuccess(result, userContext, methodName)
{
  if(userContext == "gettingData")
  {
    $get("TextFavoriteColor").value =
      Sys.Services.ProfileService.properties.FavoriteColor;
    $get("TextPetsName").value =
      Sys.Services.ProfileService.properties.PetsName;
    $get("TextNews").value =
      Sys.Services.ProfileService.properties.HomePageSettings.News;
    $get("TextWeather").value =
      Sys.Services.ProfileService.properties.HomePageSettings.Weather;
    $get("TextSports").value =
      Sys.Services.ProfileService.properties.HomePageSettings.Sports;
  }
}

function onFailed(result, userContext, methodName)
{
  alert("An error occured \n"  + result.get_message());
}
```

LISTING 9.18 Profile Preload

```
<asp:ScriptManager ID="ScriptManager1" runat="server">
  <ProfileService LoadProperties="FavoriteColor,PetsName" />
</asp:ScriptManager>
```

Custom Application Services

As we worked with the application services in the previous section, you might have wondered just where the services that we are calling are. There were no web services that had to be copied to our project, and aside from a few configuration entries in the web.config file to turn the services on, there was really no setup on our part. So, how was this done?

The authentication, role, and profile application services are provided as internal services accessed by submitting a request using the *_AppService. axd URL pattern, with the beginning of each URL entry containing the authentication, role, or profile name. The `ScriptResourceHandler` is configured by default to listen for requests with this type or URL and automatically processes them. From the client perspective, we are using the web service proxy infrastructure we used for our WCF services. However, instead of calling a web service, we are calling an internal service contained in the `System.Web.Extensions` DLL. The alternative to this approach requires that we set up a web service for each of these services in every application we create. This laborious task is fraught with implementation issues as each developer works through potential issues of an incorrectly configured service. This internal service approach to creating application services is the topic of this section as we cover how to develop a custom application service.

> **■ NOTE   Already Covered Material**
>
> This section touches many of the concepts described in Chapter 8, including HTTP handlers, application services architecture, web services, and web service proxies. If you have not had a chance to read Chapter 8, which covered the ASP.NET AJAX communication architecture, we suggest you read it before continuing with this section. If it has been a while since you worked with HTTP handlers, you should also read Appendix C, "ASP.NET Handlers and Modules."

The composition of a custom application service builds on much of what we have covered already in this chapter, Chapter 8, and Appendix C.

The diagram in Figure 9.14 shows the server architecture for the custom application service. The layers are built using the same technologies described in Chapter 8, with the custom application services being built as WCF services, the JSON serialization being provided by WCF, and the ServiceHandlerFactory HTTP handler providing the processing for the request. It might seem odd that we would build our application service using WCF, but this is similar to how application services are implemented internally. The application services are actually ASMX web service classes used to provide the functionality for each service. The ScriptHandler Factory uses reflection to instantiate and call the service based on the *_ApplicationService.axd-based URL passed in. The service then calls the Membership, Roles, or ProfileBase class to process the various requests. The other aspect of this approach is that we are following a familiar and repeatable pattern to building the custom application service, which builds on a rich attribute-based approach that has made WCF so popular.

The diagram in Figure 9.15 shows the client architecture for the custom application service. The client architecture also builds on the same technologies, such as the WebServiceProxy class, the WebRequest class, and the web request core classes. The proxy class used to call the custom application services will inherit from the WebServiceProxy class and exhibit the same behavior as any other web service proxy.

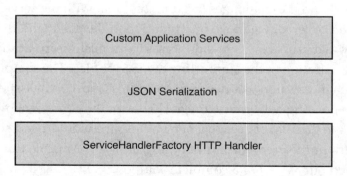

FIGURE 9.14 Custom application service server architecture

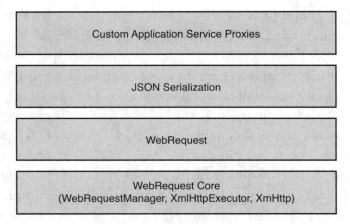

FIGURE 9.15 Custom application service client architecture

The goal of the sections to follow is to demonstrate some of the high-level components required when processing requests and some of the challenges you will face implementing a solution of this type. We start with the HTTP handler factory and its use to validate requests and create the appropriate HTTP handler. Then we turn our focus to the processing logic, where we detail the steps involved with calling the internal services and JSON serialization and the challenges faced in this area. With the server aspect of the solution covered, we move our attention to the client and the web service proxy that provides client-side access to the custom application service and the registration of the supporting JavaScript files. The sample application used in this section was designed to address most of the issues you will face when creating a custom service. However, the core functionality provided by the CommunicationSupport namespace would need some additional work in the area of error handling and performance tuning before being rolled out as part of a complete solution.

HTTP Handler Factory and Supporting Classes

The diagram in Figure 9.16 shows the ServiceHandlerFactory HTTP handler factory and the supporting ServiceRequestProcessor. The Service HandlerFactory is responsible for handling all requests that meet the *_InternalService.axd format and use the ServiceRequestProcessor as a pipeline to perform the actual processing of the request. The Service RequestProcessor consist of four main stages that comprise the actual request processing: working with the service cache to obtain a reference to the service metadata, deserializing and assigning parameters that were passed in, instantiating the service and calling the requested method, and finally serializing the result to send back as a response. As we focus on how the request is processed, we cover the ServiceHandlerFactory, the WCFHandler, and the classes in the CommunicationSupport namespace and the part they play in processing the service request.

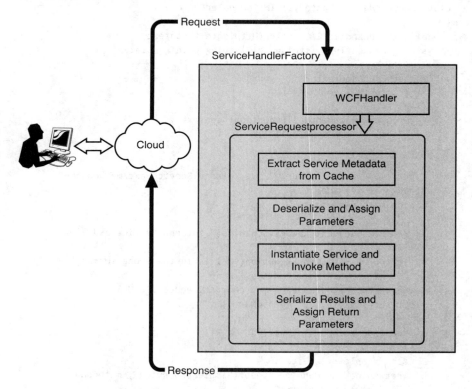

FIGURE 9.16 ServiceHandlerFactory HTTP handler

ServiceHandlerFactory Class

The ServiceHandlerFactory shown in Listing 9.19 provides the ability to validate the request URL and create an HTTP handler that can process the specific service request. The URL is expected to be in the format Service Name_InternalService.axd/methodname, with the ServiceName being the name of the service to call, and the methodname being the name of the method. The factory uses this information to determine the service type that will be used, and instantiates a handler that can process the request. The simple URL format that we are using is similar to the one used by the application services and makes it really easy to work with any number of services using a common URL pattern.

LISTING 9.19 Service Handler Factory

```
class ServiceHandlerFactory : IHttpHandlerFactory
{
  public IHttpHandler GetHandler(HttpContext context,
    string requestType, string url, string pathTranslated)
  {
    //check for context
    if (context == null)
    {
      throw new ArgumentNullException("context",
        "Context can't be null");
    }

    //get class name from url "/xyz_InternalService.axd/methodname"
    string serviceName;
    string methodName;

    if (context.Request.RawUrl.Contains("_InternalService.axd") ==
      false)
        throw new ArgumentException("Url is in the wrong format");

    GetServiceAndMethodNameFromUrl(context.Request.RawUrl,
      out serviceName, out methodName);

    switch (serviceName.ToLower())
    {
      case "simplewcfservice":
        return new WCFHandler(typeof(SimpleWCFService), methodName);
      case "complexwcfservice":
        return new WCFHandler(typeof(ComplexWCFService), methodName);
      default:
        throw new InvalidOperationException("Invalid Service
          Operation");
    }

  }

  public void ReleaseHandler(IHttpHandler handler)
  {
  }

  void GetServiceAndMethodNameFromUrl(string rawUrl,
```

```
    out string serviceName, out string methodName)
  {
    int lastForwardSlash = rawUrl.LastIndexOf("/");
    int firstUnderScore = rawUrl.IndexOf("_");

    serviceName = rawUrl.Substring(1, firstUnderScore - 1);
    methodName = rawUrl.Substring(lastForwardSlash + 1);


  }
}
```

WCFHandler Class

The WCFHandler class shown in Listing 9.20 provides the implementation for the IHttpHandler interface-based class returned from the Service FactoryHandler. The handler implements the ProcessRequest method of the IHttpHandler interface, which is called by the ASP.NET runtime as the request is processed. It is during this call that the handler calls into the RequestProcessor to perform the actual request processing. The IRequire SessionState interface is used to indicate that the handler will work with session state. The inclusion of this interface can come in handy if any of your code needs to access session state. If you choose not to include this interface, session state will not be available in your services, which might not be expected in the services themselves. When designing the Service HandlerFactory and WCFHandler classes, references to the services are needed to get the type information from them. In most cases, the partnership between the handlers and the services is so tight that they are included in the same project, ensuring you have a proper reference. This is the approach we used by including the services and handlers in the Service Communication project shown in Figure 9.17.

LISTING 9.20 WCF Handler

```
internal class WCFHandler : IHttpHandler, IRequiresSessionState
{
  public WCFHandler() { }
  public WCFHandler(Type serviceType, string serviceMethodName)
  {
    ServiceType = serviceType;
    ServiceMethodName = serviceMethodName;
  }

  public Type ServiceType { get; set; }
  public string ServiceMethodName { get; set; }
```

LISTING 9.20 continued

```
public bool IsReusable
{
   true;
}

public void ProcessRequest(HttpContext context)
{
   ServiceRequestProcessor.ProcessRequest(context,
     ServiceType, ServiceMethodName);
}
}
```

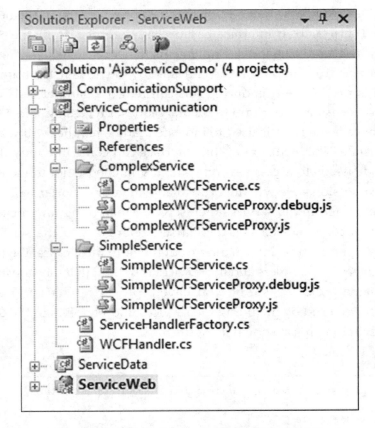

FIGURE 9.17 ServiceCommunication project structure

CommunicationSupport Namespace Classes

The classes contained in the CommunicationSupport namespace provide all the functionality needed to process the request (see Figure 9.18). The

ServiceHandlerFactory and the WCFHandler classes provide the ASP.NET pipeline hooks needed to capture the request, but the RequestProcessor class and the other supporting classes in this namespace are the ones that do the actual work.

The ProcessRequest method of the RequestProcessor is the entry point for processing the request and serves as the orchestrator for the various steps required in the request processing pipeline (see Listing 9.21). The individual stages shown in Figure 9.16 of the RequestProcessor are performed in this function and will serve as our guide as we walk through processing a service request.

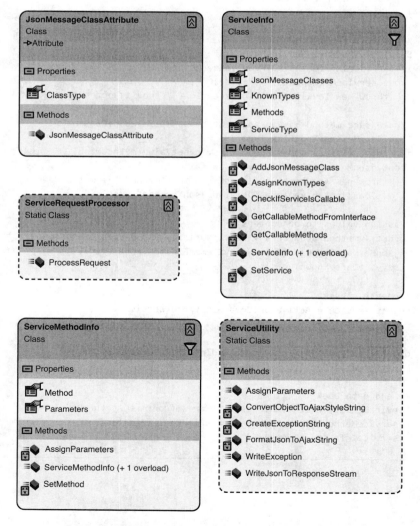

FIGURE 9.18 CommunicationSupport namespace classes

LISTING 9.21 ProcessRequest Method

```
public static void ProcessRequest(HttpContext context, Type
  serviceType, string methodName)
{
  //check for service info in cache
  ServiceInfo serviceInfo = context.Cache.Get(serviceType.Name) as
    ServiceInfo;
  if (serviceInfo == null)
  {
    serviceInfo = new ServiceInfo(serviceType);
    //save service to cache
    context.Cache.Add(serviceType.Name, serviceInfo, null,
      DateTime.Now.AddYears(5), Cache.NoSlidingExpiration,
      CacheItemPriority.AboveNormal, null);
  }

  //get reference to method
  ServiceMethodInfo serviceMethodInfo;
  if (serviceInfo.Methods.TryGetValue(methodName,
    out serviceMethodInfo) == false)
      throw new InvalidOperationException("Method is not supported");

  //make sure method has an associated JsonMessageBodyClass
  Type jsonMessageBodyClassType;
  if (serviceInfo.JsonMessageClasses.TryGetValue(methodName,
    out jsonMessageBodyClassType) == false)
      throw new ArgumentOutOfRangeException("Method " + methodName +
        "does not have an associated JsonMessageClass");

  //assign values to parameters
  object[] methodParameters = ServiceUtility.AssignParameters(context,
    jsonMessageBodyClassType, serviceMethodInfo.Parameters,
    serviceInfo.KnownTypes);

  //create class
  object service = Activator.CreateInstance(serviceType);

  //Invoke Method
  object returnValue = serviceMethodInfo.Method.Invoke(service,
    methodParameters);

  //Send data back to client
  ServiceUtility.WriteJsonToResponseStream(context, returnValue,
    serviceMethodInfo.Method.ReturnParameter.ParameterType,
    serviceInfo.KnownTypes);
}
```

Using Service Metadata

The use of reflection is a slow process. Therefore, when you need to reflect into a class numerous times, caching the values for later use is a recommended approach. The `ServiceInfo` class does just that by reflecting into the service and extracting out the `OperationContract`-decorated methods and the `KnownType` and `JsonMessageClass` attribute entries associated with the methods and the service as a whole. The `OperationContract` and `KnownType` entries should be familiar to you by now, but the `JsonMessage Class` attribute is something new. This attribute is a custom attribute created for this solution that is placed along with the `OperationContract` attribute on the operation of the service contract. The attribute is used during the parameter assignment phase of processing to inform the `Data ContractJsonSerializer` of the overall data type that it will be working with. Without this attribute, it becomes extremely difficult to dynamically determine the desired data type from the JSON data passed in.

The inclusion of the service metadata in the `ServiceInfo` class makes working with the service a lot easier. The `ServiceInfo` class categorizes the service information by method, making it easy to determine whether the method passed in is valid, the associated `JsonMessageClass` for deserializing parameters, and the actual parameters of the method. This combined set of information can then be used to build up the actual parameter list that is then passed into the service method.

Reconstructing Method Call

The one real trick when working with JSON data is getting it into a format that the `DataContractJsonSerializer` can use. The JSON data in Listing 9.22 represents the data passed to a call to `SaveCustomer` shown in Listing 9.23. The format of the data consists of the parameter name and the data to assign to the parameter. If we were to try to deserialize this data using the `DataContractJsonSerializer`, passing in `CustomerEntity` as our type, the call would fail because the composition of the data does not follow the correct `name:value` format for the type. What we really need is a wrapper type that contains a customer property of the type `CustomerEntity`. This added type would then be correctly aligned with the JSON data, and the deserialization would work correctly. This is where the `CustomerEntitySave Customer` type shown in Listing 9.24 and the `JsonMessageClass` attribute come into play. The CustomerEntitySaveCustomer type directly matches the JSON data format and ensures that the DataContractJsonSerializer will properly deserialize the data. The use of the JsonMessageClass attribute is how the correct data type for the JSON data is determined. By assigning this attribute to the operation contract, you are specifying in the contract the data type for the message to be received. The AssignParameters method then uses this information along with any known types during the deserialization process to ensure a proper conversion to the CustomerEntity type (see Listing 9.25).

The parameter array created as a result of the parameter assignment is then passed into the invoke method that is called on the MethodInfo of our service method. This reflection call executes our service and returns the results of the operation.

LISTING 9.22 JSON Parameter

```
{"customer":{"__type":"CustomerEntity:#ServiceData.Complex",
"FirstName":"Joe","LastName":"Dirt","Address":"1525 Faraday Suite
250","City":"Carlsbad","State":"CA","Zip":"92009"}}
```

LISTING 9.23 SaveCustomer Contract

```
[ServiceContract]
public interface IComplexWCFService
{
  ...
  [OperationContract]
  [CommunicationSupport.JsonMessageClass(
    typeof(CustomerEntitySaveCustomer))]
  CustomerEntity SaveCustomer(CustomerEntity customer);
  ...
}
```

LISTING 9.24 CustomerEntitySaveCustomer Type

```
[DataContract]
public class CustomerEntitySaveCustomer
{
  [DataMember]
  public CustomerEntity customer { get; set; }
}
```

LISTING 9.25 Parameter Assignment

```
public static object[] AssignParameters(HttpContext context,
  Type messageBodyClassType, Dictionary<string, ParameterInfo>
  methodParms, Collection<Type> knownTypes)
{
  DataContractJsonSerializer jsonSerializer = new
    DataContractJsonSerializer(messageBodyClassType, knownTypes);

  object jsonMessageBodyClass = jsonSerializer.ReadObject(
    context.Request.InputStream);

  object[] assignedParms = new object[methodParms.Count];
  int i= 0;
  ParameterInfo parmInfo;
  PropertyInfo propertyInfo;

  foreach (KeyValuePair<string, ParameterInfo> parmInfoDictionary in
    methodParms)
  {
    parmInfo = parmInfoDictionary.Value;
    propertyInfo = jsonMessageBodyClass.GetType().
      GetProperty(parmInfo.Name);
    assignedParms[i] = propertyInfo.GetValue(jsonMessageBodyClass,
      null);
    i++;
  }
  return assignedParms;
}
```

Processing Method Result

The challenges presented when serializing the data returned from the service method call are similar to the ones during deserialization. The JSON format needed by the `Sys.Serialization.JavaScriptSerializer` can't be created by the `DataContractJsonSerializer` (see Listing 9.26). The JSON emitted by the `DataContractJsonSerializer` does not contain any type information and is not in the correct format (see Listing 9.27). To create the correct JSON format, we need to construct the JSON using the combined functionality provided by the `WriteJsonToResponseStream` method and the `DataContractSerializer`. The `WriteJsonToResponseStream` method, shown in Listing 9.28, builds up the JSON data by first serializing the returned data from the service method call using the `DataContractJson Serializer` and then formatting the response into the JSON representation shown in Listing 9.26. When the JSON is in the correct format, we can send it back to the client, where the `JavaScriptSerializer` will convert it back to the `Customer` type.

LISTING 9.26 JSON Format Expected by the Sys.Serialization.JavaScriptSerializer

```
{"d":{"__type":"Customer:#ServiceData.Simple",
"Address":"1525 Faraday Suite 250","City":"Carlsbad",
"CustomerId":1901817923,"FirstName":"Joe","LastName":"Dirt",
"State":"CA","Zip":"92009"}}
```

LISTING 9.27 DataContractJsonSerializer JSON String

```
{"Address":"1525 Faraday Suite 250","City":"Carlsbad",
"CustomerId":570278328,"FirstName":"Joe","LastName":"Dirt",
"State":"CA","Zip":"92009"}
```

LISTING 9.28 WriteJsonToResponseStream Method

```
public static void WriteJsonToResponseStream(HttpContext context,
    object data, Type dataType, Collection<Type> knownTypes)
{
    StringBuilder ajaxAdditions = new StringBuilder();

    ajaxAdditions.Append("{");
    ajaxAdditions.Append("\"");
    ajaxAdditions.Append("d");
    ajaxAdditions.Append("\"");

    //check data for null
    string json = ConvertObjectToAjaxStyleString(data,
                    dataType, knownTypes);
    if (json == "null")
    {
        ajaxAdditions.Append(":");
        ajaxAdditions.Append(json);
    }
    else
    {
        ajaxAdditions.Append(":{");
        ajaxAdditions.Append("\"");
        ajaxAdditions.Append("__type");
        ajaxAdditions.Append("\"");
        ajaxAdditions.Append(":");
        ajaxAdditions.Append("\"");
        ajaxAdditions.Append(dataType.Name);
        ajaxAdditions.Append(":");
```

```
            ajaxAdditions.Append("#");
            ajaxAdditions.Append(dataType.Namespace);
            ajaxAdditions.Append("\"");
            ajaxAdditions.Append(",");
            ajaxAdditions.Append(json);
        }
        ajaxAdditions.Append("}");

        context.Response.AddHeader("Content-Type", "application/json");
        context.Response.Output.Write(ajaxAdditions.ToString());
    }
```

Service Proxy

The generation of the proxy class for each web service we create has until now been done by registering the WCF web service with the `Script Manager`. This registration instructed the `ScriptManager` to add a reference to a dynamically created proxy class that we could use on the client to call our web service. In the case of our custom application services, this proxy class will not be created for us automatically and will require us to create our own proxy class.

Creating and Using the WebServiceProxy Base Class

The `SimpleWCFService` proxy class shown in Listing 9.29 represents the `SimpleWCFService` that was created in our example. The class contains many of the same sections we have seen before with the namespace registration, the class constructor, and the class prototype. In previous discussion of the proxy class, the namespace was generated by the `ScriptManager` and was pulled from the `ServiceContract` namespace setting. In the case of our custom application service, this namespace name must be created manually, and any name will do as long as it's unique within the application. Another automatic setting that we must address is the path of the service. The path of the service must match the URL pattern that our `Service HandlerFactory` handler is expecting. In the case of a proxy, the path points to the `SimpleWCFService`, which tells the handler that we want to use that application service. The remaining portion of the URL creation actually happens by the `WebServiceProxy` class, which appends the name of the method called to the end of our path to complete the URL. This complete buildup is performed during our call to the _invoke method of the Web ServiceProxy base class for each of our service operations, which are created in the class prototype. An entry for each service operation supported by the proxy must be created. In our case, we have a method for the Save Customer and LookupCustomer service operations, which are the two operations supported by our service. The format of these method signatures is the same as in the previous proxies because all of them inherit from the same base class. The last thing we discuss concerning the proxy class is the registration of the supporting types that will be passed back and forth between the client and the server. Again referring back to the automatic proxy generation, the types used by the web service operations were automatically added to the proxy class. In this case, however, the entries again need to be added by hand. This requires a multistep process that consists of creating a reference to the WebServiceProxy type generator, adding a namespace entry for the type, and registering the type. The use of the custom type name in the format Type:#Namespace is required by the DataContract JsonSerializer on the backend to properly deserialize the type.

LISTING 9.29 SimpleWCFService Proxy Class

```
Type.registerNamespace('ServiceCommunication');

ServiceCommunication.SimpleWCFService=function() {
  ServiceCommunication.SimpleWCFService.initializeBase(this);
  this._timeout = 0;
  this._userContext = null;
  this._succeeded = null;
  this._failed = null;
  this._path = "/SimpleWCFService_InternalService.axd";
}

ServiceCommunication.SimpleWCFService.prototype={
  saveCustomer:function(customer,succeededCallback, failedCallback,
    userContext) {
      return this._invoke(this.get_path(),'SaveCustomer',
        false,{customer:customer},succeededCallback,failedCallback,
        userContext);
  },

  lookupCustomer:function(customerId,succeededCallback, failedCallback,
    userContext) {
      return this._invoke(this.get_path(), 'LookupCustomer',false,
        {customerId:customerId},succeededCallback,failedCallback,
```

```
            userContext);
    }
}

ServiceCommunication.SimpleWCFService.registerClass(
  'ServiceCommunication.SimpleWCFService',Sys.Net.WebServiceProxy);

var gtc = Sys.Net.WebServiceProxy._generateTypedConstructor;

Type.registerNamespace('ServiceData.Simple');

if (typeof(ServiceData.Simple.Customer) === 'undefined') {
  ServiceData.Simple.Customer=gtc("Customer:#ServiceData.Simple");
  ServiceData.Simple.Customer.registerClass(
    'ServiceData.Simple.Customer');
}
```

The use of the `SimpleService` proxy class shown in Listing 9.30 should be familiar enough by now. The service calling code is in the save function and follows the same pattern of supplying the parameter data and the call-back functions. The one difference between the proxy class created here and the one generated by the `ScriptManager` is the optional static usage pattern. This implementation requires the new operator to instantiate the class, but a simple modification to the proxy class can easily solve this if needed.

LISTING 9.30 SimpleService Proxy Calling Code

```
/// <reference path="../SimpleService/SimpleService.aspx" />
...
function saveForm(e)
{
  //create new customer
  var customer = new ServiceData.Simple.Customer();

  //get data from form
  customer.CustomerId = ("customerId").value;
  if(customer.CustomerId === "")
    customer.CustomerId = 0;
  customer.FirstName = $get("firstName").value;
  customer.LastName = $get("lastName").value;
  customer.Address = $get("address").value;
  customer.City = $get("city").value;
  customer.State = $get("state").value;
  customer.Zip = $get("zip").value;

  save(customer);
}
```

LISTING 9.30 continued

```
function save(customer)
{
  var service = new ServiceCommunication.SimpleWCFService();
  service.saveCustomer(customer,onSuccessSave,onFailed);
}

function onSuccessSave(result)
{
  //send new date to table builder
  createTableEntries(result);
  clearForm();
}

function onFailed(error)
{
  alert("An error occured \n"  + error.get_message());
}
...
```

Script Files and Assemblies

The proxy class that you create needs a mechanism to pass it to the client, and the combination of registering the script file with the assembly using the WebResource attribute and registering the script file with the Script Manager achieves this. You can see the registering of the script file with the assembly in Listing 9.31, where we register both the debug and release versions of the proxy class. If you recall from our discussions about registering scripts in Chapter 8, the ScriptManager will use the appropriate script file based on a debug or release build of the source code. When you are creating library classes, the project that has the script files in it will be the one that has the WebResource attribute applied to its assembly file. The second part of this process is registering the proxy file with the ScriptManager, which is shown in Listing 9.32. The most likely method for this registration will be using the APIs rather than a declarative method. The reason behind this is that you will most likely be doing this inside your controls class, and you won't want to expose this out to the consumer of your control. You can get a reference to the ScriptManager via the contained page object using the static ScriptManager.GetCurrent method. This method returns a reference to a `ScriptManager` without having to know what the ID is and provides a clean and dynamic way to get a reference. With the `ScriptManager` reference, all you need to do is add the script file to the Scripts collection by creating a `ScriptReference` class and using the verbose overloaded constructor syntax consisting of the full name of the script file as it was entered using the `WebResource` attribute and the name of the assembly that contains the script resource. With these two steps completed, your script proxy class is now available on the client.

LISTING 9.31 WebResource Assignment in Assembly

```
[assembly: WebResource(
  "ServiceCommunication.SimpleService.SimpleWCFServiceProxy.js",
  "text/javascript")]
[assembly: WebResource(
  "ServiceCommunication.SimpleService.SimpleWCFServiceProxy.debug.js",
  "text/javascript")]
```

LISTING 9.32 ScriptManager Registration of Proxy Class

```
ScriptManager scriptManager = ScriptManager.GetCurrent(this);
scriptManager.Scripts.Add(new ScriptReference(
  "ServiceCommunication.SimpleService.SimpleWCFServiceProxy.js",
  "ServiceCommunication",
  "ServiceCommunication"));
```

Configuration

When using HTTP handlers, you must configure them in your web.config file for them to be included in the processing. The configuration fragment in Listing 9.33 is simple and requires only a single entry in the HTTP handlers section of your web.config file. The path for the handler is *_Internal Service.axd, which means that any URL that follows this pattern will be handled by this handler. The type for the handler is `ServiceCommunication.ServiceHandlerFactory`, which resides in the `ServiceCommunication` assembly where the handlers and application services are located. This simple one-line configuration entry is all that is needed to enable communication with the service.

LISTING 9.33 HTTP Handler Configuration

```
<configuration>
  <system.web>
    <httpHandlers>
      <add verb="*" path="*_InternalService.axd" validate="false"
        type="ServiceCommunication.ServiceHandlerFactory,
        ServiceCommunication, Version=1.1.0.0, Culture=neutral,
        PublicKeyToken=null"/>
    </httpHandlers>
  </system.web>
</configuration>
```

SUMMARY

The work that Microsoft has done with ASP.NET membership, role, and user profile services and their integration with the ASP.NET AJAX application services demonstrates a strong commitment to extending these feature-rich service-based technologies to the client. The services that are now available on the client provide much more flexibility when designing solutions that need to tightly integrate with the server.

The new world that application services opens for us also extends to custom service development, where we can apply the techniques of integrated services to provide a cleaner and more resilient service-based approach to programming on the client.

PART IV
AJAX Control Toolkit

10

ASP.NET AJAX Control Toolkit Architecture

T HE ASP.NET AJAX CONTROL TOOLKIT is a shared source joint project between Microsoft and the developer community that is hosted on CodePlex, www.codeplex.com, which is the Microsoft open source project hosting website. The Toolkit builds on the foundation of ASP.NET AJAX to provide a framework that simplifies the development of extender and script controls we covered in Chapter 5, "Adding Client Capabilities to Server Controls." In addition to the framework, the Toolkit also comes with numerous pre-built extender and script controls that provide varying levels of functionality that can be used on your projects.

The power of the Toolkit is in the increased productivity that the framework provides, in comparison to coding against the raw API as we did in Chapter 5. Features like attribute-based programming, rich design-time support, and support for animation provide a compelling reason to choose the Toolkit as a basis for building your controls. In this chapter, we cover the overall architecture of the Toolkit, including many of the building blocks you need to understand to use it.

Overview of the Toolkit

The ASP.NET AJAX Control Toolkit provides a framework for building ASP.NET AJAX extenders and script controls that run on a wide range of browsers. The idea behind the framework was to provide a rich foundation that abstracts some of the more mundane details associated with creating extenders and script controls, making it easier to develop feature-rich components. This section provides a high-level overview of the Toolkit and what it has to offer. The following sections address the three key areas of the Toolkit: reliance on attributes, rich set of .NET classes, rich set of JavaScript classes, and support for animations. It provides you with an overall understanding of how the Toolkit is composed, setting the stage as we delve deeper into the architectural details later in the chapter.

Reliance on Attributes to Simplify Development

The Toolkit relies heavily on attributes for things such as registering scripts, determining which properties to include in your `ScriptComponent` `Descriptor`, and much more. This reliance on attributes simplifies the development approach compared to coding directly against the `Extender` `Control` and `ScriptControl` base classes. The use of these classes directly requires the developer to add overrides for the `GetScriptDescriptor` and `GetScriptReferences` methods and build up `ScriptComponentDescriptor` and `ScriptReference` entries by hand, which can be tedious and error prone. The use of attributes simplifies this approach by relying on attributes to decorate your classes and properties, instructing the Toolkit to apply those values appropriately when constructing `ScriptComponent` `Descriptor` and `ScriptReference` entries.

Rich Set of .NET Classes

The Toolkit builds on the class structure provided by the ASP.NET 2.0 AJAX Extensions, providing the additional functionality required to build controls in the Toolkit. The `System.Web.UI.ExtenderControl` and `System.Web.UI.ScriptControl` classes have been replaced with the `AjaxControl` `Toolkit.ExtenderControlBase` and `AjaxControlToolkit.ScriptControl` `Base` abstract classes, which are designed to support the increased functionality that the Toolkit provides to inheritors of these classes. The Toolkit version of these classes provides support working with ASP.NET themes, building `ScriptReference` and `ScriptComponentDescriptor` entries, working with client state, working with control view state, working with client callbacks, and working with form-based data during postback, just to name a few. The Toolkit also comes with classes that support a rich design-time experience, adding functionality such as editing extender properties on the target control without writing any code.

Rich Set of JavaScript Classes

The JavaScript class structure has changed, too, with the Toolkit, providing its own base classes for `Sys.UI.Behavior` and `Sys.UI.Control`. The `AjaxControlToolkit.BehaviorBase` class provides additional support for working with client state and interacting with the `Sys.WebForms.PageRequestManager` class during postbacks. The `AjaxControlToolkit.ControlBase` class includes support for client state and interaction with the `PageRequestManager`, too, but also provides support for working with client callback, which was introduced in ASP.NET 2.0. There are also JavaScript classes that provide support for working with drag and drop and timers, providing a clean API for implementing this type of functionality.

Support for Animations

The ASP.NET AJAX Control Toolkit comes with a framework that provides rich animation support for creating visual effects on your pages. The animation framework consists of a set of JavaScript and .NET classes that you can use to build up animations of all types. There is support for building animations using the JavaScript API directly or using a declarative approach, animations that run sequentially or run in parallel, and a vast array of animation types ranging from animations that fade the opacity of a control in and out to animations that transition from one color to the next.

Composition of the Toolkit

The ASP.NET AJAX Control Toolkit is a shared source project that developers can use from the standpoint of a consumer of the controls included or as a foundation that can be built on to develop your own controls. In this section, we cover installing the Toolkit and the layout of the solution. The layout of the solution is of most concern to us because it will make it easier to understand where things are as we detail the architecture in later sections.

Installation

You can download the Ajax Control Toolkit from the CodePlex website, www.codeplex.com, as a stand-alone DLL installation or as an installation that includes source code. The stand-alone version is great if you want to use the control Toolkit as a consumer of the controls or do simple control development. It even comes with the sample test website that the source version uses. The installation for the stand-alone version is as simple as extracting the Zip file to a directory and optionally running the Ajax ControlExtender.vsi file contained in the `AjaxControlExtender` subdirectory to add the project and item templates to Visual Studio. The version that includes source contains not only the Toolkit library project but also a sample website project, unit test harness project, and a template project. This version contains everything you need to create your own controls and fully debug and test them. The installation for this version also includes extracting the Zip file to a directory and optionally running the AjaxControl Extender.vsi file located in the same directory. After you complete this, you can open the AjaxControlToolkit.sln file contained in the root directory you extracted to and run the application with all the projects contained in one solution.

Layout of the Solution

The solution file for the Toolkit is broken into three main projects, consisting of the Toolkit library project, the sample website, and the ToolkitTest website.

Toolkit Library Project

The Toolkit library project contains all the currently created controls and the foundation classes that you will use to create your own controls. As we look at this project, the Animation, Common, and ExtenderBase folders are of most interest to us since we will cover how to use the framework to build custom controls.

Animation Folder

The Animation folder contains not only the `Animation` extender but also all the animation-related classes that you will use when creating animations. The files in this folder that you will use the most are the animation.cs and the animation.js files. The animation.cs file represents the object model for the animations and is used to convert the XML representation of an animation to JavaScript Object Notation (JSON). The animation.js file contains all the animation-related JavaScript code used to perform the various animations on the client.

Common Folder

The Common folder is used to place files that provide common functionality that can be used by all the controls in the Toolkit. If you are creating a control you might consider to be included by the Toolkit, you would place your common code in this folder. The common.js file can be used to place simple scripts, or you can create a separate file like DateTime.js, which contains a rich timer API, and Threading.js, which contains a rich asynchronous API, and add them to the folder.

ExtenderBase Folder

The ExtenderBase folder contains the vast majority of .NET and JavaScript files you will use when developing controls. We cover many of the files in this folder as we dive into the Toolkit, so we do not list them individually here, but do note that all the base classes, helper classes, and JavaScript classes used by the Toolkit are contained in this folder. The classes that support the rich designer features for the Toolkit are also included in this folder in the Design subfolder.

Sample Website

This website contains the samples for all the controls in the Toolkit and is a great way to see the controls in action. If you are considering adding controls to the Toolkit, you will want to add them to this project, making sure they operate in the site.

ToolkitTest Website

This website contains the test scripts for all the controls in the Toolkit and demonstrates a nice approach for unit testing web controls. Just as with the sample website, if you are considering adding controls to the Toolkit, you want to create unit test and add them to this website.

Server-Based Architecture

The ASP.NET AJAX Control Toolkit comes with many classes, interfaces, and attributes that support the rich foundation that the Toolkit provides. These classes, interfaces, and attributes can be broken into three main areas: attributes, base classes, and designer classes. In this section, we cover these three areas, describing how they fit into the overall foundation of the Toolkit and its code structure.

Attributes

The use of attributes to describe functionality has become common in frameworks such as Windows Communication Foundation (WCF), and ASP.NET AJAX Control Toolkit continues with this trend to simplify creating extenders and script controls. The Toolkit comes with many attributes, as shown in Figure 10.1, that help in reducing the amount of code you need to write. As an example, refer back to Chapter 5, when we were creating the `ImageRotator` extender. If we take a look at Listing 10.1, we can see that we create properties that captured values on the server side and then override the `GetScriptDescriptors` method to add those values to the `Script BehaviorDescriptor`. If we contrast that experience to Listing 10.2, we can see that when working with the Toolkit all we need to do is add the `ExtenderControlProperty` attribute and the `ClientPropertyName` attribute to the same properties, and the functionality provided by the Toolkit takes care of creating the `ScriptBehaviorDescriptor` entries for us, greatly simplifying our development experience.

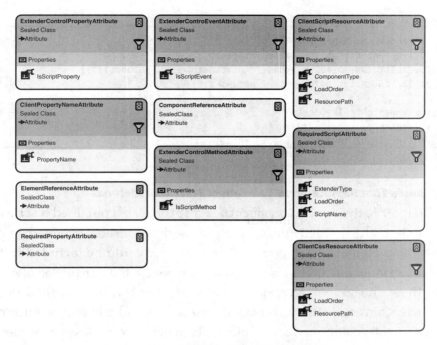

FIGURE 10.1 ASP.NET AJAX Control Toolkit attributes

LISTING 10.1 Code without Attributes

```
//Property Signatures
[DefaultValue(3), DisplayName("RotationInterval(seconds))")]
public int RotationInterval { get; set; }

public string ImageList { get; set; }
....
//GetScriptDescriptors method override
protected override IEnumerable<ScriptDescriptor>
  GetScriptDescriptors(System.Web.UI.Control targetControl)
{
  ScriptBehaviorDescriptor descriptor =
    new ScriptBehaviorDescriptor(
"ImageRotatorExtender.ImageRotator",
targetControl.ClientID);

    descriptor.AddProperty("rotationInterval", RotationInterval);
    if (!string.IsNullOrEmpty(ImageList))
    {
      descriptor.AddProperty("imageList",ImageList.Split(','));
    }
    yield return descriptor;
    }
}
```

LISTING 10.2 Code with Attributes

```
[ExtenderControlProperty]
[ClientPropertyName("rotationInterval")]
[DefaultValue(3), DisplayName("RotationInterval(seconds))")]
public int RotationInterval { get; set; }

[ExtenderControlProperty]
[ClientPropertyName("imageList")]
public string ImageList { get; set; }
```

Attributes That Replace ScriptComponentDescriptor Methods

In Chapter 5, the ScriptComponentDescriptor class contained a series of methods that provided functionality to add properties, events, components, and element references to it so that they could be included in the $create statement that was generated for us by the ScriptManager. To add these entries, we override the GetScriptDescriptors method in the ExtenderControl- or ScriptControl-based class and add entries for properties, events, components, and elements matching our class properties to the Sys.Component-based classes on the client. This type of work was tedious and is where attributes provide a simpler approach. The Toolkit comes with a series of attributes that are applied to a property that simplify the registration of properties with the ScriptComponentDescriptor. The list in Table 10.1 compares the attributes to their ScriptComponentDescriptor method counterparts and provides a good reference as we detail the attributes.

TABLE 10.1 Attributes and ScriptComponentDescriptor Methods Comparison

Attribute	ScriptComponentDescriptor Method
ExtenderControlProperty	AddProperty
ExtenderControlEvent	AddEvent
ElementReference	AddElementProperty
ComponentReference	AddComponentProperty

The `ExtenderControlProperty` attribute shown in Listing 10.3 is used to decorate a property that is going to be registered with the `Script ComponentDescriptor`. If the `ClientPropertyName` attribute is not used, the name of the property with its current casing is used by the `Script ComponentDescriptor`. If the `ClientPropertyName` attribute is used, the name provided to the attribute is used instead.

> ▪ **NOTE** **Property Names**
>
> The naming structure for JavaScript is a little different from .NET, which should be taken into consideration if you leave the `Client PropertyName` attribute blank. In .NET, a property for a person's first name would be `FirstName`, whereas in JavaScript it would be `firstName`.

LISTING 10.3 ExtenderControl and ClientPropertyName Attribute Usage

```
[ExtenderControlProperty]
[ClientPropertyName("rotationInterval")]
public int RotationInterval
{
  get { return rotationInterval; }
  set { rotationInterval = value; }
}
```

The `RequiredProperty` attribute (not shown in Table 10.1) enables you to ensure that a particular property has a value. In fact, the Toolkit goes through a validation check before continuing with the attribute-processing step to ensure that all fields that require a value actually have one. If you do not add a value, you receive an error during runtime as the page containing the control is rendered.

To round out the remaining attributes, the `ExtenderControlEvent` attribute is used to decorate a property that contains the name of a function that will be handling an event. The `ElementReference` attribute is used to decorate a property that contains the name of an HTML element that will be referenced. Finally, the `ComponentReference` attribute is used to decorate a property that contains the name of a control that will be referenced.

ScriptReference-Related Attributes

In Chapter 5, we were forced to add script entries by building up a strongly typed collection of ScriptReference values and return them in our GetScriptReferences override. Just as in the case with the Script ComponentDescriptor, this method was tedious and error prone. The Toolkit comes with three attributes that are applied at the class level that make adding script references easy (see Table 10.2).

TABLE 10.2 ScriptReference-Related Attributes

Attribute	Description
ClientScriptResource	Creates a ScriptReference for the specified script
RequiredScript	Ensures referenced script is included
ClientCSSResource	Includes a CSS file in the control

The ClientScriptResource attribute is used to create a ScriptReference entry for the specified script. The attribute assigns the script type to the Assembly property and path to the Name property of the ScriptReference and leaves all the other values at their defaults. The one nice feature about this attribute is the ability to order the scripts so that they are loaded in a specific order, which can help in situations where dependencies occur.

The RequiredScript attribute shown in Listing 10.4 is designed to ensure that the referenced script is included before the scripts that are included with the ClientScriptResource attribute. This attribute can accept a type or a script name and is mostly used with the type overload, which provides the ability to drill down into the type and extract associated ClientScriptResource attributes applied to the type. The attribute also enables you to set the order that it is loaded, which again helps in situations where dependencies occur.

LISTING 10.4 RequiredScript Attribute Usage

```
[RequiredScript(typeof(TimerScript))]
public class ImageRotatorExtender : ExtenderControlBase
{
    ...
}
```

The `ClientCssResource` attribute brings in a particular CSS file using a full resource name or a type and a resource name. The attribute supports the ability to dictate the load order, just like the other script-related attribute we have discussed so far, assisting in situations where dependencies occur.

Base Classes for Extenders and ScriptControls

The Toolkit comes with its own extender and script control base classes that build on the functionality provided by the `ExtenderControl` and `Script Control` classes (see Figure 10.2). The `ExtenderControlBase` class provides the base functionality for creating extender controls, and the `ScriptControl Base` class provides the base functionality for creating script controls.

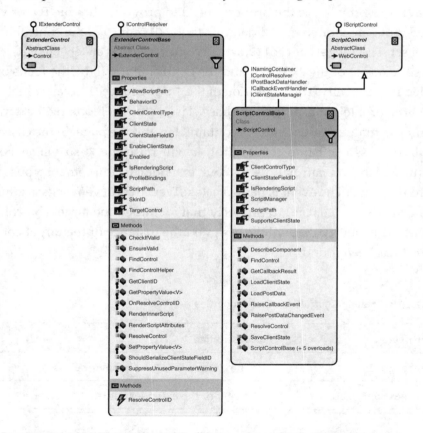

FIGURE 10.2 ASP.NET AJAX Control Toolkit extender and ScriptControl base classes

ExtenderControlBase Class

The ExtenderControlBase abstract class provides the base functionality to extender controls in the Toolkit and is the class your extender will inherit from. The class builds on the functionality of the System.Web.UI. ExtenderControl class to provide support for working with ASP.NET themes, building ScriptReference and ScriptComponentDescriptor entries, working with client state, and working with control view state, to name a few. In this section, we cover how you can take advantage of these features when building an extender control and show how these features are implemented.

The ExtenderControlBase class provides a couple of core properties to the inherited extender that we will talk about first (see Table 10.3). The BehaviorID property is the property used to provide a unique ID for your JavaScript behavior class and defaults to the ClientID of the control if one is not set. The TargetControlID, which comes from ExtenderControl, identifies the target of the extender and the control that will be the focus of its added functionality. The resolution of the TargetControlID can sometimes be a little problematic, despite the base class's efforts of looking for it in the naming container the extender is contained in and the page. In the case that the base class can't find the control, it will raise the ResolveControlID event, which you can handle in your extender to implement your own searching logic. The event is passed a ResolveControlEventArgs argument that consists of a ControlID property that identified the target control and a Control property that will be assigned the instance of the target control after it has been found.

TABLE 10.3 ExtenderControlBase Core Properties

Attribute	Description
BehaviorID	The unique ID of the behavior class
TargetControlID	Target of the extender control

A property can be accessed in many ways, such as by the designer engine, in HTML source, and in your code behind class. If we look at the designer engine and HTML source, they are both the same, using the default persistence mechanism of the designer to store the entries so that they are available when the page is accessed. The code behind class approach is a little different because the value you set in code by default will not be persisted by the extender. This is where control view state comes into the picture and the functionality the base class provides for using it. The base class provides two generic methods `GetPropertyValue<T>` and `SetPropertyValue<T>` that are used to access view state values in a type-safe way. By using these methods in your property setter and getter, you are ensuring that your property values will be available on subsequent post-backs (see Listing 10.5). The one drawback of this approach is its dependence on view state being enabled. If view state is disabled, this approach will not work.

> ■ **NOTE**   Control State versus View State
>
> The concept of control state was introduced in ASP.NET 2.0 and is designed to give developers of a control a "view state"-like storage mechanism intended for critical data that is guaranteed to be there even if view state is turn off for a page or the control. You can find more information about this topic at http://msdn2.microsoft.com/en-us/library/1whwt1k7.aspx, which includes a sample application contrasting the use of both approaches.

LISTING 10.5 Property Setter and Getter Using the GetPropertyValue<T> Approach

```
[ExtenderControlProperty]
[ClientPropertyName("rotationInterval")]
public int RotationInterval
{
    get { return GetPropertyValue<int>("RotationInterval", 3); }
    set { SetPropertyValue<int>("RotationInterval", value); }
}
```

In some cases, you need to work with client state on both the client and on the server in a clean way, and the base class, in conjunction with the `BehaviorBase` JavaScript class, provides a way to work with data on both sides. To work with client state, you need to set the `EnableClientState` property on the base class to `true` and then use the `ClientState` property to interact with the string-based data. The base class implements this functionality using a hidden field and will take care of creating the field, giving it a unique ID, and reading and writing to it during postbacks. The `BehaviorBase` JavaScript class then provides access to this value, providing support for reading and writing on the client. At first you might think that storing a string value is a little limiting, but if you use JSON to represent your data, the sky is the limit as to what type of data you can work with. All you need to do is handle the JSON serialization and deserialization on both ends and you are done.

The need to validate the data your extender is based on can sometimes be a little tricky, especially in cases where the interaction between multiple values comes into play. The base class provides a nice overload that works in conjunction with the `RequiredProperty` attribute to ensure that your extender data is valid. The `EnsureValid` method can be overloaded to add additional validation logic to your extender, and when used in conjunction with the base implementation also ensures that you have entered all required data.

The concept of themes and skins was introduced in ASP.NET 2.0 and greatly simplifies the approach of styling web applications. Themes provide a common foundation for storing skins, CSS information, images, and other resources that can be applied at the page level or globally so that they can be used by all sites on a web server. Skins are applied to controls and consist of the control markup with the properties you want to be part of a theme. The base class has all the appropriate attributes and properties to support themes and skins and provides a `SkinID` property that can be used to override a page-level or global-level theme's skin setting to a new value.

Our final topic in this section is debugging. The base class supports script debugging by enabling you to specify a different script path than the one specified in your `ClientScriptResource` attribute applied to your class. This enables you to set breakpoints and debug script without having to recompile your application to the debug version. If this behavior is not desired or you want to provide additional logic to determine whether the `ScriptPath` property value should be used, override the `AllowScriptPath` property and implement your custom logic there.

ScriptControlBase Class

The ScriptControlBase abstract class provides the base functionality to script controls in the Toolkit and is the class your script control will inherit from. The class builds on the functionality of the System.Web.UI.Script Control class to provide support for working with ScriptReference and ScriptComponentDescriptor entries, working with client state, support for a naming container, enabling the control to be the target of a callback, and ensuring that the ScriptManager is present to name a few. In this section, we cover how you can take advantage of these features when building an extender control and explain how these features are implemented.

> ■ **NOTE**   Duplicate Functionality
>
> The ScriptControlBase class provides all the same functionality the ExtenderControlBase class did for working with attributes, Script ComponentDescriptor, and ScriptReference entries and working with client state, so we do not address these topics again in this section.

The main features that the ScriptControlBase class provides are a naming container and support for client callbacks. The ScriptControlBase class implements the INamingContainer interface, creating a new namespace, and ensuring that all container elements have a unique ID throughout the page. The use of this interface eases development when adding additional child controls to your script control by providing an infrastructure that eliminates the risk of ID collisions on the page. The base class also provides support for client callbacks, which were introduced in ASP.NET 2.0, to provide a mechanism for the client to call back to the ASP.NET web page, where it runs in a modified version instantiating the ICallbackEvent Handler.RaiseCallbackEvent and ICallbackEventHandler.GetCallback Result methods to process the request.

Designer Classes

The introduction of the Extender Wizard in Visual Studio 2008, which we talked about in Chapter 5, has enhanced the design-time experience for working with extenders, and this section covers the supporting classes that provide the ability to add design-time features to extender controls, giving them that professional feel users have become accustomed to (see Figure 10.3).

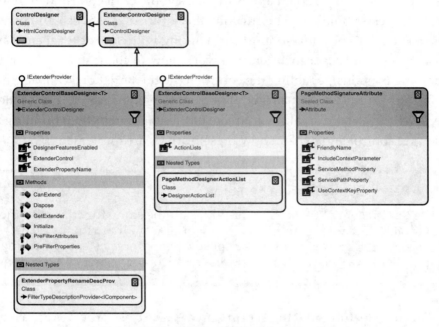

FIGURE 10.3 ASP.NET AJAX Control Toolkit design-time classes

> **NOTE**   Designer Support Limitations
>
> Currently, the Toolkit offers only designer support for working with extenders, so our discussion in this section is limited to extenders only.

> **NOTE**   Designer Changes in Visual Studio 2008
>
> The bulk of the functionality in ExtenderControlBaseDesigner<T> was developed to work with Visual Studio 2005; in Visual Studio 2008, however, the implementation for extending properties is now included, so that functionality is no longer needed.

ExtenderControlBaseDesigner<T>

This class is the base class that all extender designers will inherit from. This class was designed to make it possible for the properties of your extender control to show up in the Properties window while the design-time focus was on the control you were extending. This ability to project the properties onto the extended control provides one-stop editing for the control being extended and the control providing the added behavior. If we take a look at Figure 10.4, we can see the design-time experience for working with extenders as we look at the user experience with the `TextBoxWaterMark` extender on a textbox. In this figure, the `Text1` control is selected in the designer, and the Properties window for the `Text1` control is shown on the right with an arrow pointing to the `TextBoxWaterMark` extender property, which contains all the subproperties for the extender. Exposing properties for the `TextBoxWaterMark` extender while keeping the focus on the `Text1` control simplifies the experience of working in the designer and reduces context switching between control and extender. If you take a look at Figure 10.4, one thing you might also notice is the UI representation for the extender is gone. Extenders in Visual Studio 2008 no longer show up in the design surface, which makes page layout much easier.

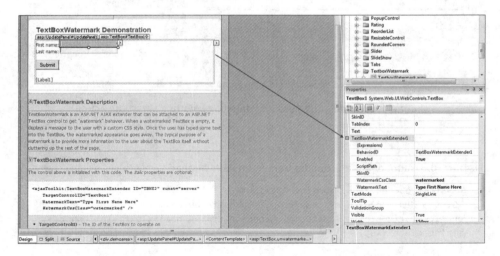

FIGURE 10.4 Design-time experience with extender controls

If you look at the class declaration, you will realize that it is a partial class that has a second counterpart in the ExtenderControlBaseDesigner. PageMethodSignatures.cs file. This partial class is responsible for adding designer actions to the smart tags that are associated with the control you are extending. The class works in conjunction with the `PageMethod` `Signature` attribute to build up a set of commands that can be invoked in the smart tag. If we take the `AutoComplete` extender as an example, it requires a callback to the server to get lookup values. During design, if you choose to implement that call as a page method, you select the Add Auto-Complete page method action item from the smart tag (see Figure 10.5), which generates the code fragment in the code behind of the page (see Listing 10.6), when the link is selected, giving you a method signature to then code against.

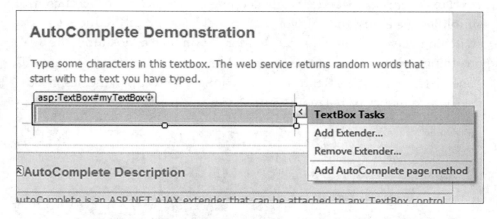

FIGURE 10.5 Adding the AutoComplete page method smart tag action

LISTING 10.6 AutoComplete Extender Generated Page Method

```
[System.Web.Services.WebMethodAttribute(),
 System.Web.Script.Services.ScriptMethodAttribute()]
public static string[] GetCompletionList(string prefixText, int count,
string contextKey)
{
  return default(string[]);
}
```

To get this functionality to work, you need to add some code to the designer class of your extender. In your designer class (see Listing 10.7) for the `AutoCompleteDesigner` class, add a delegate that contains the signature needed for the page method and decorate that delegate with a `PageMethod Signature` attribute that contains the display name shown in the designer's smart tag action item, the name of the `ServicePath` property on your extender (which is used to verify that a path does not already exist), and the name of the `ServiceMethod` property on your extender (which is used to set the page method name). After you have added this code, the designer will show a smart tag action item (refer to Figure 10.5), which will allow you to generate a page method (see Listing 10.7) in the code behind of your page, providing a simple method signature that you can then code against.

LISTING 10.7 `AutoCompleteDesigner` Class

```
public class AutoCompleteDesigner :
ExtenderControlBaseDesigner<AutoCompleteExtender>
{
    /// <summary>
    /// Signature of the page method for AutoComplete's web service
    /// that is used to support adding/navigating to the page
    /// method fromthe designer
    /// </summary>
    /// <param name="prefixText">Text already entered</param>
    /// <param name="count">Number of items to return</param>
    /// <param name="contextKey">Optional user specific
    ///   context</param>
    /// <returns>Possible completions of the prefix text</returns>
    [
PageMethodSignature("AutoComplete", "ServicePath",
                        "ServiceMethod", "UseContextKey")
    ]
    private delegate string[] GetCompletionList(string prefixText,
                                        int count, string contextKey);

}
```

Client-Based Architecture

The Ajax Control Toolkit comes with a set of JavaScript classes that build on the Microsoft AJAX Library to provide the added functionality the Toolkit provides for developing extenders and script controls. The class diagram in Figure 10.6 shows the structure of the `BehaviorBase` and `ControlBase` base classes that the JavaScript behavior and control classes for your extenders and script controls are based on. In this section, we cover these base classes and the functionality they provide.

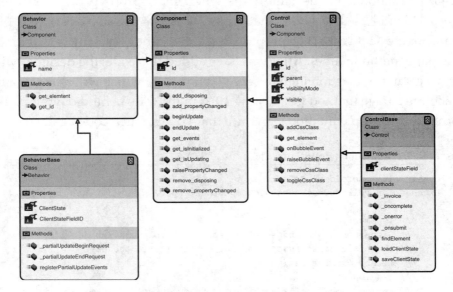

FIGURE 10.6 ASP.NET AJAX Control Toolkit JavaScript class hierarchy

> ## ▪ NOTE   Property and Method References
>
> Throughout this section, we refer to properties using the single property name rather than functions with the `set_` and `get_` prefixes and methods to refer to all other functions associated with a JavaScript class.

BehaviorBase Class

The `BehaviorBase` class is the base class for the JavaScript behavior classes that are associated with your extender controls. This class inherits from the `Sys.UI.Behavior` class and provides functionality for working with client state and interacting with the asynchronous request events of the `Sys.Web Forms.PageRequestManager`. The client state functionality, which we talked about earlier, is supported by the `ClientState` and `ClientStateFieldID` properties, which are set by the `$create` statement that is generated by the `ScriptComponentDescriptor` entry for the `ClientState` and `ClientState FieldID` properties. The `ClientStateFieldID` property contains the name of the hidden field and interacting with the `ClientState` field reads or writes values to this hidden field. During postback, the hidden field is read, and the contents are assigned to the `ClientState` field where they are available on the server. The `_partialUpdateBeginRequest` and `_partialUpdate EndRequest` are methods called when the `beginRequest` and `endRequest` events are raised by the `PageRequestManager`. The base class registers these methods as handlers for those events, in turn providing the inheritor a set of override methods that can be used to implement custom logic when the events occur.

ControlBase Class

The `ControlBase` class is the base class for the JavaScript control classes associated with your script controls. The `ControlBase` class inherits from `Sys.UI.Control` and provides functionality for working with client state and working with client callbacks. Client callbacks are supported by both the `ControlBase` and `ScriptControlBase` classes, with each of them providing a complementary piece of functionality. The `ControlBase` class provides functionality to compose the callback parameter, call the web page, and process the return value. The `_invoke` method is responsible for building up the JSON data, consisting of the client state and the arguments passed in, and calling back to the web page. The `_oncomplete` method is the callback method that processes the return value and assigns the client state value back to the hidden input element on the page.

Animations

The animation support in the ASP.NET AJAX Control Toolkit is extensive and constitutes the largest grouping of JavaScript classes in the Toolkit. In this section, we look at animations, what they are and how they work. Then, we look at the JavaScript classes that make up the animation foundation and how they are used. Finally, we look at how developers can use the Toolkit for animation support as they build their classes.

Animation Structure and Types

The animations in the Toolkit can be used in many different ways, ranging from declaring and executing a simple animation from your behavior or control to creating a complex sequence of animations declaratively in your page. In this section, we cover the different types of animations and the options the Toolkit provides for working with them.

Execution Structure

An animation can be run as a single animation or a group of animations that are run either sequentially or in parallel. The ability to create a group of animations, which can be a mix of sequential and parallel execution paths, contributes to the rich foundation the Toolkit provides for building complex visual effects on your pages.

The basic concepts of setting up and running an animation are simple. An animation will contain a target that is the ID of the DOM element it will be working with, a duration that specifies in seconds how long the animation will last, and the number of frames per second that will be played during the animation. All animations also have start, pause, and stop methods that are used to manipulate the animation after it has been created. As stated previously, the power of animations is the ability to group them together to construct an animation sequence, and this is where the `Sequence` and `Parallel` animations come into play.

The `Sequence` and `Parallel` animations are parent animations that contain children animations inside them that they run. They are designed to run the animations sequentially, one by one, or in parallel, running them all at the same time, providing a rich containment model capable of running any number of animations. As you build up these complex animations, you will soon need the ability to add some type of control flow to them (a dynamic way to control the flow of the animations as they run). The `Condition` and `Case` animations, which are also considered parent animations, are used to control which of their containing child animations will play. The `Condition` animation is designed to run either the first or second animation, depending on the `true` or `false` result of an external script that is run similar to an "if then else" statement. The `Case` animation is designed to run the child animation that contains the matching index returned from an external script that is run, which is similar to a `case` statement in .NET.

Animation Types

The Toolkit comes with two categories of animations: those that perform animations, and those that perform an action and are nonanimating. The types that perform some type of animation include the `Fade` animation, which is used to fade an element in and out of view, the `Color` animation, which transitions the value of a property between two colors, and the `Pulse` animation, which repeatedly fades an element in and out to create a pulsating effect. The actions include the `EnableAction`, which changes whether an element is disabled, the `HideAction`, which hides an element from view, and the `ScriptAction`, which runs a script. These two categories of animations are what you use when adding animations to the `Sequence`, `Parallel`, `Condition`, and `Case` parent animations we have discussed so far.

Client Architecture

The client architecture for animations consists of a rich set of JavaScript classes that provide the animation functionality on the client. The classes come with animations that can contain other animations, animations that can be run sequentially or in parallel, animations that perform explicit actions, and animations that can scale and fade elements. In this section, we cover the base animation class, animation containers, various discrete animations, and animations that perform actions.

Animation Base Class

The animation, which inherits from `Sys.Component`, is the base class for all animations in the Toolkit. The class comes with a set of properties that are shown in Table 10.4, methods that are shown in Table 10.5, and events that are shown in Table 10.6 and are common to all animations.

TABLE 10.4 Animation Properties

Property	Description
target	The element ID of the target of the animation.
duration	The duration of the animation in seconds. The default is 1.
fps	Frames per second, which defaults to 25.

TABLE 10.5 Animation Methods

Method	Description
play	Plays the animation
pause	Pauses the animation, with the ability to start again from the point it was paused
stop	Stops the animation and resets it to the beginning

TABLE 10.6 Animation Events

Event	Description
started	Raised when the play method has been called
ended	Raised when the stop method is called

Containers

The animation foundation comes with animations that can contain other animations, providing a model for extremely versatile configurations. In this section, we detail these parent animations and the functionality they provide. The class diagram in Figure 10.7 shows the hierarchy for the ParallelAnimation, SelectionAnimation, and SequenceAnimation classes, which support child animations. The `SequenceAnimation` class is designed to run its child animations one at a time until they all have been completed. In some cases, it might be desired to run the sequence multiple times or maybe even in a repeating loop. The `iterations` property controls the number of times a `SequenceAnimation` series will run, and providing a value greater than 1 will cause the sequence to run more than one time; a value of 0 will cause the sequence to run indefinitely. The `Parallel Animation` is designed to run its child animations concurrently and can be used in situations where you need to have many items run at one time. The `SelectionAnimation` is really just a base class for the `ConditionAnimation` and `CaseAnimation` classes, which provide control flow for child animations. The `ConditionAnimation` provides the functionality to execute one of two child animations, depending on the result of the script set in the `conditionScript` property. If a value of `true` is returned, the first animation is run; if a value of `false` is returned, the second one runs. The `Case Animation` provides the functionality to run one of many child animations, depending on the index value returned from the script set in the `selectScript` property. If the script returns a valid index value, the corresponding animation at that index position will run; otherwise, no animations will run.

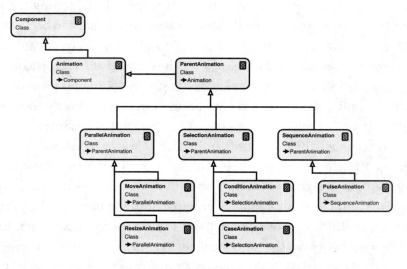

FIGURE 10.7 ASP.NET AJAX Control Toolkit animation containers

Animations in the Toolkit

The animations that come with the Toolkit provide a wide range of functionality that can add amazing visual effects to your web page (see Figure 10.8). In this section, we cover the animation class and what animations offer.

The `ScaleAnimation` is designed to scale the size of the target element by setting the `scaleFactor` property to a specific value. The animation will scale the element down in size if the `scaleFactor` property is set to a value less than 1, and up in size if the value is greater than 1. The animation also has a `scaleFont` property that controls whether the font size associated with the element will scale, too. A value of `true` will size the font; `false` will leave it alone. Finally, the animation has a `center` property that controls whether the element's center will move when it is scaled. A value of `false`, yes `false`, causes the element's center to move, but only if the target element was positioned using absolute positioning; otherwise, the effect will not work.

The `FadeAnimation` is a generic fade animation designed to fade an element into or out of view depending on the value of the effect property. Setting the property to `FadeEffect.FadeIn` causes the element to fade in to view, and setting it to a value of `FadeEffect.FadeOut` causes the element to fade out of view. If you are targeting Internet Explorer, setting the `forceLayoutInIE` property to `true` will handle some issues that can occur on that browser. If you already know the direction of the fade, you can use the more direct versions `FadeInAnimaiton` or the `FadeOutAnimation` to simplify things a bit, especially when you are declaratively setting up the animation.

The `PropertyAnimation` is a base animation that enables you to assign a value to a specified property. The `DiscreteAnimation` and the `InterpolatedAnimation` inherit from this class to provide property-assigning functionality in their animations. The `PropertyAnimation` enables you to assign a value to a specified property using the property name. This animation also enables you to assign the name of the property, which is useful in situations where the property takes the format `property[propertyKey]`. The `DiscreteAnimation` is designed to set the value of the targeted element's designated property to an array of values using the property-assignment properties of the `PropertyAnimation` base class.

The InterpolatedAnimation is a base class designed to assign a range of values to a specified property. The startValue property is used to assign the starting value, and the endValue property is assigned the ending value. The property the value is assigned to is set using the property options of the PropertyAnimation base class. The ColorAnimation, which inherits from the InterpolatedAnimation, is designed to transition a color value between two seven-character hex string values assigned to the startValue and endValue properties. The LengthAnimation, which also inherits from InterpolatedAnimation, is designed to assign a range of values that have been converted to units to the assigned property.

The MoveAnimation and ResizeAnimation, shown previously in Figure 10.7, inherit from the ParallelAnimation to provide functionality for moving and resizing elements. MoveAnimation is designed to move the target element both horizontally and vertically. The animation treats the horizontal and vertical entries, as long as absolute positioning is used, as offsets if the relative property is set to true, and a coordinate if the value is set to false. The ResizeAnimation is designed to change the target element's size from its current height and width value to the height and width set in the corresponding properties on the animation.

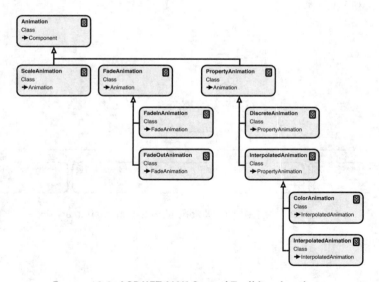

FIGURE 10.8 ASP.NET AJAX Control Toolkit animations

Actions

Sometimes you will need to make a property assignment or possibly call a script that doesn't fall into the standard structure of an animation. In these cases, you use what is called an action to perform a task. An action is an animation that does not animate; instead, an action executes it function instantaneously, not progressively over time. In this section, we cover the actions that come with the Toolkit and what they have to offer (see Figure 10.9).

The `ActionAnimation` is the base class that all actions inherit from. The `EnableAction` changes the target element to disabled depending on the value of the enabled property (`true` or `false`) and is useful at the beginning and ending of a `Sequence` animation when you want to disable an element such as a button. The `HideAction` is a simple action that sets the style's display attribute of the target element based on the visible property setting. The `StyleAction` is designed to set the style attribute on an element. The attribute property contains the attribute to change, and the value property is set to the value to change it to. The `OpacityAction` is designed to set the opacity of the target element to the value set on the opacity property. The valid values for this property are `0` to `1`. The final action we cover is the `ScriptAction`, which is designed to execute the JavaScript contained in the script property.

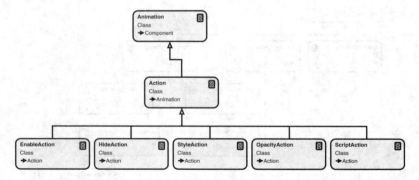

FIGURE 10.9 ASP.NET AJAX Control Toolkit animation actions

Server Architecture

The server architecture for animations enables you to add animation script references to your controls to enable client-side programming, create JSON representation of the animations, and declaratively create animation sequences in the HTML source editor. In this section, we cover how to add script references and declaratively create animations in the HTML source editor.

Script Registration for JavaScript API -Based Programming

The act of registering script references for client-side programming is simple. If you are creating an extender that will use the client-side functionality only, all you need to do is add a `RequiredScript` attribute to your class with a reference to the `AnimationScripts` type as a parameter. This will include all the animation scripts as part of the script references for the control, making them available on the client. Once the scripts are on the client, the animations are now available for you to use, enabling you to create and run animations using the JavaScript animation API.

Declarative Animations

The ability to work with the animation API on the client is powerful, but not all developers like to write JavaScript. This is where the declarative approach to animations comes in and the base classes that support this functionality. The `AnimationExtenderControlBase` class, the `Animation` class, and the `AnimationJavaScriptCoverter` class shown in Figure 10.10 provide the declarative animation functionality for the Toolkit and will be the classes you will use as you create an extender that supports declarative animation. Before we get started discussing the classes, let's cover the overall approach to working with animations declaratively in the Toolkit.

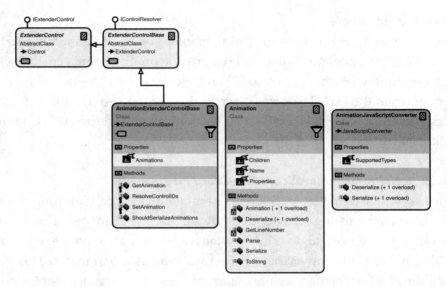

FIGURE 10.10 ASP.NET AJAX Control Toolkit declarative animation support classes

The declarative approach to working with animations follows a pattern of creating a series of animations related to an event on the target element. The HTML fragment in Listing 10.8 shows an AnimationExtender designed to work with the OnClick event. The listing shows how an animation is created that will respond to an OnClick event of the element the extender is associated with. If we walk through the sample, each animation begins with an Animations tag that is the parent for all the events and subsequent animations they contain. In the case of our example, we have created a Sequence animation that has a target element of info to which the animation will be applied. This Sequence animation then contains a series of child animations that will be applied to the target element. The following is a list of actions that occur in the Sequence animation:

- The StyleAction sets the overflow property to hidden.
- A nested Parallel animation simultaneously scales the element to 5 percent of its size and fades out the opacity of the element to 0.
- A series of StyleActions sets the display to none, the width to 250px, the height to nothing, and the font size to 12px.
- An OpacityAction sets the opacity of the btnCloseParent button to 0.
- An EnableAction enables the btnInfo button.

The style of adding these tags is similar to other patterns we have seen in ASP.NET, making this approach familiar to someone who has been programming in ASP.NET for a while. Now let's look at how the Toolkit classes in Figure 10.7 enable us to work with this declarative data.

LISTING 10.8 AnimationExtender Sample

```
<ajaxToolkit:AnimationExtender id="CloseAnimation" runat="server"
  TargetControlID="btnClose">
  <Animations>
    <OnClick>
      <Sequence AnimationTarget="info">
        <StyleAction Attribute="overflow" Value="hidden"/>
          <Parallel Duration=".3" Fps="15">
            <Scale ScaleFactor="0.05" Center="true"
              ScaleFont="true" FontUnit="px" />
            <FadeOut />
          </Parallel>
          <StyleAction Attribute="display" Value="none"/>
          <StyleAction Attribute="width" Value="250px"/>
          <StyleAction Attribute="height" Value=""/>
          <StyleAction Attribute="fontSize" Value="12px"/>
          <OpacityAction AnimationTarget="btnCloseParent"
            Opacity="0" />
          <EnableAction AnimationTarget="btnInfo"
            Enabled="true" />
      </Sequence>
    </OnClick>
  </Animations>
</ajaxToolkit:AnimationExtender>
```

The `AnimationExtenderControlBase` class contains support for working with declarative animations in the form of the `Animations` property and the `GetAnimation` and `SetAnimation` properties. The `Animations` property is tied to the `Animations` tag in the declarative animation that is created and handles converting the XML representation of the animation to an `Animation` class representation. The `GetAnimation` and `SetAnimation` methods are used in the properties that represent each event being handled and provide functionality to convert animations to and from JSON. The `OnClick` event handler property in Listing 10.9 comes from the `AnimationExtender` and shows how the methods are called inside the property.

The `Animation` class provides the functionality to convert the XML representation of animations into an object format. The class provides a `Parse` method that is called from the `Animations` property to parse the XML string into an `Animation` class and then assigns the individual event handler animations to the event handler properties on the extender. The class is also designed to convert its representation to and from JSON, which, by the way, happens when the `GetAnimation` and `SetAnimation` methods on the `AnimationExtenderControlBase` class are called by the inherited extender. This last step is important because a .NET developer can code against your extender, in which case they would be working with `Animation` classes rather than XML.

LISTING 10.9 OnClick Event Handler Property

```
[DefaultValue(null)]
[Browsable(false)]
[ExtenderControlProperty]
[DesignerSerializationVisibility(DesignerSerializationVisibility.Hidden)]
public Animation OnClick
{
    get { return GetAnimation(ref _onClick, "OnClick"); }
    set { SetAnimation(ref _onClick, "OnClick", value); }
}
```

SUMMARY

The Ajax Control Toolkit comes with a tremendous amount of functionality that not only assists in the development of controls but also adds additional features that are needed in most of your development scenarios. The reliance on attributes to decorate your classes and properties greatly simplifies the task of interacting with the `ScriptComponentDescriptor` and `ScriptReference` classes, by providing a no-code solution for creating entries of those types. The designer support also stands out as one of the features that give your controls the professional feel, and the new wizards in Visual Studio add to that experience. Finally, the animation support provides a fantastic foundation for building complex visual effects for your pages. In the next chapter, we cover how to build extender controls using the ASP.NET AJAX Control Toolkit that utilizes many of the features described in this chapter.

■ 11 ■

Adding Client Capabilities to Server Controls Using the ASP.NET AJAX Control Toolkit

I N THE PRECEDING CHAPTER, we covered the architecture of the AJAX Control Toolkit, describing at a high level what it has to offer and the attributes, classes, and interfaces that make it all happen. The enhanced functionality you get in the toolkit, from attribute-based programming to rich animations, provides a compelling alternative to coding against the ASP.NET 2.0 AJAX Extensions and the Microsoft AJAX Library directly. In this chapter, we delve into the details of the toolkit a little further as we develop as series of extender controls that demonstrate the rich features the toolkit provides.

Adding Client-Side Behavior Using the ExtenderControlBase

The ASP.NET AJAX Control Toolkit provides many features to assist in the development of extender controls, such as the automatic creation of `$create` statements, the use of attributes to decorate extender control properties that should be included in the `$create` statement creation, built-in designer support, and many more. In this section, we revisit the `Image Rotator` extender we created in Chapter 5, "Adding Client Capabilities to Server Controls," and re-create it using the ASP.NET AJAX Control Toolkit. This approach enables us to compare the alternatives as we build the new extender.

The process of building an extender control using the ASP.NET AJAX Control Toolkit consists of four main steps.

1. Create the template classes.

2. Provide implementation for the inherited extender control class.

3. Provide implementation for the `Sys.UI.BehaviorBase`-based JavaScript class.

4. Attach the extender control to an existing server control.

Visual Studio 2008 Extender Control Library Template

The ASP.NET AJAX Control Toolkit comes with full support for Visual Studio 2008 in the form of a project template that is geared toward creating an extender control library project. The template, shown in Figure 11.1, creates a library project structure (see Figure 11.2) that contains an extender control class, a designer class, and a JavaScript behavior class. In this section, we look at the ImageRotatorExtender.cs, ImageRotatorDesigner.cs, and ImageRotatorBehavior.js files that the template generated for us as we begin to discuss creating a new and improved `ImageRotator` extender.

> ### ■ NOTE   Additional Template
>
> The toolkit also comes with a template that generates the same files that can be used when you need to add additional extenders to an existing project, which can be found when you select Add New Item from a project.

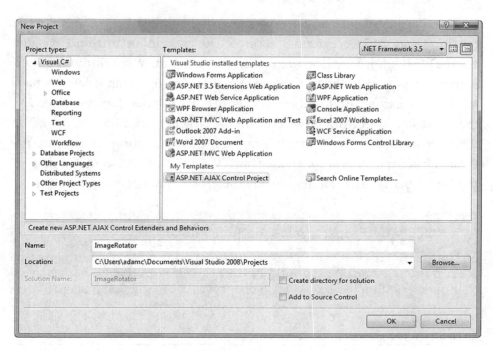

FIGURE 11.1 Extender control project template

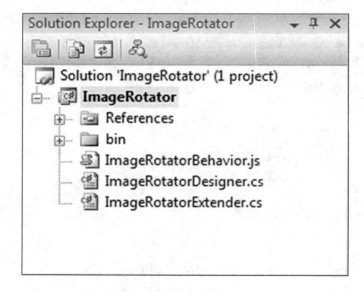

FIGURE 11.2 Extender control project template structure

The `ImageRotatorExtender` class shown in Listing 11.1 serves as the basis for our `ImageRotator` extender control. The class inherits from `Extender ControlBase` and provides a template that contains most of the required entries for us, such as the web resource registration of our associated behavior class, class attributes that associate the designer for the extender, the client script to be downloaded, and the target type for the extender. The template also creates a default property, demonstrating the use of the `ExtenderControlProperty` and `DefaultValue` attributes and the use of the `GetPropertyValue` method inside the property setter and getter.

> **■ NOTE   GetPropertyValue Method Version**
>
> The version of the `GetPropertyValue` method used by the template is an outdated one. When building out the class, we will change the implementation to use the `GetPropertyValue<T>` version instead.

LISTING 11.1 ImageRotatorExtender Class

```
[assembly: System.Web.UI.WebResource(
"ImageRotator.ImageRotatorBehavior.js","text/javascript")]
namespace ImageRotator
{
  [Designer(typeof(ImageRotatorDesigner))]
  [ClientScriptResource("ImageRotator.ImageRotatorBehavior",
    "ImageRotator.ImageRotatorBehavior.js")]
  [TargetControlType(typeof(Control))]
  public class ImageRotatorExtender : ExtenderControlBase
  {
    [ExtenderControlProperty]
    [DefaultValue("")]
    public string MyProperty
    {
      get
      {
        return GetPropertyValue("MyProperty", "");
      }
      set
      {
        SetPropertyValue("MyProperty", value);
      }
    }
  }
}
```

The `ImageRotatorDesigner` class shown in Listing 11.2 will be the designer class for our `ImageRotator` extender control. The designer class provides default designer functionality for our extender control during design time. We associate the designer with our `ImageRotatorExtender` class by using the `Designer` attribute, which is automatically added when we use the template. The `ExtenderControlBaseDesigner<T>` class that the `ImageRotatorDesigner` class inherits from makes it possible for the properties of our extender control to show up in the Properties window while the design-time focus is on the image control we are extending. This default behavior provides a more efficient way of working with extenders and the controls they are extending.

LISTING 11.2 ImageRotatorDesigner Class

```
namespace ImageRotator
{
  class ImageRotatorDesigner : AjaxControlToolkit.Design.
    ExtenderControlBaseDesigner<ImageRotatorExtender>
  {
  }
}
```

The `ImageRotatorBehavior` class shown in Listing 11.3 will be the client-side behavior class for our `ImageRotator` extender control. The class consists of the same structure we used in Chapter 5, but now inherits from the `AjaxControlToolkit.BehaviorBase` class, which provides added functionality for working with client state and interacting with the asynchronous request events of the `Sys.WebForms.PageRequestManager`.

LISTING 11.3 ImageRotatorBehavior Class

```
/// <reference name="MicrosoftAjaxTimer.debug.js" />
/// <reference name="MicrosoftAjaxWebForms.debug.js" />
/// <reference name="AjaxControlToolkit.ExtenderBase.BaseScripts.js"
    assembly="AjaxControlToolkit" />

Type.registerNamespace('ImageRotator');

ImageRotator.ImageRotatorBehavior = function(element) {
  ImageRotator.ImageRotatorBehavior.initializeBase(this, [element]);
```

LISTING 11.3 continued

```
    // TODO : (Step 1) Add your property variables here
    this._myPropertyValue = null;
}

ImageRotator.ImageRotatorBehavior.prototype = {
  initialize : function() {
    ImageRotator.ImageRotatorBehavior.callBaseMethod(this,'initialize');
    // TODO: Add your initialization code here
  },

  dispose : function() {
    // TODO: Add your cleanup code here
    ImageRotator.ImageRotatorBehavior.callBaseMethod(this, 'dispose');
  },

  // TODO: (Step 2) Add your property accessors here
  get_MyProperty : function() {
    return this._myPropertyValue;
  },
  set_MyProperty : function(value) {
    this._myPropertyValue = value;
  }
}

ImageRotator.ImageRotatorBehavior.registerClass(
  'ImageRotator.ImageRotatorBehavior', AjaxControlToolkit.BehaviorBase);
```

Inheriting from the ExtenderControlBase Class

The ASP.NET AJAX Control Toolkit comes with its own version of the System.Web.UI.ExtenderControl class, which provides additional functionality that supports the development pattern the toolkit is designed to work with. The AjaxControlToolkit.ExtenderControlBase class provides the inheritor support for serialization of property values, support for working with the toolkit-based attributes, seamless integration with control-based view state, support for working with client state, and the ability to specify an alternate script path for debugging and working with themes. The ImageRotatorExtender class in Listing 11.4 shows a much different-looking class than we saw in Chapter 5. The class no longer requires overrides for the GetScriptDescriptors and GetScriptReferences methods, it has class-level attributes, it has property-level attributes, and the property setters and getters are referencing their values through a method. So, let's go over these changes and see how we develop an extender control building on the structure the template provided for us.

The setting of the assembly-based `WebResource` attribute in our extender class is a pattern that all the extenders and script controls in the toolkit follow. This pattern helps centralize all the pieces for the component in one location instead of having to add an entry to the assembly when a new control is added to the toolkit. The attributes applied to the class that we cover in this section are the `Designer`, `ClientScriptResource`, `RequiredScript`, and `TargetControlType` attributes. The `Designer` attribute is used to specify the class that will provide design-time services to our extender. The `ClientScriptResource` attribute is used to include the client-side scripts for our extender and consists of the resource type and the full resource name and should refer to an embedded resource. The `RequiredScriptResource` attribute brings in the timer script file that is associated with the `Timer Script` class that we will use in our behavior class. Finally, the `Target ControlType` attribute is used to limit the types of controls our extender can be associated with.

The `RotationInterval` and `ImageList` properties of our class have also changed with the use of attributes and the reliance on the `GetProperty Value<T>` and `SetPropertyValue<T>` methods to access our property data. The `ExtenderControlProperty` attribute is used to indicate that the property should be added to the `ScriptComponentDescriptor` as a property and later included in the `$create` statement that creates the behavior class on the client. The `ClientPropertyName` attribute is used to change the name of the property that is used when the property is added to the `Script ComponentDescriptor` from the default value of the property name to the name provided to the attribute. The `DefaultValue` attribute, which comes from the `System.CompnentModel` namespace, is used to indicate to designers and code generators the default value of the property. The `Extender ControlBase` class provides the `GetPropertyValue<T>` and `GetProperty Value<T>` generic methods that get and set the property value directly from the control view state. By using these methods in our property setters and getters, a consumer of our extender can work with it in the designer, declaratively in the HTML editor, or in code and be assured that during a postback the values will be available.

LISTING 11.4 ImageRotatorExtender Class

```
[assembly:System.Web.UI.WebResource("ImageRotator.ImageRotatorBehavior.js",
"text/javascript")]
namespace ImageRotator
{
  [ParseChildren(true, "ImageList")]
  [Designer(typeof(ImageRotatorDesigner))]
  [ClientScriptResource("ImageRotator.ImageRotatorBehavior",
     "ImageRotator.ImageRotatorBehavior.js")]
  [RequiredScript(typeof(TimerScript))]
  [TargetControlType(typeof(Image))]
  public class ImageRotatorExtender : ExtenderControlBase
  {
    [ExtenderControlProperty]
    [ClientPropertyName("rotationInterval")]
    [DefaultValue(3), DisplayName("RotationInterval(seconds))")]
    [DesignerSerializationVisibility(
      DesignerSerializationVisibility.Visible)]
    public int RotationInterval
    {
      get { return GetPropertyValue<int>("RotationInterval", 3); }
      set { SetPropertyValue<int>("RotationInterval", value); }
    }

    private ImageUrlList _imageList;
    [ExtenderControlProperty]
    [ClientPropertyName("imageList")]
    [DesignerSerializationVisibility(
      DesignerSerializationVisibility.Content)]
    [PersistenceMode(PersistenceMode.InnerDefaultProperty)]
    public ImageUrlList ImageList
    {
      get
      {
        if (_imageList == null)
        {
          _imageList = GetPropertyValue<ImageUrlList>(
            "ImageList", null);
          if (_imageList == null)
          {
            _imageList = new ImageUrlList();
            SetPropertyValue<ImageUrlList>(
              "ImageList", _imageList);
          }
        }
        return _imageList;
      }
    }
  }
}
```

Creating the AjaxControlToolkit.BehaviorBase Class

The ASP.NET AJAX Control Toolkit comes with its own version of the `Sys.UI.Behavior` class, which provides additional functionality and supports the development pattern the toolkit is designed to work with. The `AjaxControlToolkit.BehaviorBase` class provides inheritor support for working with client state and interacting with the asynchronous request events of the `Sys.WebForms.PageRequestManager`. The support for working with client state is provided by the `get_ClientState` and `set_ClientState` methods that can be used to work with the string-based hidden field associated with your extender. The class also provides two methods tied to the `beginRequest` and `endRequest` events of the `PageRequestManager`, which can be overridden to provide specific functionality in your behavior in situations where an UpdatePanel is being used.

The `ImageRotatorBehavior` class shown in Listing 11.5 inherits from the `BehaviorBase` class and provides the client-side behavior for our extender control. The structure of this class is exactly the same as in Chapter 5, with the `rotationInterval` property used to set the interval at which the images will be swapped out and the `imageList` property containing an array of the images. The one change to the class is in the use of the `Sys.Timer` class, which is part of the ASP.NET AJAX Control Toolkit. This class, which is contained in the Compat/Timer folder, wraps the `window.setInterval` call, providing a cleaner interface for this timer-specific functionality. The `Sys.Timer` class is just one of many that come with the toolkit that provide added functionality to the existing Microsoft AJAX Library. If you look in the Compat and Common folders in the toolkit library project, you will find classes for working with dates, drag and drop, and threading, just to name a few.

LISTING 11.5 ImageRotator Behavior Class

```
Type.registerNamespace('ImageRotator');

ImageRotator.ImageRotatorBehavior = function(element) {
  ImageRotator.ImageRotatorBehavior.initializeBase(this, [element]);

  this._imageIndex = 0;
  this._imageList = new Array();
  this._rotationInterval = null;
  this._timer = null;
```

LISTING 11.5 continued

```
}
ImageRotator.ImageRotatorBehavior.prototype = {
  initialize : function() {
    ImageRotator.ImageRotatorBehavior.callBaseMethod(this,
      'initialize');

    var element = this.get_element();

    if(this._imageList)
    {
      this._imageList =
        Sys.Serialization.JavaScriptSerializer.deserialize(
          this._imageList);
      this._imageList[this._imageList.length] = element.src;
    }

    if(this._rotationInterval == null)
      this._rotationInterval = 3;

      if(this._timer == null)
        this._timer = new Sys.Timer();

      this._timer.set_interval(this._rotationInterval * 1000);
      this._timer.add_tick(Function.createDelegate(this,
        this._rotateImage));
      this._timer.set_enabled(true);
  },

  dispose : function() {
    ImageRotator.ImageRotatorBehavior.callBaseMethod(this, 'dispose');
    if (this._timer)
    {
      this._timer.dispose();
      this._timer = null;
    }

    this._imageList = null;

  },
  get_rotationInterval: function(){
    return this._rotationInterval;
  },
  set_rotationInterval: function(value){
    this._rotationInterval = value;
  },
  get_imageList: function(){
    return this._imageList;
  },
```

```
    set_imageList: function(value){
      this._imageList = value;
    },
    _rotateImage: function(){
      var element = this.get_element();
      if(element)
      {
        element.src = this._imageList[this._imageIndex++];
        if(this._imageIndex > this._imageList.length - 1)
          this._imageIndex = 0;
      }
    }
  }
ImageRotator.ImageRotatorBehavior.registerClass(
    'ImageRotator.ImageRotatorBehavior', AjaxControlToolkit.BehaviorBase);
```

Attaching the Extender to a Control

You can attach the `ImageRotator` extender to an image control by using the new Extender Control Wizard (see Figure 11.3) that comes with Visual Studio 2008 and thus provide the same design-time experience we saw in Chapter 5. The wizard is available from the smart tag of the image control by selecting the Add Extender option, which opens the wizard. The wizard enables the user to select an extender control from a list and associate it with a control. In our case, we would select the `ImageRotator` extender to associate it with the image control. After we do that, we add values to the `RotationInterval` property and `ImageList` property using the Properties window of the image control.

Final Thoughts

If we compare our experience of creating extender controls using the ASP.NET AJAX Control Toolkit to using the classes provided by the ASP.NET 2.0 AJAX Extensions, we can see that our development experience is much simpler. The use of attributes to register our properties to be included in the `$create` statements and to register our associated script files dramatically reduces the complexity of our code compared to implementing logic in the `GetScriptDescriptors` and `GetScriptReferences` methods. This convenience alone makes it worth using the toolkit, but if we tack on the added design-time features, support for working with client state, and the numerous added JavaScript files such as the `Sys.Timer` class, the reasons to switch get greater. The use of the toolkit can be compared to the use of the ActiveX Template Library (ATL) that was used to create ActiveX controls in C++. The template provided a ton of base classes and Visual Studio templates that made creating them a lot easier.

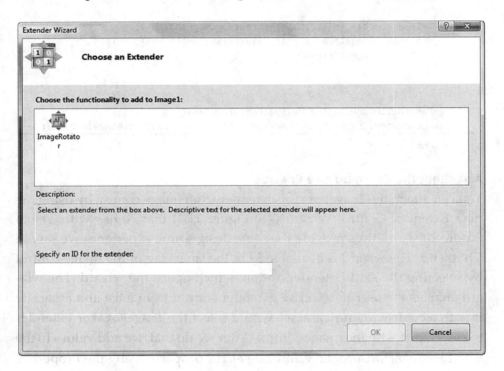

FIGURE 11.3 Extender Control Wizard

Adding Design-Time Support to Your Extender Control

The introduction of the Extender Wizard in Visual Studio 2008 has enhanced the design-time experience with regard to working with extender controls, and this section explains how to add design-time features of your own to give your controls that professional feel that users have become accustomed to.

Default Design-Time Experience

The ImageRotatorDesigner class shown in Listing 11.2 provides everything we need to get a basic design-time experience for our extender control. The ExenderControlBaseDesigner<T> that it inherits from makes it possible for the properties of our extender control to show up in the Properties window while the design-time focus is on the image control we are extending. Figure 11.4 shows the RotationInterval and ImageList properties that appear in the Properties window while the image control has focus in the designer. This default feature addresses one issue, which is being able to work with the ImageRotator properties in an integrated way, but still does not address the issue of data entry for the properties themselves and how that experience can be enhanced.

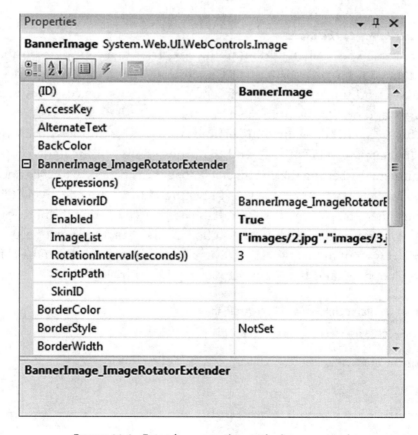

FIGURE 11.4 Extender properties on the image control

Adding Designers and Editors to Properties

In this section, we look at how to extend the design-time behavior of our `ImageRotator` `ImageList` property. The `ImageList` property that we worked with in Chapter 5 was rudimentary and prone to errors as a user entered in the values. In this version of the extender, we want to extend the functionality to support design-time editing and HTML source editing.

The road to these modifications requires a few steps as we add the functionality:

1. Add attributes to the class.
2. Add attributes to the property.
3. Add editors to assist in assigning values.
4. Create a type converter to support serialization.

Add Attributes to the Class

Most users expect when adding multiple entries to a control to be able to add them in the body of the HTML element. This is the experience we have when adding web service references or script references to the `Script Manager` and one we want to have in our control.

The `ParseChildren` attribute enables us to add multiple entries inside our `ImageRotator` HTML tag and treat those entries as a single property assignment. By setting the `ChildrenAsProperties` property to `true` and the `DefaultProperty` to `ImageList`, as in Listing 11.6, we are effectively telling the designer that we want to have all the items contained in the body of our `ImageRotator` tag parsed and assigned to the `ImageList` property. The HTML fragment in Listing 11.7 shows what this looks like when the HTML editor is opened and the `ImageRotator` tag has entries.

LISTING 11.6 ParseChildren Attribute Assignment

```
[ParseChildren(true, "ImageList")]
...
public class ImageRotatorExtender : ExtenderControlBase
{
    ...
}
```

LISTING 11.7 ImageList Assignment in HTML

```
...
<asp:Image ID="BannerImage" runat="server" ImageUrl="~/images/1.jpg" />
<cc2:ImageRotatorExtender ID="BannerImage_ImageRotatorExtender"
  runat="server" Enabled="True" TargetControlID="BannerImage">
  <cc2:ImageUrl Url="~/images/2.jpg" />
  <cc2:ImageUrl Url="~/images/3.jpg" />
  <cc2:ImageUrl Url="~/images/4.jpg" />
</cc2:ImageRotatorExtender>
...
```

> **▪ NOTE ASP.NET Server Control Designer References**
>
> The addition of designer features to your extenders requires some knowledge of how designers work. MSDN has some great information about this at http://msdn2.microsoft.com/en-us/library/aa719973%28VS.71%29.aspx that covers adding design-time support to ASP.NET server controls.

Add Attributes to the Property

To fully implement the ability to add nested image entries to our Image Rotator extender, we need to add a couple of attributes, as shown in Listing 11.8, to our ImageList property, which provides hooks for the designer to integrate with our property and properly assign the image values.

The DesignerSerializationVisibility attribute is added to the property to ensure that the designer will serialize the contents of the property during design time. The setting of DesignerSerializationVisibility. Content instructs the designer to generate code for the contents of the tag and not the tag itself.

The PersistenceMode attribute is the other piece to this puzzle and is responsible for adding the <ImageUrl .. /> entries inside our ImageRotator tag as we add values to the property in the Properties window. The setting of PersistenceMode.InnerProperty specifies that the property is persisted as a nested tag inside the ImageRotator, as shown in Listing 11.7.

LISTING 11.8 Designer-Specific Attributes for the ImageRotatorExtender Class

```
[ParseChildren(true, "ImageList")]
...
public class ImageRotatorExtender : ExtenderControlBase
{
    ...

    [DesignerSerializationVisibility(
      DesignerSerializationVisibility.Content)]
    [PersistenceMode(PersistenceMode.InnerDefaultProperty)]
    public ImageUrlList ImageList
    {
        ...
    }
}
```

Add Editors to Assist in Assigning Values

The use of editors in your extenders can greatly enhance the user experience during design time and in some cases can lead to more accurate entry of data. Recall from Chapter 5 that we entered images to the ImageList property by adding URL entries and separating them using commas. This rudimentary approach would not be expected by a consumer of a professional control. In this version of the ImageRotator, we want to enhance the data entry of the images by providing an editor that can be used to add image URL entries and have those entries placed into the body of our ImageRotator HTML tag. If we go back to the ScriptManager control, this is the experience it provides when adding web service or script references while in the Properties window.

The ImageList property in this version of the ImageRotator uses two editors to provide a rich design-time experience when adding ImageUrl entries. The first editor is a Collection editor, shown in Figure 11.5, and is designed to assist in adding, editing, and removing values that are based on a Collection. The editor is automatically associated with our ImageList property because the type of the property is a Collection. The second editor we will use is the ImageUrlEditor, shown in Figure 11.6, which the ImageUrl entry uses to assist the user in entering a URL. This editor is associated with the Url property of the ImageUrl class, as shown in Listing 11.9, by adding the Editor attribute to the property. We use the Editor attribute to configure which editor to use when adding values to the property in the designer. In our case, we are using the `ImageUrlEditor` to provide the user with a clean way to find an image located in a web application and assign the value to the `ImageUrl` property. The use of the associated `UrlProperty` attribute provides a filter that identifies specific file types that can be used to filter against the `ImageUrl` property.

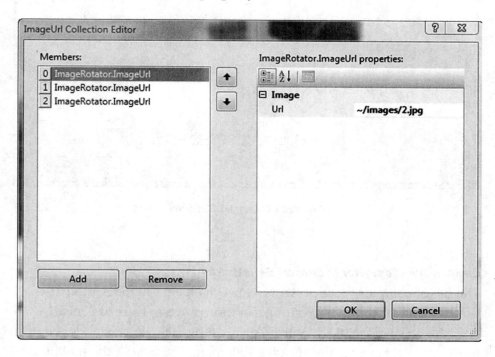

FIGURE 11.5   Image URL Collection Editor

LISTING 11.9 ImageUrl Class

```
[Serializable]
public class ImageUrl
{
  [DefaultValue(""),Bindable(true),
    Editor("System.Web.UI.Design.ImageUrlEditor,
      System.Design, Version=2.0.0.0, Culture=neutral,
      PublicKeyToken=b03f5f7f11d50a3a", typeof(UITypeEditor)),
    UrlProperty]
  public string Url { get; set; }
}
```

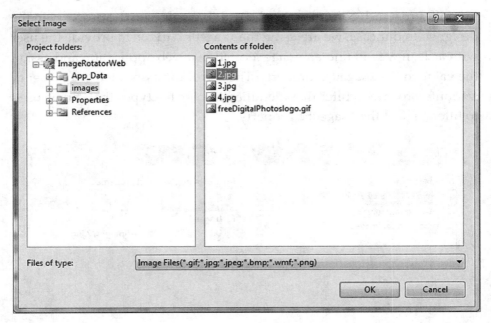

FIGURE 11.6 Image URL Editor

Create a Type Converter to Support Serialization

The use of complex types presents a few challenges in the ASP.NET AJAX
Control Toolkit during the script generation process. The problem arises in
how the ASP.NET AJAX Control Toolkit serializes your extender control
properties as it creates the $create statement. By default, the toolkit tries
to get the default string representation of the value your property represents. In most cases, this is an easy task because most simple types convert
to a string relatively easily. If you are using complex types, however, this
can present a problem because the default ConvertToString() representation of a complex object is its type name. To resolve this issue, you must create a type converter and associate it with the complex type. When the
ASP.NET AJAX Control Toolkit encounters a type during script generation,
it looks to see whether the type has a converter. If it does, it uses the converter to convert the data instead of using the default ConvertToString()
method. In this section, we walk through creating a System.Component
Model.TypeConverter that will be used to convert our ImageUrlList type

into a JavaScript Object Notation (JSON) string that can be consumed on the client.

The `ImageListConverter`, shown in Listing 11.10, is designed to convert the `ImageList` to a JSON array of image URLs that are then passed back to the client. The creation of this type converter now enables us to return a data format that the client can use instead of a string that contains the type name of the `ImageList`. For the type converter to be used, we need to associate it with the `ImageList` type. We do this by adding the `TypeConverter` attribute to the `ImageList` class, as shown in Listing 11.11, and assigning the type of the `ImageList` to it. Now when the toolkit performs a `Convert` `ToString` on the `ImageList`, the JSON string representation of the `Image` `List` will be returned.

> **▪ NOTE   Use of the DataContractJsonSerializer**
>
> In more complex situations, you might use the `DataContract` `JsonSerializer` that we discussed in Chapter 8, "ASP.NET AJAX Communication Architecture," which replaces the`System.Web.UI.` `JavaScriptSerializer` class as the new JSON serializer to convert your data to JSON format.

LISTING 11.10 ImageListConverter Type Converter Class

```
public class ImageListConverter : TypeConverter
{
  public override object ConvertTo(ITypeDescriptorContext context,
    System.Globalization.CultureInfo culture, object value,
    Type destinationType)
  {
    Collection<ImageUrl> imageList = value as Collection<ImageUrl>;
    if (imageList != null && destinationType == typeof(string))
    {
      StringBuilder builder = new StringBuilder();
      builder.Append("[");
      bool first = true;
      foreach (ImageUrl imageUrl in imageList)
      {
        if(first)
        {
          first = false;
        }
        else
```

LISTING 11.10 continued

```
        {
          builder.Append(",");
        }

        builder.Append("\"");
        builder.Append(imageUrl.Url.Replace("~/", ""));
        builder.Append("\"");
      }
      builder.Append("]");
      return builder.ToString();
    }
    return base.ConvertTo(context, culture, value, destinationType);
  }
}
```

LISTING 11.11 ImageUrlList Collection Class

```
[Serializable]
[TypeConverter(typeof(ImageListConverter))]
public class ImageUrlList : Collection<ImageUrl>
{

}
```

Adding Animations to Your Extender Control

The ASP.NET AJAX Control Toolkit comes with a rich animation framework that provides support for creating cool visual effects on your pages. The animation framework consists of a set of JavaScript and .NET classes that enable you to build up animations of all types, including animations that run sequentially or in parallel, animations that fade the opacity of a control in and out, and animations that transition from one color to the next. The framework provides support for building these animations using the JavaScript API directly or using a declarative approach that consists of adding markup in the HTML editor. The following sections examine how to add animation functionality to extender controls.

Animations Using the JavaScript API

The ImageRotator extender we created earlier provided little in the area of effects as the images switched and resulted in very fast transition from one image to the next, which wouldn't catch a viewer's attention. In this section, we create a new version of the ImageRotator, called the Animated ImageRotator, that fades in the image as it switches from one image to the next and provides this feature in addition to the existing functionality of the ImageRotator. As we cover how to add this new animation functionality, we gloss over the topics we have already covered, focusing only on implementing the animation pieces.

To add this functionality to the AnimatedImageRotator, we need to register the animation scripts with the AnimatedImageRotatorExtender class and add logic to the behavior class to call the animation when the image changes.

Registering the Animation Scripts

To register the script files so that they are downloaded to the browser, we need to add the RequiredScript attribute to the AnimatedImageRotator Extender class, as shown in Listing 11.12. We use the RequiredScript attribute in this case to ensure that the animation.js, timer.js, and common.js script files associated with the AnimationScripts type are included with the scripts brought down to the browser for our control. This style of adding scripts associated with a type is a common practice in the toolkit and is clean way to include dependent scripts associated with a type.

LISTING 11.12 AnimatedImageRotator Extender Class

```
...
[RequiredScript(typeof(AnimationScripts))]
...
public class AnimatedImageRotatorExtender : ExtenderControlBase
{
    ...
}
```

Calling Animation APIs

The ASP.NET AJAX Control Toolkit contains a JavaScript API that you can use to provide animation support on the client. In the case of our `Animated ImageRotator` extender, we will use the `FadeAnimation`, which is part of the animation API, to provide a fade-in effect when the images on our image control change. The JavaScript code to implement this functionality will be contained in our behavior class and will integrate with the existing features of the `ImageRotator`.

The `AnimatedImageRotator` behavior class, shown in Listing 11.13, takes the `ImageRotator` behavior and adds a fade animation when the image changes, to fade the image into view. The constructor of the `FadeAnimation` takes the target of the animation, the duration of the animation, the number of steps per second, the effect, the minimum opacity, the maximum opacity, and whether to adjust for layout in Internet Explorer. In our case, the `BannerImage` image control will be the target of our animation, and the duration of our animation will be hard coded to 20% of the time the image is visible. To provide a clean animation, we will set the animation steps to 150, and combine that with a fade-in effect that will cause the image to transition in when the image changes. During this transition, we will start off with an opacity of 0, which will give us a full view of the image background, and then through the 150 steps work our way to a full view of the image with an opacity of 1. Table 11.1 lists some of the `FadeAnimation` properties and provides a little more information about what they do.

After we associate the animation to the element, starting, stopping, and pausing the animation is just a method call away, making it simple to manipulate the animation. In the `AnimatedImageRotator`, the load event of the image is used to trigger the animation to play because it will be fired each time our `Sys.Timer` calls the `_rotateImage` method. To do this, we associated the `_onLoadImage` event handler with the `onLoad` event of the image and called the play method on the animation inside the function. Now each time the load event occurs, the animation plays, transitioning the image into view. One of the side effects of working with an animation in a situation like this is a potential race condition if the duration was set too long. When working with transition-type animations like the `FadAnimation`, pay close attention to how you are using it to ensure the animation will work in all cases.

LISTING 11.13 AnimatedImageRotator Behavior Class

```
...

AnimatedImageRotator.AnimatedImageRotatorBehavior = function(element) {
  ...
  this._fadeAnimation = null;
  this._timer = null;
  this._onImageLoadHandler = null;
}
AnimatedImageRotator.AnimatedImageRotatorBehavior.prototype = {
  initialize : function() {
  ...

    if(this._fadeAnimation == null)
    {
      this._fadeAnimation =
        new AjaxControlToolkit.Animation.FadeAnimation(
          element, this._rotationInterval/20, 150,
          AjaxControlToolkit.Animation.FadeEffect.FadeIn,
          0, 1, true);
    }
    if (element)
    {
      this._onImageLoadHandler = Function.createDelegate(this,
        this._onImageLoad);
      $addHandler(element, 'load', this._onImageLoadHandler);
    }
    ...
  },

  dispose : function() {
    ...
    var element = this.get_element();
    if (element) {
      if (this._onImageLoadHandler) {
        $removeHandler(element, 'load',
          this._onImageLoadHandler);
        this._onImageLoadHandler = null;
      }
    }

    ...

    if (this._fadeAnimation)
    {
      this._fadeAnimation.dispose();
      this._fadeAnimation = null;
    }

    ...
```

LISTING 11.13 continued

```
    },
    _onImageLoad: function(){
      if(this._fadeAnimation)
        this._fadeAnimation.play();
    },
    ...
  }
  ...
```

TABLE 11.1 Partial List of Fade Animation Class Properties

Property	Description
target	Target of the animation.
duration	Length of the animation in seconds. The default is 1.
fps	Number of steps per second. The default is 25.
effect	Determine whether to fade the element in or fade the element out. The possible values are AjaxControlToolkit.Animation.FadeEffect.FadeIn and AjaxControlToolkit.Animation.FadeEffect.FadeOut. The default value is FadeOut.
minimumOpacity	Minimum opacity to use when fading in or out. Its value can range from 0 to 1. The default value is 0.
maximumOpacity	Maximum opacity to use when fading in or out. Its value can range from 0 to 1. The default value is 1.
forceLayoutInIE	Whether we should force a layout to be created for Internet Explorer by giving it a width and setting its background color (the latter is required in case the user has ClearType enabled). The default value is true.

Animations Using the Declarative Method

The declarative approach to animation in the toolkit provides a nice extensibility path for consumers of your extender. In our previous example, we hard coded all the animation functionality inside our extender, providing little support for developer customization. In some cases, this might be all that is needed. In other cases, however, you might need to provide a more robust solution that provides a JavaScript-free way to customize animations. In this section, we replicate the same functionality we created in the preceding section, but we provide a more extensible approach consumers of our extender can use when they are configuring it in the designer. The extender we create has just one feature: the capability to run a FadeIn animation when the onLoad event of an associated image control occurs. This new extender will be used in addition to the ImageRotator extender we created earlier, which had no animation functionality. This refined approach to adding animation support builds on the principle that many extenders can be placed on a single control to provide combined client-side capabilities. To get started, let's take a look at what the declarative syntax or our control will look like before we go into the implementation details. Just as in the preceding section, as we cover how to add this new animation functionality we gloss over the topics we have already covered, focusing only on implementing the declarative animation pieces.

Overview of Declarative Syntax

To get started, let's look at the HTML source we will be working toward being able to work with in our ImageAnimation extender. The source in Listing 11.14 contains an ImageAnimationExtender tag that contains in its body an Animations tag. As you might guess, the approach here is to add various animations that are driven by events raised by the image control we are extending. In our case, we are working with the OnLoad event and adding a Sequence animation that will call a child Fade animation. A Sequence animation is designed to run all its child animations one at a time until all have finished. So, what this source tells us is that our extender will have an animation that will be tied to the OnLoad event of the image control and will run the child Fade animation whenever the OnLoad event occurs.

LISTING 11.14 AnimationImageExtender Declarative Syntax

```
<asp:Image ID="BannerImage" runat="server" ImageUrl="~/images/1.jpg" />
<cc3:ImageAnimationExtender ID="Banner_ImageAnimationExtender"
  runat="server" Enabled="True" TargetControlID="BannerImage">
  <Animations>
    <OnLoad>
      <Sequence>
        <FadeIn AnimationTarget="BannerImage" Duration=".3"/>
      </Sequence>
    </OnLoad>
  </Animations>
</cc3:ImageAnimationExtender>
<cc2:ImageRotatorExtender ID="Image1_ImageRotatorExtender"
  runat="server" Enabled="True" TargetControlID="Banner">
  <cc2:ImageUrl Url="~/images/2.jpg" />
  <cc2:ImageUrl Url="~/images/3.jpg" />
  <cc2:ImageUrl Url="~/images/4.jpg" />
</cc2:ImageRotatorExtender>
```

Providing Declarative Support in Your Extender Class

The AnimationExtenderControlBase class provides most of the functionality we need to parse the Animation tag and all its contents. This class provides internal methods that convert the XML representation of the animation into JSON format, which our behavior will then use to run the animation, and also provides the Animation property that we see in Listing 11.15. The following sections cover the steps needed to ensure the extender will work correctly.

1. Add attributes to the class.

2. Create a property for the event.

3. Add attributes to the property.

Add Attributes to the Class

This type of extender has a couple of added class attribute entries of interest to us. The first is the inclusion of the RequiredScript attribute for the AnimationExtender type. The AnimationExtender class provides a lot of the client-side functionality we will be using in our extender control, and by using this type in our RequiredScripts attribute, we are guaranteed that the scripts will be present on the client for us to use. The second attribute is the `System.Web.UI.Design.ToolboxItem` attribute, which enables our control to show up in the toolbox of Visual Studio. It might seem strange that we have to add this because all our other extenders didn't. If we look at the attributes on the `AnimationExtenderControlBase` class, however, the support for viewing in the toolbox has been turned off. Therefore, we must reset this value on our control so that it will show up in the toolbox.

Create a Property for the Event

The pattern when creating extenders of this type is to add a property for each event you want to interact with. In our case, we are working with the `OnLoad` event, so we create a property named `OnLoad` (to make it easy to understand what the event is). If we were to choose other events, we would name them based on the DOM event they represent. The property accessor for these events must use the `GetAnimation` and `SetAnimation` methods to ensure proper data conversion into JSON as the data is stored and retrieved out of the extender's view state.

Add Attributes to the Event Property

The event property must have the `Browsable`, `DefaultValue`, `Extender ControlProperty`, and `DesignerSerializationVisibility` attributes applied to it. The `Browsable` attribute stops the property from showing up in the Properties window and therefore excludes the property from being assigned in the Properties window. This is needed because no editor is associated with this property, and we don't want users to try to add anything into the Properties window that would corrupt the values. The `Designer SerializationVisibility` attribute with a value of `DesignerSerialization Visibility.Hidden` is used to indicate that the property value should not be persisted by the designer because the `Animation` property will take care of that for us. The `DefaultValue` attribute indicates to the designer that the default value will be null, and the `ExtenderControlProperty` attribute is used to register the property with the `ScriptComponentDescriptor`.

LISTING 11.15 ImageAnimationExtender Class

```
[Designer(typeof(ImageAnimationDesigner))]
[ClientScriptResource("ImageAnimation.ImageAnimationBehavior",
  "ImageAnimation.ImageAnimationBehavior.js")]
[RequiredScript(typeof(AnimationExtender))]
[ToolboxItem("System.Web.UI.Design.WebControlToolboxItem, System.Design,
Version=2.0.0.0, Culture=neutral, PublicKeyToken=b03f5f7f11d50a3a")]
[TargetControlType(typeof(Image))]
public class ImageAnimationExtender : AnimationExtenderControlBase
{
  private Animation _onLoad;

  [DefaultValue(null)]
  [Browsable(false)]
  [ExtenderControlProperty]
  [DesignerSerializationVisibility(
     DesignerSerializationVisibility.Hidden)]
  public new Animation OnLoad
  {
    get { return GetAnimation(ref _onLoad, "OnLoad"); }
    set { SetAnimation(ref _onLoad, "OnLoad", value); }
  }
}
```

Adding Declarative Support to Your Behavior Class

The ImageAnimationBehavior class, shown Listing 11.16, provides all the client-side functionality for our extender with support from the animation script files associated with the AutomationExtender class. These associated scripts provide support for converting the JSON representation of the FadeIn animation that was captured on the server to an actual animation, support for associating the animation with the high-level OnLoad event, and support for playing the animation when the OnLoad event occurs.

You need to complete a few steps for each event you plan to work with:

1. Add variables to the class.

2. Create functions.

3. Add handlers.

Add Variables to the Class

Each event that your behavior will work with needs a variable that references the GenericAnimationBehavior for the event and a delegate that will be called for the event that will be processed. In the `ImageAnimation` `Behavior` class, we use the `_onLoad` variable to store a reference to the `GenericAnimationBehavior` class and the `_onLoadHandler` variable to store a reference to the delegate that will handle the `onLoad` event. The guidelines established so far in the toolkit use a naming convention that includes the event name in all the variable names.

Create Functions

The behavior needs a series of functions for each event you will work with. The `get_OnLoad` and `set_OnLoad` functions in our case take care of working with the JSON-based data for the `FadeIn` animation and utilize the functionality provided by the `GenericAnimationBehavior` class to store and retrieve that data. The `get_OnLoadBehavior` function returns a reference to the `GenericAnimationBehavior` instance that was created for our `FadeIn` animation, providing the ability to work with the behavior that directly exposes the play, stop, and quit methods common to all animations.

Add Handlers

Handlers must be added for each event the behavior will process and should correspond to the events exposed on the extender control. In our case, we are working with the `onLoad` event, so we need to create the `_onLoadHandler` delegate and associate it with the `onLoad` event of the image using the `$addHandler` shortcut. The opposite of this must happen in the dispose of our behavior, when we use the `$removeHandler` shortcut to ensure proper memory cleanup.

LISTING 11.16 ImageAnimationBehavior Class

```
Type.registerNamespace('ImageAnimation');

ImageAnimation.ImageAnimationBehavior = function(element) {
  ImageAnimation.ImageAnimationBehavior.initializeBase(this, [element]);
  this._onLoad = null;
  this._onLoadHandler = null;
}
ImageAnimation.ImageAnimationBehavior.prototype = {
  initialize : function() {
    ImageAnimation.ImageAnimationBehavior.callBaseMethod(this,
      initialize');
    var element = this.get_element();
```

LISTING 11.16 continued

```
    if (element)
    {
      this._onLoadHandler = Function.createDelegate(this,
       this.OnLoad);
      $addHandler(element, 'load', this._onLoadHandler);
    }
  },

  dispose : function() {
    ImageAnimation.ImageAnimationBehavior.callBaseMethod(this,
      'dispose');

    var element = this.get_element();
    if (element) {
      if (this._onLoadHandler) {
        $removeHandler(element, 'load', this._onLoadHandler);
        this._onLoadHandler = null;
      }
    }

    this._onLoad = null;

  },
  get_OnLoad : function() {
    return this._onLoad ? this._onLoad.get_json() : null;
  },
  set_OnLoad : function(value) {
    if (!this._onLoad) {
      this._onLoad = new
        AjaxControlToolkit.Animation.GenericAnimationBehavior(
          this.get_element());
      this._onLoad.initialize();
    }
    this._onLoad.set_json(value);
    this.raisePropertyChanged('OnLoad');
  },
  get_OnLoadBehavior : function() {
    return this._onLoad;
  },
  OnLoad : function() {
    if (this._onLoad) {
      this._onLoad.play();
    }
  }
}
ImageAnimation.ImageAnimationBehavior.registerClass(
  'ImageAnimation.ImageAnimationBehavior',
  AjaxControlToolkit.BehaviorBase);
```

Final Thoughts

The HTML source for our sample, shown Listing 11.14, contains a Fade animation that targets the BannerImage control and runs for a duration of .3 seconds. We could have chosen almost any type of animation as long as it occurred when the OnLoad event fired on the BannerImage image control. This flexibility provides a JavaScript-free way to set up animations of any type when a pattern such as this is used. In fact, this is exactly how the Animation extender works; and if it weren't for the way it handles the OnLoad event, we would have used it in our example.

SUMMARY

The AJAX Control Toolkit comes with quite a bit of functionality that you can use to create truly interactive extenders that require much less coding than if you were to use the ASP.NET 2.0 AJAX Extensions directly. As you learned in this chapter, the toolkit provides a much richer environment for creating extender controls than using the ASP.NET 2.0 AJAX Extensions alone. In addition, the toolkit includes myriad controls you can either use or build on, making the toolkit a compelling alternative.

PART V
Appendixes

▪ A ▪
JavaScript in Visual Studio 2008

U P UNTIL VISUAL STUDIO 2008, JavaScript support in the Visual Studio IDE was at best bad, and at worst you switched to a different development environment for JavaScript programming and debugging. Microsoft has made great JavaScript support improvements in Visual Studio 2008 and has fully integrated it with ASP.NET AJAX. Let's go over the main JavaScript upgrade in Visual Studio 2008: IntelliSense.

IntelliSense

We've had good IntelliSense in Visual Studio for the non-JavaScript languages for years. It's gotten better with each subsequent release, but the JavaScript IntelliSense didn't improve equally compared to other languages. With Visual Studio 2008, we finally get improved JavaScript IntelliSense, and it's a good thing, too, because we now have to deal with a large file in the Microsoft AJAX Library, and we'll be writing a lot more JavaScript as our AJAX-enabled applications expand.

IntelliSense works much better, but there are some specific techniques that are important to know to make it work to its fullest capabilities. Let's cover those.

Referencing Libraries and Web Services

One of the great things about Visual Studio 2008 IntelliSense is its capability to provide IntelliSense on objects that aren't present in the current working file. Visual Studio does this through two different methods: an explicit reference directive and inference.

References

References work on external JavaScript files. They link the working JavaScript file to other JavaScript files or service definitions (web or Windows Communication Foundation [WCF]) so that the objects and methods contained within the linked files and definitions are available through IntelliSense when developing in the working file.

To link to another file or a service definition, you place a reference directive for each link at the top of the working JavaScript file. Listing A.1 demonstrates the three different types of references supported.

LISTING A.1   Referencing External Files from an External File

```
/// <reference path="Books.js" />
/// <reference path="~/DataService.asmx" />
/// <reference name="EmbeddedBooks.js" assembly="Books" />
/// <reference name="MicrosoftAjax.js" />
```

> **■ NOTE   Placement**
>
> You must place references at the top of your JavaScript files for them to work. As soon as nonreference code is parsed by Visual Studio, it no longer picks up any new references.

Reference Types

1. A free-standing JavaScript file: Books.js.
2. A reference to a web service: ~/DataService.asmx.
3. A reference to an embedded JavaScript file, EmbeddedBooks.js, located in the Books assembly.
4. A reference to the embedded MicrosoftAjax.js assembly. When no assembly is listed, the reference automatically uses the System.Web.Extensions assembly.

Inferences

The inference method reads the files that have been registered on the page and adds them to the IntelliSense list. Registering the files can occur in two ways. One is to use the HTML `script` tag. The other is to use the `Script Manager` server control to add `ScriptReferences` and `ServiceReferences` to the page. Listing A.2 demonstrates the two ways of registering files.

LISTING A.2 Referencing External Files from a Page

```
<html>
<head>
  <script type="text/javascript" src="Books.js" />
</head>
<body>
<form id="form1" runat="server">
  <asp:ScriptManager id="SM1" runat="server">
    <Scripts>
      <asp:ScriptReference Path="Books.js" />
      <asp:ScriptReference Name="EmbeddedBooks.js" Assembly="Books" />
    </Scripts>
    <Services>
      <asp:ServiceReference Path="~/WebService.asmx" />
    </Services>
  </asp:ScriptManager>
</form>
</body>
</html>
```

■ NOTE   ASP.NET AJAX Client Libraries

When a `ScriptManager` server control is added to the page, the Microsoft AJAX Library files, MicrosoftAjax.js, MicrosoftAjaxWeb Forms.js, and others, are automatically available through IntelliSense.

When we include references to external resources, our JavaScript programming becomes easier. Figure A.1 and Figure A.2 show IntelliSense examples after we've referenced a JavaScript file that contains the `Books.Publishers.Publisher` type and a web service method that contains the method `ProcessData`.

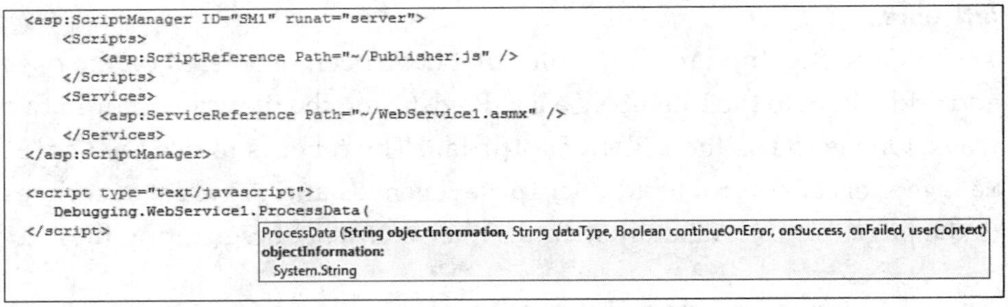

```
<asp:ScriptManager ID="SM1" runat="server">
    <Scripts>
        <asp:ScriptReference Path="~/Publisher.js" />
    </Scripts>
    <Services>
        <asp:ServiceReference Path="~/WebService1.asmx" />
    </Services>
</asp:ScriptManager>

<script type="text/javascript">
    Debugging.WebService1.ProcessData(
</script>
```

ProcessData (**String objectInformation**, String dataType, Boolean continueOnError, onSuccess, onFailed, userContext)
objectInformation:
  System.String

FIGURE A.1 ProcessData IntelliSense

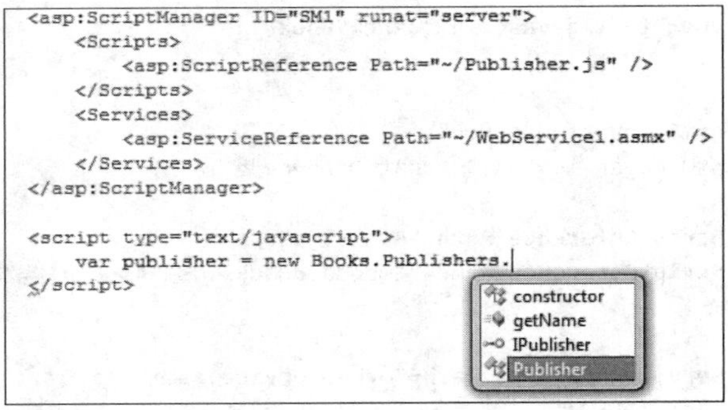

```
<asp:ScriptManager ID="SM1" runat="server">
    <Scripts>
        <asp:ScriptReference Path="~/Publisher.js" />
    </Scripts>
    <Services>
        <asp:ServiceReference Path="~/WebService1.asmx" />
    </Services>
</asp:ScriptManager>

<script type="text/javascript">
    var publisher = new Books.Publishers.
</script>
```

```
constructor
getName
IPublisher
Publisher
```

FIGURE A.2 Books.Publishers.Publisher IntelliSense

Problems with JavaScript IntelliSense

Although JavaScript IntelliSense in Visual Studio is much improved, there
are some issues with it:

1. When working with external files, IntelliSense isn't fully available on
   ASP.NET AJAX style types from within the file they are declared. For
   instance, if we declare type A inside MyTypes.js, there will be almost
   no IntelliSense available on type A and instances of type A inside the
   MyTypes.js file. If Type A is attached to a namespace, then no
   IntelliSense is available on the type at all. Normal functions and
   variables declared in that file do have IntelliSense capabilities. This is
   a huge issue, and we hope Microsoft will release a patch that
   addresses it.

2. IntelliSense information is updated only when the file you're working in "reparses" the references. Reparsing doesn't happen automatically when a referenced file changes. From our experiments, it definitely occurs when the working file is reopened, and it occurs at other times, too, but inconsistently. The referenced file must be saved for the changes to be seen by other files. You can also force JavaScript IntelliSense to update by pressing Ctrl+Shift+J or selecting Update JScript IntelliSense from the Edit ﹥ IntelliSense menu.

XML Comments

XML comments are now available to JavaScript methods. Just as with .NET methods, we follow a specific schema to create the comments, and when our JavaScript methods appear in IntelliSense, the comments appear in both the completion list and underneath the function as we complete the method call. The following statements hold true for XML comments too:

1. They start with a triple slash.
2. They go *inside* the method body, unlike for .NET comments, which go outside.
3. They can be applied to all JavaScript methods, not just methods that are declared using ASP.NET AJAX programming style.
4. They are localizable.
5. The listed parameters should be in the same order as the method's parameters.

The schema for XML comments is actually large, and we're not going to be able to cover all of it. Let's walk through a few common situations that will appear in your code.

In Listing A.3, we comment our class by adding a summary tag. When we bring up our type's constructor in IntelliSense we're shown the summary comment. Figure A.3 shows the IntelliSense we receive when we're completing our constructor selection, and Figure A.4 shows the IntelliSense we receive as we complete the constructor call.

LISTING A.3 Comments Applied to a Type Declaration

```
Books.Publishers.Publisher = function(name, city) {
/// <summary>
/// A business class that holds attributes related to a publisher.
/// </summary>
}
```

FIGURE A.3 Constructor's IntelliSense for completion list

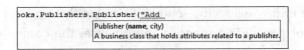

FIGURE A.4 Constructor's IntelliSense underneath during selection

In Listing A.4, we comment a method using three different tags: summary, param, and returns.

LISTING A.4 Comments Attached to a Method

```
changeInformation: function(newName, newCity) {
/// <summary>Updates the publisher's information</summary>
/// <param name="newName" type="String" optional="false" mayBeNull="false">
///    The publisher's new name
/// </param>
/// <param name="newCity" type="String" optional="false" mayBeNull="false">
///    The publisher's new city
/// </param>
/// <returns type="Boolean">A Boolean value indicating if the update was
successful </returns>
}
```

The summary element is the same as it was in the class constructor and appears when we display the method in the completion list and underneath the function as we type.

The `param` elements match the method's parameters. The element's inner text describes the parameter's use, and the attributes we used in this example, `name`, `type`, `integer`, `mayBeNull`, and `optional`, provide additional parameter details. Table A.1 describes the attributes we used.

TABLE A.1 Param Element Attributes

Attribute Name	Description	Default Value
`name`	Associates the parameter to the parameter in the arguments list.	None
`type`	The type of the parameter. This can be a built-in type such as `Number` or `String`, but can also be a user-defined type such as `Books.Publishers.Publisher`.	None
`integer`	Indicates whether the `Number` parameter is expected to be an integer or a double.	`false`
`mayBeNull`	Indicates whether the method will accept a null value for the parameter.	`false`
`optional`	Indicates whether the method will work appropriately if the parameter is not included in the method call.	`false`

The `returns` element provides information on what the method returns. If the method returns nothing, the `returns` element shouldn't be used. The inner text can provide some description of the return information, and the two attributes we used, `type` and `integer`, serve the same purpose as they did for the `parameter` element.

Figure A.5 shows the method completion IntelliSense, and Figure A.6 shows the parameter information for the method. Notice how the return type, `Boolean`, is also available during this IntelliSense phase.

FIGURE A.5 IntelliSense completion list

```
var publisher = new Books.Publishers.Publisher("A&W",
publisher.changeInformation("Addison",
        ┌──────────────────────────────────────────────────────┐
        │ Boolean changeInformation (String newName, Float newCity)│
        │ newCity:                                                 │
        │   The publisher's new city                               │
        └──────────────────────────────────────────────────────┘
```

FIGURE A.6 Parameter IntelliSense

Listing A.5 shows how we should comment properties.

LISTING A.5   Comments on an ASP.NET AJAX Property and Event

```
get_name: function() {
/// <value>The name of the publisher</value>
/// <returns type="String" />
…
},
set_name: function(value) {
// no commenting here
…
},
add_updated: function(handler) {
/// <summary>Adds handler for the Updated event, which fires
///          whenever the Update method is called.
/// </summary>
/// <param name="handler" type="Function" >
…
},
remove_updated: function(handler) {
// no commenting here
…
}
```

Because properties are split into separate get_ and set_ methods, only the get_ method needs to be commented. Likewise, because events are split into separate add_ and remove_ methods, only the add_ method needs to be commented.

▪ B ▪
Validating Method Parameters

WITH XML COMMENTS, we can annotate our methods with information on the parameters we expect and their valid range of values using the `param` element and its attributes. However, the `param` element is informational only and does not enforce the requirements it specifies in its markup. If a parameter was expected to be a non-null integer, we could pass a null or a string in on that parameter, and our method would happily accept the parameter. To us .NET statically typed developers, this is undesirable because the method might behave unexpectedly with unexpected values for inputs. Microsoft must have felt the same way and built a mechanism to perform parameter checking at the beginning of the method that we can use, too.

> **▪ WARNING**   **Private Function!**
>
> The method we're about to discuss, `Function._validateParams`, is a private method attached to the `Function` type (notice the underscore). This means that Microsoft can change its functionality at any time or even completely eliminate the method. Because using it is such a common practice among ASP.NET AJAX developers, we believe that the risk is minimal that Microsoft will eliminate it or change it in a major way as to compromise the code written against it. But be warned!

If we've been able to write XML comments that specify the variation of parameters our method can accept, we can create a call to the `Function._validateParams` method fairly easily. We just need to translate the information that is stated in our comments into a method call. Listing B.1, which shows the `fancyParameterChecker` method, demonstrates how we convert our IntelliSense parameter information into actionable code.

LISTING B.1   Checking a Function's Parameters

```
function fancyParameterChecker (val1, val2, val3, val4, val5) {
/// <summary>Adds two integers</summary>
/// <param name="val1" type="Books.BookType" />
/// <param name="val2" type="Books.Publishers.IPublisher" />
/// <param name="val3" type="Number" integer="true" mayBeNull="true" />
/// <param name="val4" optional="true" />
/// <param name="val5" type="Array" elementType="String" />

  var e = Function._validateParams(arguments, [
    {name: "val1", type: Books.BookType },
    {name: "val2", type: Books.Publishers.IPublisher },
    {name: "val3", type: Number, integer: true, mayBeNull: true},
    {name: "val4", optional: true},
    {name: "val5", type: Array, elementType: String}
  ]);
  if (e) throw e;
}
```

The `_validateParams` method takes two parameters: `params` and `expectedParams`. We pass the method's special `arguments` parameter in as the `params` parameter and an array of `expectedParam` objects in as the `expectedParams` parameter. Each `expectedParam` object in the `expected Params` array represents one of the `param` tags in the method's comment.

> **■ NOTE   Using Function._validateParams**
>
> Microsoft only uses the Function._validateParams method in the debug version of the library. They don't validate parameters in the release version. If you use both debug and release versions of a script this is something you might consider doing to eke out the last bit of performance.

When the _validateParams function executes, it performs a number of steps ensuring that the parameter values passed in through the params argument meet the criteria defined by the expectedParams values. If during the execution of a step the code recognizes a parameter value that does not meet the criteria set forth by the related expectedParam, an Error object is created and returned. The type of error that is created depends on the type of criteria that wasn't met, but the errors are similar to the ones we might throw during argument checking in a .NET method: ArgumentException, ArgumentNullException, ArgumentTypeException, and others. When an Error is created, it is returned as the method's return value, and execution control is returned to the calling method. From there, it is up to the method to determine what to do with the Error object, but most of the time the method throws the Error and lets the code's error handling mechanism handle the error.

But, if the method finds no errors in the parameters, it returns null.

The basic steps of the _validateParams method are as follows:

1. Determine whether the number of arguments included in the params parameter is valid based on the definition of the expectedParams. The number of parameters and expected parameters may not match exactly because some parameters may be optional or may be a special kind of parameter called a parameterArray.

2. Loop through the params and compare the current param against the expectedParam at the same array position.[1]

    a. Type and value comparison is performed on each param:

    - Ensures that if the parameter isn't allowed to be null, the value isn't

    - If the expected type is an enumeration, that the value is a valid value of the enumeration

    - If the expected type is a DOM element, that the value is a valid DOM element

    - If the expected type is not an enumeration or DOM element, that the value is an instance of the expected type (i.e., the value is a valid Books.Publisher.IPublisher)

---

[1] When the expected parameter is a parameterArray, the actual compared parameter is a parameter in the correct position within that array.

b. If the expected type is an `Array`, it loops through the array elements and executes step (a) for each array element.

> ### ■. NOTE   What's a parameterArray?
>
> A `parameterArray` is a concept in the Microsoft AJAX Library that's used only for validation. If an `expectedParam` is marked as a `parameterArray`, the validation routine knows to treat any parameter that isn't directly assigned to a named parameter as a member of an array of ending arguments. For instance, in the `registerClass` method, we can pass in 0 to *n* interface types that our class implements. We do this by providing the interface types in a comma-separated list at the end of the method. Simply put, we just pass them in to the method as we would a normal parameter. In the `registerClass` method, the `interfaceTypes` `expectedParam` is marked as a `parameterArray`. When the validation routine loops through the `expectedParams` array and reaches the `interfaceTypes` `expectedParam`, it validates the remaining arguments passed in to the method call against the `interfaceTypes` `expectedParam` definition. In this case, the definition states that if the parameter passed in isn't an interface, throw an error.
>
> The `parameterArray` idea is similar to the `params[]` keyword in C#, but C# uses the `param` keyword to define a method that can take 0 to *n* parameters. As we now know, JavaScript doesn't care how many arguments are passed in to a method; so unlike C#, where the `params[]` keyword changes how the method accepts parameters, the `parameterArray` idea is used only for validation purposes.
>
> Finally, for the `parameterArray` validation to occur properly, the `parameterArray` must be the last parameter of the method.

■ C ■

ASP.NET Handlers and Modules

A SP.NET handlers and modules provide the underlying support that makes ASP.NET AJAX function, and a good understanding of how they work can go a long way. In this appendix, we cover how HTTP handlers and modules work and how they fit into the overall ASP.NET 2.0 application lifecycle.

ASP.NET Application Lifecycle

The application lifecycle that ASP.NET 2.0 goes through when processing a request consists of quite of few layers. As shown in Figure C.1, the flow of a request from a client starts with the request coming into IIS and logic being applied to determine whether the ASP.NET runtime will be processing the request. If the file extension of the request ends with .aspx, .ascx, .ashx, .asmx, or .svc, the ASP.NET 2.0 runtime will handle the request, and the ApplicationManager will create an application domain for the request. This application domain is used to provide isolation between the various web applications in IIS and allows each web application to be managed separately. The byproduct of creating an application domain is the creation of the HTTP runtime, which consists of the HttpContext, HttpRequest, HttpResponse, and HttpApplication objects that work together to processes the request. The HttpContext class contains objects that are specific to the current application request, such as the `HttpRequest` and `HttpResponse` objects. The `HttpRequest` object contains information about the current request, including cookies and browser information. The `HttpResponse` object contains the response that is sent to the client, including all rendered output and cookies. It is the `HttpApplication` pipeline that is contained in the `HttpApplication` object that is of most interest to us because the pipeline is responsible for the instantiation of the HTTP handlers and modules for ASP.NET 2.0.

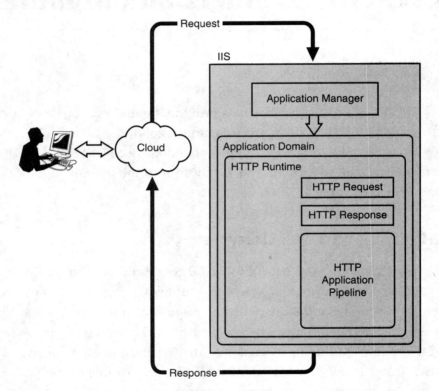

FIGURE C.1 ASP.NET application lifecycle

HTTP Handlers

In their simplest form, HTTP handlers run in response to a request into an ASP.NET application and are part of the `HttpApplication` pipeline illustrated in Figure C.1. In the course of processing the request, the

HttpApplication pipeline loads the specific handler based on the file extension of the request and uses it to process the request.

Overview of HTTP Handlers

HTTP handlers are custom classes you create in any .NET language to process specific types of HTTP requests. These handlers provide a low level of interaction, much like ISAPI extensions but with a simpler programming model. To create a handler, you need to create a class that implements the IHttpHandler interface and provide implementation for the IsReusable property and ProcessRequest method. The IsReusable property is called by the ASP.NET 2.0 runtime to determine whether this instance of the HTTP handler can be reused for processing another request of the same type. The property returns either true if it can be reused or false if not. The ProcessRequest method is the workhorse of the handler and is responsible for processing the request. The method takes one parameter of type HttpContext that encapsulates all the HTTP-specific information about the request, providing access to everything from the Application object to the Request and Response objects. With access to this kind of information, it's not hard to see how powerful handlers are. In Listing C.1, we show a simple HTTP handler designed to write back "Hello World" to the output stream. In the ProcessRequest method, you can see that we are setting the content type to text/plain, which sets the Content-Type HTTP header of the response, and then writing "Hello World" to the response buffer. The IsReusable property in our case is returning false, which means that it can't be shared across all requests of its type. The next topic we cover is how we set the types of requests a handler can process.

LISTING C.1 HTTP Handler

```
namespace SimpleHandler
{
  public class MyHandler : IHttpHandler
  {
    #region IHttpHandler Members
    public bool IsReusable
    {
      get { return false; }
    }
    public void ProcessRequest(HttpContext context)
```

LISTING C.1 continued

```
    {
      context.Response.ContentType = "text/plain";
      context.Response.Write("Hello World");
    }
    #endregion
  }
}
```

The types of requests a handler can process are determined when you register the handler in the web.config file of your application. Handlers can be registered to respond to specific HTTP verbs such as POST and GET and a specific path that can be represented by a specific URL or by using wild-card strings such as *.axd. In Listing C.2, we show a handler being added to the HttpHandlers section of the web.config file with a verb of *, which means all, a path of Handler.axd, and finally a type of SimpleHandler. MyHandler, which is the name of the class including the namespace. With this registration in place, the handler is set up to handle all types of requests that contain a path of MyHandler.axd.

LISTING C.2 HTTP Handler Registration

```
<system.web>
  <httpHandlers>
    <add verb="*" path="MyHandler.axd" type="SimpleHandler.MyHandler"/>
  </httpHandlers>
</system.web>
```

> ### ■ NOTE   Path Does Not Have to Exist
>
> In Listing C.2, the path is MyHandler.axd, but in the Web project, that file does not exist. The path used does not have to physically exist for the handler to respond to it. This is how ASP.NET AJAX processes all the ASP.NET 2.0 application services because the URL references don't physically exist.

Overview of HTTP Handler Factory

If you look at the common web.config file located in your Windows direc-tory under \Microsoft.NET\Framework\[version]\CONFIG, you will notice an entry under the `HttpHandlers` section that relates to the handler that processes ASPX pages:

```
<add path="*.aspx" verb="*" type="System.Web.UI.PageHandler
Factory" validate="True"/>
```

The interesting thing about this entry is that it refers to a class called `PageHandlerFactory` and not `Page` (as you might think, because `Page` does implement the `IHttpHandler` interface). This is because the creation of the `Page` class is delegated to the factory, which in this case knows how to create the class and return an instance of it. This factory pattern is used throughout ASP.NET 2.0 by classes that implement the `IHttpHandler` `Factory` interface. The `IHttpHandlerFactory` interface is implemented by classes that create and manage HTTP handlers for processing requests. It is possible, therefore, to create a class that implements the `IHttpHandler` `Factory` interface, and then use that class just as you would use an HTTP handler. This approach can allow finer control over the processing of an HTTP request by mapping a URL to an HTTP handler factory that creates different handlers based on a complex set of conditions. For example, with an HTTP handler factory, you can create a limited number of HTTP handler objects that access expensive or limited resources, such as a database, and then reuse those handler objects in future requests.

In Listing C.3, the `MyHandlerFactory` class provides implementation for the `GetHandler` and `ReleaseHandler` methods of the `IHttpHandlerFactory` interface. The `GetHandler` method is responsible for creating and returning a handler that implements the `IHttpHandler` interface. The method accepts an `HttpContext`, which as we have stated before encapsulates all the HTTP-specific information about the request, a string that represents the request type, a string that represents the raw URL for the request, and a string that represents the physical file system path of the request. In our example, the `GetHandler` method determines what the request type is and returns a handler for a `POST` or `GET` request type and a null reference for any others. The `ReleaseHandler` method in our example does nothing because both of our handlers are simple. In cases where the handlers have references to expensive resources, however, this is where you would clean things up.

LISTING C.3 HTTP Handler Factory

```
namespace SimpleFactory
{
  public class MyHandlerFactory : IHttpHandlerFactory
  {
    #region IHttpHandlerFactory Members
    public IHttpHandler GetHandler(HttpContext context,
      string requestType, string url,
      string pathTranslated)
    {
      switch (requestType)
      {
        case "POST":
          return new PostHandler();
          break;
        case "GET":
          return new GetHandler();
          break;
      }
      return null;
    }
    public void ReleaseHandler(IHttpHandler handler)
    {
      //not implemented
    }
    #endregion
  }
}
```

The second part to working with the factory handler is the same as handlers and relates to registration in the web.config file of your application. Factories, just like handlers, can be configured to respond to specific HTTP verbs such as POST and GET, and a specific path that can represented by a specific URL or by using wildcard strings such as *.axd. In Listing C.4, we show a factory being added to the HttpHandlers section of a web.config file with a verb of *, which means all, a path of MyFactory.axd, and finally a type of SimpleFactory.MyFactory, which is the name of the class including the namespace.

LISTING C.4 HTTP Handler Factory Registration

```
<system.web>
 <httpHandlers>
  <add verb="*" path="MyFactory.axd"
      type="SimpleFactory.MyHandlerFactory"/>
 </httpHandlers>
</system.web>
```

HTTP Modules

An HTTP module is similar in concept to the HTTP handler in the sense that it runs in response to a request into an ASP.NET application. In the case of a module, however, it runs with every request regardless of the HTTP verb or the path of the URL. The HTTP module works with the `Http Application` pipeline as it goes through the various events that occur during processing, providing extensibility points as events occur, much like an event handler.

Overview of HTTP Modules

An HTTP module is a managed class that implements the `IHttpModule` interface. An HTTP module can preprocess and post-process a request by intercepting and handling system events and events raised by other modules. The `IHttpModule` interface defines two methods: `Init` and `Dispose`. The `Init` method initializes the module and prepares it to handle requests. It is during this method call that you subscribe to the events (see Table C.1) that you want to work with, which in turn plugs the module into the ASP.NET 2.0 request processing pipeline and enables the ASP.NET 2.0 runtime to invoke the event handlers so that they can participate in the request processing. The `Dispose` method of the module is where you clean up resources that the module uses.

TABLE C.1 HttpApplication Events

Event	Description
BeginRequest	Occurs as the first event in the HTTP pipeline chain of execution when ASP.NET responds to a request.
AuthenticateRequest	Occurs when a security module has established the identity of the user.
PostAuthenticateRequest	Occurs when a security module has established the identity of the user.
AuthorizeRequest	Occurs when a security module has verified user authorization.
PostAuthorizeRequest	Occurs when the user for the current request has been authorized.
ResolveRequestCache	Occurs when ASP.NET completes an authorization event to let the caching modules serve requests from the cache, bypassing execution of the event handler (for example, a page or an XML web service).
PostResolveRequestCache	Occurs when ASP.NET bypasses execution of the current event handler and allows a caching module to serve a request from the cache.
PostMapRequestHandler	Occurs when ASP.NET has mapped the current request to the appropriate event handler.
AcquireRequestState	Occurs when ASP.NET acquires the current state (for example, session state) that is associated with the current request.
PostAcquireRequestState	Occurs when the request state (for example, session state) that is associated with the current request has been obtained.
PreRequestHandlerExecute	Occurs just before ASP.NET begins executing an event handler (for example, a page or an XML web service).
PostRequestHandlerExecute	Occurs when the ASP.NET event handler (for example, a page or an XML web service) finishes execution.

Event	Description
ReleaseRequestState	Occurs after ASP.NET finishes executing all request event handlers. This event causes state modules to save the current state data.
PostReleaseRequestState	Occurs when ASP.NET has completed executing all request event handlers and the request state data has been stored.
UpdateRequestCache	Occurs when ASP.NET finishes executing an event handler to let caching modules store responses that will be used to serve subsequent requests from the cache.
PostUpdateRequestCache	Occurs when ASP.NET completes updating caching modules and storing responses that are used to serve subsequent requests from the cache.
EndRequest	Occurs as the last event in the HTTP pipeline chain of execution when ASP.NET responds to a request.

Listing C.5 shows a class that inherits from IHttpModule and provides implementation for the Init method. In this method, a handler is created that responds to the PostAcquireRequestState event, which is an Http Application-level event that occurs after the request state has been acquired. In this handler, we are adding a value to the session object that contains a simple string that incorporates the request path so that this value would be available for a page to use as it is processing.

LISTING C.5 HTTP Module

```
namespace SimpleHttpModule
{
  public class MyModule : IHttpModule
  {
    #region IHttpModule Members

    public void Dispose()
    {
      //not implemented
    }
```

LISTING C.5 continued

```
public void Init(HttpApplication context)
{
    context.PostAcquireRequestState +=
       new EventHandler(context_PostAcquireRequestState);
}

void context_PostAcquireRequestState(object sender,
    EventArgs e)
{
    HttpApplication application = sender as HttpApplication;
    if (application.Context.Session != null)
    {
        application.Context.Session.Add("ModuleData",
           "hello for a request path of " +
            application.Request.Path.ToString());
    }
  }

 #endregion
 }
}
```

The second part of this example, shown in Listing C.6, relates to the registration of the module in the web.config file of your application. The registration entry is simpler than the handlers or factories and requires only a name, which in this case is SimpleHttpModule, and a type, which in our case is SimpleHttpModule.MyModule, which is the name of the class including the namespace.

LISTING C.6 HTTP Module Registration

```
<system.web>
 <httpModules>
  <add name="SimpleHttpModule"
       type="SimpleHttpModule.MyModule"/>
 </httpModules>
</system.web>
```

D

Client Error Handling Code

AS WE MENTIONED IN CHAPTER 3, "Components," here's the full
source code for creating the ErrorHandler client and server controls.
Included at the end of this appendix is a sample ASPX page that tests the
error handler's capabilities.

ErrorHandler Client Class

```
/// <reference name="MicrosoftAjax.js"/>
/// <reference name="StackTrace.js" assembly="ErrorHandlerLibrary"/>

ErrorHandler = function ErrorHandler() {
  ///<summary>
  ///Publisher for handled and unhandled exceptions
  ///</summary>
  ErrorHandler.initializeBase(this);
  this._disableErrorPublication = false;
};

ErrorHandler.prototype = {
  initialize: function ErrorHandler$initialize() {
    ErrorHandler.callBaseMethod(this, 'initialize');
    window.onerror =
      Function.createDelegate(this, this._unhandledError);
  },
  dispose: function ErrorHandler$dispose() {
    window.onerror = null;
    ErrorHandler.callBaseMethod(this, 'dispose');
  },
```

```
get_disableErrorPublication: function() {
  return this._ disableErrorPublication;
},

set_disableErrorPublication: function(value) {
  if (!this.get_updating()) {
    this.raisePropertyChanged("disableErrorPublication");
  }
  this._disableErrorPublication = value;
},

_unhandledError:
  function ErrorHandler$_unhandledError(msg, url, lineNumber) {
  try {
    var stackTrace = StackTrace.createStackTrace(arguments.callee);
    if (!this._disableErrorPublication) {
      ErrorDataService.PublishError
        (stackTrace, msg, url, lineNumber);
    }
    var args = new ErrorEventArgs(stackTrace, msg, url, lineNumber);
    this._raiseUnhandledErrorOccured(args);
  }
  catch (e) { }
},

add_unhandledErrorOccurred: function(handler) {
  this.get_events().addHandler("unhandledErrorOccurred", handler);
},

remove_unhandledErrorOccurred: function(handler) {
  this.get_events().removeHandler("unhandledErrorOccurred", handler);
},

_raiseUnhandledErrorOccured: function(args) {
  var evt = this.get_events().getHandler("unhandledErrorOccurred");
  if (evt !== null) {
    evt(this, args);
  }
},

publishError: function ErrorHandler$handledError(error) {
  /// <summary>Publishes a handled error to the server</summary>
  /// <param name="error" type="Error" />
  try {
    var e = Function._validateParams(arguments, [
      {name: "error", type: Error }
    ]);
    if (e) throw e;
```

```
        var stackTrace;
        if (error.stack) {
          stackTrace = error.stack;
        }
        else {
          stackTrace = StackTrace.createStackTrace(arguments.callee);
        }
        ErrorDataService.PublishError(stackTrace, null, null, null);
      }
      catch (e) { }
    }
};
ErrorHandler.registerClass ('ErrorHandler', Sys.Component);
```

ErrorEventArgs Client Class

```
ErrorEventArgs = function(stackTrace, message, url, lineNumber) {
  ErrorEventArgs.initializeBase(this);
  this._message = message;
  this._stackTrace = stackTrace;
  this._url = url;
  this._lineNumber = lineNumber;
}
ErrorEventArgs.registerClass("ErrorEventArgs", Sys.EventArgs);
```

ErrorHandler Server Control

```
using System.Collections.Generic;
using System.Web.UI;
using System;

namespace ErrorHandlerLibrary
{
  public class ErrorHandler : ScriptControl
  {
    protected override IEnumerable<ScriptReference>
      GetScriptReferences()
    {
      yield return new
       ScriptReference("ErrorHandlerLibrary.ErrorHandler.js",
       typeof(ErrorHandler).Assembly.FullName);

      yield return new
        ScriptReference("ErrorHandlerLibrary.StackTrace.js",
        typeof(ErrorHandler).Assembly.FullName);
```

```
      }

      protected override IEnumerable<ScriptDescriptor>
        GetScriptDescriptors()
      {
        ScriptComponentDescriptor scd =
          new ScriptComponentDescriptor("ErrorHandler");
        scd.ID = "ErrorHandler";
        yield return scd;
      }

      protected override void OnPreRender(System.EventArgs e)
      {
        base.OnPreRender(e);
        ScriptManager.GetCurrent(this.Page).Services.Add(
          new ServiceReference("~/ErrorDataService.asmx"));
      }

      protected override void OnInit(System.EventArgs e)
      {
        base.OnInit(e);
        if (Page.Items.Contains(typeof(ErrorHandler)))
        {
          throw new InvalidOperationException(
            @"Only one ErrorHandler control is
              allowed on the page at a time.");
        }
        Page.Items.Add(typeof(ErrorHandler), this);
      }
    }
  }
```

StackTrace Client Class

```
/// <reference name="MicrosoftAjax.js"/>
// StackTrace adapted from www.helephant.com/Article.aspx?ID=675

_StackTrace = function() {
  _StackTrace.initializeBase(this);
  this._maxRecursion = 20;
};

_StackTrace.prototype = {
  _getFunctionName: function _StackTrace$_getFunctionName (func) {
    if(func.name) {
      return func.name;
    }
    var fnText = func.toString();
```

```
      var fnName = fnText.substring(
        fnText.indexOf('function') + 8, fnText.indexOf('('));
      if(fnName !== null && fnName !== "") {
        return fnName;
      }
      return "anonymous";
    },

    _getSignature: function _StackTrace$_getSignature(func) {
      var signature = new Sys.StringBuilder(this._getFunctionName(func));
      signature.append("(");
      for(var i=0; i < func.arguments.length; i++) {
        var nextArgument = func.arguments[i];
        if(nextArgument.length > 30) {
          nextArgument = String.format("{0}...",
                         nextArgument.substring(0, 27));
        }
        signature.append(String.format("'{0}'", nextArgument));

        // parameter separator
        if (i < func.arguments.length - 1) {
          signature.append(", ");
        }
      }
      signature.append(")");
      return signature.toString();
    },

    createStackTrace: function
                      _StackTrace$createStackTrace(startingPoint) {
      /// <summary>Creates a Stack Trace from the startPoint</summary>
      /// <param name="startingPoint" type="Function" />
      var e = Function._validateParams(arguments, [
        {name: "startingPoint", type: Function }
      ]);
      if (e) throw e;

      var numberOfRecursions = 0;
      var stackTraceMessage = new Sys.StringBuilder("Stack Trace");
      stackTraceMessage.appendLine();
      var nextCaller = startingPoint;

      while(nextCaller && (numberOfRecursions < this._maxRecursion)) {
        stackTraceMessage.appendLine(this._getSignature(nextCaller));
        nextCaller = nextCaller.caller;
        numberOfRecursions++;
      }
      stackTraceMessage.appendLine();
      stackTraceMessage.appendLine();
```

```
      return stackTraceMessage.toString();
    }
};
_StackTrace.registerClass("_StackTrace");

Sys.Application.add_init(
  function() {
    StackTrace = new _StackTrace();
  }
);
```

ErrorDataService Web Service

```
using System.Web.Script.Services;
using System.Web.Services;

[ScriptService]
public class ErrorDataService : WebService
{
  [WebMethod()]
  public bool PublishError(
              string stackTrace,
              string message,
              string url,
              int? lineNumber)
  {
    // Do whatever you want at this point.
    // Log it, create an exception, etc.
    return true;
  }
}
```

Test Error Page

```
<%@ Page Language="C#" AutoEventWireup="true"
                  CodeBehind="ErrorHandlerTest.aspx.cs"
                  Inherits="ErrorHandler.ErrorHandlerTest" %>

<%@ Register Assembly="ErrorHandlerLibrary"
            Namespace="ErrorHandlerLibrary"
            TagPrefix="cc1" %>

<html>
<head runat="server">
  <title>Error Handler Test Page</title>
```

```
    </head>
    <body>
      <form id="form1" runat="server">
      <asp:ScriptManager ID="SM1" runat="server" />
      <cc1:ErrorHandler ID="ErrorHandler1" runat="server" />
      <asp:Button runat="server"
                  OnClientClick="tester();"
                  Text="Test Client Error Handling" />
      <asp:Button ID="Button1"
                  runat="server"
                  OnClientClick="testHandled();"
                  Text="Test Handled Error Handling" />

      <script type="text/javascript">
      function testHandled() {
        $find("ErrorHandler").publishError(Error.create("test", "error"));
      }
      function tester() {
        var test = null;
        test.err = 4;
      };
      </script>
      </form>
    </body>
    </html>
```

Index

Microsoft .NET Development Series

.NET Framework Standard Library Annotated Reference
Volume 1: Base Class Library and Extended Numerics Library

Brad Abrams

978-0-321-15489-7

.NET Framework Standard Library Annotated Reference
Volume 2: Networking Library, Reflection Library and XML Library

Brad Abrams
Tamara Abrams

978-0-321-19445-9

Essential Windows Presentation Foundation

Chris Anderson

978-0-321-37447-9

.NET Web Services
Architecture and Implementation

Keith Ballinger

978-0-321-11359-7

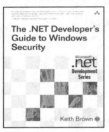

The .NET Developer's Guide to Windows Security

Keith Brown

978-0-321-22835-2

Visual Studio Tools for Office
Using C# with Excel, Word, Outlook, and InfoPath

Eric Carter
Eric Lippert

978-0-321-33488-6

Visual Studio Tools for Office
Using Visual Basic 2005 with Excel, Word, Outlook, and InfoPath

Eric Carter
Eric Lippert

978-0-321-41175-4

Graphics Programming with GDI+

Mahesh Chand

978-0-321-16077-5

Software Engineering with Microsoft Visual Studio Team System

Sam Guckenheimer
with Juan J. Perez

978-0-321-27872-2

The C# Programming Language
Second Edition

Anders Hejlsberg
Scott Wiltamuth
Peter Golde

978-0-321-33443-5

ASP.NET 2.0 Illustrated

Alex Homer
Dave Sussman

978-0-321-41834-0

The .NET Developer's Guide to Directory Services Programming

Joe Kaplan
Ryan Dunn

978-0-321-35017-6

Smart Client Deployment with ClickOnce
Deploying Windows Forms Applications with ClickOnce

Brian Noyes

978-0-321-19769-6

Essential ASP.NET 2.0

Fritz Onion
with Keith Brown

978-0-321-23770-5

Essential Windows Communication Foundation
For .NET Framework 3.5

Steve Resnick
Richard Crane
Chris Bowen

978-0-321-44006-8

.NET Internationalization
The Developer's Guide to Building Global Windows and Web Applications

Guy Smith-Ferrier

978-0-321-34138-9

Visual Studio Team System
Better Software Development for Agile Teams

Will Stott
James Newkirk

978-0-321-41850-0

A Developer's Guide to SQL Server 2005

Bob Beauchemin
Dan Sullivan

978-0-321-38218-4

Essential .NET
Volume 1
The Common Language Runtime

Foreword by James S. Miller

Don Box
with Chris Sells

978-0-201-73411-9

Domain-Specific Development
with Visual Studio DSL Tools

Steve Cook
Gareth Jones
Stuart Kent
Alan Cameron Wills

978-0-321-39820-8

Framework Design Guidelines
Conventions, Idioms, and Patterns for Reusable .NET Libraries

Krzysztof Cwalina
Brad Abrams

978-0-321-24675-2

Effective Use of Microsoft Enterprise Library
Building Blocks for Creating Enterprise Applications and Services

Len Fenster

978-0-321-33421-3

Essential C# 2.0

Mark Michaelis

978-0-321-15077-6

The Common Language Infrastructure Annotated Standard

James S. Miller
Susann Ragsdale

978-0-321-15493-4

Enterprise Services with the .NET Framework
Developing Distributed Business Solutions with .NET Enterprise Services

Christian Nagel

978-0-321-24673-8

Data Binding with Windows Forms 2.0
Programming Smart Client Data Applications with .NET

Brian Noyes

978-0-321-26892-1

Designing Forms for Microsoft Office InfoPath and Forms Services 2007

Scott Roberts
Hagen Green

978-0-321-41059-7

eXtreme .NET
Introducing eXtreme Programming Techniques to .NET Developers

Dr. Neil Roodyn

978-0-321-30363-9

Windows Forms 2.0 Programming

Chris Sells
Michael Weinhardt

978-0-321-26796-2

Essential Windows Workflow Foundation

Dharma Shukla
Bob Schmidt

978-0-321-39983-0

The Visual Basic .NET Programming Language

Paul Vick

978-0-321-16951-8

Pragmatic ADO.NET
Data Access for the Internet World

Foreword by Chris Sells

Shawn Wildermuth

978-0-201-74568-9

.NET Compact Framework Programming with C#

Paul Yao
David Durant

978-0-321-17403-1

.NET Compact Framework Programming with Visual Basic .NET

Paul Yao
David Durant

978-0-321-17404-8

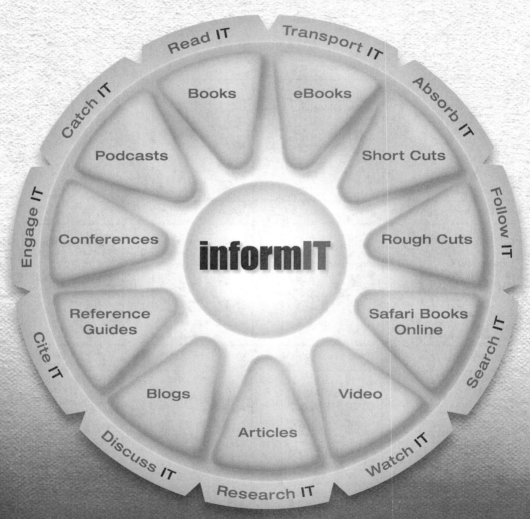

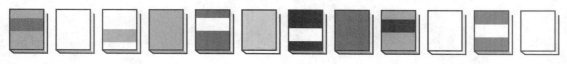